THREE FILMS OF WOODY ALLEN

Other Books by
WOODY ALLEN

Getting Even

Without Feathers

Side Effects

Four Films of Woody Allen

Hannah and Her Sisters

THREE FILMS OF WOODY ALLEN

ZELIG

BROADWAY DANNY ROSE

THE PURPLE ROSE OF CAIRO

VINTAGE BOOKS
A DIVISION OF
RANDOM HOUSE
NEW YORK

A Vintage Original, August 1987
First Edition

Published in the United States by Random House, Inc., New York, and
simultaneously in Canada by Random House of Canada Limited, Toronto.

Library of Congress Cataloging-in-Publication Data
Allen, Woody.
Three films of Woody Allen.
Contents: Zelig—Broadway Danny Rose—The purple rose of Cairo.
1. Moving-picture plays. I. Title.
PS3551.L44A6 1987 791.43'75 86-40462
ISBN 0-394-75304-6 (pbk.)

Photographs on pages 87 and 95 by Kerry Hayes.
All other photographs by Brian Hamill/Photoreporters.
Manufactured in the United States of America
10 9 8 7 6 5 4 3 2

CONTENTS

The italicized passages that describe the action have been provided by the publisher.

ZELIG

White-lettered title credits fade on and off a black screen. There is no sound.

Orion Pictures and Warner Bros.
Present

ZELIG

The following documentary would
like to give special thanks to
Dr. Eudora Fletcher, Paul Deghuee,
and Mrs. Meryl Fletcher Varney.

The camera abruptly cuts to:

A 1920s ticker-tape parade, shown in a black-and-white newsreel. Thousands line Fifth Avenue, cheering and waving. Streamers are flung out of office windows. An American flag waves in a foreground window. Militia marches in regalia in the background. The noise of the enthusiastic crowd is deafening.

The camera cuts to the actual parade on the street, to an open-car procession. Paparazzi run in front of the first car, where two men stand, waving to the crowds and camera. Closed military jeeps slowly drive next to them. The roar continues as Susan Sontag's voice is heard.

SUSAN SONTAG'S VOICE-OVER He was *the* phenomenon of the . . .

CUT TO:

The present day, in living color. Susan Sontag is sitting at an outdoor cafe, a coffee cup in front of her. She faces the camera, still talking, as behind her an idyllic glimpse of Venice is seen: a bright blue sky, gondolas on the canal, sea gulls flying by the slanted roofs. Her name pops on the bottom of the screen: SUSAN SONTAG.

SUSAN SONTAG *(Continuing, fingering her napkin)* . . . twenties. When you think that at that time he was as well known as Lindbergh, it's really quite astonishing.
The film cuts back to the 1920s parade, back to the procession of cars, the cheering throng, and the reporters flashing their cameras.

The camera then moves in on the main car, where a beaming Leonard Zelig and a smiling Eudora Fletcher wave to the crowd. Two other men, one in military costume, share the open car with them. The crowd continues to cheer as Irving Howe's voice is heard.

IRVING HOWE'S VOICE-OVER His story reflected the nature of our civilization, the character of our times . . . yet it was also one man's story . . .
As Irving Howe speaks, the film cuts abruptly back to the present day in color. Irving Howe sits in a comfortable leather chair in a residential living room. Behind him is a small desk with a framed photograph on its top and an unlit fireplace. A microphone sits on his shirt, interview style. As he talks, his name pops on the screen: IRVING HOWE.

IRVING HOWE *(Continuing, gesturing)* . . . and, um, all the themes of our culture were there—heroism, will, things like that. But when you look back on it, it was very strange.

CUT TO:

The 1920s parade in black-and-white. The crowd is cheering, the ticker tape is falling, the American flag waves in the breeze as the camera moves in closer, to a cavalcade of cars driving down the street. Saul Bellow begins to speak over the cheers.

SAUL BELLOW'S VOICE-OVER Well, it is ironic . . .

As Saul Bellow continues to speak, the cavalcade of cars is seen at a slightly different angle. Zelig's car enters the screen along with several other vehicles. He and Dr. Fletcher are still waving at the enthusiastic crowd.

SAUL BELLOW'S VOICE-OVER . . . to see how quickly he has faded from memory, considering what an astounding record he made.

CUT TO:

The present day in color. Saul Bellow is sitting in his library. Books line the shelves behind him. A microphone is attached to his plaid shirt. He addresses an offscreen interviewer as his name pops on the screen: SAUL BELLOW.

SAUL BELLOW He was of course fairly amusing, but at the same time touched a nerve in people. *(Pauses)* Perhaps in a way which they would prefer not to be touched. *(Nodding)* It certainly is a very bizarre story.

A big-band rendition of "Charleston" and a staccato noisemaker are heard as the film cuts back to black-and-white, in the 1920s. A young woman is dancing to the music. The camera, starting at her black, bow-tied tap shoes, moves up her body, revealing the band behind her. She's wearing a two-piece sequined costume; her hair is bobbed '20s style.

The camera then moves to the crowded audience, to a blonde woman in a glamorous evening dress. She smiles and shakes her noisemaker in rhythm with the band. The men around her, in tuxedos, clap their hands in time to the music as they watch the offscreen dancer.

The nightclub is now seen from a different angle. Beyond the heads of the audience seated at tables, the Charleston flapper continues to dance. People throw small ball favors at her in fun. A showgirl, standing, tries to catch the balls before they land on the stage. The music continues.

The music swells as the film cuts to several women in bobbed hair and a tuxedoed man sitting at a table near the wall in the club. They are smiling and shaking their noisemakers, obscuring a sign on the wall.

The camera moves back to the flapper, now wearing shimmery streamers over her sequins. She dances and spins in front of the "Charleston"-playing band as balls from the audience fall at her feet.

CUT TO:
EXTERIOR. PARAMOUNT THEATER—DAY.

"Charleston" is heard over a view of a crowded, rainy street. The theater marquee is lit up. Trolley cars pass each other, and crossing pedestrians carry umbrellas. The sidewalks are filled with milling people; Model T–like cars add to the congestion. The film moves in a cranked-up fashion, giving the impression of silent-movie motion. A narrator speaks over the screen in a well-modulated, educated voice. As he talks, the screen cuts to various film clips of a bygone era. We see:

—A biplane flying in the sky. A sax player and a trumpeter play, standing up on each wing. The pilot beats a rhythm with drumsticks on the wing above the cockpit.
—A couple dancing before a simple, small band to the tune of the background "Charleston." A woman, watching, claps her hands in time to the music.
—Four simply dressed women standing in a row, smiling as they kick their heels to the music.
—A man and woman in a passionate embrace in front of a framed painting. They are seen through an open doorway of a private library.
—Two men in Panama hats and suits sitting in a parked car. While the driver looks out his window impatiently, the man in the passen-

ger seat takes a pint-size bottle of liquor out of his pocket and begins to drink.

—President Calvin Coolidge pinning a medal on a beaming Charles Lindbergh on a presidential platform. Around them, a well-heeled crowd, including some men in uniform, clap their hands and smile.

—Al Capone, in a three-piece suit, walking away from a car towards the camera. Flashbulbs go off.

—A man sitting precariously on a chair balanced on another *chair —both of which are balanced on the edge of a tall building's roof. A tiny city street and sidewalk are seen several stories below.*

—A close-up of a thumb popping a champagne cork.

—A close-up of bubbling champagne being poured into a glass.

—A small party in session. A woman plays the banjo while a man next to her bounces his head in rhythm to her music. A few women are dancing the Charleston. Everyone is smiling and upbeat.

NARRATOR'S VOICE-OVER The year is 1928. America, enjoying a decade of unequaled prosperity, has gone wild. The Jazz Age, it is called. The rhythms are syncopated; the morals are looser; the liquor is cheaper—when you can get it. It is a time of diverse heroes and madcap stunts, of speakeasies and flamboyant parties.

CUT TO:
EXTERIOR. LONG ISLAND SUMMER HOUSE—DAY.

The camera shows an elegant mansion set back on a well-manicured lawn, then moves closer to its front door. As the narrator continues to speak, the screen shows a 1920s-model limousine parked in front of the canopied entrance. Several people alight from the limo and walk into the house. The sedan drives away, revealing a few liveried footmen and great stone vases filled with flowering plants.

NARRATOR'S VOICE-OVER One typical party occurs at the Long Island estate of Mr. and Mrs. Henry Porter Sutton, socialites, patrons of the arts.

The film moves to a party in progress on the mansion's great lawn. The camera pans across the lawn, revealing some chairs and several oversize striped umbrella tables where well-dressed guests are sitting, chatting, and enjoying themselves. Other guests mill around, standing on a porch, walking around the tables. "Charleston" plays on.

NARRATOR'S VOICE-OVER Politicians and poets rub elbows with the cream of high society. Present at the party is . . .

CUT TO:

F. Scott Fitzgerald in solitude, writing at a table in a lovely, lush garden. As the narrator continues to speak, the film dissolves to a close-up of Fitzgerald, deep in thought, as he writes in a leather-bound diary.

NARRATOR'S VOICE-OVER . . . Scott Fitzgerald, who is to cast perspective on the twenties for all future generations. He writes in his notebook . . .
The movie cuts to a photograph taken at the party. There, among a chatting group of summer-white-dressed men and women, is Zelig. The camera moves closer to his face as the narrator speaks. "Charleston" is still heard.

NARRATOR'S VOICE-OVER . . . about a curious little man named Leon Selwyn, or Zelman, who "seemed clearly to be an aristocrat and extolled the very rich as he chatted with socialites."
The film goes back to the party in progress as the narrator speaks. The camera first shows an overview of the party, with its umbrellas and milling guests; it then moves towards the patio, which is crowded with animated guests. Gradually, the camera moves back to the manicured entrance as a limousine departs and another one drives up. People stand by the doorway, chatting as they wait for their cars.

NARRATOR'S VOICE-OVER "He spoke adoringly of Coolidge and the Republican party, all in an upper-class Boston accent. An

hour later," writes Fitzgerald, "I was stunned to see the same man speaking with the kitchen help. Now he claimed to be a Democrat, and his accent . . ."
The camera cuts outside the Long Island estate. People walk by its tall stone fence while a crowd eagerly lines up at its gate to catch a glimpse of the socialite guests. "Charleston" changes to a somber "Leonard the Lizard."

NARRATOR'S VOICE-OVER ". . . seemed to be coarse, as if he were one of the crowd." It is the first small notice taken of Leonard Zelig.
The music changes to the "Ballpark Theme" as an old-fashioned newsreel title card is seen over a black screen. Under the Hearst Metrotone News credit is the headline GEHRIG AND RUTH JOIN YANKS IN DIXIE—WITH TWO SLUGGERS ON THE JOB, YANKS GET DOWN TO REAL WORK AT ST. PETERSBURG, FLA.

The narrator starts to speak as the newsreel titles dissolve to an old film clip of Lou Gehrig at the bat in a Yankee practice session. The bleachers are crowded with men in suits and hats. Gehrig hits the ball and starts for first as the camera cuts to the pitcher. He catches a ball and turns towards home base. Behind him is a large pavilion.

NARRATOR'S VOICE-OVER Florida—one year later. An odd incident occurs at the New York Yankees' training camp. Journalists, anxious as always to immortalize the exploits of the great home-run hitters, notice a strange new player . . .
The camera moves back to home base. Babe Ruth is now at bat. Behind him, waiting his turn, is baseball player Zelig.

NARRATOR'S VOICE-OVER . . . waiting his turn at bat after Babe Ruth. He is listed on the roster as Lou Zelig . . .
The film cuts quickly back to the pitcher, who is moving into his throw.

NARRATOR'S VOICE-OVER . . . but no one on the team has heard of him. Security guards are called . . .

The camera is back on Babe Ruth, who hits the pitcher's ball. Zelig, bat in hand, still in the background, takes off his cap and wipes his forehead.

The movie cuts to a newspaper page while the narrator continues to speak. It's a nondescript inside page, with columns, various headlines, a photo of some cars, and some ads. As the narrator talks, the camera moves in on a small article on the page, headlined IMPOSTOR CHASED FROM YANKEE CAMP; *the story underneath begins,* AN UNIDENTIFIED MAN, POSING AS A BASEBALL PLAYER . . .

NARRATOR'S VOICE-OVER *(Continuing)* . . . and he is escorted from the premises. It appears as a small item in the next day's newspaper.

The music changes to "Chicago, That Toddlin' Town," played with a heavy drumbeat, as the film cuts to a hand knocking on a speakeasy door. A secret window slides open and the camera reveals an extreme close-up of bushy-eyebrowed eyes looking out. The knocking hand puts some folded-up dollar bills through a door slot and into the waiting hand of the eyebrowed man.

As the narrator speaks, the film cuts inside to a crowded party scene. A black man in top hat and tails dances while the well-dressed speakeasy patrons watch at linen-covered tables—drinking, clapping their hands, and enjoying themselves thoroughly. Tuxedoed waiters stand at the wall; all eyes are on the dancer. Streamers hang down from the ceiling.

NARRATOR'S VOICE-OVER Chicago, Illinois—that same year. There is a private party at a speakeasy on the South Side. People from the most respectable walks of life dance and drink bathtub gin.

The camera moves to the musicians at the party as the narrator speaks. In quick succession, the screen shows:

—*A black drummer banging out "Chicago." Patrons crowd around him, bouncing and dancing to the rhythm.*
—*A straw-hatted black trumpeter blowing his horn to the delight of the crowd. A sax player in the background accompanies him.*
—*The black drummer again, seen closer up. He's smiling and really going at his drums. The patrons stand behind him, moving to the beat.*
—*Couples dancing cheek to cheek on the crowded dance floor, the men in suits, the women in flapper dress. Waiters scurry about in the background.*

NARRATOR'S VOICE-OVER Present that evening was Calvin Turner, a waiter.
The film abruptly cuts to an aging Calvin Turner, in full color. It's the present day. He's sitting at a table in a sparse dining room. A coffee cup near his elbow is the only decoration.

CALVIN TURNER *(To offscreen interviewer)* And a lotta, lotta customers—a lot of gangsters—come in the place, 'cause they always good tippers and take good care of us, and, of course, we try to take care of our customers. But on this particular night, I looked over and here's a strange guy comin' in. I'd never seen him before . . .
As Calvin Turner continues to speak, the film shifts to a snapshot taken at the speakeasy party. There, surrounded by fellow gangsters at a table covered with a checkered tablecloth, is Zelig. He wears a three-piece suit and a paunch. One hand, holding a cigar, rests on the arm of the gangster next to him. The men, all in suits, all with drinks, smile for posterity as the camera moves in closer and closer on Zelig's face.

CALVIN TURNER'S VOICE-OVER . . . so I asked one of the others, I said "John, you know this guy? You ever seen him?" So he

looked, and, "No. I ain't never seen him before, man. I don't know who he is, but I know one thing, he's a tough-looking hombre!" So I looked over and then, next thing, the guy had disappeared. I don't know where he went to! But about this time, you know . . .
The film cuts back to color, to Calvin Turner in his dining room in the present day.

CALVIN TURNER *(Continuing, gesturing)* . . . the music usually gets started, and the band started dra-da-dra-da-dra-da-dra playing, and I looked, and here's a guy—a colored guy in the ba-, a colored boy over there playin' the trumpet. Man he was playin' back!
The movie leaves the present, cutting back to the 1920s speakeasy, to a still photograph of the band. Everyone is smiling, the sax player, the banjo player, the drummer—and the black trumpeter. It's Zelig. The camera moves closer and closer in on Zelig's black face as the close-up photo of Zelig, the white gangster, moves halfway onto the screen. The two Zeligs, one white, one black, appear side by side on the screen as Calvin Turner continues to reminisce.

CALVIN TURNER'S VOICE-OVER And I looked at the guy and I said, "Well, my goodness! He looks just like that gangster, but the gangster was white and this guy is black!" So I don't know what's, I don't know what's, what's happening.

CUT TO:
EXTERIOR. NEW YORK CITY—DAY.

Times Square, in black-and-white, is jumping in the 1920s. People scurry across the street, up and down the sidewalks. Cars and trolleys move slowly past the buildings, through the square, as a fast-tempoed "Sleuthing in Chinatown" plays in the background.

NARRATOR'S VOICE-OVER New York City. It is several months later.

The narrator continues to speak as the film cuts first to an office where three hardworking detectives examine the files of fingerprints, then to one of the detectives as he studies a page of prints through an old-fashioned magnifying glass. The film then jumps to a view of Washington Square Park in Greenwich Village circa the 1920s. A few cars and pedestrians pass through its bright white arch.

NARRATOR'S VOICE-OVER Police are investigating the disappearance of a clerk named Leonard Zelig. Both his landlady and his employer have reported him missing.
The movie cuts to a row of charming town houses bordering Washington Square Park. A few passersby are seen on the clean-looking street as the scene dissolves to the front door of one of the houses. Its white frame and steps fill the screen.

NARRATOR'S VOICE-OVER They tell police he was an odd little man who kept to himself. Only two clues are found in Zelig's Greenwich Village flat . . .
A more serious-sounding "Vesti la Giubba" is heard as the film cuts to a still photograph of a casually attired Eugene O'Neill, a young child, and an equally casually dressed Zelig. The camera moves in on Zelig's face as the narrator speaks.

NARRATOR'S VOICE-OVER *(Continuing)* . . . one a photograph of Zelig with Eugene O'Neill . . .

A second photograph is seen. This time it is Zelig as Pagliacci, complete with clown costume and big bass drum.

NARRATOR'S VOICE-OVER . . . and one of him as Pagliacci.
The camera moves closer and closer in on Zelig's Pagliacci face before the scene shifts to a narrow Chinatown street. A CHOP SUEY *sign in Chinese and English dominates the street; a few people in shirt-sleeves pass by. The music returns to "Sleuthing in Chinatown," the*

narrator continues his tale, and the film cuts to a photograph of a tenement-lined Chinatown street. Lanterns hang at entranceways; carts packed with goods line the street. The camera moves in on one of the doorways.

NARRATOR'S VOICE-OVER Acting on a tip, they trace his whereabouts to Chinatown, where, in the rear of a Chinese establishment . . .

The film shifts inside, to a still photograph of several reclining, languishing Chinese men smoking opium, all wearing coolie caps and pajamas, all lined up in a row. In the group is Zelig. The camera moves closer and closer on Zelig's Oriental face as the narrator speaks.

NARRATOR'S VOICE-OVER . . . a strange-looking Oriental who

fits the description of Leonard Zelig is discovered. Suspicious, the detectives try to pull off his disguise . . .

A photograph of several hats and fedoras fills the screen. As the camera moves back, the hats are seen to belong to a group of detectives crowded around the door of a truck. Throngs of people look on, a part of the frozen tableau.

NARRATOR'S VOICE-OVER . . . but it is not a disguise, and a fight breaks out.

The narrator continues to speak as an old-fashioned black ambulance speeds down a city street; a doctor sits in its open back. A curious policeman watches it pass. The ambulance drives through the covered entranceway to the hospital. In jerky newsreel style, the doctor hops off the back and enters the building as several attendants come out to help bring Zelig inside.

NARRATOR'S VOICE-OVER He is removed by force and taken to Manhattan Hospital. In the ambulance, he rants and curses in what sounds like authentic Chinese. He is restrained with a straitjacket.

Zelig's hospital admitting record fills the screen. The camera moves from top to bottom, revealing the official petition letterhead, the admitting detective agency, the date, Zelig's name and personal data, diagnosis, and the contents of his wallet and other valuables.

NARRATOR'S VOICE-OVER When he emerges from the car twenty minutes later, incredibly, he is no longer Chinese but Caucasian. Bewildered interns place him in the emergency room for observation.

The film cuts to Dr. Fletcher's serious-looking face. Her hair is braided; she fiddles with her glasses. She stands in front of the hospital.

NARRATOR'S VOICE-OVER At seven A.M., Dr. Eudora Fletcher, a psychiatrist, makes her usual rounds.

The movie abruptly cuts to the present, in color. An older Dr. Fletcher, with glasses and gray hair, sits on a comfortable sofa in her living room. Behind her are bookshelves, a lamp, and a green plant.

OLDER DR. FLETCHER *(To offscreen interviewer)* When I first heard about this emergency case that had been brought in, I didn't think anything peculiar. And when I first laid eyes on him, it was a bit . . . um . . . strange because I . . . I took him—mistook him—for a doctor.
The film cuts back to black-and-white in the '20s as the older Dr. Fletcher speaks. Zelig's head and shoulders fill the screen. He's wearing intern greens and he's deep in conversation with offscreen doctors.

OLDER DR. FLETCHER'S VOICE-OVER He had a very professional demeanor about him.

CUT TO:

The young Dr. Fletcher sitting at a paper-cluttered conference table. Two other doctors are with her, one seated to her right, the other leaning over the table and pointing to some papers. Other doctors, in suits, fill the background. The room is heavy with cigarette smoke and debate.

NARRATOR'S VOICE-OVER As a young psychiatrist, Eudora Fletcher is fascinated by Leonard Zelig. She convinces the conservative staff of the hospital to allow her to pursue a study of the new admission.
The film cuts to a photograph of a dazed Zelig in shirt and jeans; he is sitting in a rocking chair in Dr. Fletcher's office, leaning forward with his mouth open. As the camera moves closer to Zelig's face, a scratchy recording of Dr. Fletcher's conversation with him is heard.

DR. FLETCHER'S VOICE-OVER So wha-what do you do?

LEONARD ZELIG'S VOICE-OVER Oh me? Uh . . . I'm uh, I'm a psychiatrist.

DR. FLETCHER'S VOICE-OVER Oh yes?

LEONARD ZELIG'S VOICE-OVER Oh yes, yes, I-I, I work *(Coughs)* um, mostly with delusional paranoids.

While the scratchy recorded conversation continues, the film cuts to a photograph of Dr. Fletcher seated at her desk and listening to Zelig. An old-fashioned phone sits on her otherwise bare desk. The camera moves back and reveals Zelig, still in his rocking chair but now wearing a robe. A cigarette is frozen in his hand. The photograph dissolves to a different photo of the same scene. The cigarette is now frozen at Zelig's lips. The recording continues as the camera moves closer and closer in on Zelig's still face.

DR. FLETCHER'S VOICE-OVER Tell me about it.

LEONARD ZELIG'S VOICE-OVER Ach . . . there's not much to tell, I, I w-work mostly on the continent and uh . . . I've written quite a few, uh, psychoanalytic papers . . . I uh . . . studied, uh, a great deal, I worked with Freud in Vienna. Um yes, we, we broke over the concept of penis envy. Freud felt that it should be limited to women.

The film cuts to Dr. Fletcher in coat and hat, leaving the hospital with a male colleague. She appears to be talking intensely; she is gesturing, pulling on her gloves, and nodding while she walks. Her colleague listens. Two other men pass them on the hospital walkway as they turn a corner and walk offscreen. The older Dr. Fletcher is heard over the silent scene.

OLDER DR. FLETCHER'S VOICE-OVER It's not that he was making any sense at all. It was just a conglomeration of psychological double-talk that he had apparently heard, or perhaps was familiar with through reading.

The older Dr. Fletcher continues her narrative as the film cuts to her younger self, flipping through a hospital file cabinet; she holds a lit cigarette in one hand. The young doctor pulls out the file she's been looking for, places it on top of the cabinet, and begins to read through it.

OLDER DR. FLETCHER'S VOICE-OVER And the funny thing was that his delivery was quite fluid and might have been really quite convincing to someone who did not know any better.

CUT TO:

A still photograph of Zelig with a man a head taller. Both are in shirt-sleeves, tie, and suspenders. Behind them is a building and some streets. They stare into the camera as it moves closer and closer in on Zelig's face. The minor keys of "Ukrainian Joys" are heard in the background.

NARRATOR'S VOICE-OVER Who was this Leonard Zelig that seemed to create such diverse impressions everywhere?
Zelig's face dissolves to a baby Zelig with the same facial expression, as seen in a framed partial photograph.

NARRATOR'S VOICE-OVER All that was known of him was that he was the son of a Yiddish actor . . .

The film cuts to an old film clip showing a stage with a forest setting. There, a heavyset woman with massive curls and wearing a draped costume with long, loose sleeves emotes and gestures. Near her, a group of Jewish, heavily bearded men in cavalry costumes act out their parts. Zelig's father, as Puck, in breeches and Orthodox-style heavy beard, bounds thickly out of the "forest" wings.

NARRATOR'S VOICE-OVER . . . named Morris Zelig, whose performance as Puck in the Orthodox version of *A Midsummer Night's Dream* was coolly received . . .
The screen next shows a framed photograph of a formidable, stocky woman wearing an old-fashioned, modest dress with lace trim; her dark hair is pulled back from her face. The camera moves closer and closer in on her face as the narrator continues his story.

NARRATOR'S VOICE-OVER The elder Zelig's second marriage is marked by constant violent quarreling, so much so that although the family lives over a bowling alley, it is the bowling alley that complains of noise.

Next seen is a still photograph taken on the turn-of-the-century Lower East Side. A group of boys in knickers and caps play around a fire hydrant. A little girl in tights and dress watches. Behind the group are some tenements and a storefront with Hebrew lettering. The camera moves closer in on one of the little boys. It's Zelig with a black eye and dirty face, looking at the camera.

NARRATOR'S VOICE-OVER As a boy, Leonard is frequently bullied by anti-Semites. His parents, who never take his part and blame him for everything, side with the anti-Semites.

The film cuts to a posed class photo revealing two rows of serious-looking young men, all wearing suits and bowler hats. The camera moves in on one young man in the second row. It's Zelig. The narrator continues.

NARRATOR'S VOICE-OVER They punish him often by locking him in a dark closet. When they are really angry, they get into the closet with him.

The film moves to another photograph in the Zelig family album. Here, an aging white-haired Morris somberly sits holding a violin. He is wearing a yarmulke and dark suit. Around him are other Jewish musicians, including a flutist, a cellist, and another violinist. All wear serious expressions, dark suits, yarmulkes, and beards.

NARRATOR'S VOICE-OVER On his deathbed, Morris Zelig tells his son that his life is a meaningless nightmare of suffering, and the only advice he gives him is to save string.

The next photo, a fuzzy blow-up of a group shot, shows brother Jack in a tuxedo.

NARRATOR'S VOICE-OVER Though brother Jack has a nervous breakdown . . .

Next is sister Ruth, posed near some potted plants in a photographer's studio. She wears a serious expression and suit. The background shows painted sky and molded wainscotting.

NARRATOR'S VOICE-OVER . . . and sister Ruth becomes a shop-lifter and alcoholic . . .

The film cuts back to a photo of Zelig, once more in a posed class portrait. Here his head is bare and he has the same neat, clean look as his other classmates. They all have white handkerchiefs in their breast pockets. As the narrator speaks, the class photo dissolves to a different class photo. Zelig's a bit older here; he sits in the front row behind a table. He now wears glasses. He and the other students, posed behind the table with two on either end, stare into the camera, which moves closer and closer in on Zelig's face.

NARRATOR'S VOICE-OVER . . . Leonard Zelig appears to have adjusted to life. Somehow, he seems to have coped. And then, suddenly, increasingly strange behavior.

With "Leonard the Lizard" playing in the background, the film cuts back to the outside of the hospital with its brick-walled fence topped with iron bars. Dr. Fletcher gets out of a black sedan taxi and holds the door for three distinguished-looking men. All four walk towards the entrance. The narrator speaks over the scene.

NARRATOR'S VOICE-OVER Fascinated by the Zelig phenomenon, Dr. Fletcher arranges a series of experiments and invites the skeptical staff to observe.

The screen next shows a series of portraits while the narrator speaks. First is seen the close-up face of a self-assured-looking Zelig in a sweater and pants, sitting in a chair by his hospital bed. One arm is casually draped over the edge of the bed. The camera moves back to reveal two psychiatrists sitting on either side of him.

NARRATOR'S VOICE-OVER With the doctors watching, Zelig becomes a perfect psychiatrist.

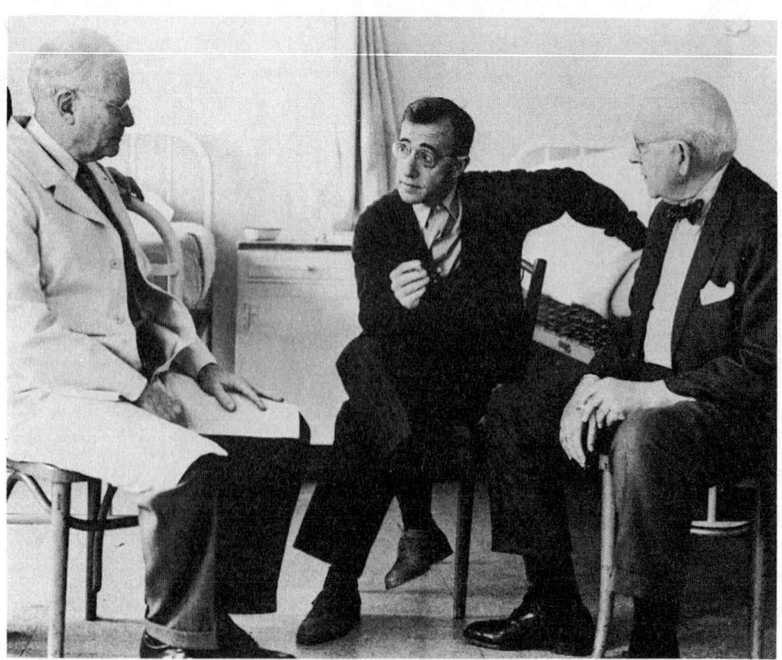

The photo dissolves to another photo taken at the hospital. This time, Zelig is standing next to two visiting Frenchmen. He looks very French himself, with slicked-back hair, dark brows, and pencil-thin mustache.

NARRATOR'S VOICE-OVER When two Frenchmen are brought in, Zelig assumes their characters and speaks reasonable French. *Appearing on the screen next is a hospital corridor. An Asian man wearing a robe stands next to a gurney, where a robed Zelig is sitting. Zelig too looks Oriental. A nurse, starting to walk across the corridor, steps back to avoid ruining the photograph about to be taken for posterity. She and another waiting nurse chatter silently, looking at the stock-still Zelig and the Asian.*

NARRATOR'S VOICE-OVER In the company of a Chinese person, he begins to develop Oriental features.

A series of newspaper clippings appear on the screen while the narrator speaks. The first is headlined BIZARRE DISCOVERY AT MANHATTAN HOSPITAL *and is a half-page spread. The second is a* New York Times–*style column headlined* MIRACULOUS CHANGING MAN PUZZLES DOCTORS. *The third shows a line drawing of Zelig and is entitled* HUMAN WHO TRANSFORMS SELF DISCOVERED.

NARRATOR'S VOICE-OVER By now, word has gotten out to the press—and a public thirsting for thrills and novelty is immediately captivated.

CUT TO:
EXTERIOR. MANHATTAN HOSPITAL—DAY.

A press conference is under way. Dr. Allan Sindell, in topcoat and suit, stands at a podium cluttered with microphones. He's surrounded by colleagues, observers, and reporters. His voice is heard scratchily over the music and the narrator's introduction. Flashbulbs go off.

NARRATOR'S VOICE-OVER The clamor is so great that Dr. Allan Sindell is forced to issue a statement.

DR. ALLAN SINDELL *(Simultaneously, with the narrator)* What I have to say is very important . . . *(Speaking now without music or narration)* We're just beginning to realize the dimensions of what could be the scientific medical phenomenon of the age, and possibly of all time.
The film cuts to an old-fashioned printing press, churning out finished newspapers ready to be sold. A printer in cap and apron is next seen as he hands a large batch of papers to a co-worker. Next, a man carrying a heavy bundle of newspapers over his shoulder scurries across a busy New York City street.

He passes several pedestrians and moves out of the way of a moving truck. The narrator speaks over the scenes and over the background sounds of "Hot off the Presses."

NARRATOR'S VOICE-OVER Fresh stories roll off the press every day about Zelig and his puzzling condition.

The film cuts to four doctors, in topcoats and fedoras, leaving the hospital, walking down the front steps, and turning down the street. They are deep in conversation. A couple passes them, oblivious. "Hot off the Presses" continues in the background.

NARRATOR'S VOICE-OVER Although the doctors claim to have the situation in hand, no two can agree on a diagnosis.

The scene shifts to inside the hospital, where a Dr. Houseman is issuing a statement to the press. A microphone is standing in front of him; flashbulbs go off. Behind him stand other doctors and observers, including Dr. Fletcher.

DR. HOUSEMAN *(His voice scratchily heard)* I'm convinced that it's glandular in nature, and although there's no evidence now of any misfunction, I'm sure that further tests will show a problem in the secretions.

The film cuts to another doctor in a three-piece suit, his hands clasped behind his back. Next to him is a medical apparatus circa the 1920s.

DOCTOR IN THREE-PIECE SUIT I'm certain it's something he picked up from eating Mexican food.

Yet another authority, Dr. Birsky, is now seen on the screen. He's outside the hospital wearing a topcoat and fedora. A microphone looms in front of him. Observers and colleagues stand behind him.

DR. BIRSKY *(His voice heard as if on a scratchy recording)* This manifestation is neurological in origin. Now this patient is suffering from, uh, brain tumor. *(Nodding)* And I should not be surprised if within several weeks he died. Now, we have not as yet been able to locate the tumor *(Emphatically)* but we're still looking.

The film cuts to the front of a large home. Several pallbearers are carrying a floral-draped coffin out the front door, past a columned front porch, and down some steps. The somber sounds of a funeral dirge are heard; snow is on the ground.

NARRATOR'S VOICE-OVER Ironically, within two weeks' time, it is Dr. Birsky himself who dies of a brain tumor. Leonard Zelig is fine.

The scene shifts to Dr. Fletcher, her back to the camera. She is walking purposefully up the steps to the hospital, passing several nurses in caps and capes. In old newsreel style, the film skips as she opens the door. A doctor steps out, tipping his hat. He holds the door for her. She nods and enters.

The narrator continues to speak as the film moves to Dr. Fletcher in her office. She no longer wears her coat; she walks over to a cluttered bookshelf and picks up a book, flipping through the pages. She is deep in thought as, reading, she moves across her office, past a window and her desk, then settles down on a sofa. All the while, her eyes are on the book. Near the couch are a window and, hanging on the wall, a diploma.

NARRATOR'S VOICE-OVER Throughout the weeks of testing and speculation, Eudora Fletcher begins to feel that the patient might be suffering not from a physiological disorder but from a psychological one. It is Zelig's unstable makeup, she suggests, that accounts for his metamorphoses. The governing board of doctors is hostile to her notion.

The film cuts to a pained Zelig in hospital pajamas. He is lying on his back on a hospital gurney while two strong-looking orderlies pull at his arms and legs. A medicine cabinet and a clock are seen on the otherwise bare white-brick background wall. Zelig grimaces; the men push and grab, turning him to and fro.

NARRATOR'S VOICE-OVER They conclude that Zelig's malady

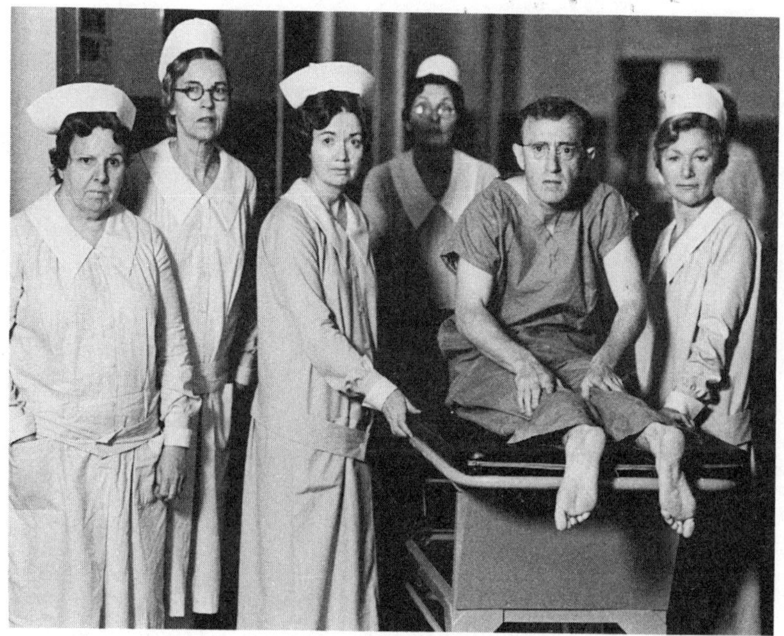

can be traced to poor alignment of the vertebrae. Tests prove them wrong and cause a . . .

CUT TO:

A hospital corridor. Surrounded by smiling nurses seemingly posing for a photographer, a less-then-happy Zelig sits up on a hospital gurney. He's massaging his legs—which are upside down and reversed.

NARRATOR'S VOICE-OVER *(Continuing)* . . . temporary problem for the patient.

The film shifts to the outside world, to a bustling New York City street corner. A newsstand vendor is busy selling paper after paper to the crowds of people walking by. Magazines line one wall of his stand.

NARRATOR'S VOICE-OVER Now the press and public hang on every bit of news, thoroughly absorbed in the real-life drama.

As a tinny radio announcer's broadcast is heard, the screen shows quick cuts of a bygone America—groups of people gathered around the radio and listening:

—A couple sitting in their living room, the woman cross-legged on a sofa, the man on a chair facing the radio.
—A mother relaxing in a big easy chair, her two daughters and the family dog on the floor around her. All face the radio; one of the girls pets the dog, the other holds a doll.
—An older couple sitting in two armchairs, their backs to the radio, the chairs almost touching. The man smokes a pipe; he holds a dog on his lap.
—An intense couple gathered close to the radio. The man, in a smoking jacket, leans forward in his chair, his ear to the radio; he looks up at his wife, then at the radio, a cigarette in his hand. The woman, wearing a long robe, her face offscreen, her legs crossed, sits in a chair; a magazine, unread, is on her lap.
—A father facing the radio, his back to the camera. Over his shoulder, his two sons are seen. One boy is sprawled on the floor, his head in his hands. The other little boy sits restlessly on the sofa in the lap of his mother; only her legs are seen.
—An elderly couple sitting looking up at a radio with a horn speaker. The man, partially off-camera, rocks back and forth in a rocker; a fan blows in the background.
—A couple sitting in front of their radio, reading different sections of the paper. The woman sits up very straight in her chair; a large photo sits on top of the radio.
—An enthusiastic couple right next to their radio. While the man fiddles with its tuning the woman leans forward on the edge of the sofa, nodding her head and smiling; a newspaper is spread on her lap.

RADIO ANNOUNCER'S VOICE-OVER The continuing saga of the strange creature at Manhattan Hospital goes on. This morning doctors report experiments were conducted and several women of varying types were placed in close proximity to the subject. But no change occurred, leading authorities to conclude that the phenomenon does not occur with women. Later today doctors will be experimenting with a midget and a chicken.

CUT TO:

A newsreel card bearing the headline NEW YORK CITY, *and underneath, the words* HOSPITAL PATIENT ASTONISHES MEDICAL WORLD. ORDINARY MAN DISPLAYS REMARKABLE TRAITS. *On the bottom, on either side of the Pathe News credit, is a rooster. The sounds of "Art Card Music for New York City" are heard as the newsreel begins.*

First seen is the front entrance of Manhattan Hospital, with its wrought-iron fence. A doctor briskly walks out its door; a few people pass by. Some cars are parked in front.

NEWSREEL ANNOUNCER'S VOICE-OVER Leonard Zelig continues to astound scientists at New York's Manhattan Hospital . . .
The newsreel next moves to an examination room, where Zelig sits in a hospital gown holding his arm. Four doctors stand next to him holding hypodermic needles and waiting their turn. Zelig looks up in fear as the first doctor, holding a giant needle, prepares his solution. He tries to inject Zelig's arm, but the latter turns around on his stool, refusing to sit still.

NEWSREEL ANNOUNCER'S VOICE-OVER . . . where numerous tests have led nowhere in determining the nature of this astonishing manifestation.
The screen then shows two obese men standing on either side of an equally obese Zelig. They chatter together; in the background of the hospital room, a nurse smiles for the camera.

NEWSREEL ANNOUNCER'S VOICE-OVER He is confronted by two overweight men at the request of the doctors. As the men discuss their obesity, an initially reticent Zelig joins in, swell-

ing himself to a miraculous two hundred and fifty pounds. Next, in the . . .
Zelig is next seen standing with two black men. He puts his arms around them, chatting and smiling. Zelig, too, is black. A serious-looking Dr. Fletcher stands in the background of the hospital room.

NEWSREEL ANNOUNCER'S VOICE-OVER . . . presence of two Negro men, Zelig rapidly becomes one himself. What *will* they think of next?
The newsreel moves back outside, to the entrance of a subway station. People crowd the stairs and the street, entering and exiting and quickly walking past the camera.

NEWSREEL ANNOUNCER'S VOICE-OVER Meanwhile, Americans all over have their own reactions.
The newsreel stops and the film cuts to a barbershop for some "Man in the Street" reactions. A customer, sitting in a chair, stares straight at the camera and talks. The chubby barber stands stiffly near him. A crowd of bystanders peer through the shop's window; cars pass on the street.

CUSTOMER I wish I could be Leonard Zelig, the changing man, and be different people. And maybe someday my wishes will come true.
Next, a stocky man in cap and overcoat addresses the camera. He is standing in a park; he stares straight ahead. There is some sculpture nearby; a couple, watching, stands in the background.

MAN Leonard Zelig is one of the finest gentlemen in the United States of America! He is the cat's pajamas!
The film moves to a close-up of Dr. Fletcher holding a spinning spiral apparatus at face level. Her eyes peer intensely over the apparatus; she looks straight at the camera as the spiral begins to spin.

NARRATOR'S VOICE-OVER Trying a new approach, Dr. Fletcher places the subject under hypnosis.

The movie cuts to a still photograph of a hypnotized Zelig in a trance. His eyes are closed; he sits fully dressed in a chair. As the camera moves back, more of the photo is seen, revealing Zelig's extended arm. A scratchy tape-recorded dialogue between doctor and patient ensues as the film moves to a different photo. Dr. Fletcher's face is seen,

staring intently at Zelig. The camera leaves her and moves past the spiral apparatus to Zelig's hypnotized face, seen now from a different angle. The scratchy recording continues.

DR. FLETCHER'S VOICE-OVER All right, now, tell me why you assume the characteristics of the person you're with.

LEONARD ZELIG'S VOICE-OVER *(In a trancelike voice)* It's . . . sss-safe.

DR. FLETCHER'S VOICE-OVER What do you mean? What do you mean safe?

LEONARD ZELIG'S VOICE-OVER S-safe . . . t-to be like the others.

DR. FLETCHER'S VOICE-OVER Uh-hum. You w-, you want to be safe?

The camera moves closer and closer in on Zelig's face in the still photograph.

LEONARD ZELIG'S VOICE-OVER I want to be liked.

DR. FLETCHER'S VOICE-OVER Uh-huh.

CUT TO:
INTERIOR. HOSPITAL CORRIDOR—DAY.

Dr. Fletcher opens a swinging door and enters the corridor, deep in conversation with two of her colleagues. She nods, talking silently, as the narrator speaks over the scene. She wears a coat. They pass out of the corridor, leaving through another swinging door. The narrator continues as a nurse and a woman swathed in furs walk towards the camera.

NARRATOR'S VOICE-OVER Probing Zelig's unconscious, Dr. Fletcher gradually puts together the pieces of Zelig's behavioral puzzle.

The film cuts to 42nd Street, outside the New York Public Library, circa the 1920s. People walk across the street, down the sidewalks. Cars pass. The library and bare tree branches are clouded in mist.

NARRATOR'S VOICE-OVER Dividing her time between the hospital and the Forty-second Street library, she writes her report.

CUT TO:
INTERIOR. HOSPITAL—DAY.

Dr. Fletcher is pacing in front of a hospital classroom filled with her peers. She holds some notes, glancing down at them occasionally as she talks silently. Behind her is a large blackboard. The doctors, sitting at desks, their backs to the camera, listen; some smoke cigarettes.

As the narrator speaks, the screen shifts to a close-up of Dr. Fletcher, standing in front of an anatomy chart. She has stopped pacing.

While the narration continues, the camera moves over the faces of the listening doctors. Some nod their heads; some look arrogant, even hostile. One of them takes notes; another mutters. They all wear suits.

NARRATOR'S VOICE-OVER A closed meeting of doctors listens as Dr. Fletcher describes Zelig as a human chameleon. Like the lizard that is endowed by nature with a marvelous protective device that enables it to change color and blend in with its immediate surrounding, Zelig, too, protects himself by becoming whoever he is around. The doctors listen and their reaction is skeptical: "Impossible," they claim, "preposterous." "If he's a lizard," quips one doctor, "then we should not spend good hospital money feeding him but simply catch him some flies."

The minor tones of "Leonard the Lizard" are heard once again as the film cuts to a series of newspaper articles. The first, in a New York Times *print style, is headlined* HUMAN CHAMELEON FOUND ACCORDING TO WOMAN DOCTOR. *The second article is first seen on an entire newspaper page, the camera moving quickly in on the pertinent column, entitled* ZELIG SAID TO SUFFER UNIQUE MENTAL DISORDER. *The third reads* IT'S ALL IN THE HEAD.

The film then abruptly cuts to the present day in living color. Ted Bierbauer and Mike Geibell are in a cluttered office talking to an off-screen interviewer. Behind some packed, open shelves is a large window. The men wear suits. As they talk, the legend MIKE GEIBELL AND TED BIERBAUER, FORMERLY OF THE NEW YORK DAILY MIRROR *flashes on the screen in white lettering.*

TED BIERBAUER *(Sitting in a chair)* Well, we knew we had a good story this time, 'cause it had everything in it. It had romance and it had suspense . . . then this fella, Zelig, you know . . . he grew up poor. *(Nodding)* I remember my city editor came to me and he said, "Ted . . . we want this story on page one every day."

MIKE GEIBELL *(Standing next to Ted)* And in those days, you'd do anything to sell papers. *(Gesturing)* You'd . . . to get a story, you'd jazz it up, you'd exaggerate; you'd even maybe play with the truth a little bit . . . but . . . *(Pauses)* here was a story. It was a natural. You just told the truth and it sold papers. It never happened before.

As the energetic sounds of "Hot off the Presses" are heard, the film switches back to black-and-white, in the 1920s. New York City's theater district is ablaze with flashing marquees, crowded with pedestrians walking up and down its sidewalks, and jam-packed with cars causing traffic snarls. A marquee in the foreground proclaims a Patsy Kelly attraction. It's a daytime rush hour.

As the narrator begins anew, the movie cuts to a crowd of men in topcoats and hats, out on the street, talking as traffic goes by, then cuts to a closer view of the men in twos and threes in intense conversation.

NARRATOR'S VOICE-OVER Overnight, Leonard Zelig has become the main topic of conversation everywhere and is discussed with amusement and wonder.

It's night now on the screen. A marquee, complete with hot lights, spells out VARSITY DANCE HALL. *The camera moves down from the marquee as the narrator continues his tale, to the entrance door, blazing with light, its sign out front headlining the night's main event:* CHAMELEON DANCE CONTEST.

NARRATOR'S VOICE-OVER No social gathering is without its Leonard Zelig joke, and in a decade of popular dance crazes, a new one sweeps the nation.

The film moves inside, to a rocking dance floor. Couples—the men in suits, the women in flapper dresses, cloche hats, and bobbed hair—dance to "Doin' the Chameleon" while a band on the stage plays. The sounds of the song, in an old-fashioned recording, is heard.

SINGER'S VOICE-OVER "There's a brand new dance come up the river. / Just jerk your head and shake your liver. / You're doin' the Chameleon! / Vo-do-do-de-o. / Make a face that's like a lizard / And feel that beat down in your gizzard. / You're doin' the Chameleon! / (Pah!)"

As the song continues, the camera moves in closer on one of the couples, showing the finer details of the dance: clasping hands, looking pop-eyed at each other, and sticking out their tongues lizard-style. They strut in and out, still clasping hands, dancing to the music. People watch in the background.

SINGER'S VOICE-OVER "Stick out your tongue the way the reptiles do / Tryin' to catch a fly. / Inflate your lung like big crocodiles do. / Hey hey, my, oh, my!"

The camera next focuses on a flapper really into the Chameleon. She kicks up her heels, her hands angled out as if she were a strutting lizard. Her skirt swirls, her long rope of pearls bounces. Behind her, the saxophonist and the piano player in the band are seen, as well as watching patrons.

SINGER'S VOICE-OVER "Throw your best gal down right on the floor, / She'll be beggin' you for more, / And you're doin' the Chameleon!"

Still "Doin' the Chameleon," the film cuts to a Harlem street corner. Four black children, the girls in white pinafores, the boys in knickers, dance to the song near an elevated-subway entrance—to the delight of several watching adults. The camera moves closer to two of the dancing children. They're in perfect form: hands clasped, eyes open wide, and tongues flicking out.

SINGER'S VOICE-OVER "If you hold your breath till you turn blue / You'll be changing colors like they do, / And you're doin' the Chameleon! / Vo-do-do-de-o."

The song still playing in the background, the movie cuts to a man on the street wearing a sandwich sign that reads LEARN THE LATEST STEPS, THE CHARLESTON, THE CHAMELEON. *He wears a cap and smokes a cigarette as people pass by. He chatters to the offscreen newsreel cameraman.*

SINGER'S VOICE-OVER "Wiggle like a salamander, / Go this way, that way . . ."

The screen now shows a close-up of three light bulbs attached to a mechanical device. They start to glow as the film cuts to Zelig, who is attached to the device, which looks like one of Dr. Frankenstein's creations. He's strapped in a chair, a helmet on his head. A nurse quickly passes as two doctors, one on either side, prepare for the "experiment." One, observing, writes on a clipboard. The other, in a white lab coat and dark glasses, pulls a switch on the chairlike apparatus. Electric sparks start to fly across Zelig's torso; his body tenses. The music continues.

SINGER'S VOICE-OVER ". . . all meander. / You're doin' the Chameleon! (Pah!) / Stick out your tongue the way reptiles do / Tryin' to catch a fly."

While the music plays on, the film cuts to a hospital room, where Zelig is stretched out on a bed. Five doctors standing in a tight row from his head to his feet listen to his heart via a giant stethoscope with five attachments—one for each doctor. Dr. Fletcher peers over the shoulder of the doctor closest to Zelig's head.

SINGER'S VOICE-OVER "Inflate your lung like big crocodiles do."
The film cuts to a storefront that prominently displays a sign advertising WE HAVE PHOTOS OF ZELIG, *under which is a partial list:* CHINESE, INTELLECTUAL, OVERWEIGHT . . . *People gather at the window, looking at the sample photos on display and reading the sign. A couple passes by in front of the camera.*

SINGER'S VOICE-OVER "Hey hey, my, oh, my! / Shake your shoulders, move your seat around, / Get right down and . . ."
"Doin' the Chameleon" continues as the film moves back to the hospital. There, in full kilt costume, is a bearded Scotsman. And there, next to him, posing for a photo, is Zelig—the Scot. He too is in a kilt and beard. In the background, a doctor in a labcoat, holding a clipboard, stares at the offscreen newsreel camera. The two "Scots" are chattering together as the camera moves in on Zelig's bearded face.

SINGER'S VOICE-OVER ". . . kick your feet around, / Doin' the Chameleon! / Vo-de-o-do."
The song stops as the film cuts to four college freshmen, complete with beanies and white sweaters, posed on the stone stairs of their school. They stare into the offscreen newsreel camera as two of them recite a Zelig joke. They barely move.

FIRST FRESHMAN *(His hands in his pockets)* What's brown and white and yellow and has four eyes?

SECOND FRESHMAN *(His hands in his pockets)* Leonard Zelig at the League of Nations.
They all laugh, the third freshman turning to look at the second freshman beside him.

CUT TO:

A large parade in progress down a city street. Men carrying Russian flags march by, in front of a marching band in formation. Onlookers line the sidewalks. A trolley car goes by in the distance. Over the paradelike sounds of "The Internationale," the narrator begins anew.

NARRATOR'S VOICE-OVER Not everyone, however, was entranced by the human . . .

The movie switches to a protest march. Crowds carrying placards proclaiming HEARST A FASCIST, BUILD A MASS LABOR PARTY, *and other pro-labor and anti-fascist signs march past uniformed policemen and curious onlookers. The narrator continues.*

NARRATOR'S VOICE-OVER . . . chameleon, and amongst the fanatics, he was a handy symbol of inequity.

The film cuts to a giant crowd of people. As a speaker yells into a microphone, the camera moves across the mass of humanity to an American flag–draped soapbox. There, the speaker is pontificating, shouting his message, while people press all around and below him; some carry placards.

SOAPBOX SPEAKER *(Offscreen, his voice reverberating over a loudspeaker)* This creature personifies capitalist man. A creature *(Onscreen)* who takes many forms, to achieve *(Film skips)* ends, the exploitation of the workers by deception.

As the crowd cheers and applauds, the camera cuts to some of the faces in the crowd, to a group of men applauding and listening. One of the men holds up a sign that reads: ZELIG UNFAIR TO WORKERS, HOLDS FIVE JOBS.

CUT TO:
EXTERIOR. FIELD—NIGHT.

White-robed Ku Klux Klan members silently and sinisterly march down a dark country road; the leader holds a burning cross. Ominous music is heard as the narrator speaks, as the members file past the camera, as the film cuts to the Klan members gathered around a towering burning cross, an ominous mountain in the background. The camera moves to a closer glimpse of the large group. Some of the white-robed members wave at the camera.

NARRATOR'S VOICE-OVER To the Ku Klux Klan, Zelig, a Jew who was able to transform himself into a Negro or Indian, was a triple threat.

CUT TO:

Dr. Fletcher getting out of a cab in front of the courthouse. The camera follows her as she briskly walks up the courthouse stairs; she carries her pocketbook and gloves. As she leaves the cab, a reporter snaps her picture; another reporter follows her up the stairs and a couple stare after her in recognition. She's become a celebrity.

NARRATOR'S VOICE-OVER Meanwhile, Dr. Fletcher, certain that her findings are correct, begs for time with her patient to put her theories into operation.

The film abruptly cuts to a still photograph of Zelig. His face, in the throes of an hypnotic trance, fills the screen. The camera moves back, farther and farther, until he is seen sitting in a spindle-backed chair in his hospital room. His arm is extended. A scratchy recording of his

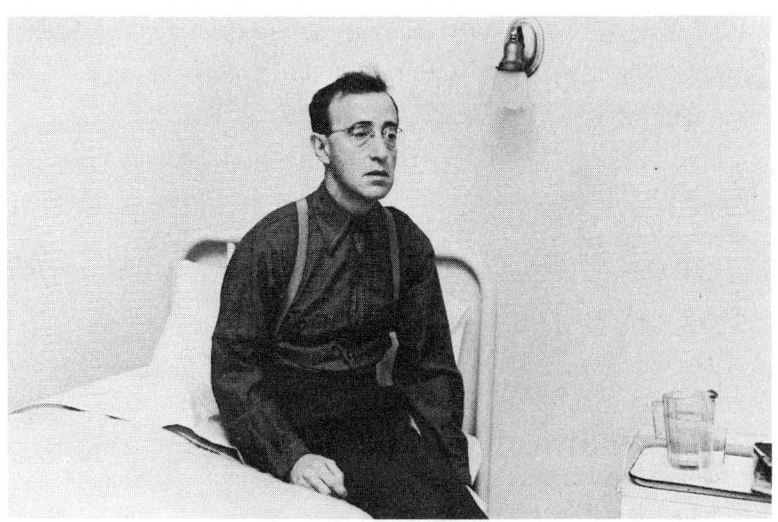

psychiatric session with Dr. Fletcher is heard over the scene, continuing as the film cuts to a different photo of Zelig. He is slumped on the edge of his hospital bed, a sad, lost expression on his face; his eyes are closed. The camera moves closer and closer in on his face.

DR. FLETCHER'S VOICE-OVER You recall the first time you began behaving like the people you were around?

LEONARD ZELIG'S VOICE-OVER *(In a trancelike voice)* In school . . . some very bright people . . . asked me if I read *Moby Dick.*

DR. FLETCHER'S VOICE-OVER Yes?

LEONARD ZELIG'S VOICE-OVER I was ashamed to say I never read it.

DR. FLETCHER'S VOICE-OVER And you pretended?

LEONARD ZELIG'S VOICE-OVER Yes.

DR. FLETCHER'S VOICE-OVER When did the changes begin happening automatically?

LEONARD ZELIG'S VOICE-OVER Years ago . . .
While the scratchily recorded dialogue continues, the film cuts to Dr. Fletcher sitting at her desk, listening intently to the dialogue on an old-fashioned tape recorder. She is alone; she smokes a cigarette.

LEONARD ZELIG'S VOICE-OVER *(Continuing in a trancelike, recorded voice)* St. Patrick's Day . . . wandered into a bar . . . wasn't wearing green.
As the scratchy recording continues, the film cuts to various hospital scenes:

—*Two nurses leaving the hospital, walking down the stairs and out the gate. They pass a couple walking in. A car is parked on the street; another car drives by.*
—*A weak-looking, subdued Zelig shuffling down a hospital corridor in a robe. Dr. Fletcher holds his arm, supporting him. Another*

doctor walks alongside them. He and Dr. Fletcher exchange silent concerned looks.

—*A close-up of Zelig's medical record with a section entitled* TRANSFUSION RECORD. *The file cover is quickly flipped over it. The cover is stamped* MANHATTAN HOSPITAL. ACCESS 01212 LEONARD Z.

LEONARD ZELIG'S VOICE-OVER *(Continuing in a trancelike voice)* They made remarks . . . I turned Irish.

DR. FLETCHER'S VOICE-OVER You told them you were Irish?

LEONARD ZELIG'S VOICE-OVER My hair turned red . . . my nose turned up . . . spoke about the great potato famine . . . and the little people.

CUT TO:
EXTERIOR. MANHATTAN HOSPITAL—DAY.

Dr. Fogey, in hat and topcoat, stands stiffly on the hospital steps, facing the camera. In front of him are two old-fashioned microphones. As he issues his statement to the press, flashbulbs go off.

DR. FOGEY We do not agree with Dr. Fletcher's ideas. We believe those ideas are pipe dreams. We believe that any change in Zelig's condition is going to be brought about through certain experimental drugs, which although risky have been known to work wonders.
The narrator begins anew as the film cuts to a hospital storeroom. Bottles, in different sizes and shapes, line the floor-to-ceiling rows of shelves. A lab technician works in the background as the film cuts to a close-up of several corked medicine bottles on one of the shelves.

NARRATOR'S VOICE-OVER Zelig is treated with the experimental drug Somadril Hydrate.
The scene shifts to Zelig's hospital room. An attendant stands near his bed, taking notes, as Zelig begins to walk up the wall. The spindle-backed chair, a lamp, and a window are in the background.

NARRATOR'S VOICE-OVER He undergoes severe mood changes, and for several days, will not come off the wall.

CUT TO:

An expectant crowd, their backs to the camera, are gathered outside the gates of the hospital entrance. The anticipatory sounds of "A New Twist" are heard as Zelig is escorted out the door by his sister Ruth and her lover, Martin Geist. Two plainclothes policemen lead the way; behind them are several uniformed policemen who help clear a path through the crowd. Zelig and company walk out the entranceway to a waiting car. Zelig, Ruth, and Martin get into the car while the policemen keep the crowds back.

NARRATOR'S VOICE-OVER Then, suddenly, as Dr. Fletcher is beginning to make some progress, the question of Zelig's fate takes a new twist as his half sister, Ruth, shocks everyone by removing him from the hospital. He can be better cared for at home, she tells the doctors. He will be looked after, she explains, by her dubious-looking lover, Martin Geist, a businessman and ex–carnival promoter. There is very little resistance amongst the doctors, who are relieved to be rid of the frustrating case.

The film cuts to a worried Dr. Fletcher walking down a hospital stairwell with her colleague Dr. Sindell. They are deep in silent conversation as they pass a man in a cap and coat who stares at the offscreen camera, and a uniformed nurse who stares after the retreating doctors.

NARRATOR'S VOICE-OVER Only Dr. Fletcher cares about Zelig as a human being. She insists he desperately needs special care, but it is to no avail.

The music stops and the film suddenly cuts to full color, in the present day; newspapermen Ted Bierbauer and Mike Geibell continue their interview in their cluttered office.

TED BIERBAUER *(Sitting in his chair, nodding)* No . . . ah . . . no one was questioning her legal right to Zelig—I mean, she was his half sister and his guardian, but she had a strange boyfriend called . . .

The film cuts to a blow-up of a black-and-white still photograph of Martin Geist, circa the 1920s. He stands next to another man whose face is only half-seen. Behind them is a car; they are outside. Ted Bierbauer continues to speak.

TED BIERBAUER'S VOICE-OVER . . . Geist that, ah . . . he'd been in jail for real estate fraud, he was . . .

The scene shifts back to the present day, to color, in Ted Bierbauer's cluttered office. The interview continues. Ted is still speaking and Mike Geibell, standing, his arms crossed, looks at Ted, listening.

TED BIERBAUER . . . selling the same piece of property to a lot of the same people and . . . matter of fact, a congressman from Delaware bought it twice.

The film cuts to traffic of the late 1920s, in black-and-white. Cars are inching their way towards a tollbooth as a camera moves across them, past some ratty flag streamers, to the booths themselves. "Runnin' Wild" is heard in the background as the narrator begins anew. As he speaks, the traffic scene shifts, showing policemen on motorbikes escorting a line of buses down a parking lot packed with cars. A few trees and telephone poles line the lot.

NARRATOR'S VOICE-OVER The crowds that line the roads to glimpse the human chameleon tie up traffic for days. He is a sight to behold for tourists and children. People from all over the country fight for space to peek at this new wonderment.

The camera moves across a crowd of parked cars and milling people. Men, women, and children are seen; balloons bob in the air. The camera moves up from the crowded lot to a huge billboard framed by bare trees. On it is a drawing of a lizard, above which is printed: MARTIN GEIST AND RUTH ZELIG PRESENT THE PHENOMENON OF THE AGES.

The music continues as the film cuts to a serious-looking uniformed guard standing in front of a shingled building. A nearby sign, nailed to the building, reads SEE THE LIVING CHAMELEON 35¢ *and in smaller print on the same sign,* A MARTIN GEIST PHENOMENON.

The narrator begins anew and the film cuts to Ruth Zelig standing outside the exhibition arena. She is facing the camera and proudly holding up a flier with a sketch of Zelig's face and the caption SEE LEONARD—GEIST FARM. *From a pile of fliers in her hand, she flips up another one, identical to the first, and holds them both up, side by side. She smiles at the watching bystanders.*

NARRATOR'S VOICE-OVER Selling mementos while her brother is allowed to be on exhibition is only the beginning for Ruth Zelig and Martin Geist.
Ruth is next seen standing proudly in front of a chain-link fence bearing the sign: REQUESTS—SEE ZELIG TURN INTO YOU—$1.00. *She is smiling; people pass by on the other side of the fence.*

The narrator continues to speak as the film cuts to Martin Geist in a suit, standing and barking behind the chain-link fence. A crowd of people, their backs to the camera, stand on the other side of the fence, watching, as the camera moves across their backs to another section of the chain-linked arena. There, behind the fence, is an American Indian standing next to Zelig, who is also an Indian—complete with blanket shawl, braids, and feathers.

NARRATOR'S VOICE-OVER Admission is charged to twice-daily demonstrations of Leonard's stunning prowess. He does not disappoint, changing appearance over and over upon demand.
The camera moves over the fence, and close up to the Indian's quietly dignified, solemn face, then moves to an equally stoic Zelig; his eyes are lined with deep circles.

NARRATOR'S VOICE-OVER Overnight, he has become an attraction, a novelty, a freak.
The movie cuts to a film clip from The Changing Man. *A telephone switchboard operator is seen on the screen, busily plugging in countless telephone lines on her board. The sophisticated tones of "The Changing Man Concerto" are heard in the background.*

OPERATOR *(In the film clip)* Yes, I'll connect you, sir. I'm sorry—
The narrator's voice is heard over the clip's dialogue. Superimposed on the bottom of the screen is the legend "THE CHANGING MAN," WARNER BROS., 1935.

NARRATOR'S VOICE-OVER *(Over the operator's dialogue)* In this 1935 film based on the life of Zelig . . .
The legend still superimposed on the screen, the clip cuts to an elegant-looking older woman talking on the telephone, her frame filling the left side of the dark screen.

OLDER WOMAN *(Into the phone, in the film clip)* Have you heard about Leonard Zelig?
Next is seen an older suited man, also talking on the phone; his frame

fills the right side of the dark screen. The legend "THE CHANGING MAN," WARNER BROS., 1935 *still appears.*

MAN *(Into the phone, in the film clip)* Oddest thing you ever saw!
The clip next shows the older woman's mouth, still talking into the telephone.

WOMAN'S MOUTH *(Into the phone, in the film clip)* I've got to see it to believe it!
While the dialogue in the telephone-talking clip goes on, the narrator continues to speak over it.

NARRATOR'S VOICE-OVER *(Overlapping the clip's dialogue, continuing)* . . . called *The Changing Man*, the atmosphere is best summed up.
The film cuts to a different scene from the 1935 movie. A glamorous, dark-haired actress playing Dr. Fletcher is seen on the screen in a hospital interior set. Behind her is a medicine cabinet on which sit models of a brain and a head.

ACTRESS FLETCHER We can't give up custody of Leonard. I know if I'm given the chance I can cure him.
An actor doctor, smoking a pipe, moves onscreen. He stands next to her.

ACTOR DOCTOR It's no use. Even our attorney says it's hopeless.
The camera cuts across the office. Standing in the doorway is another actor, playing a lawyer. He leans on the door frame, his arms folded. On the wall next to him is a telephone. He wears a suit.

ACTOR LAWYER *(Offscreen)* Really, Dr. Fletcher . . . *(Onscreen)* uh . . . *(Pauses)* May I call you Eudora?
The camera is back on the Dr. Fletcher actress and her male colleague.

ACTRESS FLETCHER I tell you, somewhere behind that vacuous face, that zombielike . . .
As her male colleague turns, the camera shows his point of view: a

cute, well-built actor playing Zelig is sitting on a gurney in the office. He stares off into space. The music swells.

ACTRESS FLETCHER *(Continuing, offscreen)* . . . stare, is a real human being—and I can bring it out.
The camera moves back to the actress Dr. Fletcher and her male colleague.

ACTOR DOCTOR *(Brandishing his pipe)* How?

ACTRESS FLETCHER I'll think up some new way. Some technique! *(Turning to look at the actor doctor)* Whatever it is, it'll have to be personal.
The camera moves to the lawyer in the doorway.

ACTOR LAWYER There's not much I can do legally. I'll try but, uh— *(Shrugs)*

ACTRESS FLETCHER *(Interrupting, the camera back on her face)* They don't care about him. They'll exploit him—all they see in him is a chance to make more money. Look at this. *(Picking up a doll that looks like a lizard dressed in a tuxedo)* Already they're selling this Leonard Zelig doll.
As the clip from The Changing Man *ends, the film cuts back to the chronicle of Zelig's life. With "Chameleon Days" playing in the background, the narrator begins to speak. The camera moves across a tabletop filled with Zelig-inspired gifts and souvenirs, including a clock with an elaborate curlicue design, a box with Zelig's face on the cover, a game, an ashtray, a toy holding black Zelig and white Zelig figures, a clock with three different Zelig heads on its top. The camera continues to show the items as the narrator speaks; an arm wearing a wristwatch is seen onscreen. Its face bears a chameleon body and a Zelig human head. A hand enters the screen and winds the watch.*

NARRATOR'S VOICE-OVER The film did not exaggerate. There were not only Leonard Zelig pens and lucky charms but clocks and toys. There were Leonard Zelig watches and books and a famous Leonard Zelig doll. There were aprons, chameleon-shaped earmuffs, and a popular Leonard Zelig game.

As Helen Kane in a Betty Boop–like voice begins the up-tempo "Chameleon Days" vocal, more Zelig items flash on the screen: a children's book titled The Little Chameleon Boy *showing Zelig and a chameleon strolling through a fantasy land; three mystery books in a series, entitled* Leonard Zelig and the Belfry Bats, Leonard Zelig and the Haunted Mountain, *and* Leonard Zelig and the Mischievous Mummy; *the box for the Leonard Zelig doll, which states on its cover,* CHANGE THE HEADS WITH A TWIST OF YOUR WRIST; *and a young, smiling boy holding up the Zelig doll, dressed in pants and a flannel shirt, with a black Zelig head. He takes off the head and puts on an Asian Zelig head in a coolie cap.*

HELEN KANE'S VOICE-OVER *(Singing)* "Ev'rybody go chameleon, / Ev'rybody show chameleon, / Take it fast or slow, chameleon, chameleon . . ."

As Helen Kane continues to sing, the film shows a montage of Americans "going chameleon":

—*A woman, facing the camera and smiling, standing in her well-stocked kitchen. She wears a Zelig-inspired apron bearing the words* CHANGE FOR DINNER *with a drawing of a chameleon wearing glasses. She holds the ends of the apron out and turns to laugh with an offscreen observer.*

—*A young woman, facing the camera and dressed in a warm coat, standing on a busy street corner. She smiles broadly, showing off her chameleon-shaped mittens and earmuffs—which resemble a chameleon cut in half. A boyfriend jumps onscreen behind her, teasing her. She turns, laughing and talking; a pocketbook hangs from her arm.*

—*A crowded store display window that prominently displays a chameleon-bodied meat thermometer with a Zelig head. A sign next to it informs the public that the thermometers are in stock.*

—*An elaborately drawn board for the Chameleon Game. The camera slowly moves down the board, which shows a giant chameleon cut into sections, the finish line at its tail. Small figures of Zelig are drawn on the lizard, in the sections and in the background.*

—*A pet shop window with puppies bouncing inside and a huge sign saying* SALE: LEONARD ZELIG APPROVED CHAMELEONS. *Three people stand posed in the doorway, facing the camera; they start to smile.*

—*A still photo of a huge billboard advertising cigarettes. Zelig, wearing a suit and his ever present glasses, is drawn face-front on the right; a badly drawn hand holds a cigarette. On the left are the words* LEONARD ZELIG SAYS . . . WE SMOKE CAMELS. *The camera moves back, revealing the billboard's prime location—atop a busy Times Square frozen in time.*

—*A photograph of a print ad, headlined with the words* WHEN I'M THROUGH CHANGING INTO OTHER PEOPLE I LIKE TO CHANGE INTO PENDLETON UNDERWEAR. *The camera moves down the page to reveal a drawing showing a chameleon man in a shirt. He stands by a dressing room with* MR. ZELIG *above a star and* CHANGING ROOM *below.*

—*A phonograph record with an RCA Victor label, which identifies it as* "CHAMELEON DAYS FOX TROT"—VOCAL: HELEN KANE. *The camera moves closer and closer.*

HELEN KANE'S VOICE-OVER *(Singing, continuing)* ". . . chameleon days! / Ev'rybody think chameleon, / Ev'rytime you blink, chameleon, / In your kitchen sink, chameleon, chameleon, chameleon days! / They're so much fun, they'll even jump right through a hoop, *(Gasps)* / And they change color when they're swimming in your soup. / Boop-boop-ee-doop! / Flying in the air, chameleon, / Crawling in your hair, chameleon, / Take away all your care, chameleon, chameleon, chameleon days!"

Helen Kane finishes her song as the film cuts to a sheet music cover for "You May Be Six People, But I Love You." The camera moves in closer to the cover; within its design is a center circle—and within that circle is a drawing of Zelig as himself.

NARRATOR'S VOICE-OVER There were many popular songs inspired by Leonard Zelig—tunes that swept the nation.

The song "You May Be Six People, But I Love You" begins as the narrator finishes for the moment. The drawing of Zelig as himself within the sheet music cover dissolves to a photo of Zelig as an American Indian. As the song continues, the photos of Zelig within the circle continue to change: His Indian dissolves to a photo of Zelig as the fat man, a nurse's face in the background; Zelig as an intellectual, eyes down, in front of a framed picture; then a photo of Zelig as himself again, looking right at the camera.

SINGER'S VOICE-OVER *(Overlapping the narrator)* "You may be six people, but I love you, / I want you for myself alone . . ."
The music changes to "Leonard the Lizard" as the camera moves closer and closer to the photo of Zelig as himself in the sheet music cover's circle. As if the camera has gone "inside" the circle, the screen dissolves to another sheet music cover—with that photo of Zelig as himself a part of the design. This cover is for "Leonard the Lizard."

SINGER'S VOICE-OVER "Leonard the Lizard, / See him running across the floor, / See him skittering out the door . . ."
The "Leonard the Lizard" sheet music cover dissolves to the cover for "Reptile Eyes." The camera moves closer and closer to a drawing of Zelig on the cover as a woman sings the song—until the cover dissolves to a still photograph of Zelig, looking trim but intensely sad in a suit and tie. The camera moves in closer to his face. The woman continues to sing.

FEMALE SINGER'S VOICE-OVER "You have such reptile eyes, / Eyes like a lizard that weave their spell . . ."
The narrator speaks anew as the film cuts to a crowded, busy New York City street. People walk down the sidewalk; cars line the streets.

In the foreground, a theater marquee is seen, proclaiming: TONIGHT ONLY—LEONARD ZELIG *and underneath his name,* EDDIE CANTOR. *"Endless Exhibitions" and "Leonard the Lizard" are heard in the background in sweeping orchestration.*

NARRATOR'S VOICE-OVER In addition to the products and endorsements, there are the endless exhibitions.
The film cuts to Hollywood, to Grauman's Chinese Theatre, spectacularly lit up in the night sky. Searchlights frame the entrance, with its mobs of roped-off people, its guards, and its limousines stopping to let off stars. As the narrator continues, the film cuts to the theater lobby—dramatically decorated with palm trees and huge pillars. More people are gathered here, milling about, as the film moves in on a formally dressed Zelig, standing with his sister Ruth and Martin Geist; they too are in evening dress. They pose for pictures, smiling as flashbulbs go off and people walk by. Zelig, seemingly uncomfortable, scratches his nose.

NARRATOR'S VOICE-OVER In Hollywood, he is a great favorite and is offered a film contract. Clara Bow invites him for a private weekend and tells him to bring all his personalities.
The film leaves Hollywood and cuts to a still photo of Jack Dempsey and Zelig—wearing a leather boxing cap on his head. They sit on a stoop of a house at Dempsey's training camp. The camera moves closer and closer in on Zelig's face.

NARRATOR'S VOICE-OVER In Chicago, he meets heavyweight champion Jack Dempsey, who clowns with Zelig at his training camp.
Zelig's "boxing" face dissolves to a more distinguished-looking, serious face. The camera moves back to reveal a suited Zelig standing between Calvin Coolidge and Herbert Hoover.

NARRATOR'S VOICE-OVER In Washington, D.C., he is introduced to both Calvin Coolidge and Herbert Hoover.
The film cuts to a photograph taken in Paris. Three men in suits stand

in a row, looking at a nearby poster advertising Zelig's Parisian show and "L'Homme Caméléon." Half of a different poster, under Zelig's ad, is posted on the board. "Paree" plays in the background.

NARRATOR'S VOICE-OVER In France, he is hailed as "Le Lezard." He is the toast of the . . .

A Parisian revue starring Zelig is next seen on the screen. The stage has an elaborate Art Deco backdrop; spotlights scan the proscenium;

the audience is full. Zelig stands in the middle, flanked by women in ornate sequined costumes and the Parisians he'll later become as the chameleon. The background music is "La Sorella." The narrator continues to speak as the screen cuts to Zelig, later in the show, flanked by two Hassidic rabbis. They talk and gesture as Zelig looks from one to another. He slowly begins to grow a Hassidic beard.

NARRATOR'S VOICE-OVER . . . Parisian music halls. His performance endears him as well to many leading French intellectuals, who see in him a symbol for everything.

The film cuts quickly to the audience, clapping wildly and whistling enthusiastically, then back to the stage. The narrator continues to speak as Zelig is now seen complete with long beard, hat, and coat—a perfect replica of the two Hassidic rabbis on stage with him. A woman in a body-hugging sequined costume and headdress flourishes her cape, presenting him and his feat to the audience. Spotlights twirl madly on the stage. The applause continues.

NARRATOR'S VOICE-OVER His transformation into a rabbi is so realistic that certain Frenchmen suggest he be sent to Devil's Island.

A jazz rendition of "Doin' the Chameleon" begins to play as the film cuts to a montage of Gay Paree at night, including:

—A lit-up marquee advertising the Bal du Moulin Rouge Art Deco entrance.
—Glittering, prancing ponies, bordering a corner of a nightspot.
—The simple lit-up marquee of the Folies Bergère, in script and in blazing, bold letters.

CUT TO:

Josephine Baker, on stage at the Folies Bergère, dancing her version of "Doin' the Chameleon" in a glittering, slinky costume, surrounded by costumed and choreographed men and women. They dance on a rope-bordered platform.

NARRATOR'S VOICE-OVER At the Folies Bergère Josephine Baker does her version of the Chameleon dance and later tells friends she finds Zelig amazing . . .

The film cuts backstage, to Josephine Baker's dressing room, where the performer, in her banana costume, puts her arm around Zelig. She

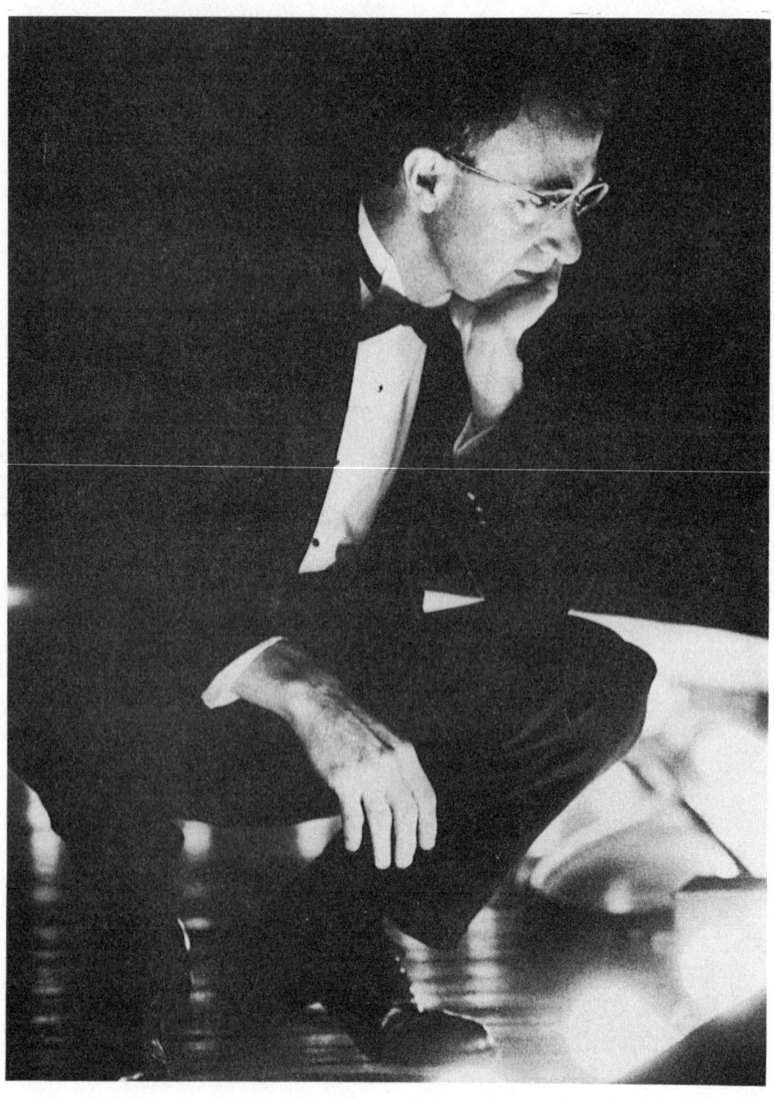

chatters, motioning to a nearby Ruth Zelig to join the picture. Ruth, smiling, shakes her head, staying in the background.

NARRATOR'S VOICE-OVER . . . but a little lost.

The film cuts to the present day in color; Bricktop sits by a window in a huge, high-backed chair. As she talks to an offscreen interviewer, the legend BRICKTOP, OWNER OF BRICKTOP'S, A PARIS NIGHTCLUB IN THE 1920'S *is superimposed on the bottom of the screen in white lettering.*

BRICKTOP *(Her hands folded on her lap)* Everyone used to be at my place, that is everyone who was someone. And ah . . . ah occasionally ah . . . someone would bring um . . . Zelig in—Leonard in. *(Shaking her head)* Cole Porter was fascinated by ah . . . Leonard and he once wrote a line in a song . . . uh, "You're the tops, you're Leonard Zelig." But then he couldn't find anything to rhyme with Zelig.

The film cuts back to the past, to a newsreel title card headlined MANHATTAN. *Underneath is the news item:* ZIEGFELD STAR FANNY BRICE AND HER HUSBAND BILLY ROSE SERENADE LEONARD ZELIG ATOP WESTBURY HOTEL. *On the bottom of the card is the Pathe News credit with its rooster logos in the bottom left and right corners. Up-tempo newsreel music plays, turning to "I've Got a Feeling I'm Falling," sung by Fanny Brice, as the film cuts to the roof of the Westbury. Fanny Brice, in culottes and snood, sings while Billy Rose beats time with his foot. A group of women stand behind them, smiling and bouncing to the music; one woman snaps her fingers; a breeze blows their clothes.*

As Fanny Brice sings, the film cuts to Zelig and Ruth, sitting in chairs, their legs crossed, listening and watching the show. Martin Geist stands in the background, chatting with a couple. A piano player, his back to the camera, is half-seen in the background as well. Zelig smiles, enjoying the song; he pushes his glasses back.

FANNY BRICE *(Gesturing, singing)* "I'm flying high, 'cause I've got a feeling I'm falling, / Falling for nobody else but you. / *(Pointing to Zelig)* You . . ."

The film cuts back and forth between Fanny Brice, moving in on her face as she sings and emotes, and the Zeligs, enjoying the show. Ruth's legs are still crossed. Zelig's are uncrossed; he sits with his hands clasped over his knees. Martin still chatters away in the background. The song ends in a rousing finish with a close-up of Fanny Brice's face.

FANNY BRICE *(Continuing, singing and moving)* ". . . caught my eye, / Now I got a feeling I'm fallin', / Show me that ring and I'll jump right through. / I used to travel single-oh, / We chanced to mingle-oh, / Now I'm a-tingle over you. / Hey, Meester *(Offscreen)* Zelig stand by, 'cause I've got a feeling *(Onscreen)* I'm fallin', / Falling for nobody else but you-w-w-wow!"

CUT TO:
INTERIOR. HOTEL CORRIDOR—DAY.

Zelig sits in a chair by a window at the end of the hall. Nearby, an empty chair faces the camera. Zelig's legs are crossed; he munches on a roll, staring into space. A man walks by, ignoring him. Other people scurry past the camera. Zelig continues to eat; he crosses and uncrosses his legs. The man who walked past him before scurries past in the other direction.

NARRATOR'S VOICE-OVER Though the shows and parties keep Zelig's sister and her lover rich and amused, Zelig's own existence is a non-existence. Devoid of personality, his human qualities long since lost in the shuffle of life, he sits alone quietly staring into space, a cipher, a non-person, a performing freak. He who wanted only to fit in—to belong, to go unseen by his enemies and be loved—neither fits in nor belongs, is supervised by enemies, and remains uncared for.

The film cuts to hands replacing a file in a cabinet drawer and closing it.

NARRATOR'S VOICE-OVER The board at the hospital has all but forgotten Zelig.

As the narrator continues to speak, Dr. Fletcher is seen on the screen. She is reading a prepared statement; microphones stand in front of her. As she reads, she turns her head, distracted for a moment.

NARRATOR'S VOICE-OVER Only Dr. Fletcher continues to fight for his custody.

The film cuts to the front of a courthouse in lower Manhattan; people pass near its great stone steps. As the narrator speaks, the film moves inside, to a packed courtroom filled with men in shirt-sleeves; some of them fan themselves.

NARRATOR'S VOICE-OVER The court turns her final appeal down. Throughout her valiant legal battle she is frequently in the company . . .

The film cuts back outside, to a park near the courtroom where Dr. Fletcher and her attorney, Charles Koslow, walk together, deep in conversation. He holds her arm. Several pedestrians walk past them; one man turns back to look at them; another looks back at the offscreen camera. Dr. Fletcher puffs on a cigarette as the film cuts to them standing in front of the courtroom building. They continue to talk; Dr. Fletcher continues to smoke. A couple, in the corner near the stone wall, looks at them. A wind blows.

NARRATOR'S VOICE-OVER . . . of her attorney, Charles Koslow. He falls in love with her and presses for her hand in marriage. She is ambivalent. Reluctantly, she is beginning to abandon all hope of recovering Leonard Zelig.

The Latino sounds of "Leonard's Fandango" and "Españo Cani" are heard as the movie cuts to Spain. A cable car passes a beautiful stone archway, revealing a Spanish tower in the background, framed by the arch. People pass by in the foreground. Castanets click in the background, and the narrator continues his tale as the film cuts to two Spanish men in suits, capes, and hats standing on a sunny street corner, talking and smoking cigarettes. People walk by them on the crowded street as the film cuts to another Spanish street scene. Here, the sidewalks are packed with people, cars jam the streets, and the buildings look clean and white with elegantly carved trim.

NARRATOR'S VOICE-OVER That summer, Geist has booked them in Spain. It is the last leg of a European tour that has been wildly successful.
As the narrator speaks, the film cuts to the entrance of Zelig's hotel. Ruth, Martin, and several successful-looking Spanish men in white suits and fedoras walk briskly out of their building to a waiting car. They enter and a uniformed driver who's been holding the door open closes it.

NARRATOR'S VOICE-OVER Relations between Martin Geist and Ruth Zelig have grown strained.

The screen next shows a still photograph of several bullfighters in full regalia. The camera moves in on one of the bullfighters in the back row. It is Luis Martinez.

NARRATOR'S VOICE-OVER They have become bored with one another and quarrel frequently. The situation grows worse when she meets Luis Martinez . . .
Luis Martinez's posed bullfighting face dissolves to another close-up of his face. This time his eyes are closed and he looks pained. The camera moves back, revealing that this is a photo of Martinez in the ring. He is backed up against the wall as the bull charges; his image is caught as he throws his cape wildly.

NARRATOR'S VOICE-OVER . . . a mediocre and cowardly bullfighter with whom she falls in love.
The film next shows Ruth, Martinez, and several other expensively dressed, suave-looking people sashaying through a Spanish walkway. Martinez "hams" for the camera, strutting and smiling, as the film moves to the arena. Martinez is no longer strutting. After a few weak attempts to wave the bull by with his cape, Martinez gives up. He

rushes to the wall and climbs up into the stands. The bull leaps in after him.

NARRATOR'S VOICE-OVER Though he wishes to impress Ruth Zelig, Martinez displays his usual panic in the arena. Good fortune is with him, however, as the bull gives himself a brain concussion.

The screen shows Martinez back in the arena; he struts around the ring, followed by his two assistant matadors. When someone throws a hat into the ring, he flings it proudly back into the stands. He bounds offscreen, smiling; the bull is nowhere to be seen.

NARRATOR'S VOICE-OVER Martinez takes credit for the kill, and cutting off the bull's ear, presents it to his lover with great bravado.

The film cuts back to a Spanish street outside the Zelig hotel. A cable car stops for passengers; people mill about as the camera moves up the hotel's tall, gleaming white façade.

The film moves inside, to a photo of Ruth and Martin's hotel room, elegantly decorated with stained-glass windows, low Spanish chairs, and a bed and desk in Spanish style.

NARRATOR'S VOICE-OVER That evening, in a jealous rage, Martin Geist returns to his hotel room and confronts Ruth Zelig. He demands that she give him the ear.

As the narrator continues to speak, the photograph of the hotel room dissolves to a different photo of the same room. This time a low table is seen across from the wide bed. The tabletop is cluttered; a Zelig flier is wedged up against the wall; a wall decoration hangs down. The camera moves closer and closer to the tabletop as the photo dissolves to yet another view of the same room. This time an elegant armoire is seen, its door open. A low Spanish chair stands nearby; part of the bedpost is seen.

NARRATOR'S VOICE-OVER She refuses. Geist insists upon possession of the ear. They quarrel furiously, and Martinez is dis-

covered hiding in the closet. Geist pulls a revolver and shoots him.
The photograph dissolves to a photo of the wall behind the bed. A detective's hand points to a series of bullet holes in the wall; the camera moves in on the wall, closer and closer.

NARRATOR'S VOICE-OVER He turns the gun on Zelig's half sister and kills her. Then he takes his own life.
The screen dissolves to another photo; this time the floor of the hotel room is seen, with its Oriental rug and dark wood. The corner of the bed is seen as well. Zelig fliers litter the floor. The camera moves closer in on one of the fliers, holding still on his sketched face.

NARRATOR'S VOICE-OVER In an orgy of jealous violence, Leonard Zelig's life is turned upside down.
Next, the screen flashes to a final edition of the Daily Mirror *front page. Its top headline, in large letters, screams:* LOVE TRIANGLE ENDS IN DEATH. *Underneath the headline are two photographs. The one on the right shows the barrel of a gun, pointed out at the reader; the one on the left shows the murder scene—the notorious hotel room. The camera moves down the page, to a photo of Martinez in matador regalia, then to photos of Geist and Ruth.*

The Daily Mirror *dissolves, and in its place is the front page of the Washington, D.C.,* Sunday Times. *Prominently displayed is a column headlined* HUMAN CHAMELEON ZELIG IS MISSING. *The camera moves closer and closer to the headline as a different front page flashes on the screen; the* Philadelphia Voice *is headlined* DEATH IN THE AFTERNOON: ZELIG MISSING. *In smaller letters right underneath are the words* STORY ON PAGE . . . *Two photographs complete the tabloid page, each pertaining to a different story: one of a smiling gent, the other, a building under construction.*

The film abruptly cuts to Times Square at night. Marquees are lit up; buildings glow with light and neon. In fast motion, cars and trolley cars zoom across the screen. An up-tempo "Five Foot Two, Eyes of Blue" plays in the background.

NARRATOR'S VOICE-OVER At first, the news reverberates around the world.

The film cuts to a dance hall where a marathon dance is in progress. Couples cling to each other, half-asleep, while a band plays in the background; a large woman in white sits in a chair watching the dazed, somnambulent dancers.

NARRATOR'S VOICE-OVER Then, just as quickly, the thrill-hungry public becomes apathetic.

The screen quickly shows the back of a car. A man leans out the backseat window, brandishing a machine gun.

NARRATOR'S VOICE-OVER Fresh scandals appear . . .

The film cuts to a scene outside a brownstone, where policemen are dragging out less-than-happy men and women; the camera moves jerkily across the crowd; a reporter turns and looks at the offscreen camera.

NARRATOR'S VOICE-OVER . . . and make headlines. Events in the Jazz Age . . .

The scene quickly changes to a football field, where Red Grange runs with the ball, scrambling past the other muddied football players.

NARRATOR'S VOICE-OVER . . . move too rapidly . . . like Red Grange.

A couple of quick cuts are seen as the narrator continues his tale:

—In a large, open field, men twirl themselves around inside big, man-size hoops.

—On a Berlin street, with a columned façade in the background, six women, with one man in the middle, pedal extremely tall unicycles in unison.

NARRATOR'S VOICE-OVER A population glutted with distractions is quick to forget.

The film cuts to the very crowded, busy floor of the New York Stock Exchange. Circular counters are manned by harried workers; mobs of men scurry in all directions as the screen quickly shifts to a close-up of the New York Times *front page with an ominous headline:* STOCKS COLLAPSE IN 16,410,030–SHARE DAY, BUT RALLY AT CLOSE CHEERS BROKERS. BANKERS OPTIMISTIC, TO CONTINUE AID. *The page fills only three-quarters of the screen. The top of the screen is black. The movie then jumps to a headline from a* Daily News *page:* STOCKS CRASH 10 BILLIONS *and, in smaller print,* SOUND ISSUES DROP 10 TO 50 POINTS. *The paper itself is on an angle, covering other newspaper pages, as if it were tossed on a pile.*

NARRATOR'S VOICE-OVER The twenties come to a crashing climax, and still Leonard Zelig is nowhere to be found.
While music continues in the background, the film cuts to a different newspaper page, filled with small print and a large line drawing of an arena. The camera moves closer and closer to a nondescript column until its headline and first few lines are clearly visible. The headline reads ZELIG STILL MISSING; *the copy talks of his disappearance in Spain after the grisly murders, how he might be ill or dead.*

The scene shifts to the front of Dr. Fletcher's country home, an idyllic stone house in the woods. She and Charles Koslow walk out the front door and walk past the front façade, past a picture window, turning a corner to go behind the house offscreen. Trees are seen in the background as the two go around the side of the house. Dr. Fletcher buttons her coat; Koslow takes her arm.

NARRATOR'S VOICE-OVER Dr. Eudora Fletcher searches in vain to locate him. When several leads prove disappointing, she gives up, discouraged.
The film cuts to the present day in color; an older Dr. Fletcher sits on her comfortable sofa, giving an interview to an offscreen reporter—more of the interview that was seen on the screen earlier.

OLDER DR. FLETCHER *(Facing the offscreen interviewer)* I felt it was a shame because here was this unique case that I could make my reputation on—not that I knew how to cure him. But if I could have him alone and, and, uh, feel my way, and be innovative and creative, I felt that I could change his life if I only had the chance.

Bells and church music are heard as a newsreel title card fills the screen. Under the Hearst Metrotone News logo is the news item HUGE TURNOUT GREETS POPE PIUS—PERFECT WEATHER AND LARGE CROWD FILL ST. PETER'S. *The screen then cuts to the newsreel itself, to a panoramic view of St. Peter's Basilica. The small figure of the Pope is seen on the balcony while thousands fill the square below.*

NEWSREEL ANNOUNCER'S VOICE-OVER *(In a somewhat scratchy recorded voice)* Three hundred thousand of the faithful are waiting before St. Peter's for the appearance of Pope Pius the Eleventh.

The newsreel cuts to the balcony where the Pope, in full regalia, stands with his entourage under a canopy, then back to the crowds, seen waiting patiently in the square. A few people pass by on the walkway in the background.

NEWSREEL ANNOUNCER'S VOICE-OVER Borne on the shoulders of twelve attendants, the seat of the adjustortoria carrying the Holy Father is drawn out to the central balcony, where he bestows his blessing on Rome and all the world. This is the first time that this ritual has been performed . . .

The newsreel cuts back to the balcony. The Pope and his entourage stand as before—until a scuffle is seen under the canopy. There is some pushing; guards charge on the balcony. A general commotion ensues.

NEWSREEL ANNOUNCER'S VOICE-OVER . . . in sixty-three years, and brings to a climax on Easter Sunday the religious ceremonies of Holy Week. Oh, but what's this? A commotion next to the Papal Father? Somebody doesn't belong up there. The guards are summoned amidst chaos, as his holiness Pope Pius the Eleventh tries to swat the intruder with his sacred decree. The faithful can't believe it.

While the Pope is seen trying awkwardly to hit a figure next to him, the film's narrator is heard over the newsreel action.

NARRATOR'S VOICE-OVER *(In a clear voice)* It is of course Zelig.

While the narrator continues as the sounds of "Return from the Vatican" are heard, the film cuts in quick succession: to an ocean liner making its laborious way across the Atlantic; to a New York City Street as seen through the front window of a rapidly moving vehicle; to the street itself, its cars and pedestrians speeding by; and to the interior of Manhattan Hospital, where a doctor and a nearby nurse, her hands on her hips, stand waiting in a corridor. At the end of the hall, in the background, people crowd a doorway, trying to catch a glimpse of Zelig. The nurse glances back at the offscreen camera.

NARRATOR'S VOICE-OVER He is returned to the United States by Italian authorities and readmitted to Manhattan Hospital.

The film next cuts to Dr. Fletcher sitting at a table filled with microphones. She reads a statement from some papers in front of her; the torsos of her standing colleagues are visible behind her.

DR. FLETCHER I welcome this opportunity to treat Leonard Zelig now that he is back as a ward of the hospital. I'm grateful that the board has given me this chance. I sincerely hope to return him to society a useful, self-possessed citizen, no longer a curiosity with no life of his own.

NARRATOR'S VOICE-OVER *(Overlapping Dr. Fletcher's speech, which is now only faintly heard)* Dr. Fletcher has no time now to think of marriage. All her attention must be devoted to Leonard Zelig.

The scene shifts to Dr. Fletcher's country home. The camera moves across the house, its trees, and its shrubbery as the narrator speaks, while the peaceful, happy sounds of "Thinking About Bix" are heard in the background. A few leaves gently fall to the ground in the breeze.

NARRATOR'S VOICE-OVER Her plan is to bring him to her country home. She will set up a neutral environment away from society. Here she will begin searching for some new way to treat him in the hopes of penetrating his unique malady.
The film moves inside Dr. Fletcher's home, to her living room, where she sits on the sofa, listening and watching, while her cousin, sitting next to her, shows her how to use a movie camera. In the background are some pieces of furniture, a secretary, a chair, and an armoire.

NARRATOR'S VOICE-OVER Aware of the significance of her work, Eudora Fletcher arranges to keep a filmed record of the proceedings. For this she contacts her first cousin, Paul Deghuee, an inventor and part-time photographer.
The film cuts to the present day in living color; an older Paul Deghuee, in fedora and suit, sits at a table in a diner. In front of him is a cup of coffee, a place setting, and salt and pepper shakers. His arms are crossed on the table. Through the window in the background, cars are seen passing by; parked cars line the street. Drapes hang down behind Deghuee's head.

OLDER PAUL DEGHUEE And she said, "I want to make a record of this case for future generations and the world of science, and I want you to keep the camera very quiet." And I said, uh, "Why don't you just take notes and write it up?" And she said, "Paul, when a man changes his physical appearance, you want to *see* it. You can't read about it. Besides which, I am planning to make history."
The film returns to the early 1930s, to Dr. Fletcher's house in black-and-white. As the camera pans across the "White Room," the study where she and Zelig will have their historic interviews, it reveals a chair, a low shelf of books, a comfortable chair next to a standing ashtray, a curtained window, an organized desk, another chair, and a lamp. A few simple pictures line the walls, and a swinging door

completes the picture. Large movie lamps mounted on the wall brighten the room; a microphone is seen nestled in the bookshelf, near the ashtray.

NARRATOR'S VOICE-OVER The White Room is carefully arranged for maximum serenity. It is a small study in Dr. Fletcher's house, sparsely furnished. Clumsy photographic lights are nailed to the wall to provide sufficient illumination. Microphones are hidden in specially selected places.
The film cuts to the movie camera Dr. Fletcher plans to use. It is on the other side of the swinging door, focused on a pane of glass in the door. While the narrator speaks, the door swings open, revealing the White Room—in particular, the camera's point of view: the easy chair where Zelig will be sitting.

NARRATOR'S VOICE-OVER The camera shoots through a pane of glass, which renders it relatively unobtrusive.
As the narrator speaks, the screen shows the camera in its little room on the other side of the swinging door. Hands drape a blanket over the camera, then a heavy coat.

NARRATOR'S VOICE-OVER Only the noise of the motor is a problem, but this is muffled with a blanket and anything else handy. From this cramped vantage point . . .
The film moves back inside the White Room to the swinging door. As the narrator speaks, the door swings open, revealing the movie camera and Paul Deghuee in the little room. He waves to the offscreen camera; he smiles and points to his movie camera, one hand holding it proudly.

NARRATOR'S VOICE-OVER . . . photographer Paul Deghuee will record the famous White Room Sessions, a remarkable document in the history of psychotherapy.
The film cuts back to the present in living color; psychoanalyst Bruno Bettelheim sits behind his desk. Books line the shelves above his head;

he sits comfortably in his leather chair as he talks to an offscreen interviewer. The legend BRUNO BETTELHEIM, PSYCHOANALYST *is superimposed on the bottom of the screen. An open book, face down, sits on the desk.*

BRUNO BETTELHEIM By today's standards, uh . . . White Room Sessions would seem very primitive, and yet they were really quite effective in developing a very strong personal relation between doctor and patient. The question whether Zelig was a psychotic or merely extremely neurotic was a question that was endlessly discussed among us doctors. Now I myself felt that . . . *(Pauses)* his feelings were really not all that different from the normal, maybe, what one would call the well-adjusted normal person, only carried to an extreme degree, to an extreme extent. I myself felt that one could really think of him as the ultimate conformist.

The film cuts back to black-and-white in the past; the White Room is seen on the screen. An interview is in session. Zelig sits in the easy chair, his legs crossed. Dr. Fletcher sits across from him; she holds a pad in her lap. Behind them is the bookshelf; a framed photo hangs above it. Their voices are heard as if recorded by a primitive machine; these talks are a part of the White Room Sessions Dr. Fletcher filmed and recorded.

DR. FLETCHER *(After a brief pause, looking at Zelig)* Leonard, do you know why you're here?

LEONARD ZELIG *(Inhaling)* To . . . discuss psychiatry, right?

DR. FLETCHER *(Resting her chin in her hand)* You're a doctor?

LEONARD ZELIG *(Fidgeting)* Yes I am, I am. Perhaps you've read my latest paper on delusional paranoia? *(Gesturing)* Turns out the entire thing is mental.

DR. FLETCHER Now— Su-suppose I tell you you're not a doctor?

LEONARD ZELIG Well, uh . . . I would say that you're making a joke. *(Looking out towards the offscreen camera)* Incidentally, is it always so bright in here?

DR. FLETCHER Oh! Y— Uh . . . I'm recording these sessions on film, if you don't mind.

LEONARD ZELIG No. *(Pointing towards the camera)* There's somebody behind there, right?

DR. FLETCHER Uh-hum, that's right.

LEONARD ZELIG *(Looking towards the offscreen camera and the swinging door)* That's a camera. *(Waves)*

DR. FLETCHER *(Nodding)* Uh-hum. L-L-Leonard . . . uh . . . Leonard, why don't we start with simple reality? Leonard, you're not a doctor.

LEONARD ZELIG *(Looking back at Dr. Fletcher)* No?

DR. FLETCHER No! Uh, you're a patient, and I'm the doctor.

LEONARD ZELIG *(Scratching his head)* Well . . . I wouldn't tell it to too many people if I were you. *(Looks at the camera, smirking and raising his eyebrows)*

DR. FLETCHER Leonard, you're *not* a doctor.

LEONARD ZELIG *(Defensively, looking towards the offscreen camera)* Is she gonna be all right? 'Cause w-what is this a, you know, because I've got to get back to town. *(Gesturing, looking at Dr. Fletcher once again)* Really I— I have an interesting case treating, treating two sets of Siamese twins with split personalities. I'm getting paid by eight people.

The film cuts to Dr. Fletcher's hands. She is writing in her journal at her desk. "Thinking About Bix" is heard in somber tones as the narrator speaks over the scene.

NARRATOR'S VOICE-OVER "The first week's sessions did not go too well," writes Dr. Fletcher in her diary. "Leonard identifies with me and is convinced that he is a doctor. He is guarded and suspicious."

As the narrator continues to recite from Dr. Fletcher's journal, the film moves outside, to the back of Dr. Fletcher's stone house. She walks out the door, carrying some papers and a cigarette, and sits down in a lawn chair. She is deep in thought; she smokes a cigarette. The day is bright; Dr. Fletcher wears a comfortable dress and a sweater.

NARRATOR'S VOICE-OVER *(Continuing)* "There is something very appealing about him, too. He is quick-witted and energetic. Perhaps it is his very helplessness that moves me. I must keep flexible and play the situation by ear."

Dr. Fletcher turns around, towards the camera, as if hearing something. The film cuts back to the White Room, to another interview in progress. Once again, the dialogue is heard as if it were recorded by a primitive, scratchy machine.

DR. FLETCHER How are you today, Leonard?

There is a brief pause before Zelig speaks.

LEONARD ZELIG *(Fidgeting, rubbing his hand on the arm of his chair)* Fine. And I . . . *(Takes a deep breath)* I, uh *(Clears throat)* got to get back to town soon. You know I . . . teach a course at the psychiatric institute and, uh . . . in masturbation and uh . . .

DR. FLETCHER *(Overlapping)* I see.

LEONARD ZELIG I'm a doctor, you know, and I uh . . .

DR. FLETCHER *(Interrupting)* I see, guilt-related masturbation.

LEONARD ZELIG *(Fidgeting)* N-n-no, no, not guilt-related, I-I-I teach advanced. *(Wringing his hands)* I'm quite a respected doctor there, you know.

While Dr. Fletcher speaks, there are several breaks in the film, making her movements jumpy and interrupting her words—and giving a very real old-documentary feel to the interview.

DR. FLETCHER Leonard, uh *(Film skips)* I'd like you to *(Film skips)* eyes follow this, this pen *(Waving a pen in front of his face)* and just let yourself breathe deeply.

LEONARD ZELIG Why? What uh . . .

DR. FLETCHER *(Moving the pen slowly from side to side)* Relax.

LEONARD ZELIG No . . . you're, you're trying to hypnotize me. Obviously.

DR. FLETCHER Do you mind?

LEONARD ZELIG Yes, of course I mind—I'm a doctor, I'm, I'm uh—

DR. FLETCHER *(Interrupting)* Leonard, you're not a doctor.

LEONARD ZELIG *(Agitated, rubbing his hands on his legs)* I *am* a doctor.

DR. FLETCHER Just relax.

LEONARD ZELIG *(Gesturing and fidgeting)* No! I uh I'm, I'm, can't I'm, I'm . . . I'm due back in town, I-I-I-I-I have this masturbation class, you know, if um, if I'm not there they start without me.

As Dr. Fletcher lowers her pen dejectedly, the interview, continuing with its documentary realistic feel, comes to a halt with a dirty film tear. The movie cuts outside, to the front of Dr. Fletcher's idyllic country house. "You May Be Six People, But I Love You" is heard in the background as the narrator begins anew.

NARRATOR'S VOICE-OVER As the weeks go by, Dr. Fletcher grows more and more frustrated.

As the narrator continues, the film cuts back inside, to Dr. Fletcher's study. She sits silently, despondently, smoking a cigarette; her diary writing is put aside for the moment. The room is dark, in contrast to the bright sun seen in the window behind Dr. Fletcher. Plants sit on the windowsill.

NARRATOR'S VOICE-OVER "Leonard continues to insist he is a doctor and even refuses to let me hypnotize him," she writes. "I believe his experiences of the past year have made him more defensive than ever. It is discouraging."

The film moves to the present day in color; an older Paul Deghuee is once again on the screen. He is in the midst of the same interview seen before, addressing an offscreen interviewer in a diner.

OLDER PAUL DEGHUEE She was under great pressure. You could tell. She was moody and nervous. He was fine . . .

As the older Paul Deghuee continues to speak in the present, the film cuts back to the past in black-and-white. Through a glass-paned French door of Dr. Fletcher's house, Zelig is seen in the garden, peacefully watering some flowers along the garden path. The room with its French door is totally black; Zelig, his watering can, and the flowers are bathed in sunshine. As Deghuee speaks, Zelig is seen turning the watering can upside down and shaking it, trying to get the last drops of water on the flowers.

OLDER PAUL DEGHUEE'S VOICE-OVER . . . napping, sitting in his chair reading. He used to refer to himself as Dr. Zelig. He was reading books on psychiatry.

The film cuts back to the present in color; the older Paul Deghuee continues to speak on-camera in the diner.

OLDER PAUL DEGHUEE I told her, you'd better get away for a day and relax. The strain is becoming too much for you.

While "Ain't We Got Fun" is heard in the background, the film cuts to black-and-white, in the past. The screen shows the outside of a Broadway theater, busily lit up with the words RKO MAYFAIR *on its marquee. Cars drive past on the street; people walk by under the huge, elaborate marquee. The narrator begins anew, and as he speaks, the film cuts inside the theater to the stage, where two women in fancy costumes bounce and dance in front of a painted backdrop of a country scene. A piano player is seen in the corner, just below the proscenium; in the darkness, only the silhouetted backs of the audience are discernible.*

NARRATOR'S VOICE-OVER Leaving Zelig alone, Dr. Fletcher takes Paul Deghuee's advice, and she and her fiancé spend some hours off relaxing. They go to Broadway—then to a well-known nightclub . . .

While the narrator and the music continue, the film cuts to a nightclub. Beyond the silhouetted shapes of the audience seated at surrounding tables, a bevy of showgirls dance in a circle on a brightly lit stage. The film cuts closer to the dancers on the stage while the narrator speaks. The dancers, in long head wraps, bounce past the watching patrons at their tables. Everyone is wreathed in smiles as another dancing scene is shown on the screen. Here the dancers are in bathing suit costumes, still smiling, still bouncing past the nightclub patrons enjoying the show, as the screen grows darker. Soon only the dancers are brightly lit; the audience is in darkness and the film cuts back to a view of the bright stage as seen over the silhouetted shapes of the nightclub patrons. The showgirls are still dancing; the lead dancer does a somersault. All the while, the narrator tells his tale.

NARRATOR'S VOICE-OVER . . . where, despite a lively stage show, Dr. Fletcher is distracted and uneasy. She is unable to think of anything but her patient. The atmosphere with her fiancé, Koslow, is awkward and strained. He is put off by her total obsession with Zelig. Ironically, it is in the noisy and smoke-filled atmosphere of the nightclub that Eudora Fletcher is struck . . .

The film cuts to a still photograph of Dr. Fletcher in evening wear and glasses sitting at a nightclub table with Koslow. The table is filled with other patrons, their bodies turned to the offscreen stage. As the narrator talks, the camera moves closer and closer to Dr. Fletcher's face. She is somber amidst the smiles and frozen gaiety of the others.

NARRATOR'S VOICE-OVER . . . by a brilliant and innovative plan that will create a major breakthrough in the case.

The film cuts back to the White Room, where Dr. Fletcher and Zelig are in the midst of another interview. There is a brief pause before they start to talk.

DR. FLETCHER *(Smoking a cigarette)* Dr. Zelig?

LEONARD ZELIG Yes.

DR. FLETCHER *(Leaning over in her chair)* I— I, I wonder if you could help me with a problem?

LEONARD ZELIG Well . . . certainly try, I . . . *(Gesturing)* of course, we can't promise anything.

DR. FLETCHER You see, last week I was— I was with a group of fairly erudite people who were discussing the novel *Moby Dick. (Shaking her head)* And I-I was afraid to admit that I hadn't read it, so I lied.

LEONARD ZELIG *(Pausing, rubbing his mouth)* Uh-huh . . .

DR. FLETCHER *(Gesturing)* You, you see I want so badly to be, to be liked, t-to be like other people so that I don't stand out.

LEONARD ZELIG *(Pausing, fidgeting uncomfortably)* That's natural.

DR. FLETCHER *(Still sitting on the edge of her chair, not noticing an ash from her cigarette dropping on the floor)* Well . . . er . . . I go to such extreme lengths to blend in.

LEONARD ZELIG Well, *(Inhales)* you're a doctor, you know, you *(Clears his throat)* should know how to handle that.

DR. FLETCHER *(Looking down for a moment)* No, but the . . . the truth of the matter is, I . . . I'm not an actual doctor.

LEONARD ZELIG *(Pausing)* You're not?

DR. FLETCHER No, doctor. No, *(Shaking her head)* I . . . I've been pretending to be a doctor to, to fit in with my friends. You see, they're doctors.

LEONARD ZELIG *(Scratching his head)* Sss . . . that's something. *(Fidgeting)* That's . . . tsss.

DR. FLETCHER But, but you're a doctor and-and you can help me, you *have* to help me.

LEONARD ZELIG Actually, I don't, I don't feel that well, actually.

Zelig looks acutely uncomfortable. He begins to squirm in his chair while Dr. Fletcher speaks.

DR. FLETCHER You . . . er uh, mm . . . my, whole life's . . . just . . . been a lie. I . . . I've been posing as one thing after another.

LEONARD ZELIG *(Squirming)* Well— You need help, lady . . . um . . . um . . . *(Takes off his glasses)*

DR. FLETCHER Last night— Last night I, I dreamt that I was falling in . . . into fire. What does that mean?

LEONARD ZELIG *(Rubbing his face)* Oh, that's terrible, I don't know, I . . . er . . . you know. I—

DR. FLETCHER Please, doctor I, I know I . . . I'm a very complicated patient.

LEONARD ZELIG *(Putting his glasses back on, still squirming)* Jesusss . . . I don't feel that well.

DR. FLETCHER What am I suffering from?

LEONARD ZELIG *(Still squirming, rubbing his hands on the arms of his chair)* How should I know, I'm not a doctor!

DR. FLETCHER You're not?

LEONARD ZELIG No. Am I?

DR. FLETCHER Who are you?

LEONARD ZELIG What do you mean who am I, I, I don't know. These are tough questions—

DR. FLETCHER *(Interrupting Zelig)* Leonard Zelig?

LEONARD ZELIG *(Nervously rubbing his thighs)* Yes. Definitely. Who is he?

DR. FLETCHER *(Emphatically)* *You.*

LEONARD ZELIG Pshaw . . . No, I'm nobody, I'm nothing . . . I . . . *(Moans)* Catch me, I'm falling. *(Slumps in his chair)*
Taking advantage of Zelig's vulnerability, Dr. Fletcher quickly grabs her pen and waves it in front of his face. She mouths hypnosis-inducing words as the narrator starts anew and "Thinking About Bix" begins to play in the background.

NARRATOR'S VOICE-OVER Playing on Zelig's identity disorder, Dr. Fletcher has manipulated him into momentary disorientation. With his guard lowered, she quickly puts him under hypnosis.
The film cuts to the outside of Dr. Fletcher's country house, peacefully nestled in the woods. A few leaves fall from the trees.

NARRATOR'S VOICE-OVER Using posthypnotic suggestion, she will now be able to induce a trance at will.

CUT TO:
INTERIOR. WHITE ROOM—DAY OR NIGHT.

Zelig, in vest and solid shirt, is sitting in his chair, his arms loosely draped on its arms. He fills the screen. His eyes are closed; he's in a trance. Dr. Fletcher is almost totally offscreen. She is furiously taking notes.

LEONARD ZELIG *(In a trancelike, singsong voice, as part of a scratchy recording)* My brother beat me . . . My sister beat my brother . . . My father beat my sister and my brother and me . . . My mother beat my father and my sister and me and my brother . . . The neighbors beat our family . . . People down the block beat the neighbors and our family . . .

The film cuts to another session with Zelig, now in a plaid shirt and suspenders, still in his chair in the same position as in the previous scene. He is hypnotized; his arm is extended in the air. Dr. Fletcher is not seen; presumably she is offscreen in her chair taking notes.

LEONARD ZELIG *(In a trancelike voice, as part of a scratchy recording)* I'm twelve years old . . . I run into a synagogue . . . I ask the rabbi the meaning of life . . . He tells me the meaning of life . . . but he tells it to me in Hebrew . . . I don't understand Hebrew . . . Then he wants to charge me six hundred dollars for Hebrew lessons.

The old-fashioned sounds of "A Sailboat in the Moonlight" are heard as the film cuts to a series of blissful outside scenes:

—Dr. Fletcher and Zelig sitting on a wooden garden bench, their backs to the camera. The garden is lush around them. They chat silently. Zelig puts his hand on Dr. Fletcher's shoulder; she rubs it reassuringly with her own hand.

—Dr. Fletcher and Zelig in the backyard, the woods all around them. They are playing with a dog. Zelig holds out a stick, the dog jumps for it. Laughing, he and Dr. Fletcher stumble backward. Zelig throws the stick; the dog runs off-camera to fetch it. Dr. Fletcher calls to the dog; she walks a few steps, clapping her hands, then returns to Zelig. She takes his arm and the two of them start to follow the dog and its stick. Dr. Fletcher holds a cigarette. The film skips a few times in realistic home-movie style. The narrator speaks over these two scenes.

NARRATOR'S VOICE-OVER Dr. Fletcher's therapy consists of a

two-pronged attack. In the trance state, the personality will be deeply probed, and then restructured. In the conscious state, she will provide love and affection—unconditional positive regard.

The music plays as more country scenes appear on the screen:

—*Zelig stands by a car, limply holding a hose, waiting for the water to run through. He starts as the water dribbles out. He holds it over the fender, the bumper, intent on the limply held hose. Dr. Fletcher's hand is seen, sponging off the hood on the other side of the car. She moves further onscreen as Zelig continues to hold the limp hose over the fender; he glances briefly at the offscreen camera. Dr. Fletcher moves over to Zelig, picks up the hose, and aims it at the hood. She pats Zelig's back, steering him closer to the car, before returning to her side. She barely misses a beat in her sponging; she smiles reassuringly at Zelig. He continues to concentrate on the hose.*

—*Zelig sits on a stool in the garden drawing on a pad. Dr. Fletcher sits nearby, watching him and smoking a cigarette. He shows her the drawing; she holds it on one side, nodding. Zelig shakes his head; he holds the drawing up for the camera. The sketch is full of arrows pointing in different directions. Zelig looks confused, almost childlike.*

The music stops as the film cuts back to the White Room, to another hypnotic session. Dr. Fletcher sits on an ottoman at Zelig's feet. She holds his hand in both of hers. He is in a trance, resting in his chair. Their voices are heard as if they are on a scratchy recording.

DR. FLETCHER *(Slowly and intensely)* You will be completely honest. You're in a deep trance. You will become not who you think I want you to be, but you'll be yourself. Now how do you feel about it here?

LEONARD ZELIG *(Slowly, in a trancelike voice)* It's the worst . . . I hate the country . . . I hate the grass and mosquitos . . .

Cooking . . . your cooking is terrible . . . Your pancakes . . . they're— I dump them in the garbage when you're not looking.

DR. FLETCHER *(Nodding)* Uh-huh.

LEONARD ZELIG And the jokes you try and tell, when you . . . when you think you're amusing, they're . . . long and pointless . . . there's no end to them.

DR. FLETCHER *(Slightly uncomfortable, touching her glasses briefly with her hand)* I see. And what else?

LEONARD ZELIG *(Pausing)* I want to go to bed with you.

DR. FLETCHER *(Taking her hands away, embarrassed and looking briefly at the offscreen camera, aware that this is being filmed)* Oh . . . uh . . . I, I . . . that surprises me. I, I didn't think you liked me very much.

LEONARD ZELIG *(Still in a trancelike voice)* I love you.

DR. FLETCHER *(Drawing away and sitting up)* You do?

LEONARD ZELIG You're very sweet . . . 'Cause you're . . . you're not as clever as you think you are. You're all mixed up . . . and nervous . . . and you're the worst cook. Those pancakes . . . oh . . . I love you . . . I want to take care of you . . . uh . . . No . . . no more pancakes.

The sounds of "A Sailboat in the Moonlight" start up anew as Zelig, exhausted, slumps back in his chair; he's asleep. Dr. Fletcher, embarrassed at his revelations, smooths back her hair, fidgeting. She glances at the offscreen camera, ill at ease, as her voice, from the present, is heard and the film cuts to Dr. Fletcher standing by the country home's French doors. She looks out, deep in thought, as her older voice continues over the scene. She takes a cigarette from a pack in her pocket and lights it. She inhales, still staring out at the sunlight; she crosses her arms.

OLDER DR. FLETCHER'S VOICE-OVER I started out by, uh, trying to use Leonard to make my reputation. And then I found that I had very strong feelings for him. I never thought I was attractive. I never had a real romance. Charles Koslow was the type of man my mother felt I should marry.

The film cuts to Zelig, Dr. Fletcher and her sister Meryl, walking through a hangar; they chatter, looking at the airplanes. "A Sailboat in the Moonlight" continues in the background as the narrator begins anew.

NARRATOR'S VOICE-OVER Feeling more confident every day with her patient, Dr. Fletcher takes him for a cautious outing, an afternoon at her sister's house in nearby Teaneck.

The scene shifts to Dr. Fletcher sitting in the cockpit of a plane outside. She fills the screen, smiling and chatting silently to the others offscreen; she looks down at the controls. While the narrator talks, a more confident, smiling Zelig walks onscreen, to the cockpit. He pats Dr. Fletcher's forehead with affection. He looks at her for a beat.

NARRATOR'S VOICE-OVER Meryl Fletcher is an aviatrix—a fine professional pilot. Eudora Fletcher is an amateur pilot, and the afternoon is spent relaxing and retelling old flying experiences.

While the narrator continues his tale, the screen shows the plane from a different angle, a bit farther away from the camera. Dr. Eudora Fletcher is still chatting to the others, turning to look over her shoulder. Her sister and Zelig walk onscreen, to the cockpit of the plane. The three talk amicably, smiling. At one point, Zelig ruffles Eudora Fletcher's hair. Meryl Fletcher turns and briefly glances back at the offscreen camera. Eudora Fletcher sits comfortably in the cockpit, one arm leaning over its side. Good feelings pervade the scene.

NARRATOR'S VOICE-OVER As the weeks pass, Zelig is encouraged to open up more and more—to give his own opinions. What was guarded at first soon becomes expansive.

The film cuts to a still photograph of Zelig, caught in a moment of deep reflection. His glasses are held in one hand; his other hand is on his forehead. His eyes are closed. He talks in a monotone, as if on a scratchy recording.

LEONARD ZELIG'S VOICE-OVER I hated my stepmother, and I don't care who knows it.

The nostalgic strains of "A Sailboat in the Moonlight" play on as still photographs appear on the screen in a montage, dissolving to one another, one at a time. Zelig continues to speak as the film first shows a blissful photograph of Zelig and Dr. Fletcher sitting on a rock in the woods. She is smiling into the camera; Zelig is petting the dog sitting happily next to him. The sun is shining. The camera moves closer and closer in on their contented faces.

LEONARD ZELIG'S VOICE-OVER *(In a trancelike voice)* I love baseball. Er . . . You know it doesn't have to mean anything, it's just very beautiful to watch.

The photograph taken at the rock dissolves into a different scene, to a moment caught in time at Meryl's Teaneck house. Dr. Fletcher sits on the running board of a car, beaming at the camera. Zelig leans over her, smiling down at her; he holds a twig. Meryl, in the background,

sits on the steps of her front porch. She too is smiling. "A Sailboat in the Moonlight" plays on as Zelig continues to speak over the screen.

LEONARD ZELIG'S VOICE-OVER I'm a Democrat. I . . . I . . . I always was a Democrat.

The Teaneck photo dissolves to a different photo, a close-up of a smiling Dr. Fletcher and Zelig, beaming for the camera. As their voices are heard over the screen, as the music plays on, the camera moves farther and farther back, revealing the couple in front of Dr. Fletcher's stone house, holding several pumpkins. Dr. Fletcher holds one up for the camera.

LEONARD ZELIG'S VOICE-OVER Is it okay if I don't agree with you about that recording?

DR. FLETCHER'S VOICE-OVER *(Softly)* Of course.

LEONARD ZELIG'S VOICE-OVER I mean, you know Brahms is-sss . . . just always too melodramatic for me.

The next photograph shows the couple in front of a car; they are dressed up. Dr. Fletcher, in hat and suit, is adjusting Zelig's tie. He looks at her with love as the camera moves closer and closer to his face.

LEONARD ZELIG'S VOICE-OVER *(Still in a trancelike voice)* You have to be your own person and, and make your own moral choices even when they do require real courage otherwise er . . . you're like a robot, or a lizard.

Zelig's still face dissolves to a new still photo, showing a smiling Dr. Fletcher standing outside her home; she holds a grocery bag. The camera moves closer and closer in on her happy face.

LEONARD ZELIG'S VOICE-OVER Are you really going to get married to that lawyer? I . . . er, I would much rather you didn't.

Dr. Fletcher's smiling face dissolves to a different still photo. Here, she and Zelig are standing outside in front of a lush tree. The sun is shining and they are laughing hysterically. Zelig's head is back in the throes of laughter. The music plays on.

LEONARD ZELIG'S VOICE-OVER No, I don't agree, I . . . I think this guy Mussolini is a . . . loser.

The laughing photo turns into the last still photo in this montage, an extreme close-up of Zelig and Dr. Fletcher standing very close together. The camera is so close that their faces are somewhat fuzzy. At first, Zelig's face is seen, looking to his right. The camera moves over and shows what he is looking at: Dr. Fletcher's face.

LEONARD ZELIG'S VOICE-OVER Eh . . . oh, we ever gonna make love?

The camera holds on Dr. Fletcher's face for a beat before the music stops, before the film cuts back to its newsreel style, to the inside of Manhattan Hospital. As the narrator begins anew, the screen shows the hospital's board of directors sitting around a conference table. The camera pans slowly around the group, past a man blowing his nose, past a cabinet jammed with books, past the board chairman, who is wearing a bow tie, his elbows leaning over a book open in front of him at the the head of the table; he points his finger for emphasis. The camera continues to move past a shelf filled with papers, then stops at a man smoking a pipe next to another man who is nodding in agreement. All the men gathered around the table are talking, deep in discussion.

NARRATOR'S VOICE-OVER It has been three months and the board wishes to examine the patient. Dr. Fletcher says Zelig is not ready to leave the premises. The doctors agree to visit him there. The date is set . . . four days hence. If progress is insufficient, she will be removed from the case.

The film cuts to the present day, in color; the older Dr. Fletcher is once again seen in her living room, talking with the offscreen interviewer.

OLDER DR. FLETCHER I was very nervous because in his waking state he never remembered anything from his trance state, and, uh, I wondered if there could be some way of locking these two things together. And then I also was worried that, uh, if he was with strong personalities, he might lose his personality.

The film moves back to the past, in black-and-white, to the driveway of Dr. Fletcher's stone house. Zelig and Dr. Fletcher stand next to a group of parked cars, greeting the just arrived board of directors. The doctors pour out of the cars, closing doors, and walk over to the waiting Dr. Fletcher and Zelig. They all shake hands and, chatting, head for the front of the house. The narrator speaks over the scene as the figures move farther away, milling about in clusters.

NARRATOR'S VOICE-OVER Sunday at noon—the doctors arrive. They are greeted by Eudora Fletcher and Leonard Zelig and are shown around the grounds. Though Dr. Fletcher is tense and alert, Leonard Zelig seems calm and at ease. Despite the fact that he is surrounded by physicians, he does not turn into one. The encounter appears to be a resounding success, when Dr. Henry Mayerson comments innocently about the weather, saying that it is a nice day. Zelig tells Dr. Mayerson that he does not agree that it is a nice day. Dr. Mayerson is taken aback at the firmness of Zelig's conviction. He points out that the sun is shining and that it is mild.

Suddenly, a figure in the background milling group starts shoving the other figures. It is Zelig, and he is quite agitated. He pushes the hat off one of the doctors; he picks up a rake and starts to swing it at the entire group. They all start chasing him, running around in a scuffle; some of the doctors fall down while trying to restrain Zelig. The narrator continues to be heard.

NARRATOR'S VOICE-OVER Zelig, trained to voice his own personal opinions fearlessly, is too aggressive. He has been molded too far in the other direction. He has become over-opinionated and cannot brook any disagreement with his own views.

The film cuts back to the present day, in color; the older Dr. Fletcher continues her interview.

OLDER DR. FLETCHER I had taken him too far in the other direction. He had struck Dr. Mayerson and several board members with a rake. *(Chuckling along with the offscreen interviewer)* This was not what we wanted, and yet I felt that I had accomplished something.

While the older Dr. Fletcher's voice continues to be heard, the film cuts back to the past in black-and-white, to the White Room, where Zelig, in a hypnotic trance, is slumped in his chair. The young Dr. Fletcher sits on an ottoman at his feet, intensely speaking to him, her hands clasping a small pad; she is leaning over, her elbows on her knees.

OLDER DR. FLETCHER'S VOICE-OVER I felt if I could have him for two more weeks I could do some fine-tuning and turn Leonard Zelig back into his own man.

Triumphant sounding music, "Chameleon Cured," is heard as the film cuts to a newsreel title card proclaiming, under the Hearst Metrotone News banner, CHAMELEON CURED BY WOMAN DOCTOR, *and, in smaller print:* SHE'S PRETTY TOO! IT TOOK HER MONTHS, BUT SHE DID IT.

The "newsreel" begins. Dr. Fletcher, decked out in hat and fur-trimmed coat, stands in front of Manhattan Hospital with an equally well-dressed Zelig. They are beaming, waving at the offscreen cheering crowds. Behind them stand several smiling doctors—some of them the very ones who had doubted Dr. Fletcher months before. Flashbulbs go off while the newsreel announcer speaks over the scene. Zelig puts his arm around Dr. Fletcher, as if asked to by the offscreen reporters. He kisses her, at first hesitantly, then again. She beams at the camera as, shrugging and chatting at the offscreen crowd, Zelig kisses her again —thoroughly enjoying himself. "Who Says Women Are Only Good for Sewing" plays in the background.

NEWSREEL ANNOUNCER'S VOICE-OVER *(In an old-fashioned newsreel recording)* Dr. Eudora Nesbit Fletcher, the hero—or should we say heroine?—of the hour. The beautiful and brilliant young psychiatrist never lost faith in her conviction that Leonard Zelig, the human chameleon, was suffering from a mental disorder. Working with her cousin . . .

The newsreel cuts to a narrow doorway of Dr. Fletcher's house. Paul Deghuee pops out, brandishing a camera. He gets down on one knee and starts filming the offscreen newsreel company, then, smiling, he stops and begins to wind up the camera. Behind him is a warmly decorated portion of the den, including shelves filled with bric-a-brac and books, a large plant, and a lit old-fashioned wall lamp. The film itself is scratchy and faded, like an old newsreel would be.

NEWSREEL ANNOUNCER'S VOICE-OVER . . . cameraman Paul Deghuee, the doctor managed to keep a vital record of the proceedings, including rare footage of Zelig hypnotized.

Next, the newsreel shows Dr. Fletcher in her home; she is feeding a bird in a cage and smiling. Zelig comes onscreen behind her. He whistles in her ear and puts his arms around her. He takes some of the seeds from her hand, and he too begins to feed the bird. Behind them is a low bookcase and a framed picture on the wall. Zelig glances at the offscreen camera briefly as he feeds the bird.

NEWSREEL ANNOUNCER'S VOICE-OVER The patient and his healer have become fast friends in the process, and enjoy one another's company even when she's not working on him. The result of maintaining a courageous minority opinion is a resounding success for psychiatry.

The newsreel next shows a peaceful-looking Dr. Fletcher sitting on her living room couch and sewing. Behind her are a curtained window and the top half of a chair. Next to the sofa is an end table with a lamp.

NEWSREEL ANNOUNCER'S VOICE-OVER Who says women are just good for sewing?

The music changes to the marching sounds of "On to City Hall," as the newsreel continues—now showing a motorcade driving through a lower Manhattan street packed with thousands of cheering and waving people. A motorcycle leads the way through the crowd, past the large government buildings, through the jam-packed streets and sidewalks.

NEWSREEL ANNOUNCER'S VOICE-OVER Now it's on to City Hall, where the town's newest celebrities are given the key to the city.

The scene shifts to the steps of City Hall, as seen from the sidelines.

The mayor and other city officials are holding umbrellas; Zelig and Dr. Fletcher stand nearby. Microphones are set up on the steps. Thousands of people look on, some holding umbrellas. As the voice of the key-presenting dignitary is heard, the film cuts momentarily to a closer view of Zelig, standing in front of a microphone. The dignitary hands him the key. They shake hands. Smiling and emotional, Zelig shows the key to the offscreen Dr. Fletcher, presumably standing next to him near the microphone. He holds it up for the offscreen camera.

PRESENTING DIGNITARY We're honored to present this key to New York City to the two of you. And . . . uh . . . Jimmy Walker did want to be here this afternoon and sing "Leonard the Lizard," but he was just too busy.

The newsreel cuts back to the steps of City Hall as seen from the sidelines. The crowds are clapping and cheering their approval as the screen next shows a group of renowned scientists sitting at a long dais during a luncheon banquet at the Waldorf. The long dais is covered with a white tablecloth; flower centerpieces and table settings are arranged on its top. As the newsreel announcer continues his narration, the camera pans slowly along the dais past the various chatting scientists, some smoking, some laughing, some looking directly at the camera, some at other tables behind the dais, some in deep conversation with neighboring scientists. All are male, all are in tuxedos or suits—until the camera stops at Dr. Fletcher, also seated at the dais, also dressed up. She is chatting with fellow scientist Nils Andersen. They both smoke cigarettes; they nod and gesture, deep in conversation.

NEWSREEL ANNOUNCER'S VOICE-OVER *(In an old newsreel style)* After City Hall, Eudora Fletcher, the beautiful genius who cured Zelig of his science-defying condition, is honored by fellow scientists at New York's Waldorf-Astoria. Present are luminaries from all over the world, not just in the field of psychiatry, but physics, biology, mathematics, and you name it. Here she is exchanging theories with Nils Andersen, the father of modern blood disease.

The camera continues past Drs. Fletcher and Andersen as the film cuts to the looming hull of an ocean liner. "Anchors Aweigh" begins to play as the camera moves down the hull, from the flag-draped deck to its bottom.

NEWSREEL ANNOUNCER'S VOICE-OVER Later in the week Dr. Fletcher is again honored by the greatest city in the world, as . . .

While the newsreel announcer speaks, the screen shows Dr. Fletcher, holding a bouquet of roses, chatting with another woman as she awaits the christening ceremony. A flag waves off to the side. The film then cuts to Dr. Fletcher on a flag-draped platform, swinging the champagne bottle against the hull of the ship. She's surrounded by dignitaries and microphones; an enthusiastic crowd is gathered around the platform.

NEWSREEL ANNOUNCER'S VOICE-OVER . . . she gets to christen her first ship. Quite a success story for a little girl from the backwoods.

The screen next shows the giant ocean liner slowly drifting out of the dry dock, amidst cheers and fanfare from the crowd. Dr. Fletcher is seen on the platform, waving good-bye and good luck; she is a small figure compared to the ship's bulk. An American flag waves in the foreground. the voice of an on-the-spot radio newscaster is faintly heard over the noise coming from the whirling cameras.

ON-THE-SPOT RADIO NEWSCASTER'S VOICE-OVER . . . pulled away from her. Dr. Fletcher has smashed the bottle. The bottle containing not champagne—

The newsreel abruptly leaves the dock and cuts to a scene in the living room belonging to Dr. Fletcher's mother. The gray-haired woman sits, looking almost shrunken, on her sofa next to a radio reporter. Huge microphones stand in front of them. Behind them is a curtained window; on the sill are several plants. While the reporter addresses the offscreen camera, Mrs. Fletcher bobs her head up and down, looking a bit overwhelmed, as if off in another world.

RADIO REPORTER I'm speaking to you from the home of Mrs. Catherine Fletcher. She's the . . . mother of Dr. Eudora Fletcher, the famous psychiatrist so much in the news these days, and I'm going to be asking Mrs. Fletcher to . . . *(Turning briefly towards Mrs. Fletcher)* . . . to begin with uh . . . to tell us something about . . . uh, what it's like to raise a medical genius, and I might ask you about the many sacrifices that you've made to put your daughter through medical school. *(Gesturing towards the microphone)* And could you speak right into the microphones, please.

MRS. CATHERINE FLETCHER *(Shaking her head as she bends over the microphone)* Sacrifices, we had none. John was a stockbroker, we had plenty of money, and I came from a wealthy Philadelphia family, so . . . *(Lifts up her hand)*

RADIO REPORTER *(Looking up at the ceiling, searching for a way out of this unsympathetic conversational course)* Well I'm, I'm sure that your daughter *always* wanted to be a doctor, ever since she could remember.

MRS. CATHERINE FLETCHER *(Shaking her head)* I don't think so. I always thought she would want to be a flier like her sister Meryl, and raise a family. But she was a very moody . . .

RADIO REPORTER *(Interrupting nervously)* But—

MRS. CATHERINE FLETCHER *(Continuing)* . . . child.

RADIO REPORTER *(Looking towards the camera, then back at Mrs. Fletcher)* But still, a mother always . . . dreams . . . uh . . . for her child to have the kind of success that your daughter has.

MRS. CATHERINE FLETCHER *(Shaking her head)* She was a very difficult girl.

RADIO REPORTER *(Uncomfortably rubbing his hands on his*

knees) Well, tell me about your husband. Uh . . . I understand that he is a simple businessman. *(Clasping his hands on his lap)* He must be so thrilled . . . an-and pleased to have his daughter achieve such recognition.

MRS. CATHERINE FLETCHER *(Shaking her head)* John had problems, depression, he drank.

RADIO REPORTER *(Taking a breath)* Well, Mrs. Fletcher, thank you so much for speaking with us today.
The film cuts to a new newsreel title card. This one is headlined SAN SIMEON. *Underneath is the copy* HEARST HOSTS ZELIG AND FLETCHER AND SHOWS HOW THE RICH AND FAMOUS SPEND THEIR LEISURE—AND HONOR THEIR GUESTS. *Below the copy is the Pathe News logo, with its encircled roosters on each side. "I Love My Baby" is heard in the background.*

The newsreel opens on a panoramic view of the San Simeon mansion, high above the California hills, beginning with the guest cottages nestled in the mountains up to the stellar towers and stucco walls of the sprawling main house, stark against the clear sky, its uppermost towers higher than its surrounding palm trees.

NEWSREEL ANNOUNCER'S VOICE-OVER *(In an old-fashioned newsreel style)* Here at San Simeon, glorious dreamland of newspaper mogul William Randolph Hearst, celebrities from all walks of society sun or play.
The newsreel cuts to the wrought-iron main entrance of San Simeon, where William Hearst, holding a Panama hat, and Marie Dressler, wrapped in fur, walk out the door, chatting. Three women guests, laughing and smiling for the offscreen camera, follow them. As the newsreel announcer continues to speak, the film, in a jumpy old-fashioned documentary style, shows several male guests walking into view. One of them hands Marie Dressler a rose; she sniffs it imperiously. A guest walks in front of the camera; another lights up a cigar. Everyone smiles and hams it up for the offscreen camera—including a

casually attired Marion Davies, who, arm in arm with another woman guest, walks up to the camera and makes a clownish face.

NEWSREEL ANNOUNCER'S VOICE-OVER There's Marie Dressler with Mr. Hearst. Always a popular guest at San Simeon, Miss Dressler accepts a flower from an ardent admirer. Along with her is Marion Davies. When she works, Miss Davies is always dead serious, but here at this fabulous playground, she shows us her fun side.
The newsreel cuts to a close-up of Marion Davies and Charlie Chaplin, clowning it up on the tennis court. He strums his tennis racquet like a guitar; Davies is laughing and talking to the offscreen cameraman.

NEWSREEL ANNOUNCER'S VOICE-OVER Here she is with you-know-who! Charlie Chaplin. *(Chuckling)* Always kidding.
The newsreel cuts back to the gated main entrance to San Simeon. Jimmy Walker hesitantly leans out of the gates. He finally moves outside. The camera zooms in on his face as he dances and sings in front of the entrance.

NEWSREEL ANNOUNCER'S VOICE-OVER Although New York is three thousand miles away, Jimmy Walker somehow appears through Mr. Hearst's enchanted gateway.
The main entrance of San Simeon is still busy. This time, the screen shows Tom Mix and a woman friend arm in arm, posing and smiling in front of the gates—as Zelig pops his head in front of the camera, mugging and smiling. He walks over to Tom Mix and his friend. The three of them laugh together. Zelig plucks Tom Mix's hat off his head and puts it on, clowning it up for the camera as the three, arm in arm, smile in bonhomie. Zelig puts the cowboy hat back on Tom Mix's head. They all wave.

NEWSREEL ANNOUNCER'S VOICE-OVER Another New Yorker is Leonard Zelig, here shown clowning with everybody's favorite cowboy, Tom Mix. Won't Tony be jealous? Tony is Tom's

horse, and we always thought they went *everywhere* together.
The newsreel cuts back to a close-up at the tennis court, where Charlie Chaplin, Adolphe Menjou, and a female guest mug and clown for the camera.

NEWSREEL ANNOUNCER'S VOICE-OVER There's that fellow Chaplin again—this time with Adolphe Menjou.
The newsreel is back for a close-up at the San Simeon gates—where a glamorous Claire Windsor and Dolores Del Rio, swathed in furs and feather boas, pose for the camera.

NEWSREEL ANNOUNCER'S VOICE-OVER There's Claire Windsor and Dolores Del Rio . . .
The scene shifts to the sprawling backyard of San Simeon, where, in jerky newsreel style, a young James Cagney chats with a well-dressed, smiling Dr. Fletcher. He affectionately pokes her chin; she laughs, touching her just-tweaked skin.

NEWSREEL ANNOUNCER'S VOICE-OVER . . . and a very charming Eudora Fletcher, chatting with Hollywood's newest dancing sensation, James Cagney.
Next, in the sunny backyard, a smiling Carole Lombard is seen, sharing a high-backed rattan chair with another woman. A dapper man drops his arms over the chair's back, tapping his glasses on the rattan. The jaunty music plays on.

NEWSREEL ANNOUNCER'S VOICE-OVER Oh, and what have we here? Only a beautiful lady named Carole Lombard.
The newsreel cuts to San Simeon's golf course, where Zelig, Dr. Fletcher, and Bobby Jones try their hand on the green. Bobby Jones is helping Zelig, giving him some pointers. Zelig, clowning, pushes the ball with his feet; Bobby Jones shakes both Zelig's and Dr. Fletcher's hands. They pose for the camera, leaning on their golf clubs. They wave.

NEWSREEL ANNOUNCER'S VOICE-OVER And there's Dr. Fletcher and Leonard Zelig, hitting a few with Bobby Jones on Mr.

Hearst's golf course. Unless Leonard can go back to his old chameleon personality and turn into a golf pro, I'd bet my money on Bobby. But who cares, if they're having fun.

The music stops, the newsreel is over, and the film cuts to an assembly hall in a club. The seats are packed with young men in suits. On the stage is Zelig, standing in front of a podium flanked with microphones. A group of adult men stand behind him against a wall with two doorways and an American flag. As Zelig, in suit and tie, speaks, the film cuts to a closer view of him at the podium, flanked by the introducing speaker and the other serious-looking, well-dressed adult men.

INTRODUCING SPEAKER *(Leaning into the microphone)* Leonard Zelig, do you want to give the kids of this country some advice?

LEONARD ZELIG *(Enthusiastically and seriously)* I sure do! Kids, you gotta be yourself. Ya know you can't act like anybody else just because you think that they have all the answers and you don't. *(Nodding his head for emphasis)* You have to be your own man and learn to speak up and say what's on your mind. Now maybe they're not free to do that in foreign countries but that's the American way. You can take it from me because I used to be a member of the reptile family, but I'm not anymore.

Zelig puts his hands on his hips as the assembly applauds and smiles enthusiastically. An Al Jolson–like voice starts to sing "I'm Sitting on Top of the World" and the movie cuts to a montage of "Zelig on the go" scenes, filmed as if being staged for a soon-to-be-released newsreel, or as if being posed for still photos. Flashbulbs go off as the screen shows:

—*A panoramic view of Atlantic City in the early 1930s: its boardwalks crowded with strollers, bicycles, and jitneys; its large, frescoed hotels; its clean, sprawling beaches; and the ocean beyond.*

—A smiling Zelig standing on the boardwalk, flanked by four bathing beauties, including Miss Los Angeles and Miss St. Louis. They all shake hands for the camera, giggling and hamming it up; Zelig puts his arms around the closest two beauties.

—An impressed Zelig shaking hands with a muscular black boxer in a crowded gym. Behind them is a boxing ring; managers and several other men in suits stand nearby. The boxer puts up his fists in a friendly challenge; Zelig does the same.

—A white boxer sparring with a punching bag in the crowded gym, with a laughing Zelig holding the bag steady. A muscular boxer, his arms crossed, a hat on his head, stands in the background, watching. Behind them is a boxing ring; the wall is cluttered with photographs and banners.

—A glimpse of Times Square, busy with cars and pedestrians. Zelig, holding a hat, walks on-camera. He smiles and motions towards the offscreen Dr. Fletcher, who, smiling and laughing, walks on-screen, over to him. Zelig puts his Panama hat on his head, his arm around Dr. Fletcher. They wave and smile at the camera; Dr. Fletcher, a bit shy, clutching her pocketbook, looks off for a moment

at the passing pedestrians, some of whom turn back to look at the camera, some of whom walk directly in its path.

SINGER'S VOICE-OVER "I'm sittin' on top of the world, / I'm rollin' along, just rollin' along. / Oh boy, I'm quittin' the blues of the world, / I'm singin' a song, just singin' a song. / Glory hallelujah, I told Leonard Zelig, / Hey Len get ready to call. / Just like Humpty Dumpty, / I'm ready to fall. / I'm sittin' on top of the world, / My my my! / Rollin' along, rollin' along!"
The music stops, and as the narrator begins anew, the film cuts to Zelig, surrounded by curious onlookers at an outdoor art show in Greenwich Village. Framed paintings are displayed on a makeshift stand; a bohemian-looking woman points them out to an attentive Zelig. Behind the group is a wrought-iron fence enclosing a park. As the narration continues, Zelig points to one of the paintings; he takes out a billfold and counts out some cash while the bohemian woman holds up his new canvas. Several of the onlookers nod; one man smokes a cigarette. One of the men, wearing a long scarf around his neck, points to the painting. Zelig, in a cap and suit, beams and nods his head, holding up his new acquisition for the camera; he shakes hands with the bohemian woman, presumably the artist.

NARRATOR'S VOICE-OVER Zelig, no longer a chameleon, is at last his own man. His point of view on politics, art, life, and love is honest and direct. Though his taste is described by many as lowbrow, it is his own. He is finally an individual—a human being. He no longer gives up his own identity to be a safe and invisible part of his surroundings.
The film cuts to the present day in color; Professor John Morton Blum is giving an interview to an offscreen reporter. He is in his office; he sits in his desk chair, his legs crossed, facing the camera. Behind him is his paper-cluttered desk. A telephone sits on its top. In the background is a printer. As the professor speaks, his name and credits pop on the screen: PROFESSOR JOHN MORTON BLUM, HISTORIAN, AUTHOR OF INTERPRETING ZELIG.

PROFESSOR BLUM Oh, his taste wasn't terrible. He was the kind of man who preferred watching baseball to . . . *(Pauses)* reading *Moby Dick*, and that got him off on the wrong foot, or so the legend goes. It was much more a matter of symbolism . . . To the Marxists, he was one thing. The Catholic Church never forgave him . . . *(Pauses)* for the Vatican incident. The American people, in the throes of the Depression as they were, found in him a symbol of possibility, of, of self-improvement and self-fulfillment. And, of course, the Freudians had a ball. *(Gesturing)* They could, they could interpret him in any way they pleased. It was all symbolism—but there were no two intellectuals who agreed about what it meant.

Still in color, still in the present day, the scene shifts to Venice, where Susan Sontag is in the middle of the same interview she was giving in an earlier segment of the movie. As she talks to the offscreen interviewer, the caption SUSAN SONTAG, AUTHOR OF AGAINST INTERPRETATION *pops on the screen.*

SUSAN SONTAG I don't know if you could call it a triumph of psychotherapy—it seems more like a triumph of aesthetic instincts. *(Gesturing)* Because Dr. Fletcher's techniques didn't owe anything to then current schools of therapy. But she sensed what was needed and she provided it, and that was, in its way, a remarkable creative accomplishment.

Still in color in the present day, the scene shifts once again, this time to Irving Howe. As in an earlier segment of the movie, he is in the midst of an interview being conducted in his living room. As he talks to the offscreen interviewer, the caption IRVING HOWE, AUTHOR OF WORLD OF OUR FATHERS *briefly appears on the screen.*

IRVING HOWE When I think about it *(Gesturing)* it seems that his story reflected a lot of the Jewish experience in America—the great urge to push in and to find one's place *(Gesturing)* and then to assimilate into the culture. I mean, he wanted to assimilate like crazy!

The film cuts back to the black-and-white past, to a dock crowded with people waving and seeing off a steamer that slowly makes its way across the screen. Aboard ship, the crowds are waving back. Excitement is in the air. On the dock, more people arrive to wish the ship a bon voyage as the narrator begins anew, as "Sunny Side Up" begins to play in the background, and as the film cuts to a beaming Dr. Fletcher and Zelig posed on the steamer's deck. They wave at the offscreen camera; Zelig keeps up a nonstop silent dialogue as Dr. Fletcher continues to smile, a bit forced. A crewman stands in a background corridor; a fellow passenger walks in front of the camera.

NARRATOR'S VOICE-OVER Eudora Fletcher's life has also changed from this experience. For her, fame and recognition are empty rewards and do not live up to the adolescent fantasies that prompted her ambition.

The film cuts to a tennis court, where Zelig and Dr. Fletcher, in old-fashioned tennis whites, play doubles across the net with another off-screen couple. The film jumps a bit in antiquated documentary-style as they take turns hitting the ball and serving. Behind them, on the other side of a wire fence, is lush woodland.

NARRATOR'S VOICE-OVER She and her patient have fallen in love, and it is no surprise when she forsakes the upwardly mobile attorney Koslow and announces wedding plans with Zelig.

As the narrator continues to speak, the film cuts to a closer view of Zelig and Dr. Fletcher on the tennis court. The game is finished; Zelig is examining Dr. Fletcher's hand. He holds up her hand, showing off a blister to the camera. She smiles; Zelig chatters silently and good-humoredly. They hold their tennis racquets under their arms.

While they smile and banter for the camera, a vocalist begins singing "Sunny Side Up," and the film cuts to a series of scenes exemplifying the happy couple at play, including:

—Zelig and Dr. Fletcher, surrounded by delighted onlookers, in a jewelry store. Zelig, looking over a tray of jewelry, picks out a cameo brooch and pins it on Dr. Fletcher's coat. She smiles and shows it off for the offscreen camera, its price tag still dangling down. Zelig kisses Dr. Fletcher's cheek once, then kisses her again. He shakes hands with the salesperson, who is only partially seen behind the jewelry counter.

—Zelig and Dr. Fletcher dancing the Charleston to the silent sounds of a big band playing in the background. The camera first shows Dr. Fletcher, demurely dancing and smiling, then moves to Zelig, who flings his arms in the air as he dances. He clowns it up, dancing closer to Dr. Fletcher, his hands waving in front of her face. She starts to laugh; she stops dancing, her hand on her mouth. Shaking her head in laughter and embarrassment, she puts her hand on Zelig's shoulder. He too stops dancing, and he laughs and fondly teases Dr. Fletcher, mouthing his curiosity as to why they've stopped. Around them, couples have an equally good time dancing on the crowded floor.

—Zelig and Dr. Fletcher on the sidelines of the dance floor, smiling and chatting with another couple. Behind them, dancers continue their energetic Charlestons. His arm linked through Dr. Fletcher's, Zelig shakes hands awkwardly with the other man, who then shakes Dr. Fletcher's hand. Zelig briefly looks up at the offscreen camera. The band is seen in the background, still playing.

—Zelig and Dr. Fletcher, smoking a cigarette, posed with several other socialites in front of the big band. A man steps on-camera, trying to join the group. He moves away; a curious woman looks on briefly, getting in the way of the camera. As the song continues, the camera moves in closer on Dr. Fletcher and Zelig. They talk silently, their lips barely moving, as they smile for the public and the camera. A portion of the band is seen behind their heads.

—Zelig and Dr. Fletcher stopping at a vendor on a New York City street to munch on some hot sweet potatoes. Zelig pays the vendor with one hand, the other holding his potato, while Dr. Fletcher munches on hers, enjoying each bite. Zelig waves to the camera with his potato. Pedestrians, some gawking at Zelig and Dr. Fletcher, walk by on the crowded streets; smoke pours out of the vendor's stove. The Washington Square arch is seen in the background as the music finally draws to a close.

SINGER'S VOICE-OVER "Now there's one thing to think of when you're blue, / There are . . . others much worse off than you. / If a load of trouble should arrive, / Laugh and say it's great to be alive. / Keep your sunny side up—up, / Hide the side that gets blue. / If you have nine sons in a row, / Baseball teams make money you know. / Keep your funny side up—up, / Let your laughter come through—do. / Stand up on your legs, / Be like two fried eggs, / Keep your sunny side up—up, / Keep your sunny side up."

The song finishes and the film abruptly cuts to the present in living color; an older Meryl Fletcher Varney speaks to an offscreen interviewer. She sits in a stark white study. Behind her are two windows, revealing the railing of an outside terrace and clear blue skies. Books line one of the window sills.

OLDER MERYL It was wonderful to . . . to see my sister and Leonard together. She drew strength from him. And . . . they were so much in love with each other . . . um, and she looked happier than she had in years. Uh . . . *(Pauses, rubbing her cheek)* I remember they decided to get married in the spring, and then of course the roof fell in.

The older Meryl puts her finger to her mouth, remembering, as the film cuts to a black-and-white still photograph of showgirl Lita Fox, clad in a skimpy sequined costume and glittery headdress. The camera moves closer and closer towards her heavily made-up face as an ominous, minor-keyed rendition of "Leonard the Lizard" plays in the background.

NARRATOR'S VOICE-OVER Two weeks before the wedding, an ex-showgirl named Lita Fox comes forth and claims that she is married to Zelig.

As the narrator continues to speak, the film cuts to a page from a New York paper dated in 1930. The headline reads ZELIG ALREADY SECRETLY MARRIED AND A FATHER. *The page dissolves to the front page of a tabloid filled with photos. The camera moves down the page, from top to bottom, quickly revealing two unrelated photos, one of a wreck, to settle on a photo of Zelig with its*

big caption, OH YOU LIZARD!, *and in smaller letters,* CHAMELEON NAMED AS HUBBY BY SHOWGIRL. *A portion of the photo next to Zelig's is seen; it shows cars stopped in traffic. The ominous music plays on.*

NARRATOR'S VOICE-OVER She also claims to have had his child. It is an immediate scandal.

The film cuts to a more conservatively dressed Lita Fox sitting on a sofa in her lawyer's office. Next to her, listening, is her lawyer. She talks directly to the camera, barely moving, telling her side of the story. On a nearby end table sits a lamp; drapes line the wall behind the sofa. The film is in a scratchy, old-fashioned newsreel style.

LITA FOX We were married a year ago. He said he was an actor, he sounded just like one, and I'm in show business too. So, we drove to Baltimore and we were married, and I have a license to prove it.

The scene shifts to the corridor outside a courtroom. Lita Fox stands in deep discussion with her attorneys; she nods her head occasionally. They are surrounded by several other men, also deep in conversation. Flashbulbs go off as they talk; one of the men turns briefly to look at the camera.

NARRATOR'S VOICE-OVER He had married her while under a different personality. When she read of the plans for his forthcoming wedding to Eudora Fletcher, she was mortified and decided to take legal action.

The film cuts to the courthouse steps outside, where Zelig's attorneys, deep in discussion, walk up towards the entrance, with Zelig and another of his lawyers closely following. Zelig runs up the last few steps and grabs the arm of an attorney who has been in front of him; they start to talk as the entire group walks past the stone columns of the entranceway. People pass on the stone steps in the background.

NARRATOR'S VOICE-OVER Zelig says he will fight it in court, but public opinion begins subtly to shift away from him.

Next, Lita Fox, demurely dressed, is seen sitting on a sofa in her living room; she plays with her baby, cuddling him on her knee. He starts to cry; she takes a toy from the nearby end table and tries to interest him in it. She bounces him on her knee. A gilded picture is framed on the wall behind the sofa. The end table holds an ornate lamp.

NARRATOR'S VOICE-OVER Clever attorneys portray Lita Fox as an abandoned woman. The child is neglected, poor, and fatherless.

The film cuts to a confident-looking Zelig standing and conversing with two Hollywood executives on a polo field. They pose for the camera in well-cut, trim suits. At a tent set up in the background various people, some in polo uniforms, are gathering; a man waves at the camera. Also behind the trio is a polo player on his horse. Lush trees frame the field.

NARRATOR'S VOICE-OVER Zelig has sold his life story to Hollywood for a large sum of money.

While the narrator continues, the film cuts to the outside of a courthouse where a group of women are demonstrating and protesting against Zelig. One woman wears a sign saying ONE WIFE—EVEN FOR REPTILES. *A small crowd is gathered on the courthouse steps, watching. A policeman stands in the midst of the demonstration; he looks towards the camera. In the background, a woman, clutching the arm of a new recruit, runs over to the demonstrators. Other people simply walk by; one man, walking in front of the camera, moves to the side—more curious about the cameras than the demonstrators. The women pose, blocking the "reptile" sign.*

NARRATOR'S VOICE-OVER When the scandal breaks, the studio demands its money back. Zelig can only return *half*, as the rest has already been spent.

The film shifts to an evening scene, to the outside entrance of a restaurant, where Zelig and Dr. Fletcher exit with a male friend. They walk quickly, in step behind another couple, towards a parked car. In the background are the elegantly curtained windows of the restaurant; its gilded poles hold up an offscreen awning and a potted plant. Zelig and Dr. Fletcher enter the car on one side; their colleague walks around the front to the driver's side. He gets in, ready to drive off. People pass by on the sidewalk.

NARRATOR'S VOICE-OVER Outraged, the studio gives him half his life back. They keep the best moments, and he is left with only his sleeping hours and mealtimes. Zelig is shaken by the scandal, but it is only the beginning.

The film cuts to a still photograph of a grim-looking Helen Gray, sitting on an oversize print chair holding two twin babies on her lap. Behind her is a plain lamp; a pair of plain candlesticks are on an otherwise bare mantel. As the narrator speaks, the camera moves closer and closer in on her face, and the film cuts to her, in coat and gloves, on a courthouse steps. She holds a marriage license, unfolding it and displaying it for the offscreen cameras and reporters. She starts to cry, talking silently as she faces the cameras. Behind her, on the steps, is a cluster of men and women; they look at the offscreen camera and mutter among themselves. A man in a suit stands next to Helen Gray; he is half on, half off the screen. Presumably, he is her lawyer.

NARRATOR'S VOICE-OVER Now another woman steps forward. Helen Gray, a salesgirl from a Wisconsin gift shop, claims that Zelig is the father of her twins. She tells her lawyers that he passed himself off as a fur trapper. Zelig has no recollection . . .

The screen next shows a large newspaper headline proclaiming CLAIMS AGAINST ZELIG MULTIPLY, *then cuts to a front page in the* New York Times *style, with a column headlined* ZELIG'S PAST CATCHES UP, *among other front page stories about a Panama highway and a killer, before cutting to the* Daily News *front page in its tabloid style, with a big* WHO ME? *headline and, in smaller print,* ZELIG NAMED IN A HOST OF LAWSUITS.

The camera moves up the page, to a huge picture of a somber-looking Zelig, next to two unrelated photos and under an unrelated partial banner saying, STATE DEMANDS CHAIR FOR BOY.

NARRATOR'S VOICE-OVER . . . but admits it could have happened when he was under one of his spells. It is the signal for the floodgates to open.

The film cuts to a black woman in a white gown, in the first of three black-and-white, newsreel-style clips. She is standing in front of a restaurant with CHINESE AMERICAN CHOP SUEY *printed in neon on its storefront. She speaks looking into the camera; she barely moves.*

CHOP SUEY WOMAN He married me up at the First Church of Harlem. He told me he was the brother of Duke Ellington.

Next, a white man in a suit, a Mr. Stoner, stands facing the camera. Behind him is a suburban house, a garage, and some shrubs. He holds his coat over his arm.

MR. STONER *(Addressing the camera in a calm voice, barely moving)* He was the guy who smashed my car up. It was brand new. Then he backed up over my mother's wrist. She's elderly, and uses her wrist a lot.

An elderly couple are the next to get on the Zelig bandwagon. They stand next to each other on the steps to the front porch of their shingled home. The woman does the speaking; her husband looks at her.

ELDERLY WOMAN *(Addressing the camera, barely moving)* He painted my house a disgusting color. He said he was a painter. I couldn't believe the results. Then he disappeared.

"Leonard the Lizard" starts to play as the film cuts to a mob scene in front of a courthouse door. As the narrator speaks, policemen, some carrying clubs, push the mobs of curiosity-seekers away.

NARRATOR'S VOICE-OVER That Zelig could be responsible for the behavior of each of the personalities he assumed means dozens of lawsuits.

The film moves inside the courthouse, where the presiding judge is seen over the shoulders of the packed room. Lawyers walk back and forth in front of the seated spectators, exchanging documents, talking among themselves in clusters, going up to the judge. As the narrator continues, the film cuts to a somber-looking Zelig, sitting at a table with his lawyer. His hands are clasped in his lap.

NARRATOR'S VOICE-OVER He is sued for bigamy, adultery, automobile accidents, plagiarism, household damages, negligence, property damages, and performing unnecessary dental extractions.

CUT TO:
EXTERIOR. BUILDING—DAY.

A humble Zelig, fingering his hat in his hands, stands in front of a cluster of microphones, flanked by his lawyers. Behind him stand several other men; one of them smokes a cigarette. Zelig is making a statement to the press as flashbulbs go off.

LEONARD ZELIG *(Speaking slowly, looking at the offscreen crowd)* I would like to apologize to everyone I . . . I'm awfully sorry for . . . for marrying all those women, it-it just, I don't know, it just seemed like the thing to do. And to the, to the gentleman whose appendix I took out . . . I . . . I'm . . . I don't know what to say. *(Gesturing)* If it's any consolation I . . . I may still have it somewhere around the house . . . I- I— My deepest apology goes to the Trokman family in Detroit . . . I, I never delivered a baby before in my life and I, I just thought that . . . ice tongs was the way to do it.
"Leonard the Lizard" begins to play in a frantic manner as the film cuts to a panoramic view of a crowded city street. Trolley cars hurry by, cars file down the street, and mobs of pedestrians walk up and down the crowded sidewalks. A policeman directs traffic, halting some people who try to cross the street.

NARRATOR'S VOICE-OVER Thriving mercilessly on loopholes and technicalities, the American legal profession has a field day.

The film cuts to a dark courtroom corridor, backlit by a bright doorway in the background, where Zelig, flanked by his two lawyers, walks briskly towards the camera. They are deep in discussion as they turn and walk up a flight of stairs, Zelig in the lead.

NARRATOR'S VOICE-OVER Zelig is branded a criminal. Despite Dr. Fletcher's insistence that he cannot be held responsible for his actions while in his chameleon state, it is no use.

The scene shifts to the insignia poster of the Holy Family Christian Association, with its cross, triangle, and eternal light motif. The camera slowly moves down the poster, leaving the HFC insignia to reveal the blasphemous text, line by line, which reads:

ZELIG'S BIGAMY
MAKES A MOCKERY
OF THE SACRAMENT
OF MATRIMONY.

LEONARD ZELIG HAS MARRIED MORE THAN
ONE WOMAN AT A TIME. THIS SINFUL BEHAVIOR
IS AGAINST THE LAW OF GOD AND MAN.
YET MANY CLAIM HE IS NOT GUILTY OF A CRIME.

POLYGAMY ATTACKS
THE HEART OF A
CHRISTIAN SOCIETY.

LEONARD ZELIG
MUST BE TRIED
AND CONVICTED.

As the camera moves over the poster's text, an elderly woman's voice slowly speaks over the screen.

VILIFICATION LADY'S VOICE-OVER *(In a dramatic voice)* Leonard Zelig sets a bad moral influence. America is a moral country. It's a God-fearing country.

The film cuts to the actual vilification lady, a sweet-looking, unassuming elderly woman, in a radio station. She sits behind a plain desk, reading her prepared speech into a microphone. Behind her, on a stark wall, is a sign bearing the station's call letters, WJCS, and a large clock.

VILIFICATION LADY We don't condone scandals. Scandals of fraud, and polygamy. In keeping with a pure society, I say, lynch the little hebe.

The film cuts to the entrance of a courthouse. Zelig, his two lawyers, and Dr. Fletcher are walking out, deep in discussion. They walk slowly, then stop, continuing to talk, Zelig to one lawyer, Dr. Fletcher to the other. She smokes a cigarette; her back is to the camera. They part, the lawyers going in one direction, Zelig and Dr. Fletcher in another, towards the camera. Behind them is the ornate door of the courthouse.

NARRATOR'S VOICE-OVER Throughout the humiliating ordeal, Eudora Fletcher stands by the man she loves valiantly. Privately, she tells friends that she is worried about Zelig's emotional condition, which seems to her to be deteriorating under the weight of conservative moral opinion.

Zelig and Dr. Fletcher, still talking, move past the camera, and after a beat, the film cuts to a city street, busy with people and cars, as seen from a high building. The middle of the sunny street is dramatically obscured by a looming shadow. The narrator continues to speak as another city street scene appears on the screen. This panoramic head-on view shows the façades of buildings, the rushing traffic, the streets and sidewalks busy with people going about their business, before the film cuts to a snazzy 1930s sedan whizzing down a city street, past a line of parked cars, past one or two pedestrians, past a row of stores.

NARRATOR'S VOICE-OVER In public, he tries to keep up an appearance of composure, but it is increasingly difficult. It is clear that he is coming apart when he and Eudora Fletcher dine at a Greek restaurant . . .

The film cuts to the entrance of a humble Greek restaurant with ATHENS *printed on its window. Dr. Fletcher is seen helping an older Greek gentleman out the door. It is Zelig. Three waiters in uniform walk out behind them, helping Dr. Fletcher bring Zelig the Greek to a parked car. They get him settled in the car. Straightening up, Dr. Fletcher turns and looks behind her, her back to the camera. One of the waiters briefly looks at the offscreen camera. Greek music plays in the background; on the tree-lined sidewalk, a few pedestrians are seen.*

NARRATOR'S VOICE-OVER . . . and in the midst of the meal, Zelig begins to turn Greek . . . He longs desperately to be liked once again—to be accepted, to fit in.

The film abruptly cuts to a factory where a crowd of men in aprons, shirt-sleeves, and sweaters are furiously tying bundles of newspapers at a long table. Behind them are more men; the pace is at a fever pitch as the film moves outside, where a mob of men, standing in line, wait for the bundles of newspapers to be flung out an open window. As one man catches a bundle, the next in line is immediately ready, and the film cuts quickly to another fast-paced street scene, where men in shirt-sleeves are directing a line of newspaper trucks. As one drives off, its open back stacked with papers, the men frantically wave to the next truck in line. People pass by on the sidewalk and the film cuts to a newsstand on a crowded street, its vendor busy selling papers, bending down to get a paper from his stack, dipping into his apron pockets for change, hawking the news. People pass in front of the cameras, walking on the sidewalk, buying papers.

NARRATOR'S VOICE-OVER Public clamor over his morality reaches a fever pitch, and on the eve of his sentencing, Leonard Zelig vanishes.

With a cacophonous blare of music, the film cuts to a close-up view of a political cartoon. The word MORALITY *appears in bold letters on a top beam. The camera quickly moves down the drawing, revealing a gallows with many nooses—all for Zelig, who is drawn in prisoner stripes emblazoned with the words* ZELIG MENACE. *He has four heads: an Asian, an Indian, a black, and his "normal" self. Below the gallows, spectators are sketched; an angry Uncle Sam points up at Zelig.*

The film cuts to a busy newsroom. In the cavernous room, lined with stone columns, men are busy in the background working at their desks, walking back and forth. In the foreground a man in suit and tie leans over a desk, talking on a telephone. Sitting at the desk is a man in shirt-sleeves typing away. As the voice of the police chief is heard, the scene shifts to the driveway of Dr. Fletcher's country house. The camera slowly moves past a row of parked police cars, past several milling detectives, some talking and smoking on the driveway, some wandering through the lawn, searching for clues, stopping as it nears the edge of the driveway, which is framed by some trees. The film then cuts to the side of the stone house, where a young Meryl Fletcher talks to a cluster of detectives; they listen and take notes as she speaks, her arms crossed, nodding her head. One of the men smokes a cigarette.

POLICE CHIEF THOMAS DOWD'S VOICE-OVER *(As broadcast over the radio)* This is Chief Inspector of Police Thomas Dowd with a national broadcasting newsbreak. Leonard Zelig is missing. On the eve of his sentencing for an assortment of crimes and misdemeanors ranging from polygamy to fraud, he has disappeared. We are searching for clues and would appreciate speaking with anyone who might have any information leading to his apprehension.

As the older Meryl Fletcher Varney's voice is heard over the screen, the film cuts to Dr. Fletcher, standing near a parked police car in her driveway. Meryl is with her, trying to comfort her sister to no avail. Dr. Fletcher, a handkerchief in hand, begins to sob. Meryl puts her arms around Dr. Fletcher; they talk silently. Ultimately, Dr.

Fletcher nods, wipes away her tears, and, holding her glasses, walks off with her sister.

OLDER MERYL'S VOICE-OVER My sister was just *shattered.* She tried, you know, she tried to keep up a calm front, but she was just too upset. And she wasn't a person who usually displayed emotion easily—except where Leonard was concerned.

The search is on—and while the narrator speaks, the film cuts to a series of scenes displaying police work in action:

—*A police car pulls up to a curb. Its door opens and a detective gets out, lending a hand to Dr. Fletcher, who is in the backseat. She too gets out of the car, followed by another detective. He closes the door; the driver exits the car on the other side, and they all move offscreen. The detectives both smoke cigars.*

—*Police stop a car on a city street. Hundreds of people, lined up behind a low wall, look on as two uniformed cops peer in the windows. They wave the car on; another is about to take its place.*

—*Two bloodhounds sniff at Zelig's jacket, which is being held out to them. They squirm on their leashes, close up to the camera, surrounded by uniformed legs.*

—*Policemen in old-fashioned jodhpurs, led by the leashed bloodhounds, roam an open field. They stumble, moving quickly through the grass.*

NARRATOR'S VOICE-OVER Dr. Fletcher and the police confer daily. Together they make public appeals to anyone who might know of his whereabouts. Apart from several crank telephone calls, there is little response. Months go by, and Zelig is not heard from. Cars are searched. False leads pour in from everywhere. His jacket is recovered in Texas. A manhunt in that state proves futile. He is reported seen in Chicago . . . in California.

The film cuts to a still photograph of a Mexican mariachi band, guitars in hand, sombreros on their heads, posed in front of a stucco wall. As the narrator speaks, the camera moves closer and closer in on one of the mustachioed guitar players: It is Zelig.

NARRATOR'S VOICE-OVER This still photo appears to have a man resembling him with a mariachi band in Mexico.
A guitar strums for a beat in the background as "A Sailboat in the Moonlight" begins. The film cuts to the outside of Dr. Fletcher's country house. Dr. Fletcher, sitting on a bench against the side of the house, sips a lonely cup of coffee. The image is wobbly, as if a hand-held camera has quickly and unobtrusively filmed the private scene. The narrator's voice is first heard; the older Dr. Fletcher then speaks over the scene.

NARRATOR'S VOICE-OVER Dr. Fletcher continues to search for Zelig, but hopes fade with each passing day.

OLDER DR. FLETCHER'S VOICE-OVER All I could think of was Leonard, and how much I missed him and loved him, and of all the terrific times we'd spent together. It was really a very painful time for me.
The film cuts to a snowy New York City street. Trolley cars and sedans slowly make their way through the snow; a few people dodge the cars and awkwardly walk through the snow-covered streets and sidewalks. It is very white; the dark marquee of a theater is seen on one side of the street.

NARRATOR'S VOICE-OVER The year ends, and Zelig is still missing.
Abruptly, the movie cuts to the present in color; the older Dr. Fletcher is in the midst of her interview with the offscreen reporter.

OLDER DR. FLETCHER I just moped around and wept. And one night after a very bad time, my sister Meryl said to me, "Come on, let's go out for dinner. Let's go to a concert," and

I said, "No, I can't do it," but she insisted. And we went out and finally ended up in a movie.
While the older Dr. Fletcher continues to speak, the film cuts back to the past in black-and-white, to a New York City street. The lit-up, flickering marquee of Loews State movie house is seen in the background, advertising Grand Hotel *as its attraction. In the foreground, parked cars line the darkened streets. People walk by in the distance; a car drives past.*

OLDER DR. FLETCHER'S VOICE-OVER We saw *Grand Hotel*, and with it, there was a newsreel.
The film cuts to a newsreel title card, stating, under its Universal Newspaper Newsreel credit, NATIONAL SOCIALISTS ON THE RISE—BERLIN, GERMANY. *German marching music plays in the background, ending as the newsreel announcer is heard and the newsreel actually begins, showing scenes of the growing Nazi party in action:*

—*A young Hitler stands to the side, in front of a large building. Near him are a group of uniformed Nazis, talking among themselves. Behind them, a crowd of people look on. A uniformed guard struts in front of them; a man walks in front of the camera.*
—*A small parade of Nazis marches down a Berlin Street, carrying a banner and several flags. On one side is a trolley stop where a crowd of people wait to board the halted trolleys. Along the other side of the street, people in the crowd wave white handkerchiefs at the Fascists. One Nazi, out of step, joins the back of the parade.*
—*A Nazi banner, with its swastika insignia, fills the screen, held by several uniformed Nazis standing at attention. Behind them are a border of flags and the façade of a large building.*

NEWSREEL ANNOUNCER'S VOICE-OVER *(In a scratchy newsreel voice)* Adolf Hitler and the National Socialist Party continue to consolidate gains in depression-ridden Berlin. Denouncing the Treaty of Versailles, the Nazis make fervent appeals to German patriotism.

The newsreel next shows a group of Nazi soldiers surrounding Hitler. The scene is a flutter of activity, with soldiers walking on- and offscreen, swastika-imprinted flags moving in the wind, and a grinning Hitler saluting his offscreen supporters. Among the cluster of soldiers is Zelig—dressed as a Nazi. The narrator is now heard, drowning out the voice of the newsreel announcer.

NEWSREEL ANNOUNCER'S VOICE-OVER Promising to rebuild . . .

NARRATOR'S VOICE-OVER *(Overlapping the announcer)* Eudora Fletcher is stunned by what she sees. Amongst the brownshirts she spots a figure who could be Zelig.
The film cuts to the present in living color; Saul Bellow is in the midst of his interview in his study.

SAUL BELLOW *(Addressing the offscreen interviewer)* Yes, but then it really made sense, it made all the sense in the world, because, although he wanted to be loved . . . craved to be loved, there was also something in him . . . that desired . . . *(Pauses)* immersion in the mass and . . .
While Saul Bellow continues to speak over the screen, the film goes back to the past, to the black-and-white newsreel scene, where Zelig as Fascist stands among Hitler and the Nazi soldiers. The scene freezes in midstream. A circle is drawn around Zelig's face—and the camera moves in closer and closer to his now fuzzy face.

SAUL BELLOW . . . anonymity, and Fascism offered Zelig that kind of opportunity, so that he could make something anonymous of himself by belonging to this vast movement.
The scene shifts to a panoramic view of an ocean liner gliding through the water. The dramatic sounds of "The Horst Wessel Song" are heard as the narrator begins anew.

NARRATOR'S VOICE-OVER She sails for Europe the following week.

The film cuts to a Berlin Street, where a crowd of women in shawls and babushkas mob a soup line manned by soldiers, busy ladling from huge vats.

NARRATOR'S VOICE-OVER Ten days later she arrives in Berlin.

The screen next shows a thin woman in a babushka accepting a filled pail at a food line. She is surrounded by other hungry people.

NARRATOR'S VOICE-OVER Germany is a country deep in the throes of the depression.

A large parade of marching Nazis fills the screen, helmeted and hundreds-strong. Some soldiers salute the offscreen crowd. They stream through an arch in the background, past the camera.

NARRATOR'S VOICE-OVER Militarism and unrest are in the air.

The screen next shows a triumphant Hitler, riding in an open jeep, his entourage behind him, moving slowly through a huge crowd of people who are saluting and frantically trying to catch a glimpse of their führer.

NARRATOR'S VOICE-OVER She searches everywhere and makes inquiries, but it is impossible.

A solid mass of people fills the screen, arms outstretched in a "Heil Hitler" salute.

NARRATOR'S VOICE-OVER After three weeks . . .

Yet another Nazi parade is seen on the screen, the troops in full regalia, their arms outstretched in salute. They march past the crowds of people that fill both sides of the streets and the balconies and windows of the surrounding buildings. Marching in unison, more and more soldiers pass the camera.

NARRATOR'S VOICE-OVER . . . the authorities begin to get suspicious. They watch her. While she is out, they search her hotel room.

Goebbels is seen next, in uniform, along with several other Nazi officials. They stand very straight, a few smiling. They salute the surrounding crowd in the street.

NARRATOR'S VOICE-OVER A fourth week goes by . . .
More crowds and more Nazi fanfare fill the screen. In this scene, Hitler towers above his officials on a platform, his arm outstretched in salute. The crowds in the background salute and wave back.

NARRATOR'S VOICE-OVER . . . and she is about to give up and go home . . .
A Nazi parade in progress fills the screen. Three Fascists in uniform lead the way, carrying a flag imprinted with a swastika. Behind them is the militia, marching in unison. Crowds line the streets on both sides, their arms outstretched in growing numbers.

NARRATOR'S VOICE-OVER . . . when news of a large rally at Munich catches her attention.
Once again, Hitler is seen, standing high above the crowds of people, lined-up soldiers, and officials. A National Socialist Party flag dominates the foreground as Hitler flings roses to his troops.

NARRATOR'S VOICE-OVER It is rumored that it will be the largest gathering to date of Nazi personnel.
Nazi soldiers are next seen marching away from the camera, their backs seen as they catch roses flung from the crowd and salute the civilians that line the streets.

NARRATOR'S VOICE-OVER Eudora Fletcher is counting on the hope . . .
The film cuts to a panoramic view of a rally in an outside square, literally filled with thousands and thousands of people—a contrast to the humble, antiquated brownstones and other aged façades that border the square. The dramatic fanfare music plays on.

NARRATOR'S VOICE-OVER . . . that Zelig may also attend . . .
The scene shifts to a strutting Hitler, walking with his officials

through an interior makeshift aisle within a surrounding crowd. Flashbulbs go off; Hitler salutes the crowds and the offscreen cameras.

NARRATOR'S VOICE-OVER . . . and that if she can confront him . . .

The rally is soon to start. Looking down on the frenzied crowd, the camera shows Hitler and company walking down a long platform. Extended arms, in aggressive salutation, are everywhere.

NARRATOR'S VOICE-OVER . . . the strong feeling he has always had for her can be awakened.

The camera quickly cuts to the crowd, to the people sitting on the edge of their seats, applauding, saluting, wild with enthusiasm.

NARRATOR'S VOICE-OVER At first, all appears hopeless.

The scene shifts back to Hitler, on the platform, as seen from the rear. Hitler's back is to the camera; he salutes the surrounding crowd. On the platform behind him are several tables covered by white tablecloths; in front of him are several soldiers in a line, looking out towards the crowd.

NARRATOR'S VOICE-OVER The crowd is huge, and it seems impossible . . .

The huge crowd is seen once again, packed wall-to-wall in the cavernous stadium. Almost everyone in the audience, in the orchestra, in the balconies, has his arm outstretched. The roar of applause is unrelenting.

NARRATOR'S VOICE-OVER . . . to locate any one particular face.

The camera is back on Hitler. He is in his element, addressing the offscreen crowd with a fiery speech. His hands are clasped; he gestures while he yells. Behind him, in front of a line of flags, are several of his chancellors, seated at the tableclothed tables.

HITLER Damals gelobte ich mir zum ersten Male, als unbekannter eisren diesen Krieg zu beginnen. Und nicht zu ruhen, bis endlich diese Entscheidung aus dem deutschen Leben . . . beseitigt sein wird.

As Hitler finishes his sentence, the narrator begins to speak anew and the film cuts back to the audience in their seats, saluting, applauding, and cheering—totally mesmerized.

NARRATOR'S VOICE-OVER Then suddenly, a figure flanking the Chancellor captures her attention.

The camera moves back to the platform, to Hitler and his seated chancellors. He continues his dramatics, the narrator speaking over his words.

HITLER Wir wollen nicht lügen, wir wollen nicht schwindeln . . .

NARRATOR'S VOICE-OVER *(Overlapping Hitler's speech)* Behind and to the right of Hitler, she spots Zelig.

The film quickly cuts back to the frenzied audience, saluting their führer.

NARRATOR'S VOICE-OVER Struggling to make contact, she manages to catch his eye.

The camera is back on Hitler, still in the midst of his fiery speech. Behind him are his chancellors, still seated behind the tables. In complete Nazi regalia, recognizable amidst the elitist group, is Zelig. As Hitler speaks, the narrator's voice is heard more distinctly.

HITLER *(Continuing)* . . . aber ich habe es abgelehnt, jemals vor diesem Volke hinzutreten, und billige Versprechungen zu geben. Glaubt niemals an fremde Hilfe, niemals an Hilfe, die ausserhalb unserer eigenen Nation, unseres eigenen Volkes liegt.

NARRATOR'S VOICE-OVER *(Overlapping Hitler's speech)* Like a man emerging from a dream, Zelig notices her. In a matter of seconds, everything comes back to him.

While Hitler emotes, larger than life, Zelig is seen pointing in the background. He begins to wave; he turns to the other chancellors, talking. A commotion begins as the film cuts to the audience in their seats once again. This time, Dr. Fletcher can be seen, in the midst of the crowd, wearing a hat, as she tentatively raises her hand and waves. Hitler's speech goes on.

HITLER'S VOICE-OVER . . . Deutschland nicht geschenkt gegeben, sondern es hat sie sich selbst erschaffen müssen.
The film cuts back to Hitler on the platform, finishing his speech. The applause is deafening as Hitler crosses his arms and gazes down at the crowd. Zelig, waving frantically now, is jostled and restrained by the surrounding officials.

The crowd is roaring now. The screen shows them shouting, "Heil Hitler!" As they calm down, settling back in their seats, Dr. Fletcher stands up, frantically waving at the offscreen Zelig.

The camera moves back to the platform, where Zelig too is frantically waving; the officials are still trying to keep him quiet. Suddenly aware of the commotion behind him, Hitler angrily turns around and the film cuts to Hollywood's version of their reunion—as seen in a clip from the Warner Bros. film The Changing Man.

The glamorous actress playing Dr. Fletcher, seen in an earlier clip, is now seen in a rally audience filled with extras. She shouts out to Zelig, waving frantically, as the legend "THE CHANGING MAN," WARNER BROS., 1935 *appears at the bottom of the screen. Romantic music swells in the background.*

ACTRESS FLETCHER *(Shouting and waving)* Leonard! Leonard!
The Hollywood movie cuts to the actor playing Zelig, also seen in an earlier clip. He is wearing a pseudo-Nazi uniform and is standing below the platform. He has a dreamy expression on his face—until something off-camera catches his attention. He turns as the "film" cuts to a celluloid version of Hitler's platform, seen over the heads of the audience. It is dramatically lit with blazing torches; a swastika banner dominates the back wall. A lone hand in the audience is silhouetted in the air. It is Dr. Fletcher's, still waving frantically.

ACTRESS FLETCHER'S VOICE-OVER Leonard!

The romantic music reaches a crescendo as the clip moves back to the actor playing Zelig. His mouth opens in amazement; he begins to wave. He grabs his hat and waves it frantically in the air. He beams as the actress playing Dr. Fletcher rushes onscreen and into his arms. They kiss in a passionate embrace, the music heightens, and the film cuts to:

INTERIOR. OLDER DR. FLETCHER'S LIVING ROOM—PRESENT DAY.

It's the present, in full color, and the older Dr. Fletcher is still seated on her couch, talking to an offscreen interviewer.

OLDER DR. FLETCHER It was nothing like . . . it . . . it happened in the movie. When, when Leonard came down from the podium, they didn't know what to think.

The film, still in color and in the present day, cuts to an interview being given by Oswald Pohl. As the caption OSWALD POHL, FORMER SS OBERGRUPPENFÜHRER *pops on the screen, the older man, in sweater and tie, talks to an offscreen reporter. He sits in a plain, straight-backed chair next to a plain dark armoire. He smokes a cigarette.*

OSWALD POHL *(In German accent, breathing heavily)* We couldn't believe our eyes. Hitler's speech was ruined. He wanted to make a joke about Poland, but just then . . . uh . . . Zelig interfered, and Hitler was extremely upset. The SS wanted . . . eh, wanted to grab Zelig, but if they would have grabbed him, they probably would have . . . uh . . . tortured him or maybe even shot him. So in the confusion, Fletcher and Zelig got out of the building through a side door. They grabbed a car, they sped away in the car *(Smoking his cigarette)* and the SS after them, shot them . . .

The film cuts to the newsreel title card for UFA films, with its revolving globe and huge block-lettered logo, with German lettering underneath. While patriotic newsreel music plays, the narrator begins anew.

NARRATOR'S VOICE-OVER In rare German newsreel footage, a quick glimpse of the escape was recorded.

The German newsreel begins with a panoramic view of a grass runway in a field airport. Hangars stand in the background, amidst various parked biplanes. One of the planes seems to be going around in circles; small figures are seen in the distance, running towards the plane. A German newsreel announcer is heard over the scene, which is shot in jumpy documentary style. The camera clumsily moves to the circling biplane, now heading down the runway. On the ground, people are scattering in all directions as the plane takes off, flying up into the sky.

GERMAN NEWSREEL ANNOUNCER'S VOICE-OVER *(In a scratchy newsreel voice)* Zwei fanatische, idiotische, amerikanische, Dummköpfe, kriminelle Schweinehunde, die Zelig und Fletcher heissen, ruinierten in einer wichtigen Rede unseres Führers Adolf Hitler den besten Witz, den er bisher über Polen machte. Die beiden . . .

The older Dr. Fletcher's voice is heard as the plane soars through the sky, the German newsreel announcer's voice growing fainter and fainter. The film cuts to the present in color; the older Dr. Fletcher sits in her garden. A breeze blows her graying hair, her print dress. She looks out at the offscreen camera, giving a different interview to the offscreen journalist. Behind her is some greenery, a stone fence, a portion of a house. Trees line the peaceful backdrop.

OLDER DR. FLETCHER'S VOICE-OVER I—I was flying! It was wonderful. And then some— *(Onscreen)* suddenly, something happened! I was frightened. I lost control. We went into a dive. Leonard was so terrified that he changed his personality, and before my eyes, because I was a pilot *(Gesturing)* he turned into one, too.

The narrator begins anew as the film cuts back to the past, to a black-and-white sky, where the biplane, looking like a toy in the distance, is seen, circling around, upside down. It goes into a tailspin, spiraling down, then slowly straightens out as the film cuts to a squadron of planes in formation in fast pursuit. They fly across the screen as the narrator continues, as the film cuts back to the lone biplane barrel-rolling through the sky above the faintly seen ocean. Dramatic escape music plays in the background; the screen shows the view of rolling earth, sky, and water as seen from the biplane's cockpit window, spinning and whirling as the plane moves through the sky. The film cuts back to the biplane, alone in the sky—flying upside down.

NARRATOR'S VOICE-OVER Zelig takes control of the airplane. Acting the role of pilot, he struggles valiantly with the aircraft. The Germans, who are stunned, take a full fifteen minutes before they follow in hot pursuit of their quarry. With Eudora Fletcher unconscious, Zelig, who had never flown before in his life, not only escapes the German pilots, but sets a record for flying nonstop across the Atlantic upside down.

The biplane does a complete roll as "America the Beautiful" begins playing proudly in the background. The film cuts to a close-up of a German soldier peering up at the sky through a pair of binoculars, then back to the biplane, a mere upside-down speck, as it flies closer and closer to the camera, growing in size, and it soars past.

The film cuts to a newsreel title card. Under its Hearst Metrotone News head is the headline ZELIG RETURNS TO BIG RECEPTION, *with its accompanying copy:* FOUND AFTER LONG SEARCH BY EUDORA FLETCHER AND WITH NO KNOWLEDGE OF HOW TO FLY —CROSSES ATLANTIC UPSIDE DOWN IN RECORD TIME.

Jaunty newsreel music plays in the background and the newsreel begins with a panoramic view of a Fifth Avenue parade—the same view that was seen in the very beginning of the movie. Crowds line the streets; people hang out the windows of the buildings flinging ticker tape. A parade of marching bands and soldiers proceeds down the street, and an American flag waves in the foreground.

NEWSREEL ANNOUNCER'S VOICE-OVER *(In a scratchy newsreel voice)* With a storm of cheers and a blizzard of ticker tape, New York welcomes back Eudora Fletcher . . .

The newsreel cuts to a closer view of the parade. A cavalcade of cars moves slowly down the street lined with cheering throngs. In the lead car are Zelig and Dr. Fletcher, perched on the backseat, waving to the crowds. Ticker tape flies everywhere; reporters and cameramen jump in front of the car, snapping pictures of the couple.

NEWSREEL ANNOUNCER'S VOICE-OVER . . . and Leonard Zelig, the human chameleon.

The newsreel moves closer still, to a similar scene glimpsed at the beginning of the movie: Zelig and Dr. Fletcher in their open sedan, waving and smiling at the crowd. This time, however, Zelig is seen with bandages on his cheek. Dr. Fletcher waves a handkerchief; flowers are in her lap. Sharing the car with them are several dignitaries, in uniform and in civilian suits.

NEWSREEL ANNOUNCER'S VOICE-OVER His remarkable feat of aviation fills the nation with pride and earns him a full presidential pardon. Forgiving multitudes flock to see him as he sits by the side of his plucky bride-to-be.

The film cuts back to the Fifth Avenue ticker-tape parade, to the slowly driving cavalcade of cars, the cheering throngs, the American flag still waving in the foreground. As the narrator speaks, the newsreel cuts in closer to the motorcade, which is surrounded by parade watchers, ticker tapes, and marching pedestrians gathered around the Zelig/Fletcher car. The newsreel then cuts to yet another view of the motorcade, in which Zelig and Dr. Fletcher, perched on the backseat of the first car, are seen waving to the crowds. The offscreen camera is looking down on them and their cavalcade of limousines, as if it is positioned in a high, offscreen window. Jaunty marching music continues in the background as the dignitaries in the car with Zelig and Dr. Fletcher throw ticker tape off their laps and onto the street.

NEWSREEL ANNOUNCER'S VOICE-OVER Their journey of triumph leads to City Hall. New York's greatest honor, the Medal of Valor, is bestowed on Zelig by Carter Dean.
The newsreel next cuts to Carter Dean, standing at a podium in front of several microphones. He is flanked by the bandaged Zelig and a partially seen Dr. Fletcher. Behind them, uniformed policemen stand at attention. The music stops.

CARTER DEAN You are a great inspiration to the young of this nation, who will one day grow up and be great doctors and great patients.
The offscreen crowd roars their approval as Carter Dean pins a medal on an overwhelmed Zelig and shakes his hand. Dr. Fletcher moves over to the microphone, in front of Carter Dean.

DR. FLETCHER *(Speaking into the microphone, smiling)* This was a great thrill. I-I'm glad we lived to see this day.
The crowd cheers. She smiles exuberantly as Zelig leans over to say a few words.

LEONARD ZELIG *(Into the microphone, gesturing and smiling)* Right —I've never flown before in my life and it shows exactly what you can do if you're a total psychotic.

The crowd cheers and roars anew. Carter Dean laughs appreciatively, the policemen in a row in the background maintain their serious, at-attention faces, a rousing march begins to play over the scene—and the film cuts to a mob of people facing the camera, trying to push past a line of uniformed policemen. The camera moves along the row of cops, their backs to the screen, as the film next cuts to a vast crowd of people, filling the street as far as the eye can see. Foremost on the screen are uniformed policemen, moving backwards into the crowd. Ticker tape flutters down and the film cuts to a snowstorm of ticker tape, swirling down, covering the screen, in a panoramic view of the parade in progress. The camera moves across the tops of the heads of the crowd, past the office building façades, past balconies draped with American flags—all barely seen through the festive rain of ticker tape.

Saul Bellow's voice is heard over the celebration on the screen and the film soon cuts to him, in color, in the present day, in the midst of his interview in his study.

SAUL BELLOW'S VOICE-OVER The thing was paradoxical because what enabled him to perform this astounding feat was his *(Onscreen, looking at the offscreen interviewer)* ability to transform himself. Therefore his sickness was also at the root of his salvation and . . . *(Pauses)* I think it's interesting to view the thing that way, that it, it was his . . . it was his very disorder that made a hero of him.

The film, still in color and in the present day, cuts to the Irving Howe interview; the author sits as before, in his living room, as he talks to the offscreen journalist.

IRVING HOWE It was really absurd in a way. I mean he had this . . . curious quirk, *(Gesturing)* this strange characteristic, and for a time everyone loved him, and then people stopped loving him, and then he did this stunt, you know, *(Gesturing)* with the airplane, and then everybody loved him again and that was what the twenties were like and you know when you think about it, has America changed so much? *(Shaking his head)* I don't think so.

The film cuts back to the past in black-and-white, to Dr. Fletcher and Zelig's wedding. Dr. Fletcher, in a simple white dress and cloche hat, holding a bridal bouquet, stands with Meryl on her sister's front porch. They smile, chatting, framed by the front door behind them. The sisters hug, then motion to an offscreen man to join them. As the narrator speaks, the well-groomed man, in suit and boutonniere, joins them, kissing Dr. Fletcher, his arm around Meryl. The trio pose for the offscreen camera, smiling. The nostalgic strains of "I'll Get By" are heard in the background.

NARRATOR'S VOICE-OVER After untangling countless legal details, Leonard Zelig and Eudora Fletcher marry. It is a simple ceremony, captured on home movies.

The film cuts to a close-up of Zelig and Dr. Fletcher, cheek to cheek in front of Meryl's house. They pose for the offscreen camera, smiling exuberantly. Zelig talks silently; Dr. Fletcher groans good-naturedly.

They look at each other. They kiss, then kiss again, Zelig's head in front of the camera. They gaze into the camera, looking very much in love, their arms around each other's shoulders.

Next, the screen shows the newly married couple, hand in hand, strolling with Meryl and her boyfriend, arm in arm. They are outside, in front of Meryl's house. Their backs are to the camera; then, as if instructed by an offscreen wedding photographer, they turn and pose for the offscreen camera, then walk back, holding hands and smiling. They stop and come in close for the camera; they reposition themselves, Zelig moving between the two sisters. The film has a home-movie quality, with jerky movements and unrehearsed action.

The film cuts to Dr. Fletcher, relaxing in a wicker rocking chair on Meryl's front porch, her legs and arms outstretched; she still holds her bouquet. She is laughing, a beautiful bride. While the narrator and the music continue, she gets up from the chair and walks over to the porch's old-fashioned swing, which holds Zelig, flanked by Meryl and an older woman in a fur stole. Dr. Fletcher stands behind the swing, leaning over, her arm around Zelig. They kiss and the film cuts to:

The bride, standing, and the groom, sitting in a chair behind her, surrounded by smiling relatives and friends on the front porch. Meryl, standing next to her, partially offscreen, tries to grab at the bouquet. Laughing, Dr. Fletcher swats the bouquet at her, then turns back to the offscreen camera. Holding the bouquet, she waits a beat, then flings it into the offscreen cluster of guests, presumably gathered on the lawn. The well-wishers around her applaud, smiling; one man jumps enthusiastically. Dr. Fletcher applauds and smiles as well, turning to Zelig, who is still in his rattan chair on the porch, chatting with an offscreen guest and beaming. Meryl moves onscreen, giving Dr. Fletcher a warm hug.

NARRATOR'S VOICE OVER "Wanting only to be liked, he distorted himself beyond measure," wrote Scott Fitzgerald. "One wonders what would have happened if, right at the outset, he had had the courage to speak his mind and not pretend. In the end, it was, after all, not the approbation of many but the love of one woman that changed his life."

The sounds of "I'll Get By" swell; a vocalist, recalling a bygone era, begins to sing the words as the film cuts to the new bride and groom walking hand in hand. Their backs are to the camera; they stroll away from the screen. Framed by a corner of the porch in the foreground, they stop and embrace, then continue strolling in the distance. They embrace once more as they disappear around the edge of the house, as the vocalist continues his song.

VOCALIST'S VOICE-OVER "I'll get by as long as I have you. / Though there be rain, and darkness too, / I'll not complain, I'll see it through. / Poverty may come to me, that's true, / But what care I, / Say I'll get by / As long as I have you."

The film cuts to a black screen. As the music continues in the background, the following words slowly roll up and off the screen:

Leonard Zelig and Eudora Fletcher lived full and happy years together. She continued practicing psychoanalysis while he gave occasional lectures about his experiences. Zelig's episodes of character change grew less and less frequent and eventually his malady disappeared completely.

On his deathbed he told doctors that he had had a good life and the only annoying thing about dying was that he had just begun reading *Moby Dick* and wanted to see how it came out.

The screen is black once again before the credits pop on and off in white letters. In the background, over the credits, the big-band strains of "I'll Get By" slowly change to "Chameleon Days," sung in a Betty Boop–like voice, which in turn becomes the high-spirited "Doin' the Chameleon," which ultimately becomes a jazzy "Charleston."

Written and Directed by
WOODY ALLEN

A
Jack Rollins and Charles H. Joffe
Production

Produced by
ROBERT GREENHUT

Executive Producer
CHARLES H. JOFFE

Director of Photography
GORDON WILLIS, A.S.C.

Production Designer
MEL BOURNE

Costume Designer
SANTO LOQUASTO

Editor
SUSAN E. MORSE

Associate Producer
MICHAEL PEYSER

Starring
WOODY ALLEN   MIA FARROW

Casting
JULIET TAYLOR

Music Composed and Adapted by
DICK HYMAN

Narrator
PATRICK HORGAN

Creative Coordinator
GAIL SICILIA

Featured Cast

GARRETT BROWN
STEPHANIE FARROW
WILL HOLT
SOL LOMITA
JOHN ROTHMAN
DEBORAH RUSH
MARIANNE TATUM
MARY LOUISE WILSON

Production Manager
MICHAEL PEYSER

First Assistant Director
FREDERIC B. BLANKFEIN

Second Assistant Director
ANTHONY GITTELSON

Unit Manager
EZRA SWERDLOW

Additional First Assistant Director
THOMAS REILLY

Additional Second Assistant Directors
DUNCAN SCOTT
JAMES CHORY

Assistant Editors

Optical and Sound Coordinator	RICHARD NORD
Stills and Duping Coordinator	PAMELA S. ARNOLD
Stock Footage Coordinator	CHRISTINE P. WILLIAMS

Film Laboratory Supervisor	DON DONIGI
	DU ART FILM LABORATORIES, INC.
Stock Research	MARY LANCE
	KATIE MEISTER
	DELL BYRNE
	JEFF GOODMAN
	CHARLIE MUSSER
Still Photography	KERRY HAYES
Photo Retouchers	KAREN DEAN
	JUDITH LAMB
Retouching Strip Printer	PHILIP MOORE
Optical Effects	JOEL HYNICK & STUART ROBERTSON
	R/GREENBERG ASSOCIATES
Stills Animation	STEVEN PLASTRIK
	COMPUTER OPTICALS, INC.
Newsreel Artcards	KAREN SIEGEL ENGEL
	COMPUTER OPTICALS, INC.
Titles	THE OPTICAL HOUSE, N.Y.
Negative Cutting	JOHN GUIDONE & EUGENIA MORRISON
	J.G. FILMS
Sound Effects	HASTINGS SOUND EDITORIAL, INC.
Supervising Sound Editor	DAN SABLE
Sound Editor	MARJORIE DEUTSCH
Script Supervisor	KAY CHAPIN
Production Coordinator	HELEN ROBIN
Assistant to Mr. Allen	GLORIA NORRIS
Unit Publicist	GAIL SICILIA
Art Director	SPEED HOPKINS
Associate Art Director	MICHAEL MOLLY
Set Directors	LES BLOOM
	JANET ROSENBLOOM
Chief Set Dresser	JOSEPH BADALUCCO, JR.
Master Scenic Artist	JAMES SORICE
Standby Scenic Artist	COSMO SORICE

Special Props Constructed by	EOIN SPROTT STUDIOS LTD.
Camera Operator	DICK MINGALONE
Assistant Cameraman	DOUGLAS C. HART
Second Assistant Cameraman	BOB PAONE
Unit Photographers	KERRY HAYES
	BRIAN HAMILL
Rear Process Photography	BILL HANSARD
Production Sound Mixer	JAMES SABAT
Boom Man	LOUIS SABAT
Sound Recordist	FRANK GRAZIADEI
Re-Recording Mixer	RICHARD DIOR
	TRANS/AUDIO INC.
Choreography	DANNY DANIELS
Music Recording Engineer	ROY B. YOKELSON
	NATIONAL RECORDING STUDIOS, INC.
Key Grip	BOB WARD
Set Grip	RONALD BURKE
Construction Grip	ARNE OLSEN
Shop Craftsman	TONY ZAPPIA
Gaffer	RAY QUINLAN
Best Boy	BOB CONNERS
Property Master	JAMES MAZZOLA
Property Man	KENNETH VOGT
Make-Up Design	FERN BUCHNER
Special Make-Up	JOHN CAGLIONE
Hair Design	ROMAINE GREENE
Hairstylist	WERNER SCHERER
Associate Costume Designer	JEFFREY KURLAND
Costume Assistants	TOM McKINLEY
	LYN CARROLL
	RICHARD HORNUNG
Men's Wardrobe Supervisor	BILL CHRISTIANS
Women's Wardrobe Supervisor	LANCEY SAUNDERS CLOUGH
Assistant Production Coordinator	TODD MICHAEL THALER

Art Department Coordinator	JOAN LOPATE
Transportation Captain	JAMES FANNING
Casting Associate	PAUL HEROLD
Extras Casting	NAVARRO BERTONI CASTING
Projectionist	CARL TURNQUEST
DGA Trainee	JAMES CHORY
Location Coordinator	TIMOTHY MARSHALL BOURNE
Location Scouts	CHERYL HILL
	CAROL NAST
	SUSAN ROLLINS
	KEN ROTHSTEIN
Studio Manager	JAMES GREENHUT
Production Assistants	JAMES A. DAVIS
	JOSEPH PIERSON
	CHARLES KAUFMAN
	KEN BERNSTEIN
Location Auditor	JOSEPH HARTWICK
Assistant Location Auditors	PETER LOMBARDI
	DAVID EPSTEIN
Production Accountants	BERNSTEIN & FREEDMAN P.C.
Insurance	ALBERT G. RUBEN INSURANCE CO., INC.
Assistant Sound Editors	RANDALL COLEMAN
	GINA ROOSE
	FRED ROSENBERG
	HARRY BOLES
	JEFFREY STERN
	DEBRA BARD
	SUZANNE PILLSBURY
Apprentice Sound Editors	LYNN SABLE
	JANET LUND

Stock Footage Courtesy of

Hearst Metrotone News
20th Century Fox/Movietone News

Sherman Grinberg Film Libraries, Inc.
John E. Allen, Inc.
National Film Archives
Library of Congress
Medical Archives of the New York Hospital/
Cornell Medical Center
Transit Film–Gesellschaft MBH

Special thanks to Ken Murray
for "Golden Days of San Simeon"
footage now appearing at the
Hearst Castle in California.

Still Photographs Courtesy of

The Bettman Archive
Culver Pictures
Frederic Lewis
J. Katz Family Private Collection
92nd Street YM-YWHA Archives
Photoworld
United Press International
Wide World Photos
Yivo Institute for Jewish Research

WOODY ALLEN	*Leonard Zelig*
MIA FARROW	*Dr. Eudora Fletcher*
JOHN BUCKWALTER	*Dr. Sindell*
MARVIN CHATINOVER	*Glandular Diagnosis Doctor*
STANLEY SWERDLOW	*Mexican Food Doctor*
PAUL NEVENS	*Dr. Birsky*
HOWARD ERSKINE	*Hypodermic Doctor*
GEORGE HAMLIN	*Experimental Drugs Doctor*
RALPH BELL	*Other Doctors*
RICHARD WHITING	
WILL HUSSONG	
ROBERT IGLESIA	*Man in Barber Chair*

ELI RESNICK	*Man in Park*
EDWARD McPHILLIPS	*Scotsman*
GALE HANSEN	*Freshman #1*
MICHAEL JEETER	*Freshman #2*
PETER McROBBIE	*Workers Rally Speaker*
SOL LOMITA	*Martin Geist*
MARY LOUISE WILSON	*Sister Ruth*
ALICE BEARDSLEY	*Telephone Operator*
PAULA TRUEMAN	*Woman on Telephone*
ED LANE	*Man on Telephone*
MARIANNE TATUM	*Actress Fletcher*
CHARLES DENNEY	*Actor Doctor*
MICHAEL KELL	*Actor Koslow*
GARRETT BROWN	*Actor Zelig*
SHARON FERROL	*Miss Baker*
RICHARD LITT	*Charles Koslow*
DIMITRI VASSILOPOULOS	*Martinez*
JOHN ROTHMAN	*Paul Deghuee*
STEPHANIE FARROW	*Sister Meryl*
FRANCIS BEGGINS	*City Hall Speaker*
JEAN TROWBRIDGE	*Dr. Fletcher's Mother*
KEN CHAPIN	*On-Camera Interviewer*
GERALD KLEIN	*Hearst Guests*
VINCENT JEROSA	
DEBORAH RUSH	*Lita Fox*
STANLEY SIMMONDS	*Lita's Lawyer*
ROBERT BERGER	*Zelig's Lawyer*
JEANINE JACKSON	*Helen Gray*
ERMA CAMPBELL	*Zelig's Wife*
ANTON MARCO	*Wrist Victim*
LOUISE DEITCH	*House-Painting Victim*
BERNICE DOWIS	*Vilification Woman*
JOHN DOUMANIAN	*Greek Waiter*
WILL HOLT	*Rally Chancellor*

COLE PALEN	*Zelig's Stunt Double*
PAM BARBER	*Fletcher's Stunt Double*
BERNIE HEROLD	*Carter Dean*

Contemporary Interviews

SUSAN SONTAG

IRVING HOWE

SAUL BELLOW

BRICKTOP

DR. BRUNO BETTELHEIM

PROFESSOR JOHN MORTON BLUM

MARSHALL COLES, SR.	*Calvin Turner*
ELLEN GARRISON	*Older Dr. Fletcher*
JACK CANNON	*Mike Geibell*
THEODORE R. SMITS	*Ted Bierbauer*
SHERMAN LOUD	*Older Paul Deghuee*
ELIZABETH ROTHSCHILD	*Older Sister Meryl*
KUNO SPUNHOLZ	*Oswald Pohl*

Announcers

ED HERLIHY	Pathe News
DWIGHT WEIST	Hearst Metrotone
GORDON GOULD	Radio
WINDY CRAIG	Universal Newsreel
JURGEN KUEHN	German U.F.A. Newsreel

Original Songs by Dick Hyman

"Leonard the Lizard"	Sung by Bernie Knee
	Steve Clayton
	Tony Wells
"Doin' the Chameleon"	Sung by Bernie Knee
	Steve Clayton
	Tony Wells

"Chameleon Days" — Sung by Mae Questel

"You May Be Six People, But I Love You" — Sung by Bernie Knee, Steve Clayton, Tony Wells

"Reptile Eyes" — Sung by Rosemarie Jun

"The Changing Man Concerto"

Additional Songs

"I've Got a Feeling I'm Falling" — By Harry Link, Billy Rose, & Thomas "Fats" Waller; Sung by Roz Harris

"I'm Sitting on Top of the World" — By Ray Henderson, Samuel M. Lewis, & Joe Young; Sung by Norman Brooks

"Ain't We Got Fun" — By Raymond B. Egan, Gus Kahn, & Richard Whiting; Performed by The Charleston City All Stars; Courtesy of MCA Records, Inc.

"Sunny Side Up" — By Lew Brown, B. G. DeSylva, & Ray Henderson; Performed by The Charleston City All Stars; Courtesy of MCA Records, Inc.

"I'll Get By" — By Fred E. Ahlert & Roy Turk; Performed by The Ben Bernie Orchestra; Courtesy of MCA Records, Inc.

"I Love My Baby, My Baby Loves Me" — By Bud Green & Harry Wilson

Performed by The Charleston City All Stars
Courtesy of MCA Records, Inc.

"Runnin' Wild" By A. H. Gibbs, Joe Grey, & Leo Wood
Performed by The Charleston City All Stars
Courtesy of MCA Records, Inc.

"A Sailboat in the Moonlight" By John Leob
& Carmen Lombardo
Performed by The Guy Lombardo Orchestra
Courtesy of RCA Records

"Charleston" By James P. Johnson & Cecil Mack
Performed by Dick Hyman

"Chicago, That Toddlin' Town" By Fred Fisher
Performed by Dick Hyman

"Five Foot Two, Eyes of Blue" By Ray Henderson,
Samuel M. Lewis,
& Joe Young
Performed by Dick Hyman

"Anchors Aweigh" By George D. Lottman, Alfred H. Miles,
Domenico Sanino, & Charles A. Zimmerman
Performed by Dick Hyman

The Producers Gratefully Acknowledge and Wish
To Thank the Following for Their Assistance:

John E. Allen
Harold Axe M.D.
Nancy Casey
Bernard Chertok
Anthony Comanda
William Everson
Ralph Friedman
Bob Gaulin
Charles Gellert
Rick Herzog
Dan Jones
Paul Killiam
Laura Kreiss
Adele Lerner

Walter Levinsky
Joe Malin
Louise Mastromano
Bill Murphy
Jack Muth
Robert Paquette
Richard Plagge
Harold Potter
John Rogers
Andrea Sheen
Bob Summers
Ted Troll
Robert Trondsen
Irwin Young

And Also Thank:

Chappell Music, Inc.
Cinema Services, Inc.
Davlyn Gallery—New York
General Camera Corp.
The Harry Fox Agency
Kaufman Astoria Studios, Astoria, New York
Killiam Shows, Inc.
Lenses and Panaflex® Cameras by Panavision®
Magno Sound and Video Center, Inc.
Mayor's Office of Film, Theatre and Broadcasting
National Medical Audio-Visual Center of the
National Library of Congress
New Jersey Motion Picture and Television Commission
Vintage Aircraft Courtesy of Old Rhinebeck Aerodrome
Warner Bros. Music
Museum of Modern Art Film Stills Archives
New York Daily News Photo Archives
Religious News Service
RCA Records Photo Archives
Museum of the City of New York Yiddish Theater Collection
Hicks Family Private Photo Collection
Kaplan Family Private Photo Collection
Lehman Family Private Photo Collection
Rivman Family Private Photo Collection
Sinreich Family Private Photo Collection

The story, all names, characters and incidents portrayed in this production are fictitious. No identification with actual persons is intended or should be inferred.

(emblem) (I.A.T.S.E. emblem)

MOTION PICTURE ASSOCIATION OF AMERICA
Approved No. 27056

AN ORION PICTURES/WARNER BROS. RELEASE

BROADWAY DANNY ROSE

The star-studded sky of the Orion logo appears on the screen, followed by the words AN ORION PICTURES RELEASE. *The screen next goes black; white credits pop on and off. At the same time, singer Lou Canova's voice is heard, accompanied by applause and laughter from an unseen audience.*

A Jack Rollins and Charles H. Joffe Production

BROADWAY DANNY ROSE

Starring

WOODY ALLEN

MIA FARROW

NICK APOLLO FORTE

Casting

JULIET TAYLOR

Associate Producer

MICHAEL PEYSER

Editor

SUSAN E. MORSE

Costume Designer

JEFFREY KURLAND

Production Designer

MEL BOURNE

Director of Photography

GORDON WILLIS, A.S.C.

Executive Producer

CHARLES H. JOFFE

Produced by
ROBERT GREENHUT

Written and Directed by
WOODY ALLEN

LOU'S VOICE-OVER Thank you, thank you. Oh, if you overate too much tonight I got a great song that the *paesans* would understand. It's "Agita." Una-two!

As Lou sings to the sound of an accordion band, the credits fade off the screen, replaced by the front of the Carnegie Delicatessen at night, lit up with a long, bright sign flashing CARNEGIE, *then* DELICATESSEN/ RESTAURANT. *People walk on the busy sidewalk; cars drive by on the street. The camera moves in, closer and closer, to the deli's front window, its inside lights glowing out onto the street.*

Lou is still singing as the front of the deli slowly dissolves to its interior. For a brief moment the window, the reflected cars, and the deli's busy kitchen area counter are one—until only the counter is seen, stacked with dishes on its top. Its mirrored front reflects some diners eating offscreen. A waiter picks up some dishes and scurries past the camera as another waiter walks down the length of the counter, his torso reflected in the mirror. The camera follows him, his back to the screen, into the dining area. Lou continues his song as the waiter stops at a table, putting down a plate of food, and walks offscreen. The dining room is hopping, the tables filled with diners; an elderly waiter takes an order and walks towards the camera and offscreen. A seasoned waitress walks through a swinging door in the background near several coats hanging on pegs; she carries a plate. Another waiter walks down the aisle; the owner gives another group their check. A man gets up from his table, his meal finished. He puts on his coat and, check in hand, walks towards the camera, offscreen.

The camera moves down the aisle, in the midst of all this activity, stopping at a table where a group of men are getting up, coats in hand, saying their farewells. Revealed when they leave is the table

behind them, where comedians Corbett Monica and Morty Gunty are sitting and eating. Lou's singing trails off, filled in with the chatter of diners, waiters, and cutlery. The two men's voices are heard over the indistinct deli noise as the camera moves closer and closer to their table. Corbett faces the camera. Morty sits opposite him, his back to the screen.

CORBETT I spent two nights in Florida.

MORTY You have to do the Miami jokes. If you're in Florida, you do Miami jokes, in Atlantic City you do—

CORBETT *(Interrupting, gesturing)* Morty, I tried Miami jokes. I don't know what works anymore.

MORTY Well, tr— Why? What happened?

CORBETT Well, you know I got that big Miami joke that I do.

MORTY *(Overlapping)* Yeah, okay.

CORBETT You know, about the hotels being expensive, and, uh . . .

MORTY *(Sipping his coffee, interrupting)* Right.

CORBETT *(Continuing, gesturing)* . . . how much it costs to stay, like a hundred and fifty dollars a day for a sleeping room. I said to the clerk, "What's cheaper?" He said, "I got a room for ten dollars, but you gotta make your own bed." I said, "I'll take it." So he gave me a hammer and a board and some nails. And that's the joke, you know.

MORTY *(Gesturing)* Yeah, it's a good joke. It works.

CORBETT Good joke? It's been working for years. Last night it died.

MORTY Really?

CORBETT Died. I tell you, Morty, *(Chuckling)* that audience sat there like they were an oil painting.

MORTY *(Shrugging)* I don't know why. It always works when I do it.

CORBETT *(Pointing to Morty)* You do that joke?

MORTY Sure, all the time.

CORBETT *(Pointing to himself)* Maybe that's where I got it from.
Corbett and Morty's faces dissolve to a different view of the same table. Morty's face is now seen. It's later that night. Three other comics, Sandy Baron, Jackie Gayle, and Howard Storm, are also gathered around the table, which is covered with bottles, napkins, and cups of coffee. A mirror hangs in the background; a waiter is first seen in the mirror; he then passes in front of the camera. Other diners and waiters are partially seen. The comedians talk among themselves, sometimes all at the same time.

MORTY Do you know that when I broke into this business in New York, that I-I could play at least twelve to twenty weeks a year without leaving the city. There was the Copa . . .

SANDY *(Interrupting)* Where?

MORTY *(Continuing)* . . . the Latin Quarter.

JACKIE The China Doll?

MORTY *(Overlapping)* I played the, uh . . . China Doll, Elegante, in Brooklyn.

JACKIE *(Overlapping)* Queen's Terrace?

MORTY I played the Boulevard. . . .

HOWARD *(Overlapping Morty)* Suburban.

SANDY *(Overlapping Howard)* San Su San.

MORTY *(Overlapping Sandy)* The Suburban out in Long Island, the San Su San.

HOWARD *(Overlapping Morty)* Well, what about Jersey? The Stagecoach. *(Mumbling)* A lot of clubs in Jersey.

SANDY *(Overlapping)* They never left. They never left at all.

JACKIE *(Overlapping)* Lamplighters, Bill Miller's, a million places.

MORTY *(Gesturing)* The Riviera, Bill Miller's, right?

JACKIE *(Overlapping, gesturing)* Look how far you have to go. You went to Washington last week. I went to Baltimore.

HOWARD Yeah.

JACKIE You gotta have good tires to work today. You know what's happening.

MORTY *(Laughing)* Or a good car.

JACKIE *(Chuckling)* Or a good car.

As all the comedians laugh, they dissolve to another scene around the table, as seen from a different angle, a bit farther away. It's even later that same night. Corbett, Morty, Sandy, and Howard have been joined by comedians Jack Rollins and Will Jordan. The swinging doors and the coats on pegs are seen in the background. An empty table is seen in the foreground.

WILL *(Gesturing)* The first impression I ever did, I went to see a film called *The Seventh Veil*, and I didn't even want to become an impressionist. *(Taking off his glasses as he inhales and begins a James Mason impersonation)* What I was trying to do was develop an English accent.

HOWARD *(Overlapping)* Yeah.

WILL *(Impersonating James Mason)* The idea of impersonating James Mason *(Snorting, primly)* was the furthest thing from my mind.

The other comics, listening and watching Will, begin to laugh appreciatively. Sandy makes an indistinct comment to Morty under the laughter.

WILL *(Overlapping the laughter, still impersonating James Mason)* And out came this impression and I've been doing impressions ever since. *(Snorts with laughter)*

HOWARD *(Sitting with his back to the camera)* But this thing is all in like the mask, right?

WILL *(Putting his glasses back on—askew)* And then I did Picasso for a few weeks.

The comics laugh anew. Will straightens his glasses and turns to Sandy, who now has center stage.

SANDY *(Gesturing, his arm resting on the back of his chair)* You know the first time I saw you do Mason? It was backstage at the Sullivan show, and you, you were brilliant. And I was there with Danny Rose. *(Looking around the table)* Remember Danny Rose?

HOWARD Yeah, yeah, yeah.

The other comics all nod enthusiastically, chattering indistinctly, all at once. An elderly male diner walks in front of the camera, putting on his coat as he walks offscreen.

SANDY Yeah. He was handling an act then, a manager, *(Gesturing)* he was handling an act then, a one-legged tap dancer, which was his normal handling. *(Overlapping an indistinct comment from Howard)* It was his normal handling. Danny Rose. Yeah. Oh, he's the best.

CUT TO:
INTERIOR. PHIL CHOMSKY'S OFFICE—DAY.

Danny Rose—in checkered sports jacket, clashing shirt, and Jewish chai *dangling on his neck—fills the screen. Behind him are windows revealing neon signs and another building outside. A lamp and a typewriter are on a desk under the windows. File cabinets are seen in the background; a framed photograph is partially seen on an offscreen desk, where Phil Chomsky is sitting. Danny, gesturing wildly, is in the midst of a conversation with the offscreen Phil.*

DANNY *(Gesturing)* May I say one word? Mi-, ca-, mi-, might I just interject one concept at this juncture? You're looking for somebody for Memorial Day weekend. *(Clears throat)* My blind xylophone player, okay? The man would be perfect for your room.

PHIL *(Offscreen)* Ah, forget it.

DANNY *(Gesturing wildly)* What? Philly, we-, p-, hear me out, will you please hear me out? The man is a beautiful man. He's a, he's a fantastic individual.

Danny starts to walk around the desk as the film cuts to his point of view: a bald Phil Chomsky, sitting behind his large desk, the window

behind him. On its sill are stacks of paper, a large fan. A desk lamp sits in the foreground, on Phil's cluttered desk.

PHIL *(Offscreen)* My *(Onscreen as the film cuts to him behind his desk)* hotel gets old Jewish people.

DANNY *(Overlapping, walking over to Phil behind the desk)* Really.

PHIL *(Gesturing)* They're blind! They ain't gonna pay to see a blind guy. *(Turns away from Danny, reacting with disgust)*

DANNY *(Standing next to Phil, gesturing)* All right, all right, *(Clears throat)* so forget that then. Phil, how 'bout, how 'bout Herbie Jayson's birds?

PHIL *(Overlapping, reacting, waving Danny away)* Awww, come on.

DANNY Herbie Jayson's birds.

PHIL *(Shaking his head)* Nah.

DANNY *(Gesturing)* They're little birds, they peck tunes out on a piano. It's a beautiful thing.
Phil sighs, still shaking his head, still turned away from the persistent Danny.

DANNY *(Under his breath, turning briefly away)* Aw, Je— . . . *(Turning back to Phil, gesturing)* All right, what about my one-legged tap dancer?
Phil groans. He continues to shake his head.

DANNY Take, take him for a weekend. My one-legged— All right, my one-armed juggler. My one-armed juggler!

PHIL *(Gesturing)* Not for my hotel!
A disgusted Phil gets up from his desk. The camera follows him as he walks over to some cardboard file boxes stacked on a table in another

area of the office. A different set of windows offers a partial view of a billboard.

DANNY *(Sighing)* All right, what about Lou Canova, my-my Ita-, Lou Canova, my Italian singer, he'd be *(Offscreen)* great.

PHIL *(Gesturing, looking briefly back at the now offscreen Danny)* Lou Canova's a dumb, fat, temperamental has-been . . . *(Pauses)* with a drinkin' problem.

The film moves back to Danny, still trying, still gesturing, as he walks back around the desk.

DANNY Shh, geez, I . . . what about, what about Eddie Clark's penguin? That's a perfect . . . Eddie Clark and his penguin. *(Gesturing, looking out at the now offscreen Phil)* Then the penguin skates on the stage dressed as a rabbi. It's hilarious. *(Gesturing)* The penguin's got a beard like a—

The film cuts to Phil as he interrupts Danny; he is standing by the file cabinets holding some publicity photos. A coffee percolator sits on a stack of papers.

PHIL *(Looking offscreen at Danny)* I'll tell ya what, Danny. Give me Sonny Chase. He's the best act you got. He's fast, he's funny.

DANNY *(Offscreen)* I don't handle Sonny anymore.

PHIL *(Gesturing, the glossies in hand)* Since when?

The film moves back to Danny near the desk, still gesturing wildly as he looks at the offscreen Phil.

DANNY D— Oh, it's a long story, Philly, really. I f-, I found, I discovered the kid, he slept on my sofa. I supported him. Eh-eh, I don't want to badmouth the kid, but he's a horrible, dishonest, immoral louse. *(Clears throat)* And I say that with all due respect.

The film cuts back to Phil as he talks to Danny; he puts down the glossies he's been looking at and walks over to a makeshift bar in the corner of the room. Photographs hang on the wall behind the bar.

PHIL *(Gesturing)* I know, Danny. They get a little success, and then they leave you. *(Pours himself a drink, his back to the camera)*

DANNY *(Offscreen)* That's wha-, that's my point! Believe me, Philly, if I had all the acts in this business that I started that made it, I'd be a rich man today. *(Briefly passes Phil as he walks on, then offscreen)*

PHIL *(Facing the bar, his back still to the camera)* I'd like to help you, Danny. But Weinstein's Majestic Bungalow Colony is a classy place, and I need a classy act.

DANNY *(Walking backwards past Phil again, briefly on, then offscreen again)* Well, that's why I want to *(Offscreen)* show you this lady. She is the Jascha Heifetz of this instrument. She is really something.
As Danny continues to talk, a blonde beehived woman briefly appears onscreen, walking past Phil as he turns, glass in hand, and looks offscreen.

DANNY *(Continuing, offscreen)* You gotta see this, Philly, it's absolutely incredible. She—
The film cuts to Phil's point of view: Danny and the blonde woman, "the water glass virtuoso," standing behind a parson's table that is covered with half-full water glasses. The table sits by the windows—having been carried by Danny and the woman when they'd quickly passed Phil, the table out of view. As Danny talks, the woman begins to play the glasses. She smiles at the offscreen Phil.

DANNY *(Continuing, over the tinkling glass-playing sounds)* Never took a lesson. *(Pointing to the woman, swaying to the music)* Ne-, self-taught. Next year, Philly, my hand to God, she's gonna be at Carnegie Hall. *(Gesturing to the offscreen Phil)* But you, I'll

let you have her now at the old price, okay? Which i-, which is anything you want to give me. Anything at all, Philly.
The film abruptly cuts back to the Carnegie Deli, to the table of comics, laughing, gesturing, and reminiscing about Danny Rose. The camera focuses first on Corbett's face, sitting near Morty, then moves across the table to Howard, Jack sitting to his right, cigarette in hand, and Jackie, to his left, his back to the camera.

CORBETT *(Laughing)* I remember that woman that played the glasses.

HOWARD You have never seen acts like this in your life. I mean, this guy would work his tail off for these acts. I mean, if he believed in an act, he would go all out.

CUT TO:
INTERIOR. REHEARSAL ROOM—DAY.

A middle-aged man in a two-toned tux and a woman in a long gown are surrounded by balloon animals on small tables; one of the tables is covered in velvet. There are several elephants; the woman holds a swan. Behind them is a door printed with an exit sign, and a partially seen window.

MALE BALLOON FOLDER *(Folding a balloon into an animal, talking over its squeaky sounds)* Danny, my partner wants me to open up with the dachshund. But I think I should open up with the, ah, swan or the giraffe.
As the man continues to create his animal, as he continues to speak, the film cuts to Danny, sitting in an aluminum folding chair in the sparse rehearsal room, his legs crossed, watching them. The man's back is partially seen. A soda can sits on the floor near his chair.

MALE BALLOON FOLDER The swan is pretty, and it fascinates the people.
The film moves back to the animal balloon folders. The man has just finished making a poodle.

MALE BALLOON FOLDER *(Holding up his balloon poodle)* Or . . . have an animal of this type.

The camera cuts back to Danny as he talks to the balloon act. The man's back and his balloon poodle are partially seen. As Danny discusses his plans, the film cuts back and forth between him, sitting in his chair, and the balloon animal couple, standing stiffly among their creations, still holding their balloon animals, listening and looking at the offscreen Danny.

DANNY *(Pointing towards the offscreen balloon creations)* Ah, *(Clears his throat)* I think your partner's right. You should open up with the dachshund, and then you should move on and build to the giraffe. *(Gesturing)* I think you should close with the giraffe 'cause it's got more impact.

MALE BALLOON FOLDER *(Holding his poodle, the camera back on him and the woman)* Really?

DANNY *(Offscreen)* If you take my advice, *(Onscreen, as the film moves back to him)* I think you're gonna become one of the great balloon-folding acts of all time. *(Gesturing and pointing)* Really. Eh, 'cause I don't see you just folding these balloons in joints, you know. You're gonna . . . you listen to me, you're gonna fold these balloons at universities and colleges. You're gonna, you're gonna make your, your snail and your elephant at, at, at, on Broadway. *(Offscreen as the camera moves back to the balloon act couple, standing stiffly as before)* You know what I mean? But the thing to remember is before you go out onstage, *(Onscreen, the camera back on him in his chair)* you gotta look in the mirror, you gotta say your three S's. *(Counting on his fingers)* Star, smile, strong. *(Nods towards the offscreen couple)*

MALE AND FEMALE BALLOON FOLDERS *(Onscreen, the camera back on them and their creations, slowly)* Star, smile, strong.

The comics' laughter is heard as the film cuts back to the Carnegie Deli, to the comics at their table. They're talking and laughing all at once. The camera is first focused on Morty, Jackie, Corbett, and Sandy. It moves across the table as the comics continue to talk, revealing Will, Jack, and Howard at the other end.

MORTY *(Overlapping the laughter, cigarette in hand)* You know Danny used to be a performer himself.

SANDY *(Overlapping Morty)* Yeah. Oh, yeah.

CORBETT *(Overlapping the others)* He was a comic.

HOWARD *(Offscreen, overlapping Corbett)* That's right. Sure. I mea-, well, he worked the Catskills. *(Onscreen as the camera moves down the table)* Yeah, he did all the old jokes . . . and stole from everybody. *(Gesturing)* He was exactly the kind of comic you'd think he'd be.
As Howard speaks, the film cuts to the inside of a large nightclub. It's packed with people squeezed around small white cloth-covered tables. Amidst the slated crowd is Danny, standing, wearing a tux, and holding a microphone. Everyone is watching him, laughing and applauding; he's seen past the heads of most of the patrons; he stands near a platform where a band is waiting, enjoying his show. The walls are decorated with mirrors. Howard's voice trails off as the sound of the laughing audience is heard. Danny is leaning down, talking to a partially seen elderly woman, her back to the camera, sitting at one of the tables.

DANNY *(Overlapping the laughter, to the elderly woman, into the microphone)* Tell me, God bless you, darling. L-, let me, let me ask you a question, sweetheart. How old are you? *(Holding the microphone out to her)* Just, just, just tell me how old you are.

ELDERLY WOMAN *(Into the microphone, her back to the camera)* Eighty-one.
The film cuts closer to Danny, standing among the nightclub patrons, working the room, his microphone up to his mouth. The people around

him are smiling at him, laughing, and interspersing his monologue with applause.

DANNY Eighty-one years old, isn't that fantastic? No, really. *(Speaking over the appreciative applause of the crowd)* She's eighty-one. This is fantastic. *(Turning around, looking around the room and nodding)* I mean that. Just . . . Unbelievable. *(To the elderly woman, into the microphone)* You don't look a day over eighty. *(Overlapping the laughter of the crowd)* No, I mean it. I'm just kidding, darling, really. I love you, sweetheart. You're really, really beautiful. What sign are you, darling? You know what sign you are? *(Holds out his microphone to the elderly woman)*

ELDERLY WOMAN *(Into the microphone, her back to the camera)* What?

DANNY *(Into the microphone, looking out at the crowd and nodding)* "What"?! She says, "What." She's great.
The audience is laughing. After a beat, Danny begins his monologue anew and the film cuts to the audience, to the crowds watching and reacting to the now offscreen Danny. First, a table of elderly, well-dressed people is seen. A woman with white curled hair and skinny eyebrows, in a lowcut evening dress, is laughing; a man nearby, in a suit and glasses, is listening, his lips pursed, looking somewhat dazed. They are surrounded by other elderly people at different tables, all watching the offscreen Danny and grinning. The film quickly cuts to another section of the audience, where a younger man in a Nehru jacket, wearing a huge medallion around his neck, is laughing. Next to him, an elderly woman in a suit drops an Alka-Seltzer into a glass of water. As it plops in, she looks up and smiles. A woman near the Nehru jacket man laughs and nods at the offscreen Danny. Behind their table, near a wall decorated with latticework, are two seated elderly men in suits; one sips his drink, his eyes wandering.

DANNY *(Offscreen, over the laughter of the crowd)* But I drove up here today. I love driving. You know, you, you run across so many interesting people. And I saw a terrible accident.

The film cuts back to Danny, in the middle of his joke, standing among the crowded tables. Cigarette smoke spirals up from the table; the heads of the surrounding patrons are seen, as well as the partially seen band members on the nightclub platform.

DANNY *(Into his microphone, gesturing)* Two taxicabs collided. Thirty Scotchmen were killed.
The audience starts to laugh, Danny looks around the room, gesturing, and the film cuts back to the Carnegie Deli, to the comics laughing and reminiscing at their table. Corbett's back is to the camera; Sandy, Will, and Jack are to his left; Howard faces the camera. To his left are the partially seen Jackie and Morty.

JACKIE *(Overlapping the comic's laughter)* That's something, I'll tell you.

HOWARD *(Overlapping Jackie, gesturing)* And I'll tell you something. The reason he stopped doing his act was because he was working the Catskill Mountains. All right?

SANDY *(Overlapping Howard, nodding)* Yeah.

HOWARD *(Continuing, gesturing)* Now, he's c— Nobody in the audience is under eighty years old.

SANDY *(Nodding, listening)* Yeah.

HOWARD *(Gesturing, looking at each comic)* Okay, he's onstage doing his act. Two people get heart attacks. Yeah.
They all start to laugh. Jackie comments indistinctly. The comics all start talking at once.

CORBETT *(Overlapping the laughter and chatter)* Oh, yeah.

WILL *(Overlapping the laughter and chatter)* So naturally he became a personal manager.
The comics all agree, nodding their heads and commenting indistinctly.

HOWARD *(Overlapping the others)* What else? Yeah, that's right. If you can't do a good act, you become a personal manager, right?

WILL But his acts were so devoted.

HOWARD Yeah.

WILL They loved him.

HOWARD Yeah, they did that.

WILL *(Overlapping Howard)* I mean, where you gonna find that kind of devotion today?
The comics all agree. Once again, they all talk at once, commenting indistinctly. Jackie takes a sip of water.

MORTY *(Overlapping the others, only his hand seen, gesturing with a cigar)* Nice kid.

HOWARD *(Overlapping the others)* I gotta tell you something, though. The funniest Danny Rose story is the time he's handling a hypnotist. Okay? He's got the guy—

JACK *(Overlapping Howard, interrupting)* Oh, right. Yeah.

HOWARD *(Overlapping Jack, continuing)* The hypnotist. *(Gesturing)* And he's got the guy working the Catskill Mountains.

JACK *(Overlapping Howard, nodding)* I remember that. Uh-huh.

HOWARD *(Overlapping Jack, continuing, looking at the comics)* And the guy brings, the hypnotist brings up *(Gesturing)* this little old Jewish lady and he . . .

SANDY *(Overlapping Howard, nodding)* Yeah.

HOWARD *(Continuing, gesturing)* . . . put the, hypn-, hypnotizes her.
Howard snaps his fingers and the film cuts to:

INTERIOR. BACKSTAGE AREA—NIGHT.

The little old Jewish lady fills the screen. She is in a trance, her eyes closed and her head down. Her arm is outstretched, partially offscreen. There are gesturing and pointing hands around her head; spotlights are seen in the background.

HUSBAND *(His face offscreen, his hands gesturing wildly)* Tessie, Tessie. *Vay iz mir.* What is this you're doing to my wife?
The film moves back as Danny begins to talk, revealing the woman sitting in a chair, her arm outstretched. Danny stands in front of her, pointing and gesturing. Her frantic husband stands next to her, on the right. To her left is the hypnotist, in turban and satin, muttering incantations. Everyone gestures and talks at once—except for the woman, who remains frozen in her chair. Backstage workers walk back and forth in front of the camera, momentarily obscuring the group each time. A man in a loud suit stands in front of a nearby ladder, his back to the camera. Other workers stand in the background, watching the group, fascinated.

DANNY *(Pointing and gesturing)* The b-b-b- . . . the body is warm. You see, it's a good sign. The body is still warm.

HUSBAND *(Overlapping Danny, talking first indistinctly in Yiddish)* Tessie, Tessie!

DANNY *(Overlapping Tessie's husband and the gesturing hypnotist, who is muttering indistinctly, to the hypnotist)* Okay, let's go, huh? *(To Tessie's husband, gesturing)* I-I promise you if your wife never wakes up again, I promise you I will take you to any restaurant of your choice, okay?

HUSBAND *(Overlapping Danny, excited, gesticulating)* He's taking me to a restaurant after he kills my wife.

DANNY *(Overlapping Tessie's husband)* I . . . *(Stutters indistinctly)*

HYPNOTIST *(Overlapping the group, gesturing in a magic trick manner, to Tessie)* Come on, come on, come on, wake up, please!

DANNY *(Overlapping the hypnotist, talking to Tessie's husband)* Do you like Chinese food? Do you like Chinese food?
Tessie's husband mutters indistinctly, upset and gesturing frantically. The hypnotist sprinkles water from a glass onto Tessie's face. The comics begin to laugh as the movie cuts back to their table in the Carnegie Deli. This time the table is seen in its entirety. Sandy, Will, and Jack face the camera; Corbett and Howard sit at either end of the table. Jackie and Morty's backs are to the camera. Everyone is laughing and talking at once. The table is littered with plates, cups and saucers, napkins, and ketchup bottles.

MORTY *(Overlapping the laughter and chatter)* He was such a failure.

SANDY *(Overlapping the group, motioning for quiet)* All right, you finished? Excuse me. Hold it, hold it. Are you finished?

MORTY *(Ignoring Sandy)* I would've paid to see him.

SANDY *(Overlapping Morty)* Are you finished?

MORTY *(Gesturing)* Yeah, yeah.

HOWARD *(Overlapping Morty, gesturing)* Yeah, yeah. What do you want?

SANDY *(Overlapping the others, continuing and gesturing)* Because I have the greatest Danny Rose story.

MORTY *(Overlapping Sandy)* Uh-huh.

HOWARD *(Overlapping Sandy, looking at the others)* He's always got the greatest story.

CORBETT *(Overlapping Howard, agreeing with him)* He's got the greatest Danny Rose story.

JACKIE *(Overlapping the others)* Oh, oh that's great . . . *(Mutters indistinctly)*

SANDY *(Overlapping, looking at the others)* Hold it, now. *(Gesturing)* Are you finished?

CORBETT *(Nodding)* Yeah.

HOWARD *(Overlapping Corbett)* Yeah.

SANDY *(Overlapping the others)* I have the greatest . . .

HOWARD *(Interrupting, gesturing)* Why don't you tell us?

JACKIE *(Overlapping Howard)* Okay, tell us.

SANDY *(Continuing)* . . . Danny Rose story, all right? *(Overlapping the others, who are nodding and making sounds of assent)* You got a couple of moments? *(Gesturing)* You wanna do anything? 'Cause this is gonna take some time.

JACKIE *(Overlapping, gesturing)* Can I go to the washroom?

SANDY *(To Jackie)* Go ahead.

MORTY *(Overlapping Sandy, to Corbett)* Corbett, order.

CORBETT *(Gesturing to an offscreen waiter)* Order. Coffee.

HOWARD *(Overlapping Corbett, gesturing to himself)* I'd like to go change my suit.

SANDY *(Overlapping the others, gesturing, to Howard)* Change your suit. *(To Corbett)* Okay, order. *(To the group at large)* Are you ready? We're gonna be here a while. Okay?

JACKIE *(Overlapping, nodding)* All right.

MORTY You're sure this is the greatest?

SANDY *(Overlapping, to Morty)* This is the, this is the greatest Danny Rose story.

Will, sitting next to Sandy, nods and takes a bite of food and a sip of water; he looks at Sandy.

SANDY *(Pointing and gesturing, overlapping Morty, who is still commenting indistinctly)* This is the one with Lou Canova.

CORBETT Oh, yeah.

MORTY *(Overlapping Corbett)* Oh, yeah.

HOWARD *(Overlapping the others, pointing)* Canova, that's the tall guy, the singer? The Italian kid?

SANDY *(Overlapping the others, nodding and pointing dramatically)* Ah.

CORBETT *(Overlapping Sandy)* Right.

MORTY *(Overlapping Corbett)* Was he the, he was the kid that had those semi-hit records in the fifties, right?

SANDY *(Nodding and gesturing)* That's right.

CORBETT Yeah, he had a record I think called "Agita." *(Chuckling, overlapping the others, who are laughing and chuckling in remembrance)* It was on the charts for about fifteen minutes.

SANDY *(Overlapping Howard and Jackie's guffaws)* This is not during those fifteen minutes. This is . . . twenty-five years later.

CORBETT *(Listening)* Ah.

The camera begins to move closer and closer to the table. As Sandy begins his tale, the camera continues to move closer, past Jackie and Morty's backs, past Corbett and Howard's profiles, moving closer and

closer to Sandy's face, until only he is seen onscreen, the coats on wall pegs behind him. Smoke from Sandy's cigarette swirls up in the corner of the screen.

SANDY *(Gesturing)* And Lou cannot get anybody to handle him. I mean, the man is in trouble. And the only one who believes in him is Danny Rose.

HOWARD *(Offscreen)* Right.

SANDY *(Looking offscreen at the group)* And by now, you gotta remember, Lou is a has-been. He's got a *big* ego, a temperament, and a slight drinking problem. *(Gesturing)* And Danny . . . has faith.

Band music begins playing a crooning standard as the film cuts to a crowded, dark nightclub. The portly Lou Canova, in a tux, is singing, a microphone in front of him, the band in back. He is lit by a spotlight, seen across the heads of the seated nightclub patrons, who are packed together at individual small tables. Scantily dressed cocktail waitresses scurry back and forth with their trays, taking orders and putting down drinks. The low din of conversation is heard over Lou's singing; cigarette smoke wafts up through the crowd.

LOU *(Into his microphone, singing)* "I like the looks of you . . ." *As Lou sings, the film cuts to various people in the audience: to a young woman in profile, looking dreamily at the offscreen Lou. She looks off and takes a puff of her cigarette . . .*

LOU *(Offscreen, singing)* ". . . The lure of you . . ."

. . . to Lou again, as seen past the crowded club . . .

LOU *(Into his microphone, continuing his song)* "The sweet of you, / The pure of you, / *(Gesturing to the band, which begins to play in a faster tempo)* The eyes, the nose, the mouth . . ."

. . . to a table where a partially seen man is sitting with two women who are dressed up, their hair and makeup perfect. Bouncing to the music, they smile at the offscreen Lou. One of the women snaps her fingers in tempo. Behind them are other patrons, drinking and enjoying the song . . .

LOU *(Offscreen, continuing his song)* ". . . of you, / The east, west, north, and . . ."

. . . then back to Lou, seen closer up now, in front of his band. He walks off the bandstand into the audience, his microphone in hand. Smiling patrons are seen in the background . . .

LOU *(Into the microphone, continuing his song, gesturing)* ". . . the south of you. / I'd like to gain complete control of you / And . . ."

. . . to a well-dressed man in a suit and glasses. He has a mustache. He listens intently, holding out a cigarette, as he watches the offscreen Lou. An enraptured woman at another table is seen in the background . . .

LOU *(Offscreen, continuing his song)* ". . . handle even the heart and . . ."

. . . then back to Lou, standing in the audience, singing his heart out. A waitress passes in the crowd behind him.

LOU *(Into his microphone, singing as he tosses the microphone from hand to hand)* ". . . soul of you. / So love at least / a small percent of me, do. / I do, I do, I do, I do. / 'Cause I love all of you. / I do, I do, I do, I do. / Yeah."

Lou finishes his song with a flourish. The enthusiastic applause begins as the film cuts to two young women, one plump, one thin, grinning and applauding wildly at their table. They are heavily made up with elaborate hairdos and earrings. The thin woman chews gum. Around them are other enthusiastic patrons, applauding and smiling at the offscreen Lou.

CUT TO:
INTERIOR. BACKSTAGE DRESSING ROOM—NIGHT.

Lou is leaning against the wall, his tie and collar open and askew. Behind him is a corkboard, busy with pinned clippings, photos, and a painting. The door is open; backstage workers are seen in the background, milling about and walking to and fro. Lou is looking out at the camera, at the offscreen Danny. There is no music.

LOU *(Gesturing)* There's a third show? I thought there's only two.

DANNY *(Offscreen)* No, there's, there's three on weekdays, and there's four on weekends.

LOU Four?! Tell 'em I'll walk! Four shows. *(Gesturing angrily, taking off his jacket)* Crazy.

DANNY *(Offscreen)* What do you mean? You *(Onscreen, walking over to Lou)* can't wa— Lou, we're not in a position yet to walk, you know. And I, and I say "yet," I used the word "yet." *(Takes Lou's jacket, trailing off)*

LOU *(Overlapping Danny, nodding, reacting)* My hair's all screwed up and everything. My tux, my pants. Everything is f—

Piano music begins offscreen. Lou fusses with his cuffs, still upset. A woman musician walks in front of the camera, past Lou and out the dressing room door.

DANNY *(Interrupting Lou, walking offscreen with Lou's jacket)* Your hair is fine. Your tux is fine. Did you do the three S's?

LOU *(Nodding)* Yeah, strong, smile, star. I know, I know. *(Gesturing)* Every time you tell me. Every time you say the same thing.

FEMALE MUSICIAN *(Walking out of the room, her back to the camera)* See you later, Lou.

LOU *(Continuing, ignoring the musician)* I got a platform—

DANNY *(Overlapping Lou, walking onscreen, carrying a robe to Lou)* Right. Here. *(Helping Lou on with the robe)* An-and what you should do is "My Funny Valentine" *after* you do great crooners from the past who are deceased.

Lou continues to nod, adjusting his robe, as a female fan wearing dangling earrings sticks her head into the dressing room.

FAN *(Smiling)* Hi, Lou, I wanted to meet you.

LOU *(Overlapping his fan, ignoring her, to Danny)* I'm discouraged. I'm down. Just down.

DANNY *(Overlapping, to Lou)* You're fine. *(To the fan, pushing her out the door)* Darling, darling, come back later. Really. God bless you, darling.

Danny pushes the fan out of the dressing room, closing the door behind her, as Lou sits down at his makeup table, which holds a cup and saucer, some food, and some liquor bottles.

LOU *(To himself, sitting at his makeup table)* All the trouble in the world. *(Shaking his head)* Shhh . . .

DANNY *(To Lou, leaning down to him and gesturing)* What are you discouraged about? Lou, you were magnificent.

LOU *(Nibbling at his food, shaking his head)* I can't pay my alimony.

DANNY *(Gesturing)* But, so, I'm telling you I'll waive my commissions till we get rolling, that's all.

LOU *(Pouring some tea into his cup, nodding)* How you gonna live? You gotta eat.

DANNY Don't worry about me so much, will ya? For God sakes. I, you know . . .

Danny, still gesturing, walks offscreen, into another area of the room. The camera stays focused on Lou, who looks offscreen at Danny, reacting. The camera moves closer and closer to his face as he listens, as he nods, as he begins to smile, his teacup frozen in his hand.

DANNY *(Continuing, offscreen)* . . . I got other acts. And, you know, I think about you in the long run. That's what I'm saying. Y-you're the kind of guy that will always make a beautiful dollar in this business. You know what I mean? You, you're what I call a perennial. You, you get better looking as you get older.

LOU *(Nodding and smiling)* That's true. I mean, when I'm out there singing, I can feel the women mentally undressing me. It's true.

Lou raises his teacup as the film cuts to the outside of a tuxedo clothing store. Danny is seen through the storefront window as he passes behind a tuxedoed mannequin, past racks of tuxedos, as he hurries through the store to Lou, who is examining some shoes in another of the storefront's windows. Danny holds a white tux trimmed in black on a hanger. He motions to Lou, holding out the tux. Lou gestures; he holds some patent leather shoes. A salesclerk is seen in the background, by a double rack of suits. A white jacket hangs in the window. A pedestrian is seen passing on the street, reflected in the storefront window. As Sandy's voice is heard over the scene, Lou puts down the shoes. He touches the tux on the hanger, gesturing. He starts to take off his jacket to try on the tux.

SANDY'S VOICE-OVER Okay, so Danny is everything to Lou. He picks his songs, his arrangements. He picks his shirts, his clothes. He eats with him. They're inseparable.

As Sandy finishes his voice-over narrative, the film cuts to the outside of the Carnegie Delicatessen and its surrounding buildings and sidewalks. It's daytime. The streets are crowded with cars and pedestrians. A man walks his dog on the sidewalk. Several taxis pass. Danny and Lou are seen from far away, walking out of the deli, underneath its awning. They are talking. They start to walk up the street, past the B.J.J. Market, next to the deli on the corner. The camera follows them as they walk, past the crowds of people walking, past the moving cars, past two pay phones on the corner. They talk, walking together and gesturing, as they wait for the light and cross the street. The New York Sheraton is seen as they cross over, as are the buildings on either side of the street. They maneuver past some turning cars. A truck passes in the background, down the cross street. People are everywhere; cars are lined up on the avenue, waiting for the light to change. A man jaywalks across the street. The sounds of traffic are heard in the background as Lou and Danny walk and talk, Danny slightly in the lead.

SANDY'S VOICE-OVER Danny's his manager, his friend, his father-confessor.

LOU *(Overlapping Sandy, indistinct at first)* Do me a favor. I wanna go across the street and get one white rose.

DANNY You want to get a white rose?

LOU *(Overlapping, gesturing)* One white rose.

DANNY Why do you want a white rose? *(Trails off indistinctly)*

LOU *(Overlapping Danny)* Danny, I met this chick. Yeah.

DANNY Ah, Lou. Lou, don't tell me about it because . . . you, you know you're gonna get caught in a hotel room, you're gonna wind up paying three alimonies, not two.

LOU *(Crossing the street)* No, no, no. This is a classy chick.

DANNY *(Crossing the street)* I-I can imagine.

LOU Classy, I mean, you know, sh-she's one of these decorators.

DANNY Yeah. With all due respect, Lou, you got a sweet wife.

LOU This is different. I mean, I'm in love.

DANNY Ah, great.

The movie cuts to the inside of a florist shop. A bouquet of white roses surrounded by other flowers fills the screen. The florist's hand is seen, plucking out a single rose.

FLORIST *(Only her hand onscreen)* The usual single white *(Onscreen, the camera moving up to reveal her face)* rose for Tina Vitale.

The camera moves with the florist and the rose, as she walks over to her counter—where Lou and Danny are standing. A cash register sits in the background; iron grillwork covers the store's glass door, through which people are seen passing up and down the sidewalk. Plants and flowers are everywhere.

LOU *(To florist, leaning down, softly hitting the counter for emphasis)* And, and just the words *(Pointing)* "I love you, my bambina."

DANNY *(Clears his throat)* Come here a minute. *(Gesturing to Lou)* Lou, Lou, come here. *(Walking away)* Lou, jus-, just step into my office for a minute.

Danny walks away from the florist, to the window. Lou follows him.

They have a "conference," surrounded by plants; people are seen through the window, walking on the sidewalk.

DANNY *(Gesturing)* Lou, Lou, what do you mean the *usual* single white rose? How long has this been going on?

LOU *(Gesturing)* For a while. I can keep a secret, you know.

DANNY *(Gesturing)* You're keeping a secret from me?

LOU *(Gesturing)* Hey, look, I knew you'd get miffed about it. I knew the whole thing, you'd get bugged because of my wife and everything. But, Danny, *(Sighing)* Danny, Tina, sh-she's beautiful. She's like, she's like a Madonna.

DANNY *(Gesturing)* I believe you, but d-, she knows you're married?

LOU Hey, I leveled with her.

DANNY *Gesturing)* Yeah, so what kind of woman is she if she knows you're married?

LOU *(Gesturing, shaking his head)* You know, I tried to introduce you to her for a long time. But I knew *(Sighing)* you wouldn't have it. Forget it.

DANNY *(Gesturing)* Ah, b-, look, have, I always tried to teach you, Lou, I've always tried to show you that sooner or later *(Pointing to Lou, then pointing towards heaven)* you're gonna have to square yourself with the big guy? Is that true? You're gonna square yourself with the bi—

LOU *(Overlapping, nodding with a sheepish grin)* Uh-huh.

DANNY *(Overlapping Lou)* You're gonna pay your dues someday. You know, you-you-you're a married man. *(Gesturing)* My Aunt Rose, take my Aunt Rose. Not, not a, a beautiful woman at all. She looked like something you'd buy in a live bait store. But why? She had wisdom. And she used to say,

you can't ride two horses with one behind. *(Gesturing)* So you see what I'm saying? You see, that's my point.
Lou gestures and shrugs, reacting, as the film cuts to a city street. Sandy's voice is heard as Danny walks down the busy street, his hands in his pockets. He looks down, then straight ahead, deep in thought. He walks quickly, passing some men standing by a building, passing several pedestrians; he carries a copy of Billboard *under his arm. He walks past some storefronts, an antique store displaying some Ming vases, a piano store. As Sandy continues to talk over the scene, Danny walks closer and closer to the camera; he resettles the* Billboard *under his arm. He walks faster, looking excited, as he passes the camera. His back now to the screen, he hurries over to a hot-dog vendor on the corner, past some pedestrians, past a building's brick wall. He motions for a hot dog, his* Billboard *in hand. A mother and child pass the vendor on his other side.*

SANDY'S VOICE-OVER Okay, now a little times passes. Danny's still struggling with the various bird acts and the blind xylophone player. Suddenly, the nostalgia craze is starting to build. And Danny finds he can book Lou a little easier.

CUT TO:
INTEROR. SHIP'S STAGE—NIGHT.

Lou, in tux and frilled dress shirt, stands in front of the stage curtain, in a circle of light. He holds a microphone and sways to the music coming from an offscreen band; the drummer is partially seen behind him.

LOU *(Into his microphone, singing)* "You may be king, you may possess / The world and all of its gold. / Oh, but gold won't bring you happiness / When you're growing old."
As Lou continues to sing, the movie cuts to an overhead view of a luxury ocean liner cruising through the water. The camera slowly moves around the ship until its bow faces the screen. As Sandy's voice is heard over Lou's singing, the camera continues to move around, to

the ship's other side, slowly moving closer to the liner, which glides through the waves.

LOU'S VOICE-OVER *(Singing)* "Oh, the world, it's still the same . . ."

SANDY'S VOICE-OVER *(Over Lou's now indistinctly heard singing)* He's working these nostalgia cruises, and the audience is eating it up, eating it up. Suddenly, an over-the-hill boy singer is starting to get some attention.

LOU'S VOICE-OVER *(Singing, now clearly heard again)* ". . . stars that shine high above."

The film abruptly cuts to The Joe Franklin Show, *in progress. Lou is in the "hot seat," sitting in the armchair next to Joe, who is partially seen behind his desk. A woman guest in an evening dress sits next to Lou on a sofa, looking towards the two men. On the stage set is a bookshelf in the background; a photo of Joe Franklin hangs on the background wall, another picture hangs alongside it. A microphone sits on Joe's desk; low coffee tables sit in front of Lou and in front of the sofa.*

JOE FRANKLIN And I am very, very honored to announce that one of America's, uh, great singing legends, a cherished musical legend, is making part of his, uh, comeback on the Joe Franklin TV show. And, uh, I-I hope my, uh, enthusiasm is generating, because I love this man. I really, I mean if you can love a man, I love Lou Canova. Lou Canova. Lou.

Joe extends his hand. As Lou reaches for it, shaking his head somewhat self-consciously, the film cuts to a close-up of his face.

LOU *(Shaking Joe's hand)* Thank you, Joe, thank you. *(Settling back in his chair)* You're very kind.

JOE FRANKLIN *(Offscreen now)* I mean that. Are you, are you sort of, uh . . .

LOU *(Gesturing)* Well, I've been on the show three, four times,

and it's, ah, it just helps. I mean, it helps everybody. Ah, you're, you're New York. What can I tell you?
The camera moves back, showing Lou in his chair looking at Joe Franklin, partially seen behind his desk. A plant is seen in a long planter underneath the hanging photo of Joe. The interview continues without missing a beat.

JOE FRANKLIN I, I always had the feeling, I don't know how I can express this, that you, y-y-y-you were never obsessed to be a superstar. *(Gesturing)* You were never driven to be a superstar. You didn't, you just let it drift and take its own course, right?

LOU *(Gesturing, sitting back in his chair)* Well, when I had a record out in the fifties, you know, it made, made some noise and everything like that. And you start to get to feel as though, hey, maybe you wanna be a bigger star, you wanna be this, you wanna be that. It-it-it didn't really bother me. B-but now I'm doing cruise ships, I'm doing bigger shows, everything like such. *(Nodding his head)* It, I-I feel, I feel great. I mean, it's a good time in life to do it.
The movie cuts to a busy Manhattan street corner. Among the crowds of passing pedestrians and the moving traffic in the streets is a gesturing Danny, deep in an indistinctly heard conversation with Milton Berle. As Sandy begins his voice-over narration anew, the camera slowly moves closer to the two men. Milton Berle smokes a cigar; a pedestrian light starts flashing DON'T WALK. *People continue to walk by obliviously; a bus waits for the light to change.*

SANDY'S VOICE-OVER *(Overlapping Danny and Milton's barely heard dialogue)* Okay, now, two days later, Danny runs into Milton Berle on Broadway. Milton is doing an NBC special, a nostalgia show. Plus, he needs a singing act to open for him at Caesar's Palace. Now Danny convinces him to come and see Lou on a club date at the Waldorf, and if Milton likes Lou, he gets the TV shot and Caesar's.

CUT TO:
INTERIOR. LOU'S DINING ROOM—NIGHT.

Lou walks through the dining room's elaborately designed door from the equally elaborate, partially seen kitchen. He wears a velour sweat-suit and a medallion around his neck. He holds a drink as he walks towards the table. The camera moves with him, revealing Danny, eating fettuccine at the table; he sits next to Lou's young daughter.

LOU *(Gesturing as he walks)* I mean, I love Milton. I mean, he's a beautiful man. *(Chuckling as he puts the drink in front of Danny)* What do you want me to say? *(Walks away offscreen)*

DANNY *(Talking with his mouth full, gesturing up at the offscreen Lou)* This is two years out of our guts.
The camera moves down the table, past Danny and the daughter, to reveal Teresa, Lou's blonde wife, at the table's head. As she talks, her fork in her hand, her young son, seated at her right, gets up with his plate and marches offscreen into the kitchen. Her daughter's hand is seen on her right picking up a water glass to drink. The table is cluttered with cutlery and soda bottles. Shimmery drapes hang behind Teresa's head.

TERESA *(Offscreen as the camera moves down the table to her)* Don't be so nervous, Lou. *(Onscreen now, to the offscreen Danny)* You know, you gotta take him out Sunday and let him relax a little bit. He's got, he's gonna be all wound up.
The film cuts to Lou, pacing in the busily decorated living room, talking to the group at large at the offscreen dining room table. He walks past an upright piano, past a decorative screen on the wall, past a few table lamps; his arms are crossed.

LOU *(Pointing with one crossed arm)* I'll open with "Volare" or "You Make Me Feel So Young."
As Lou trails off, thinking out loud, the film cuts back to the table, to Danny and Lou's daughter. Danny nods at the offscreen Lou; his mouth is full.

DANNY *(Overlapping Lou, turning and gesturing to Lou's daughter, putting his arm briefly on her shoulder)* How are you, darling?

LOU'S DAUGHTER *(Nodding, looking at Danny)* Good.

DANNY *(Gesturing)* Is everything okay? How are, how old are you, sweetheart?

LOU'S DAUGHTER Twelve.

DANNY Twelve? *(Winking at the offscreen Lou and chuckling)* Are you married?

LOU'S DAUGHTER *(Laughing)* No. *(Takes a sip from her glass, looking at Danny)*

LOU *(Offscreen)* What's the matter with this guy?

DANNY *(To the offscreen Teresa, gesturing and grinning)* Fantastic fettuccine. *(To the offscreen Lou as he wipes his lips, his mouth full)* Don't forget to do "My Funny Valentine" with the special lyrics about the moon landing.

The film cuts quickly to Lou, still pacing in the living room area.

LOU *(Gesturing)* Maybe we ought to put on a press agent for that week, though.

As Lou bends down to a table, reaching for a whiskey decanter near a vase full of flowers, the movie cuts back to the dining room table, as seen from Lou's point of view: Teresa is at its head; her daughter and Danny sit to her left. A chandelier hangs down from the ceiling. The group is busy eating and talking. Lou's daughter reaches over Danny to get some sugar. Lou's son returns from the kitchen carrying a full plate. He takes his seat on Teresa's right.

DANNY *(Gesturing, looking out at the offscreen Lou)* Um, I, I've been getting your name in the columns pretty good and it's not costing us any fee.

LOU *(Offscreen)* Not like having a steady press agent. I mean, you know, steady. Listen—

TERESA *(Interrupting, gesturing)* You know, you better take him to a movie or he's gonna be a wreck by show time.

The film is back on Lou, pacing in the living room. He holds a glass in one hand, the whiskey decanter in the other. He walks towards an armchair, then paces back again.

LOU Great idea for a TV show. Mr. Television looks at the stars of the fifties. *(Shaking his head)* Beautiful.

The movie cuts to the outside of a Broadway record store, The Colony, as seen from across the street. A man quickly walks past the camera. The sidewalks are mobbed with people; cars and taxis pass by on the street. It's daytime and the city is crowded. Danny and Lou are seen walking out of the store as Sandy starts his narration anew. People wait for the traffic light to change; the pedestrian light says DON'T WALK. *The camera moves with Danny and Lou as they walk across the street with other pedestrians, as Danny takes out some just purchased sheet music from a brown bag, as they walk in front of a line of cars and trucks, waiting for the light to change, as some cars move down the cross street in front of them. They gesture and talk as they reach the other side, where a Broadway theater is seen next to a Howard Johnson's on the corner. Lou takes some of the sheet music from Danny and looks at it. Lou is walking slightly in the lead.*

SANDY'S VOICE-OVER That week, Danny devotes to Lou exclusively. They go over the running order of his act fifteen times. What color shirts to wear, his weight, you know, he wants Lou to lose some pounds. I don't know who's more nervous, Lou or Danny. Meanwhile, his other clients by now are starting to complain about their own problems.

CUT TO:
INTERIOR. NIGHTCLUB—DAY.

An empty bird cage sitting on a chair fills the screen; its door is open. As Herbie Jayson, one of Danny's other clients, speaks, the bird cage is lifted up. The camera moves up with it—revealing an agitated Herbie holding and looking at the empty cage. The swing inside dangles in the empty air.

HERBIE *(Offscreen)* I couldn't get your service, I had a *(Onscreen, looking at the cage and reacting, looking at the offscreen Danny and gesturing)* crisis! A cat ate one of my birds! *(Putting down the cage)* I had to cancel the show, and now Ralph doesn't want to pay.

The camera moves back, and a frantic Danny walks onscreen; he stands next to Herbie, gesturing and talking to the offscreen Ralph. Behind him, some birds are seen in their cages on a background table.

DANNY *(Offscreen)* What are you talking *(Onscreen)* about, he doesn't want to pay? *(To the offscreen Ralph)* What do you mean, you don't want to pay? *(Gesturing)* A cat ate his bird! That comes under the "act of God" clause.

RALPH *(Offscreen)* He gets paid if he does his show only. That's all.

HERBIE *(To Danny, tapping him on the shoulder)* Look, it was the lead bird. Remember Pee Wee, the one who used to peck "September Song"? I couldn't reach you.

DANNY *(Reacting in shock)* Pee Wee's gone? *(Picking up the cage and walking towards the offscreen Ralph, to Ralph)* P-, Pee-, Ralph, what are you do—? Pee Wee is now be-, been eaten by a feline. Re-remember Pee Wee gave us many a laugh and tear.

The camera follows Danny as he walks over to Ralph, who is sitting at a table against a brick wall in the dim light. In the foreground are stacks of upturned chairs. Danny holds the cage, top and bottom; his back is to the camera.

RALPH Danny, I don't pay no birds that don't work.

DANNY *(Overlapping)* Yeah, b-b-b-b—

RALPH *(Gesturing)* Where were you when I needed a replacement?!

DANNY But Pee Wee—

HERBIE *(Offscreen, overlapping Danny)* Yeah, where were you, Danny?!

DANNY *(Looking out at the offscreen Herbie, gesturing)* All right, I admit it's my fault. I've been remiss lately. *(Walking back to Herbie, still holding the empty cage, the camera moving with him off Ralph)* You know, so, I've been very busy with another client. *(Gesturing as he plunks the cage down in front of Herbie)* After Sunday night, my hand to God, you have me, I'll be yours exclusively. I know how you feel. *(Looking out at the offscreen Ralph as Herbie looks down at the cage, his face sad, to Ralph)* Pee Wee, Pee Wee was the son he never had, so it's, you know. *(To the downcast Herbie, patting him on the shoulder)* Ah, I-I promise after Sunday night, really, I'm with you. *(Raising his hand in a pledge)* It's the emess.

The film cuts to a gym, where Lou's sneakered feet are seen walking on a treadmill.

LOU *(Only his feet seen)* One, two. One, two. One, two. One, two. One, two.

DANNY *(Offscreen, overlapping Lou's counting)* All right. Tomorrow night I want you to open with "You're Nobody Till Somebody Loves You" . . .

As Danny continues talking, the film cuts to a wider view of the scene. Lou walks on the treadmill, his hands grasping the rails, his head down. Danny stands nearby, looking at Lou. A poster of a woman on a beach hangs on the background wall.

DANNY *(Continuing, gesturing)* . . . and then go into, uh, "My

Bambina." And after that do great crooners from the past who are now deceased, okay? And then "Agita," if you want.

LOU *(Overlapping Danny, nodding as he turns off the treadmill)* Danny, would you do me a favor tomorrow night?

DANNY *(Gesturing, his hands outstretched)* Whatev— You name it, you got it.

LOU *(Stepping off the treadmill, walking over to Danny)* I want you to bring Tina.

DANNY Who's Tina?

LOU *(Gesturing)* Come on, I told you about Tina. I mean, I'm really crazy about her.

Danny and Lou begin to walk through the gym; the camera moves with them. A man is seen working out on a rowing machine, another is doing sit-ups on a Nautilus mat. A mirror hangs on the wall, reflecting the varied exercise apparatus in the gym. A television sits on a high wall shelf; posters line the wall. Danny and Lou talk as they amble, their backs to the camera. The sounds of the men at their machines are faintly heard in the background. Through an open doorway is the Nautilus weight room. Some equipment is partially seen; someone passes across the doorway. A poster is faintly seen on the weight room wall.

DANNY *(Gesturing, surprised)* Tha—? I thought I talked you out of that.

LOU It's no use. *(Gesturing)* I'm like a little kid. I'm still sending her a white rose every day.

DANNY *(Gesturing)* What're you—? You're nuts. Don't we have enough on our minds? What are you doing?

LOU *(Walking through the open doorway)* She's been lucky for me from the first day I met her. I mean, good things started happening.

Lou walks offscreen, towards a weight machine. Danny stands in the doorway, framed by the door. He talks to the offscreen Lou; he looks offscreen.

DANNY *(Gesturing)* Yeah, but Teresa's gonna be there. For God's sake, you're gonna get in a lot of trouble.
The film cuts to the weight room; a Nautilus apparatus fills the screen for a beat—before Lou walks in front of the machine. He looks at the offscreen Danny. A man in sweatpants is busy examining some weights in the background.

LOU *(Offscreen)* That's why *(Onscreen)* you gotta bring her. You be the beard.

DANNY *(Offscreen)* What are you *(Onscreen, walking over to Lou, also standing in front of the Nautilus)* talking about, I should be the beard? I don't want to be a beard.

LOU *(Overlapping Danny, gesturing)* Hey, come on. I'm telling ya, I'll do a great job if she's there. Without her, I'm gonna be lost.

DANNY Since when? Lou, this is business.
A man in exercise shorts, a towel draped over his neck, walks past, behind the Nautilus machine.

LOU Why are you making such a big deal of this thing?

DANNY *(Overlapping Lou, gesturing)* I'm not making a big deal.

LOU I mean, Terry goes home right after the show, then I'll take her off your hands. But when there's any people around, she's with you.

DANNY *(Gesturing)* No, it's not nice. You know, you're going to wind up in alimony jail. Uh—

LOU *(Interrupting)* I can't function without her. *(Sighing)* I-I-I'm lost.

DANNY *(Overlapping Lou, gesturing)* Since when? Since when? Who-who is this woman? Why does she have such a hold on you?

LOU *(Shaking his head)* I don't know what it is about this woman.

DANNY *(Overlapping Lou, reacting)* Jeez.

LOU *(Overlapping Danny)* I love her. Maybe it's a whole mother thing.

DANNY *(Gesturing)* A whole mother thing? Your mother's alive. Let me take her.
The film cuts to a close-up of Lou's face, looking at the offscreen Danny . . .

LOU She gives me confidence. I love her. What do you want me to say? *(Shaking his head)* I'm scared enough as it is.

. . . then cuts to a close-up of Danny, reacting. Behind him, two men in exercise garb are seen walking past, deep in conversation. Lou's shoulder and profile are partially seen.

DANNY *(After a beat)* Jesus, Lou, is this more serious than I thought?

LOU You don't listen to me when I talk.
The camera moves back to Lou's face . . .

LOU *(Continuing, shaking his head)* I haven't had a night's sleep trying to figure out what to do with my life, okay?

. . . then back to Danny's face . . .

DANNY *(Nodding and gesturing)* So, so . . . all of a sudden I gotta be the beard?

. . . then back to a close-up of Lou.

LOU I want her there. I gotta know she's there and I gotta know she loves me.

Lou's face fills the screen. Danny is quiet for a beat, then walks over to Lou, onscreen. They start to walk again, their backs to the camera, behind the Nautilus machine. A mirror hangs on the wall.

DANNY *(Offscreen, after a beat)* I can only say as your friend *(Onscreen)* and your manager, you know, you're a sick individual. But, if that's what you want, you know, all right, we'll do it.

They continue to walk behind the machinery, across the weight room, as a drum beat intro begins to play, as the film cuts to:

EXTERIOR. DANNY'S APARTMENT BUILDING—DAY.

Danny hurries out of his apartment building, which has a stone façade with an elaborately carved frame around its glass doors. A sign advertising pecan pies is hung in one of the large lobby windows. Cars are parked along the sidewalk. A few pedestrians pass as Danny bounds out into the street. The drum beat intro has become a bouncy version of "Agita."

Twirling his keys in his hand, looking briefly down the street, Danny walks over to his car, one of a line of cars parked on the other side of the street. A young woman in a miniskirt walks past as Danny leans over and reaches through the partially open window on the driver's side. He pulls up the lock button, opens the door, and gets in. Danny looks in the rearview mirror and wipes his face—as seen through the sun-obscured windshield—as the scene dissolves to a faraway view of Danny's car zooming across the George Washington Bridge. He passes a huge Mack truck and several other cars as the camera moves farther and farther away, revealing a breathtaking panoramic view of the bridge in the water, with the New York skyline in the distance. Danny's car is now a mere speck.

The music stops as the movie cuts to a closed door in a dark hallway.

The door is opened almost immediately by Tina, a bleached-blonde Italian woman in dark glasses, framed by the light from her apartment beyond the doorway. She looks out at the offscreen Danny.

DANNY *(Offscreen)* Tina? You're Tina? Danny Rose. Had no trouble getting here at all. None at all. Y-are you ready? 'Cause, you know, I'm, I'm double-parked downstairs.

TINA *(Without missing a beat, into a telephone that was previously in her offscreen hand)* Listen, Lou, you can drop dead. That's what you've been saying for months.

The film cuts to Tina's apartment at the same time she walks away from the door, still talking in the phone. She walks offscreen into the living room, her voice still heard. As she screams on the phone, Danny peeks his head into the apartment from the doorway; he cautiously enters, closing the door behind him. His eyes never leave the offscreen Tina—who passes briefly in a blur in front of the camera as she walks and talks offscreen on the phone. Danny stands in the living room, watching and listening; he wrings his hands. Pictures are scattered on the wall. A lamp sits on a corner table, along with several knick-knacks and a plant.

TINA *(Continuing, into the phone, walking into the living room)* Yeah, well, I don't buy it, and I'm damned *(Offscreen, screaming)* sick and tired of all your stories . . . Don't tell me that, Lou. Being married's one thing, but two-timing's something else! . . . Yes, yeah, well, that's just a bunch of garbage, because I don't buy it, and you'd better watch yourself! . . . I don't care how important it is! . . . It's too damned bad if you're upset. The way you treat me, you're lucky I don't stick an ice pick in your goddamn chest! . . . Like hell, I'll be there! You know what you can do! *(Slamming down the phone)* *(Offscreen)* Goddamn phoney!

DANNY *(Pointing to the offscreen Tina, smiling)* Lou tells me you're an interior decorator.

As Tina begins to speak, the film cuts to her, putting the phone down on the dining room table across the room. The table is covered with condiment holders and a vase; a lamp globe hangs down. Tina is livid. The camera follows her as she stomps past her living room window, its ledge dotted with bric-a-brac, as she throws things around and walks over to a desk, a picture hanging above it on the wall.

TINA *(Offscreen)* I don't want to *(Onscreen, storming across the room)* hear Lou's name. I don't want a runaround. I don't want any crap, goddamnit!

DANNY *(Walking over to Tina, who's leaning over the desk, rummaging through the drawer)* Uh, uh, darling, sweetheart, darling, may I, might I interject one notion at this juncture? *(Gesturing, watching Tina search through the drawer)* Sweetheart, how old are you?

TINA *(Flinging aside papers and notions from the drawer)* None of your goddamn business!

DANNY *(Looking back and forth from the papers Tina is flinging on the floor to Tina)* No, no, I'm serious, darling. Look, l-look, you're upset. Wha-, wha-, wha-, what sign are you? Gemini? Are you Gemini? 'Cause I . . .

TINA *(Overlapping Danny, finding the object of her search: a pack of cigarettes)* Shut up! Will you just shut up?! *(Walks away from Danny, offscreen)*

DANNY *(Following the offscreen Tina into the kitchen)* M-may I make one statement? Can I just say one thing, sweetheart?
The phone starts to ring. Danny and Tina are now in the small apartment kitchen. As Danny continues to talk, trying to rectify the situation, Tina is trying to light a cigarette, her back to Danny.

DANNY My father, may he rest in peace, the man would say maturity, *(Gesturing)* tha— a little tolerance, a willingness to give, that's all.
Tina mutters indistinctly as she opens a kitchen cabinet, distracted, looking for matches to light her cigarette. The phone continues to ring. Tina continues to ignore it—and the gesturing Danny.

DANNY *(Continuing, gesturing to Tina's back)* That's all. L-l-l-l-look, this is a big night for Lou. Don't ruin it for him.

TINA *(Yelling, walking out of the kitchen to her dining room table)* I don't want to talk to that creep.

DANNY *(Following Tina to the kitchen doorway, gesturing to her back)* Wha-what happened? I don't understand.

TINA *(Picking up the phone, into the receiver)* Go to hell!

Tina hangs up the phone and stomps back into the kitchen, past the agitated Danny in the doorway. He turns and follows her, once again talking to her back, as Tina begins rummaging through the kitchen cabinet anew.

DANNY *(Gesturing, to Tina's back)* Sweetheart, may I make one statement here? And I don't mean to be didactic, nor facetious in any manner.

TINA *(Overlapping, noisily rummaging through the cabinet)* What the hell are you talking about?

DANNY *(Gesturing)* But, the man's crazy about you. He's nuts for you. Why don't you—

TINA *(Interrupting, turning around to Danny)* Yeah, I got friends who told me he was out last night with a cheap blonde.

DANNY *(Reacting, gesturing and shaking his head)* A cheap blonde? Lou? A cheap blonde? *(Looks away for a beat as Tina turns back to her cabinet search)* It doesn't— Would he fall for a cheap blonde? Uh, you know, the man has class. He's got— He's got—

TINA *(Interrupting as she walks across the narrow kitchen past Danny and starts to search another cabinet on the opposite wall, her unlit cigarette still in hand)* Yeah? I thought so, too.

DANNY *(Turning around and walking over to Tina, once again talking to her back)* Yes, of course. *(Gesturing)* Sweetheart, I promise you, he's cheating with you. *(Shaking his head as Tina, searching noisily, throws a box down on the floor)* He's got integrity. He cheats with one person at a time, only. That's his style. He's—

TINA *(Stopping her search for a beat as she looks at Danny)* Yeah. My friends told me he was at the track last night with his arm around a cheap blonde. *(Turns her back as she begins to search another cabinet, throwing down box after box onto the floor)*

DANNY *(To Tina's back, more and more agitated)* Bu-but, you know, because they bother him 'cause he's cute, you know, *(Looking off as he makes a grabbing motion)* so they try and grab. So he pushes them away. *(Gesturing a push, his palm up)* So maybe when he pushes them away, *(Gesturing)* his arm goes around—

TINA *(Interrupting, turning to Danny, shaking her head)* Aw, knock it off. You think I buy that? *(Turns back to her cabinet search)*
The phone on the dining room table in the background rings again. Once more, it is ignored.

DANNY *(Gesturing, to Tina's back)* Wha-wha-, you know, uh *(Snapping his fingers)* his wife is a blonde. His wife, eh, she's not cheap. A lovely woman. Educated. *(Pushing back his hair)* She's a cocktail waitress, you know what I mean? *(Turning as Tina stomps through the doorway to answer the phone, gesturing to Tina's back)* And, and they don't all hustle. They don't. No matter what you say, they're not hustlers.

TINA *(Picking up the phone, into the receiver)* What the hell do you want?

DANNY *(Walking over to the dining room table, standing on the side opposite Tina and gesturing)* Look, please don't upset him.

TINA *(Into the phone, overlapping Danny)* Yeah? Yeah, well, I'm not coming, you got that?

DANNY *(Overlapping Tina, gesturing)* No, no, no, I want to speak to him.

TINA *(Loudly, into the phone)* Drop dead!
Tina throws the receiver on the table and walks back into the kitchen offscreen.

DANNY *(Reacting, scrambling and reaching over the table for the phone)* Ooh. Ooh. *(Into the phone)* Hello? *(Fixing his glasses and catching his breath)* Lou? Lou? Yes. Lou? I-it's me. I got here okay, Lou. *(Gesturing, trying to sound calm as he rubs the back of a dining room chair)* The directions were good. They were good. It *was* a Gulf station.
As Danny talks on the phone, his tone slow and methodical, glass is heard breaking offscreen.

DANNY *(Continuing to talk on the phone, ignoring the noise from the breaking glass)* Lou, she seems to be a little upset. *(Looking up for a beat as Tina scurries past the camera, on, then immediately offscreen, in the kitchen)* Mm-hmm.
Danny stays on the phone, his ear to the receiver, as the door is heard slamming offscreen. He looks out offscreen, reacting, as the film cuts outside to Tina's apartment building.

Tina, her coat in hand, is stridently walking away from the building down the sidewalk. It is a sunny day; a wind blows the trees and Tina's beehive hair. A few cars drive by.

DANNY *(Offscreen)* Tina! Tina! *(Onscreen, rushing out of the building towards Tina)* Hey, Tina! Ti—

TINA *(Overlapping, turning her head towards Danny as she starts to walk across the street)* Will you get lost?

DANNY *(Running up to Tina, looking out for cars as he crosses the street)* Where're you going?

TINA *(Not missing a beat as she continues to cross the wide two-way street)* I got other things on my mind besides two-timers.

DANNY *(Gesturing, just behind Tina, stepping out of the way of some passing cars)* Wait. No, the man adores you. The man is crazy about you. You're the one that he wants ringside.

TINA *(Looking straight ahead as she walks)* What the hell you come to get me so early for?

DANNY *(Gesturing)* I come every place early. I don't want to cut it close.

They cross the street, past some other buildings, past a gas station situated at a fork in the street, past a group of row houses. Cars continue to drive by as they now walk on a sidewalk dotted with telephone poles, street signs, and the row houses' street-level garages.

TINA *(Walking briskly)* You're hours early.

DANNY *(Gesturing, running next to Tina)* Yeah, I know, 'cause tonight's a big night. Milton is coming tonight. Remember when you were a little girl? Milton, Tuesday nights? He'd come out in a woman's dress. Remember? Look, he's an immortal.

Tina disappears into a stairway that leads up to one of the row houses, offscreen. Danny follows her offscreen. The camera stays focused on the row house with its street-level garage, it stairs leading up to a porch and front door, and the porch itself, situated on top of the garage. They continue to talk; their footsteps are heard on the stairs.

TINA If I'm so *(Offscreen)* important to him, why does he two-time me?

Tina appears onscreen as she walks onto the porch at the top of the stairs, followed by Danny.

DANNY *(Offscreen)* No. No. You got it wrong. You got it wrong, sweetheart. Women, women annoy him. *(Onscreen)* He sings and they mentally undress *him*, is . . . *(Trails off)*

Tina opens the front door and walks inside—leaving a spluttering Danny alone on the porch.

Gypsy violins begin to play in the background as the film cuts inside the row house, to the bedroom where Angelina the fortune-teller is sitting up in her bed; light filters in from a bamboo shade on a nearby window, which is bordered with an open print curtain. A portion of a wooden icon is seen above the bed's wooden headboard; a small drawing hangs nearby. Angelina's wide blanket is shared with her dog, a small Pekingese who walks around the blanket near her. Angelina wears glasses and a demure nightdress. She wears a cross around her neck. She looks out offscreen, her hands to her forehead in concentration.

ANGELINA *(Rubbing her forehead)* I see an adventure. *(Pointing, sitting farther up)* Yes, a trip. A man in a gray suit who owns a dog will come to see you.
As Angelina begins to pet her dog, the film cuts to her point of view: two clients, Tommy's brother and his mother, at the foot of her bed. Behind them are other clients, including Tina; they overflow out through the doorway; they all look offscreen at Angelina. A female client walks past the group; she smokes a cigarette. Tommy's brother wears a polyester suit; his ample mother wears a plain light dress.

TOMMY'S BROTHER *(Turning to his mother)* Ah. See, that's Tommy.

TOMMY'S MOTHER *(Nodding, to her son)* Tommy?

TOMMY'S BROTHER *(Nodding)* Yeah.
Tommy's mother asks him a question in Italian. Danny appears in the background, dimly seen walking over to Tina and standing next to her.

TOMMY'S BROTHER *(To the offscreen Angelina)* When is he coming?

ANGELINA *(Offscreen)* Soon. Very soon. When you least expect it, he'll be at your house.

TOMMY'S BROTHER *(Overlapping Angelina)* How soon?

DANNY *(To Tina, loudly, overlapping Tommy's mother, who is asking Angelina a question in Italian)* What are you *doing* here?

TOMMY'S BROTHER *(Overlapping indistinctly, distracted by Danny)* Shhh!

TINA *(To Danny)* Shhh!

DANNY No, I'm ser-, uh . . .

Tommy's mother, distracted, mutters in Italian; both she and Tommy's brother turn around to the source of the interruption: Danny. As he continues to talk to Tina, the film cuts to Angelina's young assistant, counting money by the bedroom window. She too is distracted; she too looks up and out towards the offscreen Danny, reacting.

DANNY *(Offscreen)* At least call Lou. Call Lou.

TINA *(Offscreen)* No.

Danny mutters indistinctly as the screen shifts to a different angle of the scene, to Danny and Tina standing by the bedroom's double door, their backs to the camera. Only one of its doors is open. Tina stands in front of the open doorway; Danny stands in front of the closed glass-paned portion. Clients stand in front of them, in the bedroom, and behind them, in the hallway. Angelina is seen through the glass panes of the closed door; she is in the background, lying in bed and foretelling the future. The line moves forward as the clients up ahead get their turn to speak to Angelina.

TINA *(To Danny)* Will you just get out of here?!

DANNY *(Gesturing, to Tina's back)* The man is nervous. Yeah, I know he doesn't seem so, but he, you know he's h— *(Indistinct)*

Danny is interrupted as a short elderly woman in a cardigan sweater (the "tropical fish lady") and her taller, round husband walk between him and Tina.

TROPICAL FISH LADY *(To Tina and Danny)* Can I get ahead?

DANNY *(Turning around to the tropical fish lady)* Oh, she wants to get ahead. *(Moving back to let her pass)* She wants . . . Let . . . let her . . .

TINA *(To the tropical fish lady)* Well, you know, I, I've been waiting.

TROPICAL FISH LADY *(Walking ahead of Tina and Danny, turning around to face them and the camera)* Umm, my nephew's ill.

DANNY Oh, he's ill? *(Pointing towards the nephew)* Look, he's ill.

TROPICAL FISH LADY *(Overlapping Danny)* Yeah, yeah, *(Nodding along with her husband, standing next to her)* and he has a, a lump on his neck.

DANNY A lump on his neck. Aw, that's terrible. *(Gesturing)* God bless you, sweetheart. God bless you. How old are you, darling?

TROPICAL FISH LADY Seventy-eight.

DANNY *(Gesturing)* You're seventy-eight years old? That's wonderful. Wh-wh-what are your hobbies?

TROPICAL FISH LADY Fish.

DANNY Fish? Tropical fish?

TROPICAL FISH LADY *(Nodding)* Tropical fish.

DANNY *(Laughing)* That's incredible. My Uncle Menachem, *(Clapping his hands)* may he rest in peace, the man, *(Gesturing)* a-a-a wonderful man, raised hamsters. You know what I mean? Hamsters. And I personally found 'em disgusting. But, uh, he, the man adored them, like you probably feel about your, you know, your-your, whatever, your guppies. You know, it's . . . *(To Tina, gesturing)* These are wonderful people.

As Danny continues to speak, the film cuts to a female client in the bedroom, reacting and looking at him offscreen. She takes a drag of a cigarette, then lights another with its tip. She sits on a chair; behind her is a bureau with some knickknacks on its top. A portion of a framed picture is seen on the wall.

DANNY *(Offscreen, continuing)* And they're of your persuasion. And Lou is of your persuasion.

TINA *(Offscreen, overlapping)* Lou's a liar.
The film cuts back to Danny and Tina, with the small tropical fish lady standing between them. Angelina's assistant walks over to them, interrupting.

DANNY *(To Tina)* No. He loves you like a mother.

ANGELINA'S ASSISTANT *(Overlapping Danny, to the tropical fish lady and her husband)* Excuse me. *(Motioning to Tina)* Okay, miss, you're next. *(To a client in front of them)* Excuse me, sir. *(To Tina)* Come on in.

TINA *(Following the assistant into the bedroom, to Danny)* All that crap about his bad marriage, and then he lies.

DANNY *(Tagging along, to the tropical fish lady as he passes her)* But-but-but the man loves her like a mother. He adores her. Worships the ground she walks on.
Another customer, a woman, walks onscreen to the end of the line at the bedroom door. Tina begins to talk to Angelina as the film cuts to the bedroom proper. Tina stands at the foot of the bed, looking down at the offscreen Angelina. She still wears her sunglasses. The chain-smoking woman sits in the background, in the corner of the room, watching. Danny walks onscreen, next to Tina.

TINA Angelina, I have a lover but I think he's unfaithful.

DANNY *(Gesturing, looking down at the offscreen Angelina)* Excuse me, Angelina, might I interject one concept at this point?

The film cuts to Angelina, sitting on her bed, stroking her dog.

ANGELINA *(Pointing with her free hand)* He *is* unfaithful. And yet he cares for you.

The camera moves back to Tina and Danny at the foot of the bed. The chain-smoker is still watching the scene. An assistant walks past the camera, carrying a tray of food over to the offscreen Angelina.

DANNY *(Relieved)* Aha! *(Moving around Tina to her other side and gesturing)* See? He cares for you. He cares for . . . *(To the offscreen Angelina, gesturing)* God bless you, da— God bless you.

ANGELINA *(Offscreen)* Don't go to him.

TINA *(Shaking her head)* I won't.

DANNY *(Dismayed)* Wait a minute. *(Looking from Tina to the offscreen Angelina)* Time out.

The camera is back on Angelina in her bed, the dog at her side under her arm . . .

ANGELINA *(Gesturing melodramatically)* See friends. Resolve all situations, even if it means traveling long distances.

. . . then back on Tina and Danny at the foot of the bed. Angelina's money-counting assistant walks over to them; Tina hands her some bills, then leaves. The assistant bows to the offscreen Tina, her hands clasped in prayer. Danny turns around and looks out at the offscreen Tina.

ANGELINA *(Offscreen)* But be careful.

DANNY *(To the offscreen Tina)* Hey, where you going? Wait. Tina!

CUT TO:
EXTERIOR. TEXACO GAS STATION—DAY.

Tina and a gas station attendant stand by the open door of her large four-door sedan. She hands him some money from her pocketbook; he hands her the car keys. Behind them is the garage. In the foreground is a gas pump island. Danny's voice is heard as the camera moves past Tina and her car, past the gas station's glass-enclosed office, past a row of houses on a tree-lined street, past a row of cars parked along the sidewalk, and across the busy street where cars are seen in the distance. The camera continues to move while Danny speaks, moving past a brick apartment house on the opposite side of the street, past a double-parked car and several other parked cars, to Danny, in a phone booth, talking into the receiver. Some trees, a few parked cars, and an apartment house are seen in the background behind the booth. A barking dog is faintly heard.

DANNY *(Offscreen)* Lou, we're into a definite type of situation here . . . *(Clears his throat)* No, L— . . . Definitely, Lou . . . Lou, definitely. We're . . . We're . . . we're into *(Onscreen, into the phone)* a complete type of situation. I'm telling you, it's a complete, definite type of situation.
The film cuts to Lou, talking on the phone in his house. Behind him is a partially seen shelf, a wall lamp, a stereo, and a corner of a framed picture. The wall is papered in a faint checkered design.

LOU *(Into the phone)* Why's she so mad at me? What, what'd I do? Won't she even speak to me? I need a drink.
The film moves back to Danny in the phone booth. Some cars and a truck pass by in the background street.

DANNY *(Into the telephone)* Lou. Lou. Lou, don't get the jitters, because if you get nervous, your whole performance goes right into the toilet. *(Gesturing)* You start drink— Lou. *(Listens, nodding his head)* Lou, I'll get her there, I promise. I, just let me work out the logistics—
Screeching tires are heard. Danny immediately reacts, throwing down the receiver and running into the street, his back to the camera. Tina's car squeals and swerves into view, speeding past Danny, who runs after it, out on the street.

DANNY *(Shouting)* Tina! Tina! Tina!

CUT TO:
INTERIOR. CARNEGIE DELI—NIGHT.

The comedians are at their table, listening to Sandy tell his Danny Rose story. His face almost fills the screen in profile; next to him on his left are Will, eating some food and then wiping his mouth with a napkin, and Jack, looking at Sandy with rapt attention. Corbett's face is barely seen on Sandy's right.

SANDY *(Gesturing)* And now, it's the big day, and things are starting to go wrong. Lou is boozing a little bit.

HOWARD *(Offscreen)* Yeah, I remember him with the Cutty Sark.

SANDY *(Looking out at the offscreen Howie)* Uh-huh. Okay. *(Pointing)* Now, she splits. She splits.

CORBETT The girlfriend.

SANDY *(Nodding, turning to Corbett and scratching his head)* Yeah.
As Sandy continues to talk, the film cuts to a country road. Danny's car is seen in the distance, moving closer and closer to the camera. No other cars are seen. Telephone poles dot the side of the road. A few billboards and some sparse trees are seen as Danny drives by. He passes the camera—which follows him now as he drives past a modern office complex, along the curving highway.

SANDY'S VOICE-OVER And Danny follows. She drives, and she drives way the hell out somewhere. Danny's right on her heels, but you know how Danny drives.
The comedians' laughter is heard as the film cuts to the outside of a country estate. Tina's car is seen moving down a circular driveway surrounded by pine trees. Parked cars line the drive. Tina parks her car between two others; two nearby men in dark suits walk over to her car. They are "party greeters," checking each car. "Funiculi, Funicula" plays in the background.

SANDY'S VOICE-OVER All right. So she winds up, an hour later, God knows where. She's taking Angelina the fortune-teller's advice. She's winding up some business with old friends.

PARTY GREETER #1 Hiya, Tina. We didn't think you were coming.

TINA *(Overlapping him, getting out of her car)* Hiya, guys.

PARTY GREETER #2 Oh, you look really nice.

TINA *(Overlapping him)* You look handsome. *(Kissing both men)* Yeah, well, I had a change in plans.

PARTY GREETER #1 *(To Tina)* Thank you. Take care.

TINA *(Walking away towards the house)* Okay, the party can begin.

The two men watch Tina walk away, their backs to the camera, as the film cuts back up the circular driveway. Through the branches of the surrounding trees, Danny's car is seen slowly driving towards the house. He moves closer and closer to the camera, past the lined-up cars, past the two party greeters standing by Tina's car. He drives over the driveway's inside curb, rights himself, then screeches offscreen. The party greeters follow him, looking offscreen at his car. They walk close to the camera. One of them smokes a cigar. Danny's car door slams offscreen; Danny rushes onscreen, about to pass the two men. They turn around to face him, their backs to the camera.

PARTY GREETER #1 *(Stopping Danny)* Can we help you, sir?

DANNY *(Facing the camera, gesturing, to the two men)* Oh, yeah, I'm I'm-I'm I'm with Tina. I'm a friend of Tina's. Yeah. Yeah. God bless you, fellas. Stay where you are. You're doing an aces job. *(Walking off towards the house, pointing back at the men)* I'll check back with you on my way out. *(Turning back for a moment, to the two men)* I'll leave something nice for you.

PARTY GREETER #2 All right.

The film cuts to the party in progress, on the expansive back lawn of the country estate. Crowds of people mingle around a pool. Umbrellaed tables are scattered throughout the horde. A statue and some shrubbery are seen in the foreground. The back of the house, a grand building with many windows, is seen; an awning is set up on the patio. The sounds of conversation are heard as the film cuts to a close-up view of Rocco, Tina's uncle; he wears a medallion around his neck and holds a drink in his hand. Trees and some milling guests are seen behind him.

ROCCO Who are you?

DANNY *(Walking onscreen next to Rocco, gesturing)* Oh, I'm here with Tina.

ROCCO *(Shaking Danny's hand)* Oh, I'm her Uncle Rocco.

DANNY *(Shaking Rocco's hand)* Oh. Lookit, Danny Rose. Danny—

ROCCO *(Interrupting, putting his arm around Danny)* Yeah. What do you do?

They start to walk, continuing their conversation, past some milling guests, past some lush trees in the background. Several guests walk by in front of them.

DANNY *(Looking over his shoulder)* Theatrical management.

ROCCO What are you looking for?

DANNY Well, I'm looking for Tina. I lost her.

ROCCO Relax. You gotta be around her every second?

DANNY No. *(Looking over his shoulder again, almost bumping into a cluster of guests)* Well, what do you do, Rocco?

ROCCO Ah, cement.

DANNY Cement?

ROCCO I own a fleet of cement mixers.

DANNY *(Ingenuously)* Oh, no kidding? Well-well is-isn't that a very big organized c— *(Stops, catching himself)* Cement. That's fantastic, cement.

As Danny continues to talk, they stop walking. They now stand near Annie, Tina's aunt. She's in conversation with a gesturing man, her back to the camera. She has a blonde beehived hairstyle; she wears a ruffled dress.

DANNY *(Continuing, putting his hand on Rocco's shoulder as a waiter passes by in front of him)* Because, cement, you always, you always need cement. That's what's great about cement. *(Gesturing, looking off for a moment)* It's not like tape recorders, which is a luxury item. Cement you use . . .

ROCCO *(Overlapping, tapping his wife on her shoulder)* Annie, Annie. Annie. This is Tina's new boyfriend.

ANNIE *(Turning to face Danny)* Oh, hello. *(Shaking Danny's hand)* How long you been going out with my niece?

DANNY *(Gesturing)* Oh, no, we don't go out, I'm— We're just friends. We're just friends, that's all.

ANNIE *(Overlapping Danny, nodding and smiling)* Yeah, well, I know Tina.

ROCCO *(Overlapping Annie and waving offscreen)* Vinnie! Vinnie!

As the group continues to talk, the camera leaves them, moving past several milling partygoers to Vincent, who is walking towards them with his wife. Vincent wears a leisure suit; his hand is on his wife's arm. They join the others; Vincent moves away from his wife. Guests mill about around them, talking and drinking. The accordion music continues. The group now includes Rocco, Annie, Vincent, and his wife. They stand in a subtle line, facing Danny and the camera.

DANNY *(Overlapping, offscreen to Annie)* No, it's true, darling.

ROCCO *(Offscreen)* Danny's in show business.

DANNY *(Offscreen)* I'm just a friend.

ROCCO *(Offscreen)* He's a manager.

VINCENT *(To Danny, joining the group)* Oh, yeah? You know Jackie Whalen?

DANNY *(Onscreen now, his face in profile)* Oh yeah, he's a comedian. He's very funny.

VINCENT'S WIFE *(Shaking her head)* I don't think he's funny. I think he's dirty.

DANNY *(Gesturing)* Oh, yeah, well, today everything is. You know, with the pornography, am I right? All the four-letter words. You know, it's all filthy. I mean—

VINCENT *(Nodding, walking towards Danny and interrupting him)* You know, I saw this guy in Atlantic City . . .

Vincent moves Danny away from the group. They talk as they walk a few steps; a guest passes in front of them. Other guests mill about in the background; one male guest, wearing a dark shirt, is chewing gum.

DANNY *(Nodding, looking down)* Yeah?

VINCENT *(Taking Danny's arm)* He had a cigar box.

DANNY Uh-huh.

VINCENT *(Gesturing)* And he cuts a hole in it, and then he goes backstage, he opens up his fly, and he sticks his thing in it.

DANNY *(Looking at his watch, then over his shoulder)* Uh-huh.

VINCENT Then he goes outside, down to ringside, to some old lady's table, opens up the box. I mean, that's humor?

DANNY *(Gesturing, to Vincent as more guests pass in front of them)* Well, you know, they call me old-fashioned, but, but, if it's old-fashioned to like Mr. Danny Kaye, *(Counting on his fingers, then pointing to Vincent's shoulder for emphasis)* Mr. Bob Hope, Mr. Milton Berle, you know what I mean, then, all right, then I'm old-fashioned. *(Putting his hand on Vincent's shoulder)* You know what I'm saying?

VINCENT *(Overlapping Danny, nodding)* Yeah. Yeah. Yeah.

The accordion music stops as the film cuts inside the house, to the darkened living room. In the foreground is a dimly seen table, its top cluttered, and other barely seen chairs and lamps. The den is visible through a doorway in the background; sun pours through its large windows and French doors. A print sofa sits in front of the French doors. The room is busy with lamps, a glass coffee table, and objets d'art. Johnny's voice is heard as he walks onscreen in the den; he is framed by the backlit doorway.

JOHNNY *(Offscreen)* Tina, can't we *(Onscreen, looking off to the right)* discuss it?

TINA *(Offscreen)* No, we discussed it a hundred times.

JOHNNY *(Gesturing, his arms outstretched)* Then why did you come here today? *(Turns and walks offscreen again)*

TINA *(Offscreen)* I don't know. I don't know. I guess I shouldn't have.

JOHNNY *(Walking back onscreen, once again framed by the doorway as he looks offscreen to the right, his arms outstretched)* Tina, I love you.

The film cuts to the den proper, to Tina, standing in front of a window, her sunglasses still in place. Framed pictures and a mirror line the wall; a large plant stands nearby.

TINA *(Gesturing, her arms outstretched)* No. No, it's over.

Tina walks over to the long bar, its top holding some filled large decanters, a plant, and a piece of sculpture. Windows line the wall behind it. Tina starts to make herself a drink; Johnny stands on the other side of the bar. An ice bucket and several bottles of liquor sit nearby on the corner of the bar; pictures hang on the wall above it. The faint sound of accordion music is heard from the party outside.

JOHNNY *(Offscreen)* If I thought that, I'd kill myself.

TINA *(Gesturing, looking under the bar for a glass)* Johnny, don't talk like that.

JOHNNY *(Leaning over the bar)* And you know I'd do it, too.

TINA *(Holding a glass, taking off the top of the ice bucket)* You know, y-y-y-you're too emotional. That's your problem.

JOHNNY *(Taking a piece of paper out of his pocket, then turning around, his back to Tina)* I wrote you a poem.

TINA *(Overlapping Johnny)* Oh, Jesus. I shouldn't have come. I'm too mixed up myself.

JOHNNY *(Standing near the light from the window)* It's about our month in Sicily.

TINA *(Pouring some liquor into her glass)* Can't you forget it?

JOHNNY *(Reading, pouring out his words as Tina, drink in hand, turns away, looking out a window behind the bar and waving)* "We strolled on cliffs of stone / Like Greeks of ancient times. / Your hair blew this way and that / Mixed with bits of sand. / Our eyes . . ."

As Johnny continues his poem and Tina continues to look out the window, the film cuts to another doorway—where Danny appears, walking from the foyer into the den. He stands in the doorway, looking at the offscreen couple. Behind him are a staircase, a chandelier, and a small glass table with a flower arrangement on its top.

JOHNNY *(Offscreen, continuing)* " . . . met and then looked out / Toward the sea, the blue Aegean."

DANNY *(Gesturing, looking out at the camera)* Uh, Tina?
The film cuts back to the bar, where Johnny is still emoting; a shocked Tina turns from the window and looks at the offscreen Danny.

JOHNNY "We laughed and ran and whispered . . . "

TINA *(Overlapping Johnny, to Danny)* What are *you* doing here?!
The camera is back on Danny in the doorway . . .

JOHNNY *(Offscreen)* " . . . vows of love undying."

DANNY *(Gesturing, to the offscreen Tina)* I know what you're thinking. Pushy, right? Pushy . . .

. . . then back on the bar. Tina stares open-mouthed.

JOHNNY *(Gesturing, to the offscreen Danny)* I'm reading a poem.

DANNY *(Offscreen)* I'm sorry. I'm sorry. I came to get you because it's so important . . . *(Trails off indistinctly)*

JOHNNY *(Overlapping Danny's mumbling)* "The sun caressed your skin . . . "

TINA *(Overlapping Johnny and Danny, to the offscreen Danny)* I want to know what you're doing here.

JOHNNY *(Overlapping Tina, reading his poem)* " . . . so fair, so gleaming white . . . "

DANNY *(Offscreen)* I want you to come with me.

JOHNNY *(Stopping his poem, to Danny)* Who are you?
The camera moves back to Danny in the doorway.

DANNY *(Gesturing, not missing a beat)* Danny Rose, theatrical management. Cou-, mi-might I just get five minutes with the young lady alone, please?

TINA *(Offscreen)* Now listen, Danny, you know I'm dying to come to the Waldorf *(Onscreen, walking over to Danny in the doorway, her drink in hand)* but it's just that I fe-, I've been hurt, that's all.

The film cuts back to Johnny at the bar as he talks. He begins to walk towards the offscreen doorway, towards the camera. He still holds the piece of paper containing his poem.

JOHNNY *(Offscreen)* So, this is who's *(Onscreen)* been sending the single white rose every day— Danny Rose.

The film cuts back to the doorway, where Danny and Tina are looking at the offscreen Johnny.

TINA *(Indignant)* How do *you* know about the white roses?

JOHNNY *(Offscreen)* I know. Believe me, I know more about you than you think I know.

DANNY *(Gesturing, to Tina)* Might I interject something here?

TINA *(Ignoring Danny, looking at the offscreen Johnny)* You know because you spy on me!

DANNY *(To Tina, trying to get her attention)* Might I interject something . . .

JOHNNY *(Offscreen, overlapping Danny)* It's *(Onscreen as the film cuts back to him at the bar)* not spying when you care about someone. How they live. What's happening to them.

TINA *(Offscreen)* Yeah. *(Onscreen as the camera moves back to the doorway)* You, you check my mailbox in my apartment when I'm not there. Admit it!

DANNY *(Trying to interrupt, gesturing)* Tina, please.

The camera is back on Johnny. He's walking closer to the doorway, closer to the camera. His voice is starting to rise.

JOHNNY So you prefer him with his white roses to me and all we were to each other?

DANNY *(Offscreen)* Please, it's getting late.

The film cuts back to an irate Tina and a disconcerted Danny in the doorway . . .

TINA *(Pointing to herself)* I-I prefer someone that has respect for me and doesn't spy!

. . . then back to Johnny, his eyes soulful . . .

JOHNNY *(Looking out at the offscreen Tina)* Are you going with him?

. . . then back to the doorway, where Tina, muttering under her breath, turns and storms out into the foyer, making a left offscreen.

DANNY *(Turning and following Tina)* Tina, w— Can I get one . . . Tina, talk . . .

CUT TO:
EXTERIOR. BACKYARD OF COUNTRY ESTATE—DAY.

The film is back at the party. An accordion player is strolling through the crowd of mingling, chattering guests; he nods and smiles. As he passes, the camera following, two fat teenage boys, identical twins, are revealed—eating from plates heaped with food. The accordion player strolls offscreen as the film moves to a chubby Mike, Mrs. Rosotti, wearing sunglasses and a hairspray-frozen do, and Angelo, with a wad of money in his hands. Behind them, a bartender is busy at an outside bar. Angelo proceeds to tear some bills in half.

MRS. ROSOTTI What are you doing with money?

MIKE *(Pulling out a wad of bills from his pocket)* What are you, a big shot, tearing up your money?

ANGELO *(Overlapping, mumbling)* It's only paper.

MRS. ROSOTTI *(Gesturing to a woman nearby)* You see what they're doing? Look at what they're doing.

MIKE *(Overlapping Mrs. Rosotti)* I been tearing up money since my first Holy Communion. See this? *(Ripping some of his bills in half)* Ten dollars. I don't care. *(Flinging it into the air)* Here. What does it mean?

MRS. ROSOTTI *(Overlapping Mike)* Wait a minute. You're absolutely crazy.

ANGELO *(Overlapping Mrs. Rosotti, ripping more of his money in half)* Twenty. Twenty. Here. *(Flinging the pieces in the air)* I don't care.

MIKE *(Overlapping Angelo, counting off some more bills from his wad)* Twenty? Twenty? A twenty, forty, sixty dollars. *(Ripping the bills in half and flinging them into the air)* What does it mean, you know?

MRS. ROSOTTI *(Overlapping the men)* Wait. They're crazy.

ANGELO *(Holding up a wad of bills)* Fifty.

MIKE *(Looking at Angelo)* It means nothing.

MRS. ROSOTTI *(Looking at Angelo)* Why don't you stop him?

ANGELO *(Ripping more bills and flinging them in the air, looking at Mike)* I'll tell you what it means. It means fascination, that's all it is.

The film cuts to the grounds of the estate, with its sprawling green lawn and lush trees. No one is in sight. The accordion music at the party can be heard in the distance as Tina first speaks over the idyllic scene. She and Danny then appear on the screen, strolling through the grounds, deep in conversation, far from the camera. Tina is holding a drink in her hand.

TINA *(Offscreen)* Yeah, I want to see Lou, but he treats me lousy.

DANNY *(Onscreen, gesturing)* W-w-, you know, Lou's crazy about you, I'm telling you. You know, tonight's a big shot for him, really. Y-you know, with all due respect for Lou, he's not a kid. He's trying to make a comeback.

TINA *(Onscreen)* When, when he sings "That's Amore," that for me is, is the end.

The camera shifts to a different angle, to a closer view of Danny and Tina from behind. They are still strolling and talking. In front of them is the expansive back lawn of the house, with its party still going strong. Guests are mingling; one of them runs across the lawn. Danny and Tina pass some tree trunks as they walk, momentarily obscuring the view of the party. Statues are seen in the background; the sounds of the accordion and the party conversations can be faintly heard over the scene.

DANNY *(Nodding and gesturing)* Is it unbelievable, what he does with that song?

TINA *(Overlapping Danny)* Oh.

DANNY *(Shaking his head)* Isn't that fantastic? *(Pushing back his hair)* Let, let me, *(Gesturing)* can, may, may I hit you with one, can, I'm gonna hit you with one word now. I'm gonna say just one word that—

TINA *(Interrupting)* Yeah?

DANNY *(Gesturing)* Sorrento. Okay?

TINA Yeah.

DANNY Sorrento. *(Nodding and gesturing to himself)* Am I lying?

TINA *(Overlapping Danny)* Oh, yeah. I like it when he takes the microphone off the stand and he walks around a little bit and sort of, sort of throws the microphone from hand to hand.

DANNY *(Pointing to himself)* That's my gesture. That's my touch. I gave him that.

TINA No.

DANNY *(Shaking his head)* No. Yes.

TINA I saw him years ago. He took the microphone off the stand.

DANNY Right. *(Pantomining a microphone moving from hand to hand)* But he didn't throw it from hand to hand.

TINA Ohhh.

DANNY *(Gesturing)* I gave him that touch. I used to do that when I was a nightclub act.

TINA So, you taught him to throw the microphone from hand to hand . . .

DANNY Yeah, I taught him everything he knows.

TINA *(Overlapping Danny)* Very good . . .

DANNY *(Hitting one hand into the palm of the other, interrupting)* I gave him his gestures. I, I handle his budget. I pick his clothes, his songs, you know—

TINA *(Crossing in front of Danny, looking back at him, smiling, still holding her drink)* And you manage his love life?

DANNY Well, you know—

TINA Hmm?

DANNY Look, you know, my father, *(Gesturing)* may he rest in peace, said, "In business, friendly but not familiar." But what am I gonna do? This is personal management I'm in. You know, it's the key word, it's personal.

TINA *(Looking at Danny)* Ooh.

DANNY So, you know I gotta get involved. Like, like my . . . Herbie Jayson, my bird act. The cat ate the, the lead bird.

(Gesturing, momentarily obscured by a tree trunk) So, I gotta leap right into the breach, you know. Or my Puerto Rican ventriloquist. The kid's a wonder, he's got everything you need to make it big, but he's a dope addict. So I, you know, I gotta get in there and help.

TINA *(Shaking her head)* What can I say?

DANNY *(Pausing, fumbling with his fingers)* You know, its funny, now that I see you, I'm the wrong guy to be the beard, because who'd believe *(Gesturing)* that, that such a beautiful girl would, would date me?

TINA *(Smiling)* Come on.

DANNY *(Shaking his head and gesturing)* No. I'm telling the truth. That's, it's the emess. *(Putting his palm up)* My hand to God.

TINA *(Overlapping Danny)* No, I'm not beautiful.

DANNY *(Overlapping Tina)* No, sweetheart. I'm telling you. *(Gesturing)* And I see a lot of singers and actresses. You are.

TINA *(Looking at Danny for a moment)* Well, you're not so terrible.

DANNY *(Gesturing)* Yeah. I-I know one thing, honey, I'm never going to be Cary Grant. I don't care what anybody says. *(Stopping with Tina as she sips her drink, and pointing to her glass)* Can I, can I get a sip of that?

TINA *(Nodding and handing Danny her glass)* Sure. All right, can I tell you a secret? *(Putting her hands in her pockets as Danny sips)* And I'm, I'm not *(Gesturing)* just trying to make you feel good or anything.

DANNY *(Handing the glass back, reacting to the strong drink)* Yeah?

TINA *(Taking her glass, shaking her head)* Handsome men never did anything for me.

DANNY *(Touching his glasses, still reacting to the drink)* No?

TINA You know what turns me on?

DANNY No.

TINA *(Nodding)* Intellectual.

DANNY *(Shaking his head, fumbling with his fingers)* Tch. Really?

TINA And I'm not, I'm not just saying this to make you feel good, or anything *(Nodding, her drink in hand)* . . . Y-y-you're a smooth talker.

DANNY Yeah? *(Looks away briefly, raising his eyebrows, and touches his glasses)*

TINA Angelina once even predicted I would marry a Jew.

DANNY *(Gesturing)* Did she, did she happen to say which Jew?

TINA No. A, a Jew or someone musical. Yeah, isn't that interesting? *(Nodding)* Kind of?

DANNY *(Overlapping Tina, gesturing)* Yeah. Well, listen, sweetheart . . . now that we're talking about something musical, could you go call Lou? Really. 'Cause the guy needs you. Go, give him a call, *(Glancing at his watch)* 'cause it's late and we'll get right out of here. Please. *(Touching Tina's shoulder)* Please, darling.

Tina nods slightly and walks off. Danny watches her move across the lawn as the film cuts inside, to the dining room, seen through the doorway of the foyer. The table is groaning with food. Two men stand near its long side, facing the camera, picking and nibbling at the platters. Two young boys chase each other around the table as Tina's voice is heard over the scene, as she walks onscreen in the foyer, pacing and talking on the phone. Another man walks into the dining room, taking food from the buffet, his back to the camera. A woman is seen in the kitchen in the background, through another doorway. The dining room walls are cluttered with a hanging mirror, a clown painting, and busy wallpaper. As Tina talks, standing near the foyer door frame, the woman in the kitchen walks through the dining room, around the table, and into the foyer, squeezing past Tina as she walks offscreen towards the camera. She carries two large loaves of bread. A waiter carrying a tray of hors d'oeuvres follows directly behind her.

TINA *(Offscreen)* No, Lou, no, it's not that I hate you. It's just *(Onscreen, into the phone, pacing)* that, you know, you get me angry sometimes . . . *(Standing by the foyer door frame)* Yeah. I-I-I'm a, I'm gonna, I'll, I was always going to be there. *(Nodding, a cigarette in her hand)* I'll be there. Will you listen to me? I'm coming, okay? It's just that s-sometimes you get me crazy . . . *(Laughing)* Yeah . . . Yeah.

CUT TO:
EXTERIOR. ESTATE BACKYARD—DAY.

Camille, a chubby dark-haired woman wearing white sunglasses, fills the screen. She is sipping her drink at the back lawn party. Around her are other guests, chattering and mingling. The accordion music plays in the background. Camille suddenly stops drinking and looks up.

CAMILLE *(Pointing upward)* Oh, my God! Look!
The surrounding party guests look up as the film cuts to another group at the back lawn party, including an older, matronly woman with teased dark hair, and two men in suits. They too stop their conversation and look up, reacting as the screen next shows their point of view: Johnny stumbling to the edge of a curved, railed balcony, his hand to his throat.

JOHNNY It's him. *(Pointing down, offscreen)* She betrayed me with him.
The film cuts to Johnny's point of view: Danny on the back lawn, surrounded by other guests. He looks up, stunned. The accordion music stops abruptly.

JOHNNY *(Offscreen)* Danny Rose!

MALE PARTY GUEST *(Offscreen)* Johnny! Hey!

The screen next shows the scene in a panoramic view, past the pool, past the backs of lined-up guests, all looking up. Johnny is seen on the top-floor balcony. He collapses as Joan, in a flowing gown, runs onto the balcony next to him. There is a slight murmur of hushed conversation. The striped umbrellas blow in the breeze. The party joie de vivre has been interrupted.

JOAN *(Dramatically)* Oh, my God. He, he drank iodine! *(Kneels down next to Johnny)*

CROWD *(Almost as one)* Oh!

JOHNNY He seduced her away from me!

Joan turns and rushes back inside as the film cuts to the party guests on the ground, as seen from the balcony. Danny is standing alone among the others; the tops of the umbrellas flutter in the breeze, their connected tables holding plates of food. Everyone is looking up—until Carmine, standing near Danny, turns and confronts him.

CARMINE Were you seeing Tina while she was going with Johnny?

The surrounding guests turn as well. All eyes are on Danny.

DANNY *(Panicky, gesturing)* No. W-why would-would I do something like that? Would I? No.

Johnny begins to speak as the camera moves back to him, sprawled out on his balcony. He grasps one of the railings as he speaks. An umbrella top is partially seen below the balcony. A nearby upstairs window is seen.

JOHNNY *(Offscreen)* Then *(Onscreen)* who sent the white roses? One every day.

Johnny's white-haired mother rushes through the balcony doors and leans over her son.

JOHNNY'S MOTHER *(Pulling at his arm)* Johnny! Johnny, what happened? *(Murmurs in Italian)* What happened? Tell Mommy. *(Helping Johnny up to a sitting position as he groans loudly, to the crowd)* My son is sensitive. He's a poet. *(Kisses him, continuing in Italian)*

The camera is back on Danny standing alone, surrounded by the others, as seen from the high balcony . . .

DANNY *(Looking up at the offscreen Johnny, pointing)* He's fantastic. H-how old are you, Johnny?

. . . then back to the balcony, where Johnny is draped over the railing, his mother propping him up . . .

JOHNNY'S MOTHER *(Shouting)* He's forty!

. . . then back to Danny on the ground.

DANNY *(Gesturing, looking up, his drink in hand)* That's really unbelievable. Wha— Are you an Aries? Just, just tell me. Are you an Aries?

CARMINE *(Addressing the surrounding crowd at large)* Johnny's been made a fool out of.

DANNY *(Turning around, to Carmine, then up towards the balcony, reacting)* No. I, I, I . . .

Danny is interrupted by Johnny's mother, who begins to shout dramatically as the film cuts back to the balcony.

JOHNNY'S MOTHER *(Offscreen)* No! *(Onscreen, looking down towards Danny)* No! They forced him to wear the horns. *(Makes the Italian sign for horns as she continues in Italian)*

The camera moves to three party guests—a fat woman wearing sunglasses, a young woman smoking a cigarette, and a little boy in glasses—sitting at an umbrellaed table, listening and watching the offscreen spectacle. An elderly man in a three-piece suit stands near them, munching on a sandwich as he listens. Others stand in the background, their heads hidden by the umbrella. All are immobile, watching.

JOHNNY *(Offscreen)* We were engaged until he put a spell on her.
Then it's back to the highly agitated Danny, standing alone amidst the others, as seen from the high balcony.

DANNY *(Looking up at the offscreen Johnny, gesturing and reacting)* I, would, I, I, you know. This man's a beautiful man. *(Turning around to the others as they begin to close in on him)* He is a fantastic individual. I, you know—
The guests, closer now, stare at Danny as the film cuts to Johnny and his mother on the balcony.

JOHNNY'S MOTHER *(Interrupting Danny)* *Vendetta! Vendetta . . . (Continues in Italian, gesturing)*
As Johnny's mother continues to rant in Italian, the film cuts to a close view of two party guests—a young man, his mouth open, and a fat woman, her hair in a tight topknot—looking up at the offscreen balcony. They are immobile, mezmerized as Johnny's mother's voice trails off. The trees in the back lawn frame their faces. After a beat, the film cuts to:

EXTERIOR. TREE-LINED STREET—DAY.

Danny's car is seen driving down the empty, tree-lined street, rattling noisily as it zooms towards the camera. As the car passes the camera, moving offscreen, the film cuts inside. Tina sits in the passenger seat, closer to the camera, chewing gum and looking out the window. Danny drives, looking straight ahead. As they drive along, trees, streetlamps, and an occasional house are seen through the window. The car's rattling is heard over their conversation.

DANNY Boy, that guy Johnny must have really been crazy about you.

TINA *(Shrugging)* Ah, you know, I, uh, I just, I-I-I like to flirt, you know? Sometimes people take it too seriously. Johnny's all right. He, he was really nice to me when my marriage fell apart.

DANNY *(Looking briefly at Tina, touching his glasses)* Yes, and what did your husband do?

TINA Oh, a little bookmaking, some loansharking, extortion, like that.

DANNY *(Looking briefly at Tina)* So, he's a professional man. What did you do, y-you divorced him or you got a separation or what?

TINA Ah, some guys shot him in the eyes.

DANNY *(Shocked)* Really? He's blind?

TINA Dead.

DANNY He's dead, of course, *(Pointing to his eye)* 'cause the bullets go right through. Oh, my God, you poor thing. Were you sh-, were you sh-, you must have been in shock.

TINA *(Rubbing her nose)* Ah, he had it comin'.

DANNY Oh, I see, it was one of those. A close marriage.

TINA It was exciting for a while, though. You n-, you never knew what was gonna happen next.

DANNY *(Nodding, looking briefly at Tina)* Well, that kind of excitement I can live without.

TINA He was really, uh, he was tough, good-lookin'.

DANNY Yeah? And what'd he tell you he did when-when you married him?

TINA A juice man for the mob.

DANNY *(Incredulous)* He made juice for the mob?

TINA Tch. Juice man. No, he collected for the loan sharks.
Soulful Italian music starts to play as the film cuts back outside, to the car driving down the country street, farther and farther away from the camera. Sandy begins his narration anew.

SANDY'S VOICE-OVER Okay, so now Danny is driving along with Tina. They're talking. What they don't know is two minutes after they left the party . . .
As Sandy speaks, the scene shifts to the country estate's porch. As a man in a suit walks away offscreen, a tall, elaborate flower arrangement is revealed, filling the foreground. In the background, past the flowers, are Johnny and his mother. They are in the midst of a heavy conversation at an umbrellaed table with wrought-iron chairs. Standing near them are Johnny's tough-looking brothers Joe and Vito. As Sandy continues his tale, the camera moves closer and closer towards the group. A waiter, carrying a tray, passes in front of them. Johnny sips some coffee. He kisses his mother's hand.

SANDY'S VOICE-OVER *(Continuing)* . . . there was this little scene with Johnny Rispoli's brothers, Joe and Vito, who are both hit men for the mob. Their mother is outraged and humiliated over what's been going on with Danny Rose, who they call Danny White Roses.
The film cuts to a closer view of Joe, standing by the table, near a sunlit French door, a portion of fringed umbrella near his head . . .

JOE *(Looking at his offscreen mother)* Don't worry, Mama. You just leave him to us.

. . . then moves to Johnny's mother, sitting at the umbrellaed table. She is framed by a potted palm and a window in the background.

JOHNNY'S MOTHER Your brother is soft. He's sensitive.
As she speaks, the film cuts to Johnny, sitting at the table, his face down, embarrassed . . .

VITO *(Offscreen)* Yeah, her husband had no respect for us either.

. . . then moves to Vito, standing by the table, partially obscured by the fringed umbrella. Behind him is a large plant.

VITO *(Continuing, gesturing)* Carmine Vitale, he was no damn good. He cheated us. And she's no better.
The camera moves back to Johnny at the table, then cuts back and forth between the family members as they talk. The scene has an almost claustrophobic feel as they talk tightly and intensely, a close-knit family ready for revenge. The Italian music plays on.

JOHNNY *(Gesturing)* She said one thing to my face and she betrayed me.

JOHNNY'S MOTHER *(Looking offscreen towards Johnny, gesturing)* It's the lover. He's got her under his spell, Johnny.

JOE *(Looking at the offscreen Johnny, nodding)* We'll fix him.

VITO *(Offscreen)* We'll chop his legs off.

JOE *(Turning to look at the offscreen Vito)* No. We'll kill him. I don't trust him.

JOHNNY *(Pointing at the offscreen Joe)* But not Tina. *(Making a fist, with intensity)* Please, not Tina.

JOHNNY'S MOTHER *(Looking at the offscreen Johnny, pointing)* Get rid of the lover. Get rid of the lover and you get her back. *(To the offscreen Joe)* He's got the evil eye. *Chi malocchio.* You understand? *(With intense feeling) Figlio mio e malocchio.*

JOE *(Looking at his mother, calmly)* Mama, he's a dead man.

CUT TO:
INTERIOR. ROADSIDE RESTAURANT—DAY.

Elaborately decorated layer cakes in a revolving display case fill the screen. As they turn, one after another, the sounds of the restaurant are faintly heard. Tina and Danny speak offscreen as the film cuts to them, dimly seen in the background of the diner. A uniformed waitress is taking their order. The display case, lit up and revolving, is seen in the foreground, near some empty tables. Some sunlight filters through heavily curtained drapes on the far wall behind Danny and Tina's table. A customer, his check in hand, walks by. Other customers sit at tables scattered around the room.

TINA *(Offscreen)* I'll just have an iced coffee.

DANNY *(Offscreen)* Yeah, and I'm gonna have a glass *(Onscreen to the waitress)* of milk, please. A large glass of milk, sweetheart. *(To Tina as the waitress walks away)* I got an ulcer. I can't help it. I shouldn'ta drank at the party, you know?

TINA *(Overlapping Danny)* Hmm.

DANNY That's my mistake.

TINA Yeah, my ex-husband had an ulcer.

The film cuts to Danny sitting opposite Tina at their table. Behind him is a coatrack.

DANNY *(Looking offscreen at Tina)* Tch. They say it's stress, you know. *(Pointing to his head)* It's an entire mental syndrome.

Tina speaks as the film cuts to her at the table, sitting opposite Danny. The diner's drapes frame her head. She smokes a cigarette. The film cuts back and forth between her and Danny as each one speaks in turn, always looking offscreen at the other.

TINA *(Smoking her cigarette)* Yep. Carmine was always afraid they were gonna shoot him in the back.

DANNY *(Inhales, shrugging, then gestures)* He was wrong, so . . .

TINA *(Offscreen)* So *(Onscreen as the camera moves back to her)* who else you handle besides Lou?

DANNY *(Pointing to himself)* Me? I, you know, I got, I got, *(Clasping his hands)* oh, I got various *(Clears his throat)* interesting artists. *(Putting his hands down on the table)* I got a, I got a very wonderful blind xylophone player, you know, that's uh . . . I got a . . . currently working with a parrot *(Adjusting his glasses)* that sings "I Gotta Be Me." And, uh *(Offscreen as the film cuts to Tina, listening, deadpan)* . . . I got some very nice balloon folders, you know? It's interesting.

TINA No big shots, right?

DANNY *(Onscreen, the camera back on his face, gesturing)* I don't know. I've, I've I've discovered certain artists that have gone on to, uh, to better things, you know.

TINA *(Shaking her head)* Yeah, but they all leave you, right? How come?

The film moves back to Danny as the waitress's hands and torso appear on the screen, placing a glass of milk in front of Danny, iced coffee near the offscreen Tina. She puts the check down and walks off as he speaks.

DANNY I got a theory about that, you know. *(To the waitress)* Thank you. *(To the offscreen Tina)* I-I-I think what happens is they get a swell head. You know what I mean? *(Gesturing)* And they, they, they, people like to forget their beginnings, you know, and they, they just split.

TINA Yeah, believe me, you must be doing something wrong if everybody leaves you.

DANNY *(Gesturing)* How? What am I doin' wrong? I, you know, I-I find 'em, I discover 'em, I breathe life into 'em, and then they, they go, you know. And then, then, no guilt. *(Shaking his head)* I mean, they don't feel guilty or anything. *(Snapping his fingers)* They just . . . split.

TINA *(Offscreen)* Guilty? What the hell is that? *(Onscreen as the film cuts to her)* You know, *(Shrugging)* they, they see something better and they grab it. Who's got time for guilt?

DANNY *(Gesturing)* What are you talking about? Guilt is important. It's important to feel guilty. Otherwise, you, you know, you're capable of terrible things. *(Scratching his nose, pushing his glasses farther up on his nose)* You know. It's very important to be guilty. I-I'm guilty all the time and I-I never did anything. *(Offscreen as the camera cuts to Tina's side of the table)* You know? My, my, my rabbi, Rabbi Perlstein, used to say we're all guilty in the eyes of God.

TINA *(Taking a puff from her cigarette, nodding)* You believe in God?

DANNY *(Adjusting his glasses, gesturing)* No, no. But uh, I'm guilty over it.

TINA *(Shaking her head)* Yeah, I never feel guilty. I-I-I-I just think, you gotta do what you gotta do, you know? Life is short. You don't get any medals for being a Boy Scout.

DANNY *(Offscreen, the camera staying on Tina)* Well, do me a favor, darling. Don't give this information to, uh, to, uh, Lou, because, uh, you know, I got enough problems.
Tina sits up straighter as she looks out the offscreen window.

TINA *(Overlapping Danny, suddenly serious)* Danny, don't move.
The film cuts to her point of view: Joe and Vito are getting out of their car in the diner parking lot. They are gesturing to each other, in heated discussion. Joe stands on the driver's side; Vito stands on the passenger side of the car; they talk to each other over the hood. They slam their car doors and start walking towards the diner entrance, Joe in the lead. Cars go by in the drab semirural background beyond the parking lot. The railing of the diner entrance as well as other empty parked cars can also be seen through the window.

DANNY *(Offscreen)* What's the matter?

TINA *(Offscreen)* Let's just get up slowly and get out of here. Out the back door.
The film cuts back inside the diner, to Danny, sitting at his side of the table.

DANNY *(Turning and looking out the offscreen window)* What? I don't understand. What-what-what's out there?
The camera cuts to Tina, still reacting, still looking out the offscreen window . . .

TINA Johnny's brothers.

. . . then back outside, in the parking lot, as seen through the diner window. Joe walks back to the car, as if remembering something. Vito is still near the passenger side. Once again, they gesture and talk over the car's hood as Danny and Tina speak over the scene.

DANNY *(Offscreen)* Johnny . . . y-you mean the, the guy with the iodine?

TINA *(Offscreen)* They're crazy. That whole family.

The film is back at the table, on Danny, looking out the offscreen window, then back at the offscreen Tina.

DANNY *(Gesturing, smiling slightly, incredulous)* W- . . . why, because they think I'm your lover?

Tina is now on the screen, on her side of the table. She fumbles with her offscreen purse.

TINA *(Looking at the offscreen Danny, then down at her purse)* They'll tear the tongue right out of your head.

The film moves back to Danny, reacting to Tina's words.

DANNY *(Gesturing)* What are you talking about? I'm just a beard. They'll tear the tongue out of the beard?

Tina starts to get up as the camera moves back, revealing both her and Danny at their table, and the diner's counter and row of windows beyond. A man works behind the counter; a shelf of magazines stands nearby. "Agita" begins to play in the background.

TINA Come on, *(Getting up from her chair, her back to the camera)* throw some money down. Let's get out of here.

Tina walks around the table, her coat in hand; she stands next to Danny, trying to hurry him along.

DANNY Hmm, what do you mean? *(Pulling some money out of his pocket, and looking at his check)* I-I only got ten bucks.

TINA *(Gesturing)* Leave it.

DANNY *(Looking up from Tina to the table, gesturing)* But . . . leave it? The tip's a dollar and . . .

TINA *(Overlapping Danny, gesturing)* Well, just leave it. *(Grabbing Danny's arm)* Come on, will ya?

DANNY *(Overlapping Tina, still looking back and forth from her to the table)* . . . the che-, the check is a dollar and a half.

TINA *(Overlapping Danny, pulling him away)* Hurry up.

DANNY *(Putting the check and the money down on the table as Tina pulls him away)* We're gonna leave an eight-and-a-half-dollar tip.

TINA *(Overlapping Danny, walking away with him in tow)* Come on. There ought to be a delivery entrance out here somewhere.

They start to walk up the aisle, their backs to the camera. They turn right at the corner and walk towards the kitchen door, past several other patrons at their table, past a waitress near a coffee and glassware area who is carrying a cup of coffee. A hostess shows a couple to a booth in the foreground.

DANNY *(Following Tina down the aisle towards the kitchen)* That's eight and a half bucks. For that kind of dough I could get the waitress to sleep with me.

Danny and Tina run through the kitchen's swinging doors, talking, as the film cuts to the kitchen proper. In front of them are open shelves, holding utensils and equipment, above an aluminum sink. A refrigerator and cabinets are scattered in the room, forming aisles.

TINA *(Looking around the kitchen for the exit)* Oh, God, where's the, the . . . There it is!

Tina and Danny dash around the shelves and appliances, maneuvering as they talk. Tina is in the lead. They pass two chefs in aprons, working at the stove area; they run offscreen as the chefs watch them go, reacting. The music plays on.

DANNY *(Turning to the two chefs, gesturing)* Oh, don't, don't get up, fellas. Just keep turnin' out the junk food.

The film cuts to the back of the diner, with its small platform and metal stairs leading from the delivery entrance to the asphalt. A truck is parked near the door, forming an alleyway. A sign printed on the building is partially seen in the foreground; a railing sits in front of it. The music continues as Danny and Tina dash out the entrance's screen door and down the stairs. Tina is still in the lead. As they talk, they run down the alleyway towards the camera, turning a corner to the side of the diner. They pass the building's sign, which now can be partially read: RESTAURANT—JERSEY CITY—14B.

TINA *(Running down the alley, breathlessly)* Come on, this way!

DANNY *(Following Tina, gesturing)* You know, I don't like this. Darling, darling, may I interject one statement? I don't like what's going on. I would—

Tina pauses near the diner, looking out at a scrubby field and the parking lot beyond—where Vito is walking towards the diner's front entrance.

TINA *(Interrupting Danny, reacting to Vito's distant figure)* Oh, Christ! *(Looking around)* Better go down there.

Tina runs into the scrubby field near the diner. A highway trestle is seen in the background.

DANNY *(Hesitating, then scurrying after Tina into the field)* Hey, I'm not going down there. What the hell did you get me into?

TINA *(Overlapping Danny, turning around and yelling at him)* Danny, do what I'm telling you. You'll wind up on a meat hook!

DANNY *(Looking around nervously)* A meat hook? A meat hook? Okay, I'll go first. *(Grunting as he starts to climb down a small ravine, holding Tina's waist)* Uh. Tch. I'm angry, Tina.

TINA *(Yelling, looking behind her)* Come on!

Danny gingerly climbs backwards down the ravine, holding Tina's waist as she starts to move down backwards, guiding her.

DANNY *(Overlapping Tina)* I'm tellin' ya, I'm angry.

TINA *(Yelling, looking behind her)* Hurry up and get down there!

DANNY *(Overlapping Tina)* I'm, I'm really fuming. Just . . . oh! Just feel free to dig your heel into my groin like that.

TINA *(Yelling)* Come on!

DANNY *(Grunting)* Just . . . oh! Oh!

They start to disappear over the edge of the shallow ravine as the film cuts to the sidewalk in front of the diner—where Vito and Joe, both carrying baseball bats, branch out in different directions, in search of their prey. Cars are parked in the lot next to the sidewalk; a portion of the diner's front façade, dotted with shrubs, is seen on the sidewalk's other side. Trucks and cars pass on a road in the background. Farther back is a boxcar sitting on some railroad tracks. As "Agita" continues to play, Vito, his back to the camera, walks offscreen to check Danny's car in the lot. Joe walks down the sidewalk, closer and closer to the camera, turning a corner to walk up the few stairs to the diner's entrance. A pay phone is on the brick wall next to the diner's glass doors.

As Joe walks up the diner's steps, the film cuts back to a panoramic view of the nearby field. Danny and Tina are seen scrambling through the narrow ravine, with the shrub-brush cliffs surrounding them, and the highway trestle, telephone poles, and highway signs in the background. As they run, the camera moves past the field, past the scattered telephone poles, past a faint Manhattan skyline; past the crowded parking lot, past a sign, to the corner of the diner's front façade, an outside lamp jutting out on the brick façade. In the glare of a large window, a beer sign hanging down near its top, is Joe, standing inside, looking out, the baseball bat in hand. As "Agita" reaches a feverish end, he reacts, noticing the offscreen Tina and Danny in the distance. He leans over for a closer view through the window and the film cuts to:

INTERIOR. CARNEGIE DELI—NIGHT.

The comedians are still gathered around their table, listening to Sandy tell his tale. His face is in profile; he smokes a cigarette. Howard, sitting across from him, has his back to the camera. He smokes a cigar. Next to Sandy is Will, eating some food, then Jack. The others are sitting offscreen.

SANDY *(Gesturing)* Okay, so Danny and Tina, they run.

JACKIE *(Offscreen)* That's the worst thing they can do, though.

The other comics start talking all at once, indistinctly commenting on the tale thus far.

SANDY *(Over the others' voices)* Wha-what's he gonna do?

HOWARD *(Over the others' voices)* What else is he gonna do? He has no choice.

SANDY *(Overlapping the others, pointing a finger up for emphasis)* Now, now, he is not only scared. *(Gesturing)* The man is pissed off.

JACK *(Gesturing)* Well, sure, because he didn't do anything.

SANDY *(Nodding, looking over at Jack briefly)* He didn't do anything. You got it. *(Gesturing)* Right.

JACK *(Overlapping Sandy)* No.

HOWARD *(Overlapping Jack)* That's right.

THE OTHER COMICS *(Overlapping Howard and Jack, on- and offscreen)* That's right.

SANDY *(Overlapping the others, putting his hands up in the air as he looks around the table)* Wait, wait, wait. Cut to a half hour later.

JACKIE *(Offscreen)* All right.

SANDY *(Overlapping Jackie)* It's a half hour later.

JACKIE *(Offscreen)* Yeah.

SANDY *(Looking around the table, one finger up for emphasis)* Now, they're lost. They're lost.

A short laugh is heard from one of the offscreen comics. He mumbles indistinctly.

SANDY *(Overlapping the offscreen comic, gesturing, drawing out the words)* And he's furious. He's getting on her nerves. She's getting on his nerves.

HOWARD What else?

One of the offscreen comics groans, then laughs, as the film cuts back to Sandy's story, to a jungle of tall reeds and grass. The leaves flutter as Tina, clutching her bag and coat, and Danny come into view, stumbling their way through the foliage. The cawing of birds and the buzzing of insects are faintly heard.

DANNY *(Offscreen)* Aw. Jesus, where the hell are we? We-we're in the middle . . . Look out!

TINA *(Overlapping Danny, stumbling into view)* All right. Take it easy.

DANNY *(Onscreen, following Tina through the grass)* And don't tell me to take it easy, sweetheart, because I've had enough already today. You know, I'm a personal manager. I-I got a big night ahead of me. I . . . meanwhile, I'm wandering around here in North Vietnam.

TINA *(Turning her head towards Danny)* We got away, didn't we?

DANNY *(Stopping momentarily, the camera moving with Tina as she stumbles through the grass)* What do you mean, we got away? I got nothing to get away from. *(Offscreen, the camera following Tina)* I didn't do anything. Jeez, I-I-I'm ru-, *(Running onscreen behind Tina, looking behind him)* running all of a sudden with, with fortune-tellers and meat hooks and . . . *(Groans and pants, looking below him)*

TINA *(Interrupting, pushing away the grass as she walks)* I'll take care of it when we hit a phone.

DANNY *(Overlapping Tina, groaning)* Where—? A phone? We're in a swamp, darling. Where we . . . where is there gonna be a phone here? She shacks up with Lou and they want to break my legs. *(Grunts)*

TINA *(Overlapping Danny, turning her head and getting annoyed)* Listen, I don't have to go tonight.

DANNY Well, that's fine with me. *(Offscreen as the camera focuses on Tina stumbling through the underbrush)* Then don't, because I'm too scared already anyhow.

CUT TO:
INTERIOR. LOU'S HOUSE—DAY.

The screen shows a framed painting of the Manhattan skyline hanging on an otherwise empty living room wall as Teresa, Lou's wife, walks onscreen. The camera moves with her as she makes her way into the adjoining dining room, talking to an at first offscreen Lou, revealing a sofa under the painting, an end table holding a lamp, and a wall hanging. She walks over to Lou, who is holding a drink and peering at himself in a hanging mirror above a buffet. A large breakfront fills the opposite wall; in the middle of the room sit the dining room table, a floral arrangement in its center, and chairs. In the background, by the curtained window, Lou's son is knocking on the glass pane, making faces at Lou's daughter, who is outside making faces back at him. A chandelier hangs from the ceiling. A background open door near the buffet leads into the kitchen.

TERESA *(Walking over to Lou in the dining room; holding a pencil)* Lou, honey, I wish you wouldn't drink like that. You've got an important show tonight. *(Soothingly)* Come on.

LOU *(Overlapping Teresa, peering in the mirror)* I got an . . . *(Grunting)* cold sore. *(Pointing to his chin)* I got a cold sore tonight. I mean, look at this thing over here.

TERESA *(Putting her hands on Lou's shoulders, playing with his hair, trying to comfort him)* Oh, it's nothing.

LOU *(Overlapping Teresa, walking towards the open door to the kitchen)* Yeah, it's gotta be tonight. *(Turning back to Teresa, gesturing)* It's gotta be tonight, believe you me.

TERESA *(Overlapping Lou, trying to comfort him)* Come on.

LOU *(Gesturing)* And those Vegas people, TV people, they notice everything. *(Offscreen as he enters the kitchen)* They're pros. They got it down to a science.

As Lou continues to rant offscreen in the kitchen, Teresa turns away and opens a drawer in the buffet. She takes out some silverware and a napkin and, still holding the pencils, walks towards the camera. In the background, Lou's daughter leaves the window and, running inside, noisily enters the dining room through the kitchen door. She races towards her brother, still at the window, as Teresa turns the corner. She talks to Lou as she passes another kitchen doorway—revealing Lou at the counter, pouring himself another drink. His kids enter the room, giggling and laughing, as Teresa walks offscreen up some partially seen stairs. The spotless kitchen, as seen through this doorway, is covered with busy patterned wallpaper.

TERESA *(Turning the corner out of the dining room)* Turn on the ball game.

LOU *(Gesturing, making himself a drink on the kitchen counter)* "Turn on the ball game." I can't even decide whether to go with "Boulevard of Broken Dreams" or "Three Coins in the Fountain" as an encore. I don't know what to do— *(Looking with amusement at his children playing tag in the kitchen)* The kids are driving me nuts over here. *(To his kids, playfully motioning them out of his way)* Wooo! Give me a break

over here. *(To the offscreen Teresa)* I wonder where Danny is? I'm waiting for his call. *(Walking towards the doorway, gesturing)* I got a million questions for him. *(Walking out of the kitchen, near the stairs)* I don't know that, what's happening. *(Shakes his head)*
The kids dash out of the kitchen behind Lou, making a beeline for the offscreen dining room. Lou walks farther into the hallway, the camera moving closer and closer to his face.

TERESA *(Offscreen)* Where is Danny?

LOU *(Gesturing, sipping his drink)* Went to pick up his date in Jersey. I guess they probably got tied up in t-traffic. What do I know?

TERESA *(Offscreen)* Who is his date?

LOU *(Looking off, gesturing)* How do I know? Some broad.

CUT TO:
EXTERIOR. A ROAD NEAR THE TALL GRASS—DAY.

Tina stands by the side of a desolate dirt road, the tall grass behind her blowing in the breeze. She brushes off her pants, then adjusts her shoe. The buzz of insects is faintly heard.

TINA Jesus, we're in the middle of nowhere.
Danny walks onscreen, talking and gesturing. They begin to walk along the edge of the road, the camera following.

DANNY *(Gesturing)* Oh, God, I never saw so many reeds in my life. I feel like Moses.

TINA Poor Lou's probably worried sick.

DANNY Darling, Lou is probably drinking out of the promotional-size whiskey bottle by now.
The tall grass abruptly ends—revealing a wide expanse of open muddy flatlands.

TINA *(Putting her hand on Danny's shoulder, pausing)* Hey, wait a minute. I know where we are. *(Looking around the flatlands)* These are the flatlands. My husband's friends used to dump bodies here.

DANNY *(Gesturing)* Great. I'm sure you can show me all the points of cultural interest.

RAY *(Offscreen)* Hey, who are you?

Tina and Danny both turn around, almost in unison, at the sound of Ray's voice, and the film cuts to their point of view: Ray Webb, an actor, in a superhero costume complete with cape and mask. He stands on the flat landscape, his cape blowing in the breeze, looking at the offscreen Danny and Tina. Birds caw in the background; one sits in a small pool. A lighthouse juts out into the sky in the far distance.

DANNY *(Offscreen)* Who are *you*?

RAY Who are *you*?

The camera moves back to a stunned Tina and Danny. They haven't moved an inch.

TINA *(Looking towards the offscreen Ray)* We're lost.

The film quickly cuts back to Ray, who begins walking towards Tina and Danny . . .

RAY *(Pointing behind him as he walks towards the camera)* We're shooting a commercial down by the river.

TINA *(Offscreen, with relief)* Huh! Oh.

DANNY *(Offscreen, overlapping Tina)* Fantastic!

. . . then back to the couple, walking towards Ray.

TINA *(Her back to the camera)* Oh!

DANNY *(Overlapping, his arm on Tina's back)* Unbelievable! What a break! I'm-I'm-I'm Danny Rose, theatrical management. *(Puts out his hand)*

The trio meets on the screen, the flatlands all around them. Tina makes noises of relief. Danny and Ray shake hands.

RAY *(Putting his arm on Danny's back)* Hey, how you doin'?

DANNY *(Overlapping Ray)* God bless you. *(Gesturing to Tina)* This is Tina . . . Tina . . .

TINA *(Overlapping Danny, nodding)* Vitale.

DANNY *(Nodding)* Vi— Right, right, Vitale.

RAY *(Overlapping Danny, taking off his mask)* Hi, I'm uh . . . Ray Webb, the actor.
Danny laughs.

RAY *(To Tina)* How you doin', baby? *(Laughs)*
Tina nods to Ray; Danny laughs with joy and relief.

DANNY *(Gesturing)* Listen, listen, we got to get a car. Is it possible? Very important.

RAY We, we, there are no cars out here till tonight.

TINA Oh.

DANNY *(Overlapping Tina, gesturing)* No, but we need one now 'cause it's an emergency. I, you know, I'm a theatrical manager, so *(Clears his throat)* I gotta see Berle at the Waldorf later. Milton Berle.

RAY *(Overlapping Danny)* Yeah?

DANNY Yeah.

RAY *(Pausing, then looking out and pointing, his mask clutched in his hand)* Uh . . . you kn-, you know what your best bet is? There's a, a guy there with a boat. Gi-give him a couple of bucks, he'll take you across.

DANNY *(Overlapping Ray, gesturing and shaking his head no)* Yeah. No. No, no, I, I . . .

TINA *(Overlapping Danny, ignoring his protestations)* Oh, great. *(Gesturing)* Great.

DANNY *(Overlapping Tina, gesturing)* I . . . I . . . I don't travel by water. It's against my religion. *(Looking from one to the other, Tina reacting with annoyance)* I'm a landlocked Hebrew. I don't go by water.

RAY *(Overlapping Danny, to Tina)* Hey, Tina, y-you ever seen me on television? I play the shaving cream man from outer space? Want to feel my cheeks, huh? *(Laughs and motions to his cheek)*

Danny laughs, pointing at Ray. Tina chuckles, then turns to Danny.

TINA Come on, Danny. We-we've gotta take this boat. Lou's waitin'. Come on.

DANNY *(Overlapping Tina)* Funny. This guy's, this . . . No, I-I . . . I don't want . . .

RAY *(Overlapping Danny)* It'll take five minutes to cross the Hudson . . . *(Mumbling)* It's nothing.

DANNY *(Overlapping Ray, growing more and more agitated)* You want me, you want me to go on the Hudson River? That's crazy.

RAY *(Gesturing, looking at Danny and Tina)* H-h-how-how did you two people get out here without a car?

TINA *(Overlapping Ray)* Oh.

DANNY *(To Tina, losing patience)* Yeah, what about that, you know? With tha— I've been through thick and thin with that car. Now I gotta leave it at the diner overnight?

TINA *(Overlapping Danny, talking at the same time, at first indistinctly, to Danny)* You'll be able to pick it up tomorrow. It'll be fine.

DANNY *(Gesturing)* Well, if anything happens to that car, I'll be furious, Tina. *(Pointing his finger at Tina)* I will be furious.

CUT TO:
EXTERIOR. ROADSIDE RESTAURANT—DAY.

Joe and Vito are noisily smashing Danny's car windows with their baseball bats, accompanied by the sounds of "Agita" in the background. The front brick façade of the diner is seen, along with its name printed on its quaint rooftopped entrance: LIBERTY VIEW. *A customer stands on the sidewalk, watching Joe and Vito destroy Danny's car. Others stand at the entrance doorway and at the diner's windows, looking on.*

CUT TO:
EXTERIOR. FLATLANDS—DAY.

Tina and Danny are running along the edge of the Hudson River, the flatlands behind him. As Sandy begins his tale anew, they make their way to a makeshift wharf where an old dinghy is moored; FREDDY K *is written on the boat's side. A crewman comes out of the cabin and greets them. He moves to the stern, where a smokestack has the letter K imprinted on it. They get aboard, rocking the boat, and make their way to the bow. The* Freddy K *is an old-fashioned fishing boat and its railing is simply secured rope. Tina sits down on a box near the front of the cabin and crosses her legs. Danny stands, holding out his hands, trying to steady himself. He rubs his face nervously. The boat continues its rocking. Danny grabs on to the boat near Tina; he grabs on to her leg; he grabs on to thin air. An oil tank, some low factories, and a lighthouse are seen in the near distance across the river. A portion of the Manhattan skyline is seen far away. "Agita" continues in the background as Sandy speaks over the scene.*

SANDY'S VOICE-OVER Okay. Now, they're gonna go back to Manhattan by boat. A *boat*, mind you. Can you picture Danny Rose on a boat? I mean, this guy is strictly pavement. He needs the smell of carbon monoxide and litter to feel good. Danny is not meant for water. So naturally, the minute he steps on the boat, he's gone. A lunch he ate in nineteen-fifty-six is beginning to come up on him. He's green, he's dizzy. Tina's fine. She's made of steel. I'll tell you what's going through *her* mind. She's thinking of a conversation that she and Lou had a week before.

CUT TO:
EXTERIOR. MINIATURE GOLF COURSE—DAY.

A miniature castle, complete with windows, ramp, and surrounding green, fills the screen. A golf ball jumps into the ramp's door.

LOU *(Offscreen, laughing)* Hey-hey! All right!
A golf club swings up as the backs of Lou and Tina's legs appear onscreen, their golf clubs trailing down. As they talk, they walk past

the castle prop, Tina on its right, Lou on its left side. They stand at the green behind the castle, their whole bodies now in view. They take turns hitting their balls into the hole, partially obscured by the castle, deep in conversation. In the background, other people play miniature golf at other holes; an employee sweeps the sidewalk near the entrance. Trees line the sky in the distance.

TINA *(Overlapping Lou, her face offscreen)* Hey, Lou. Listen, Lou. I . . . I don't, I don't want you, want you to break up *(Onscreen, walking to the green and shaking her head)* with your wife because of me. Uh, I don't—

LOU *(Interrupting)* Tina, it's not you. *(Getting ready to putt his ball)* I mean, this has been on my mind.

TINA Yeah, but you know, I . . . I-I-I'd, I'd feel like a homewrecker.

LOU *(Hitting his ball with his club)* Look, I'm telling you, baby . . .

TINA *(Overlapping Lou)* That's what I feel like.

LOU *(Continuing)* . . . what I gotta do is I gotta change my whole lifestyle. I . . . I got—

TINA *(Interrupting)* Yeah, if you ask me, the thing y-, the thing you gotta change is your management. *(Picking up her ball)* That's what you gotta change.

LOU *(Looking up at Tina, the club in his hand in putt position)* Hey, listen, Danny's all right. I mean, s-so he's no world-beater or something like that. I mean he's, he's all right, you know? *(Picks up his ball)*

Tina and Lou walk off the castle green as they continue their conversation. The camera moves in a circle around them as they stroll to the next hole, and we see the miniature golf course on a different angle. Trees still frame the background; golfers play at other holes. Identify-

ing flags stand on poles by each hole. A decorative cage stands on a pole in the center of the course. A portion of the parking lot, with its parked cars, is seen. A golfer walks in front of the camera, momentarily obscuring Tina and Lou as they talk and start to play the next hole on a plain flat green. Tina hits her ball first. Another golfer runs in front of the camera, club in hand.

TINA *(Sighing, walking to the next hole)* Okay. I-I don't know anything about show business, and I got nothing against the guy, 'cause I, I d-, I don't even know him. *(Shaking her head)* But I see the joints you work, you know, an-and the way things are going. *(Putting down her ball at the starting square)* Y-you're, you're better than all these new guys.

LOU *(Putting his ball down on the square, chuckling)* You're prejudiced 'cause you like me.

TINA *(Hitting her ball)* Yeah, sure I am.

LOU *(Aiming his club)* Listen, Danny'd be lost without me.

TINA Okay.

LOU *(Overlapping Tina)* I'm telling you, he's counting on me.

TINA Yeah, okay. *(Gesturing as Lou hits his ball, bending his legs)* You know what you're doing. Why don-, why don't you let me introduce you to Sid Bacharach?
The camera starts to circle them again, moving past the shrubbery, as they walk to the hole, holding their clubs, still talking. As they finish playing their ball, a young male golfer bends down in front of the camera, starting to play a nearby hole.

LOU How do you know Sid Bacharach?
Tina grunts, shrugging.

LOU *(Playing his ball at the hole)* Why would he give me five minutes of his time?

TINA *(Playing her ball at the hole)* Because he was very good friends with my husband. They were both very tight in Atlantic City.
As Lou and Tina continue their conversation, the film cuts to a close-up of the green. A ball rolls on to the screen, inches from the cup. It curves off, missing it. Another ball rolls on the green, misses the cup, and rolls offscreen. Lou's shadow and his club's shadow are seen in the corner.

LOU *(Offscreen)* Sid Bacharach, huh?

TINA *(Offscreen)* Yeah. He's a big guy, right?

LOU *(Offscreen)* Big gun, big gun, no two ways about it.
Soulful Italian music begins to play as the film cuts to the Freddy K, *slowly and forlornly making its way across the water. It's shrouded in fog. Nothing can be seen but the boat, the water, the fog—and the dim figures of Tina and Danny on the stern. Sandy continues his tale.*

SANDY'S VOICE-OVER Okay. Now, they're in the middle of the Hudson River. The fog has come in. Danny's face is, what color should I say? It's khaki. The man has a khaki face.

JACKIE'S VOICE-OVER And so, so what are you saying? Tina wanted Lou to leave Danny and go with Sid Bacharach?

SANDY'S VOICE-OVER *(Overlapping the other comedian)* That's exactly what I'm saying. See, three days earlier, Tina had set up a secret lunch meeting at some steak joint in Manhattan.

CUT TO:
INTERIOR. STEAK RESTAURANT—DAY.

Tina's face, with her ever-present sunglasses, fills the screen. The background is blurry. The noise of other patrons, their cutlery and conversation, can be faintly heard.

TINA Well, guys, we finally made it. *(Looking from one to the other, gesturing)* Uh, Lou Canova, Sid Bacharach. Sid, this is Lou.

As Tina talks, the camera moves back, revealing her at a table with Lou and Sid, a balding, suited man. Their places are set; water goblets sit in front of them on a white tablecloth. Other patrons are seen sitting at other tables, conversing and eating. The blurry background turns out to be a part of the bar against the wall. A simple chandelier is partially seen. The wall behind the bar is mirrored. It's a busy place. A waiter walks past their table in front of the camera.

LOU *(His face offscreen)* A pleasure, Mr. Bacharach. *(Onscreen, shaking Sid's hand, as the camera moves back)* Truly a pleasure.

SID *(Patting Tina's arm)* Nah, I've only heard wonderful things about you from my girl Tina.

TINA *(Overlapping Sid)* Yeah, well, Lou's terrific.

LOU *(Gesturing, laughing self-consciously)* She says that all the time.

TINA No. *(Gesturing, to Sid)* You remember Lou from the fifties. He's . . . he's got it.

Tina looks at Lou for a beat, smiling. He's nodding, his finger on his mouth, concentrating on Sid. A waiter puts a menu down by Tina's place; he crosses in front of the camera to put menus by Lou and Sid, his body momentarily obscuring Lou. The three put their menus to the side, resting their elbows on them.

SID *(Nodding)* I remember "Tossin' and Turnin'."

LOU *(Gesturing)* You do? Really? Th-that thing on "Perfidia," too, you know.

SID Yes. Now, I understand you already have representation.

LOU *(Offscreen, as the waiter places a menu in front of him)* Yeah, I do.

TINA Yeah, oh, he's loyal to a guy who means well, but he can't seem to move him. *(Opens her pocketbook and takes out a pack of cigarettes)*

LOU *(Overlapping Tina onscreen as a waiter exits)* Hey.

SID Well, you know, Lou, I-I know all about those things, and, uh, you know, sometimes it just doesn't work out, and *(Gesturing)* he can't, uh, he can't help you.
Tina lights a cigarette.

LOU It's my career. *(Gesturing)* I mean, it's my life. *(Looking down at the table)* I gotta . . . do what's right for it.

SID *(Gesturing)* I really want to catch your act. I know that this whole nostalgia thing is really coming on strong.

TINA *(Overlapping Sid, smoking and gesturing towards Lou)* Oh, yeah. You . . . he's hot now.

LOU *(Overlapping Tina, pointing a finger for emphasis)* Well, I'm . . . I'm gonna be at the Waldorf on the twenty-fifth.

TINA *(Interjecting, overlapping Lou)* Twenty-fifth. Be great if you could come, Sid.

LOU *(Continuing, overlapping Tina)* Right? Sunday night. Sunday night.

TINA Really, you know. He's ready. *(Gesturing)* All he needs is somebody with a little clout to open some doors.

SID *(To Lou, nodding)* I'll do my best to make it on Sunday night.

LOU Hey, that'll be great.

SID *(Overlapping Lou, nodding)* I really will.

TINA *(Overlapping Sid)* You're great. *(Touching Sid's arm and smiling)* Thanks, Sid. Great.

LOU *(Overlapping Tina, gesturing, in a lower voice)* Don't worry about . . . Listen, I'll get you in . . . in the back. I'll—

TINA *(Picking up her menu, interrupting)* You won't regret it.

LOU *(Gesturing, in a lower voice, looking at Sid)* No problem gettin' in.

SID *(Nodding, looking at Lou)* Okay.

LOU *(Gesturing, looking at Sid)* Okay?

CUT TO:
EXTERIOR. NEW YORK STREET—DAY.

Vito Rispoli is walking out of a pizza parlor; its interior, including a Coca-Cola machine, is dimly seen in its glass front façade. A miniature windmill and several beer bottles line the inside windowsill. He holds two slices of pizza. He glances about him as he walks up and across the busy sidewalk to Joe, who is leaning on the side of their car. An el is in the background; people walk underneath it. Vito hands Joe a slice of pizza. They eat and talk; one of the platform's pillars stands in front of Joe, partially obscuring him. Their voices are indistinctly heard as Sandy begins his tale anew.

SANDY'S VOICE-OVER Okay. So Tina's thinking about all this stuff while they're sailing back across the Hudson.

HOWARD'S VOICE-OVER Hm-mm.

SANDY'S VOICE-OVER Meanwhile, the two crazy brothers are in New York, lookin' to kill Danny.

HOWARD'S VOICE-OVER Hmm. I don't get it.
As Howard continues to speak, the film cuts to a phone booth at the pier. Tina is on the phone, seen through a broken window of the booth.

HOWARD'S VOICE-OVER *(Continuing)* Wasn't Tina gonna make a phone call and have 'em called off?

SANDY'S VOICE-OVER She did. The minute they got ashore. But it didn't work.

Tina hangs up the phone and walks out of the booth towards Danny, who is waiting in the background at the edge of the wharf, looking out at the river. Several seagulls fly by, their cawing heard over the screen. A partially seen pier sits in the water in the distance. Danny turns as Tina approaches.

DANNY *(Turning to face Tina)* So what's happening?

TINA *(Walking towards Danny, her back to the camera)* You're gonna have to lay low for a while.

DANNY What do you mean?!

TINA You-you got any friends out of town?

DANNY *(Reacting)* Out of town? Like where? What are you, nuts?

TINA *(Standing by Danny)* Then you better check into a hotel.

DANNY *(Gesturing)* What do you mean, check into a hotel? You said you were going to settle this with one phone call.

TINA It will be, but it's gonna take a few days. Meanwhile, they're looking for you.

DANNY *(Gesturing)* Darling, may— Can I say one thing right now? I'm going to the police.

TINA *(Shaking her head)* No. No, that's a mistake. No. You gotta lay low.

They start to move along the edge of the wharf, the long pier in the water revealed as they walk. They pass some straggly bushes in the foreground.

DANNY What are you talking about, lay low? I didn't *do* anything. My, I, uh, my whole life I never got involved in any trouble. I-I eat the right foods. Now I gotta lay low? *(Gesturing while Tina exhales)* Jesus! You-you said one phone call.

TINA Yeah, I know. It's gonna, it's gonna be taken care of. I got someone onto it. My advice is to check into a hotel.

DANNY I'm, uh, why? I've got an apartment. Why do I need a hotel?

TINA *(Overlapping Danny)* No, you can't go back there for a few days.

DANNY I'm, I'm gonna spend for a hotel while I'm carrying an apartment? Are you nuts?

TINA Yeah, all right. It's just, it's a mix-up. Just don't go home, that's all.

DANNY *(Gesturing)* What? I've g-got to go home. Y-You know, you-you're bad news, honey. I knew that when you, I came in you were starting with the ice pick on Lou. Nice girls don't screw around with ice picks. They got, they got ribbons and stuff.

TINA Just don't go home.

They walk offscreen, their voices still heard over the empty scene; the wharf, the water, and the long pier in the distance are all that is seen.

DANNY *(Offscreen)* But, what's g—? I gotta go home. I gotta get my pills and my shorts and, and Lou, the poor guy, he's probably a wreck.

CUT TO:
INTERIOR. LOU'S DINING ROOM—DAY.

The dining room set, with its spotless table topped with a floral centerpiece, fills the screen. A portion of the breakfront is seen, as well as the background drapes and hanging chandelier. The room is empty.

It is silent for a beat, then the clinking of ice is heard, and Lou's hand places a glass on the corner of the table as his voice is heard. While he speaks, the camera slowly moves across the table—to reveal Lou, sitting on the floor and talking on the phone. He is drunk. Outside noises are faintly heard in the background as he talks.

LOU *(Offscreen)* I'm not drunk . . . I'm not drunk. I mean . . . I'm okay . . . I'm gonna be all *(Onscreen, into the telephone)* right. Now where you been? I'm goin' crazy. I mean, where's Tina?

The film cuts to Danny, who is talking on his phone, standing near his sofa in his shabby apartment. A window, with chintzy curtains, is partially seen in the background, above an old-fashioned radiator. The wall behind him is filled with framed photographs; a desk sits below them.

DANNY *(Into the phone)* Lou, Lou, would you ha— *(Gesturing)* Lou, take some black coffee and get over to the Waldorf. *(Gesturing to Tina, offscreen)* R— She's here. Lou. *(To Tina, who walks onscreen to the phone, putting his arm on her shoulder)* W-would you speak to him, 'cause, 'cause he's lost. He's, he's gone already.

TINA *(Into the phone, overlapping Danny, who walks away, offscreen)* Lou? . . . Lou, I'll be there, honey . . . Yeah-ye— *(Nodding)* Just do what Danny says. We'll meet you at the place.

DANNY *(Offscreen, overlapping Tina)* Be nice to him.

TINA *(Into the phone, ignoring Danny)* All ri—? . . . Of course I miss you. But will you lay off the sauce? . . . Ch—. . . All right.

Tina hangs up the phone. Flailing her arms in frustration, she walks to the photograph-lined wall, her back to the camera, as Danny speaks offscreen.

DANNY *(Offscreen)* He's drunk. I don't know what I'm gonna do. I-I knew this was gonna happen. And where are my pills? I need a-a Valium the size of a hockey puck. It's the only thing that works for me.

TINA *(Interrupting Danny, looking at a photograph on the wall)* Who is this? Who is this here?

DANNY *(Offscreen)* What do you mean, who's that? That's Frank. That's Frank. *(Walking onscreen to Tina)* That's Frank, Tony Bennett, and me. *(Pointing at the photo)* This was a big night. See me up there? A little tiny smudge right there with the *(Indistinct as Tina speaks)* like a fingerprint?

TINA *(Overlapping Danny)* Oh, yeah.

DANNY *(Pointing)* That's my, that's my head . . .

TINA Hm-mm.

DANNY *(Continuing, pointing to another photo)* . . . over there. And there I am with Miss Judy Garland. Never a dearer woman existed and, my hand to God, she's—

TINA *(Overlapping Danny, looking at the photo)* Where are you?

DANNY Well, I'm uh-uh, you know, I'm right outside the frame. *(Pointing to the photo)* 'Cause if, uh, the picture went on another inch, I would be, I was back on the, on the, behind the dais and everything.

TINA *(Overlapping Danny)* Hm-mm.

Tina turns away from the wall. Danny, oblivious, continues to point out various photographs as she glances around the room. She's chewing gum.

DANNY *(Still pointing out the photos)* And then here's Mr. Myron Cohen, and . . . *(Opening up a desk drawer, distracted)* Jesus, where is my bottle of pills?

TINA *(Looking around as she walks offscreen)* How long have you had this joint?

DANNY *(Turning his head in Tina's direction, gesturing)* What do you mean, "joint"? This is rent-controlled. It's, this is fine. *(Turns back to the desk and rummages through the drawers)*

TINA *(Offscreen)* You ought to fix it up. You're livin' like a loser.

DANNY *(Opening a bottom drawer)* Well, wha-what am I gonna, you know, nobody ever comes over here. *(Retrieving his pill bottle and turning towards the offscreen Tina)* I live alone, so what do I care?

TINA *(Offscreen)* Nobody comes over?

DANNY *(Shaking the pill bottle to get some pills and coming up empty)* No.

TINA *(Offscreen)* You ever been married?

DANNY No. *(Examining the bottle for a stray pill, turning it upside down)* I was engaged once to a dancer, you know, but, uh . . . *(Throwing the bottle on his desk and walking away)* she ran away with a piano player and I broke off with her.

The camera follows Danny across the room until he passes Tina and walks offscreen. It stays on Tina as she begins to talk.

TINA *(Taking off her sunglasses and looking around the room)* You know what I'd do with this room?

DANNY *(Offscreen)* What?

TINA Liven it up. Do it all in, in . . .

DANNY *(Offscreen)* Hm.

TINA *(Continuing, gesturing)* . . . something up, you know. Pink, maybe.

DANNY *(Offscreen)* Pink?

TINA *(Gesturing)* Yeah. You know, y-y-y-you got to lighten it up. Pink, wi-wi-wi-with-with maybe some gold wallpaper and then . . . *(Turning around, touching a nearby lamp and shade)* y-you need fabric, you know? Big, like big purple pillows or somethin'. *(Gesturing)* Maybe some incense.

DANNY *(Offscreen)* What is this? A Turkish whorehouse? I *live* here, darling. *(Onscreen as he walks over to Tina, a glass of water and a pill bottle in hand)* What do you *(Indistinct as Tina's voice overlaps, as he swallows some pills and takes a drink of water)* think for . . .

TINA *(Overlapping Danny)* No, I'm, I'm serious. Y-y-you gotta lighten it up. Maybe some, maybe some bamboo furniture. *(Gesturing, looking at the room)* Bamboo. I always wanted to do a room in bamboo wi-with, like, zebra skins.

DANNY *(Looking around)* Really? Are you serious?

TINA Why not? It's exciting.

DANNY *(Walking to his desk, the camera leaving Tina and following him)* Yeah, you mean, like y— *(Putting the glass on the desk and placing the pill bottle in a drawer)* what you're talkin' about is like a tropical motif or something, right?

TINA *(Offscreen, overlapping)* Yeah, yeah.

DANNY *(Pointing to himself, looking towards the offscreen Tina)* Yeah, well, you know, it's funny, 'cause, hmm . . . actually, I like bamboo.

TINA *(Offscreen)* Really?

DANNY *(Pushing his glasses up on his nose, walking over to Tina, passing the window and a television set)* Yeah, I can—

TINA *(Offscreen, interrupting)* Picture, picture like . . . *(Onscreen, as Danny joins her in the middle of the room, gesturing in the air)* hanging plants, maybe . . .

DANNY *(Overlapping Tina, nodding)* Hm-mm.

TINA *(Continuing, gesturing towards the floor)* . . . and a really nice tile floor.

DANNY *(Overlapping Tina, nodding and gesturing)* Right, I can see it. Bamboo furniture. It's very, it's very beautiful . . .

TINA *(Overlapping Danny, nodding)* Yeah.

DANNY *(Continuing, walking in front of Tina, gesturing as he moves offscreen)* . . . and very dramatic. You know, you got an eye for drama.

TINA *(Looking after him)* Really? You really think so?

DANNY *(Offscreen)* I do, yeah. You sound surprised.

Tina walks towards Danny, continuing their conversation as she passes a few pictures hanging on the wall, a floor lamp, and a wall fixture, stopping in the bedroom doorway and talking to Danny, who is in the other room, offscreen.

TINA *(Walking towards the offscreen Danny and the doorway)* Well, you now, I'd, I-I . . . nobody ever liked my African jungle idea before.

DANNY *(Offscreen)* It's great.

TINA *(Overlapping Danny)* Uh, I, eh, I, eh, I'd always had this as a dream. *(Shaking her head and gesturing)* You're the first person who ever liked it.

DANNY *(Offscreen)* Well, sure. You, I-I'm, you know, I'm willing to bet that you're full of good ideas, but wha— You know what you lack? You lack confidence.

TINA *(Nodding)* Yeah.

DANNY *(Offscreen)* You don't have any confidence. You know what I mean?

TINA *(Nodding and gesturing)* I know. It's, it's my big problem as a, as a decorator. I g-, I got no confidence.
As Danny begins to speak, he walks out of the offscreen bedroom, past Tina in the doorway, to his nearby bathroom. He carries some boxer shorts in his hand. Tina turns around and follows him, standing in the bathroom doorway as he switches on the light and grabs some socks hanging on the shower rod.

DANNY *(Offscreen)* Sure, it's like the *(Onscreen, walking into the bathroom)* acts I handle. You know, if I was handling you, I could straighten you out in no time at all. *(Pulling down the socks)* You know, I d-, 'cause I don't see you, honey, just decorating little joints. *(Turning around to Tina, gesturing)* You know what I mean? And little, little, little apartments in the suburbs. I see you, you know, doing your-your gold walls and your Turkish pillows, and then y-y-y-you know, all that garbage in, in hotels and embassies and stuff. *(Walks offscreen to the bathroom sink area)*

TINA *(Standing in the doorway, her back to the camera)* Really?

DANNY *(Offscreen)* Yeah, naturally.

TINA No.

DANNY *(Offscreen)* No, you could, I can smell it.

TINA *(Turning away from the offscreen Danny, leaning against the doorway)* No, I don't think so. No, no. The boat sailed for me. *(Looking down, fingering her sunglasses)* I shoulda, I shoulda been more serious when I was younger.

DANNY *(Offscreen)* What are you talking *(Onscreen as he walks to the doorway, his boxer shorts and a toothbrush in hand)* about, younger? Y-you got your whole life ahead of you.

TINA Nah. *(Putting her sunglasses back on, sighing)* You know the trouble is, y— *(Gesturing)* I look at my work and I think it's ugly.

DANNY *(Gesturing, standing in the doorway opposite Tina)* Tch. Well, you know, m-m-m-my Uncle Morris, the famous diabetic from Brooklyn, used to say, "If you hate yourself, then you hate your work."

TINA *(Pointing to herself)* I sleep at night. It-it's-it-it's, it's you that's got the ulcer.

DANNY *(Gesturing)* Yeah, I got an ulcer, but you know, it may be, it may be a good thing there. You know, you know what my philosophy of life is? That it's important to have some laughs, no question about it, but you got to suffer a little, too. Because otherwise, you miss the whole point of life. And that's how I feel. *(Walks away from the doorway into the offscreen living room)*

TINA *(Looking at the offscreen Danny)* Yeah. You know what my philosophy of life is?

DANNY *(Offscreen)* Ach, I can imagine.

TINA It's over quick, so have a good time. *(Gesturing)* You see what you want, go for it. *(Pointing for emphasis)* Don't pay any attention to anybody else. And do it to the other guy first, 'cause if you don't, he'll do it to you.

DANNY *(Offscreen)* This is a philosophy of life? *(Onscreen as he walks over to Tina, carrying his shorts and a paper bag)* This s-this-s-this sounds like the, the screenplay to *Murder Incorporated.* *(Handing Tina the paper bag)* Here, hold this for a second. That's ridiculous. No wonder you don't like yourself.

TINA *(Looking into the bag, holding it open)* Now, what—? Stop saying that. I like myself fine.

DANNY *(Putting his shorts, toothbrush, and toothpaste into the bag)* Well, you know, I'm just saying down deep, I-I sense that you don't.

TINA *(Overlapping Danny, reacting)* You're the one that's living like a loser. *(Lets go of the bag)*

DANNY *(Gesturing, taking the bag)* Why? 'Cause I haven't made it? You see, that's the beauty of this business. That's the beauty of it. *(Snapping his fingers)* Overnight, you can go from a b-bum to a hero. *(Gesturing)* Like I-I think I'm, it's gonna happen now with Lou, and then I'm gonna—

TINA *(Overlapping Danny, nodding)* We'd better get going. Hurry up.

DANNY *(Gesturing)* Well, just let me say one thing. My Uncle Sidney, man, you know, hmm, lovely uncle—dead, completely—used to say three things. Used to say, "Acceptance, forgiveness, and love."

TINA *(Nodding as she walks away, offscreen)* Yeah.

DANNY *(Overlapping Tina, gesturing and turning towards her)* And that is a philosophy of life. Acceptance, forgiveness, and love. *(Reaching behind him in the doorway and turning off the bathroom light)* So, there, there's where it is. *(Nodding)* So tell me more about the bamboo *(Offscreen, walking towards Tina)* room. I love it.

CUT TO:
EXTERIOR. NEW YORK CITY STREET—DAY.

A cab drives down a city street, pulling up to the curb in the foreground. Danny, carrying his paper bag, gets out, followed by Tina.

He walks to the driver's window and hands him some money. They walk a few steps as Danny stops, reacting, to the offscreen hotel. "Agita" plays in the background, above the city sounds of traffic. Cars line both sides of the street. A building with a stone façade is seen on the opposite side. People walk to and fro in the background.

DANNY *(Looking up offscreen, gesturing)* Oh, Jesus. I'm gonna stay one night, one night, 'cause I don't want to incur expense.

TINA *(Overlapping Danny, nodding and gesturing as she looks away, down the street)* All right. Listen, I-I'm gonna make a phone call. I got another idea.

Tina, fumbling in her pocketbook, and Danny walk towards the hotel entrance. The camera follows them as they walk through its open doors and down a corridor to the reception desk, their backs to the screen. Tina stops at a row of pay phones; she gestures to Danny as, nodding, he continues towards the lobby. She puts some coins in the phone and starts to dial as the film cuts to:

INTERIOR. HOTEL LOBBY—DAY.

Danny approaches the reception desk; he alone is seen on the screen. A nearby small sign reads No Vacancies. *Mail slots hang on the wall behind the partitioned desk.*

DANNY *(Gesturing to an offscreen clerk)* Uh, how much is a single room?

DESK CLERK *(Offscreen)* Sorry, all filled up.

Danny snaps his fingers in annoyance and walks away. "Agita" continues to play as the film cuts back to the hotel corridor, as seen through the hotel entrance. Danny walks towards the entrance, past the row of phones. Tina is no longer there. He walks outside, looking both ways. No Tina.

DANNY *(Walking up the sidewalk, looking around)* Tina? Tina?

Danny walks back down the sidewalk. A church is seen next to the hotel; the hotel's ground-floor windows are enclosed in iron bars. He walks back to the hotel entrance; he peers in, then walks farther down the pavement.

DANNY Tina, darling?

Still no Tina. Danny turns around and walks backwards a few steps, moving past the hotel, near a row of old brownstones. He looks worried; he clutches his paper bag. He turns to the front again and continues his search, glancing about him. People walk by in the background; parking signs dot the street. A theater marquee is seen on the opposite side. Suddenly, there's a screech of tires. As Danny walks over to the curb to check it out, a car pulls up. Joe, in the driver's seat, opens the door as the car stops.

JOE Hello, Danny. *(Jumps out of the car and grabs Danny)*

VITO *(Coming around the car from the passenger side)* Come on, Danny.

JOE Come here, Danny. Come on. Come on. Get in the car!

Vito grabs Danny, too. Joe hurls Danny's paper bag to the street.

VITO Come on, get in the car.

JOE Get in the car. *(Grunts and mumbles, his arms around the struggling Danny)*

VITO Get in the car. Get in the . . . *(Grunting, mumbling as he pushes Danny into the car)* Get in the car! *Marone!*
The Rispoli brothers push Danny into the backseat. They get in themselves and slam the doors, screeching off up the street. A woman's sweater hangs out of the trunk, flapping in the air.

The car squeals offscreen as the film cuts to its interior, to a close view of Vito, sitting in the backseat, glancing briefly at an offscreen Danny. The music has stopped; the passing cityscape is seen in the rear window.

DANNY *(Offscreen, grunting)* F-fellas, fellas. Fellas, fellas, may-may, can-can I, may I just interject one thing at this particular point in time?

VITO *(Ignoring Danny, looking straight ahead at the offscreen Joe in the front seat)* Keep going straight.

DANNY *(His face offscreen, only his hands seen next to Vito, who clears his throat)* Look, uh, I like Johnny. This is what you don't underst— I like *(Onscreen as the camera moves past Vito to his face)* your brother. I got nothing against him. And I-I just met him today. He's swee— I liked his poem. *(Looking back and forth at the offscreen brother)* What's under discussion here is the girl's feelings. That's wha— The gir— Incidentally, where is the girl?
The film cuts quickly to Joe, driving the car, as seen from the backseat. An outside building fills the windshield.

JOE *(Turning his head slightly towards the offscreen Danny)* Oh, we're gonna take real good care of you, pal.
The camera cuts to Danny's anxious face.

DANNY *(Gesturing)* Wait, I want to say one thing. And I, I don't mean to be didactic or facetious in any manner. She doesn't love him. That's it, she doesn't love him anymore. What can I, you know? I know, it's hard to take. I-it, you know, because we all want what we can't have in life. This is, it's a natural thing. *(Offscreen as the film cuts to Vito, his mouth open, looking towards Danny)* But, uh, you know, take-take my cousin Ceil. *(Onscreen again, as the film cuts back to his face)* Not, not pretty like Tina at all. She looks like something in the reptile house in a zoo. So—you'll like this story—she meets this accountant.

VITO *(Offscreen, yelling)* Will you shut up?!

Danny reacts and the film cuts to a warehouse pier; a large building looms in the background. The Rispoli car careens onscreen from behind the building, its squealing tires heard over the strains of "Agita," which begins anew. The car moves closer to the camera, then veers to the left, zooming past the metal-columned base of a high bridge, past a low, smokestacked factory, past the background's low brick fence that separates the warehouse area from a row of trees. The car zooms into a huge warehouse, the number 2 painted on the side of the garage. A waiting Pete, a benchman, hurries into the warehouse behind the car.

The film cuts inside. The warehouse is dim, its only light coming from a few windows. The Rispoli car, stopped, viewed from behind, fills the screen. Joe hops out of the car; he goes to the trunk, where the woman's sweater is still dangling out. He unlocks and opens it as Vito, pulling Danny with him, scrambles out of the car on the other side. They all talk at once, shouting and struggling.

DANNY *(Refusing to leave the backseat of the car)* W-wai-wai-wait, no . . . *(Indistinct as Vito overlaps his speech)* You misunderstand me.

VITO *(Overlapping Danny, struggling in the backseat)* Open the door, would ya? *(Continues indistinctly)*

Joe drags a cramped Tina out of the trunk.

TINA Goddamn you!

JOE *(To Tina, overlapping her as he pulls her out)* Come on.

DANNY *(Struggling with Vito, getting out of the car)* I'm trying to make a point.

VITO *(Overlapping Danny, muttering as he pulls Danny away from the car)* Come on, let's go.

DANNY *(Struggling in Vito's grip)* You know what, you're just jealous. Fellas, I'm a veteran. I'm a veteran.

The struggling group make their way across the garage to an open stairwell. Tina and Danny are pulled and pushed up the stairs, their backs to the camera. They all talk at once, shouting and grunting indistinctly. The heavyset Pete follows them a few paces behind.

VITO *(Overlapping Danny)* Come on, you, come on . . . *(Mutters)*

JOE *(Overlapping Tina's grunts of protest, turning his head to Pete and pointing)* Get the axe.

DANNY *(Struggling in Vito's grip)* There's an axe?! Hey, uh, fellas, I'm the beard.

Joe and Vito mutter threateningly. Pete, holding the axe, follows the group up the stairs. They stumble to the top, turning offscreen, as the camera cuts from their backs, following them up the stairs, to their fronts, at the top of the stairwell. Tina and Danny are pushed through a doorway; they are pulled down a corridor, past a window, and, still struggling, they are shoved into a run-down office area. Tina and Joe are in the lead; Vito and the squirming Danny are right behind. The silent Pete lumbers in the rear. Everyone shouts and grunts at once. The music stops.

DANNY *(Overlapping Joe's and Vito's mutterings)* I'm just a beard. You don't understand.

TINA *(Struggling in Joe's hold)* He's tellin' the truth. He has nothin' to do with this.

JOE *(Overlapping Tina, muttering)* Come on.

VITO *(Pulling Danny)* Come on, let's go.

JOE Who's he talking to, huh?

DANNY *(Overlapping Joe, indistinctly, then clearly)* You don't believe me, right? You see, you don't believe me . . . *(Trails off)*

JOE *(Overlapping Danny, reacting behind him and pulling Danny forward)* We're gonna chop your legs off.

The group is dimly seen in the office area; light filters through some background windows. Joe and Vito shove Danny on one side of a large desk; Pete drags Tina to the other side, facing the others.

DANNY *(Struggling in the thugs' arms)* Fellas, it's the emess. I'm-I'm only the beard.

The film cuts to Tina, struggling, as Pete locks his axe-free arm around her neck, looking offscreen at the others across the room . . .

DANNY *(Offscreen)* My hand to God, I'm just the beard.

TINA *(Overlapping Danny, gesturing)* Would I, would I waste my time with a guy like this?

JOE *(Offscreen, overlapping Tina)* Oh, yeah?

. . . then moves to the other side of the room, to Joe, Vito, and Danny. Joe's back is to the camera; his arms are holding the squirming Danny. Vito holds a gun to Danny's head.

VITO *(Looking offscreen at Tina)* Okay then, who?

JOE *(Overlapping Vito, to Danny)* Shut up.

VITO Look, you want him to walk out of here, you're gonna have to give us a name.

As Joe mutters indistinctly, struggling with Danny, the film cuts back to Tina and Pete . . .

TINA I'm not talking.

. . . then back to Vito, Joe, and the cringing Danny.

JOE *(To Danny, grabbing his lapels)* No, no, you tell us, you punk.

DANNY No . . . *(Nervously)* I, you don't want me to rat on a *(Suddenly more fearful as Vito brings the gun closer to Danny's face)* f-friend, do you? I, look, *(Clears his throat, gesturing)* let me, let me quote Rabbi Hirschhorn, an extremely learned man, perhaps not of your persuasion, *(Looking from one hood to the other)* but—

JOE *(Interrupting, shaking Danny)* Who are you bearding for ?!

DANNY *(His voice shaking)* No, what the, not, I'm not the guy. Isn't that enough?
Tina begins to speak as the film cuts to her—with her head in Pete's grip.

TINA *(Offscreen)* Whatever *(Onscreen)* happens to him, you two are dead men.

PETE *(Overlapping Tina, his grip tight)* Shut up.
Then it's back to a closer view of Danny's terrified face, as seen over Joe's back. Joe still holds his lapels, shaking him; Vito's gun is pointed at his nose.

JOE *(To Danny, shaking him)* Oh, yeah? Come on, tell us. Who you bearding for, you little cheese-eater?

DANNY *(Laughing nervously and gesturing)* Cheese— He said . . . cheese, I d— I d— I don't know exactly what it means, but I *(Slapping Joe's arm as the latter grabs him tighter)* know it's not good.

VITO *(Pointing the gun at the offscreen Tina)* Who-who are you bearding for? I'll p-, I'll put a bullet right between her eyes.

Danny tries to grab the gun, grunting and struggling, as the film cuts to a close view of Tina's terrified face. She is struggling in Pete's hold.

DANNY *(Overlapping Vito, grunting)* Wait, wait, don't, don't *(Offscreen)* do that! That— I'll talk!

TINA *(Terrified)* Danny, don't. They'll kill him!
Then it's back to Danny's face—partially obscured by Joe's back and Vito's gun, which is still aimed at the offscreen Tina.

DANNY *(Gesturing)* Uh, I-I don't want to get my legs chopped off 'cause I do a guy a favor.

JOE Come on, let's go! Who is this?!

DANNY *(Grunting)* All right, all right, you want to know who it is? *(Looking from one thug to the other as Vito puts his gun down and turns to Danny)* Should I, you wan— Should I tell you who it is? Should I say? It's . . . *(Pointing emphatically with both hands)* Barney Dunn.

VITO *(Grabbing Danny, looking into his eyes)* Who's Barney Dunn?!
The film cut back to Tina's stunned face. Pete still holds her in place.

VITO *(Offscreen)* Come on, who is it?

TINA *(Playing along)* Danny, you rat!

PETE *(His face offscreen, shoving Tina)* Shut up!

DANNY *(To Tina)* Listen, listen, I don't owe you anything over this. *(To Vito and Joe)* Fellas, I swear on my, I swear on my life, it's Barney Dunn and, and, *(Gesturing heavenward)* Barney, may God forgive me.
The film shifts to the far view of the group seen earlier. Joe and Vito hold Danny on one side of the room; Pete holds Tina on the other.

CUT TO:
INTERIOR. CARNEGIE DELI—NIGHT.

The camera is on Will's face.

WILL *(Looking offscreen at Sandy, puzzled)* Who?!
The film cuts to Sandy, looking at the offscreen Will. A waiter passes in the background.

SANDY Barney Dunn.

JACKIE *(Offscreen)* I remember Barney Dunn.

SANDY *(Overlapping Jackie, looking at the other offscreen comics)* You know Barney Dunn.

MORTY *(Offscreen)* Yeah.

SANDY *(Nodding)* Barney Dunn.

CUT TO:
INTERIOR. APARTMENT—DAY.

A child's birthday party is in progress. Children in party hats are playing in a background room, laughing and chattering among the streamers, balloons, and party-decorated table and chairs. Others are sitting on the floor in an adjoining room, their backs and pointy party-hatted heads to the camera. They are watching Barney Dunn, a round, middle-aged ventriloquist, performing with Herman, his dummy, in the wide doorway between the adjoining rooms. A mother holding a little girl stands nearby. A young boy, in party hat and suit, stops playing with a balloon and stands next to Herman and Barney, watching, his balloon in hand. Sandy's voice is heard over Barney's act, over the screaming, laughing kids.

BARNEY *(As Herman)* I can't hear you.

SANDY'S VOICE-OVER Barney Dunn was the world's worst ventriloquist.

BARNEY *(Overlapping Sandy's voice, to Herman)* Well, anyhow . . .

SANDY'S VOICE-OVER *(Talking over Herman's mutterings)* If they couldn't get an animal act, they would call Barney Dunn.

BARNEY *(Overlapping Sandy's voice, turning to the back room)* Let's go back there. *(As Herman)* Yeah.

The film cuts to a closer view of Barney and his smiling dummy. Barney wears a bow tie; he moves his lips. His dummy wears a party hat. Their voices are low and indistinct as Sandy continues to speak over their act.

SANDY'S VOICE-OVER Barney would work children's parties. Five-year-old kids would boo him.

CUT TO:
EXTERIOR. COLUMBUS CIRCLE—DAY.

Danny is strolling across the street, a newspaper in hand. The entrance to Central Park is seen in the background, along with various buildings. Cars are stopped, waiting for the light to change. People pass by. It's a crowded, bright New York City day.

Sandy continues his tale as Danny jauntily hops up the opposite curb and walks over to Barney Dunn, who is standing on the corner, a pipe in hand, talking to a tall young woman with a headband who is carrying a huge shoulder bag. Cars drive by in the noisy background.

SANDY'S VOICE-OVER Now two weeks ago, Danny, who doesn't handle Barney—I mean, that'll tell you something about Barney's act, Danny didn't want to handle him—Danny meets Barney on the street.

DANNY *(Patting Barney on the back)* Hey. How you doin', Barney?

BARNEY *(Turning to Danny; he speaks with a pronounced stutter)* Oh, hi, D-Danny.

DANNY *(Overlapping Barney)* Hi, how's it goin'?

BARNEY I'm l-, I'm-I'm leaving on a c-cruise tomorrow.

DANNY Oh, you're kidding. Where for?

BARNEY Well, I'm working a sh-ship to the B-B-Bahamas.

DANNY *(Touching Barney's shoulder, gesturing)* Oh, fantastic. An-and then back here?

BARNEY N-n-no. And here's the b-b-beauty part. Uh, from the B-B-Bahamas to P-P-Puerto Rico for th-three weeks.

DANNY *(Touching Barney's shoulder)* Oh, fantastic. *(Gesturing towards the woman)* Who's your friend?
Barney introduces Danny to the young woman. They continue their indistinctly heard conversation as Sandy and Will speak over the scene. Pedestrians walk past the camera, momentarily obscuring the trio.

SANDY'S VOICE-OVER *(Overlapping the murmurs of conversation)* So Danny names Barney Dunn.

WILL'S VOICE-OVER But can't they check that?

SANDY'S VOICE-OVER They *do* check it. They tie up Danny and Tina and they go to check it.
The film cuts back to inside the warehouse; its office windows fill the screen. A wire apparatus hangs down in front of them. As Danny's voice is heard, the camera slowly moves down and across a portion of the room—to reveal Danny on top of Tina. They are tied together, face to face, lying prone and immobile on the desk. Light filters in from the windows in the background.

DANNY *(Offscreen)* What am I doing here? How did I get into this? What, what, *(Onscreen)* why me? Why, what did I do to deserve this that I'm here now? Wh—

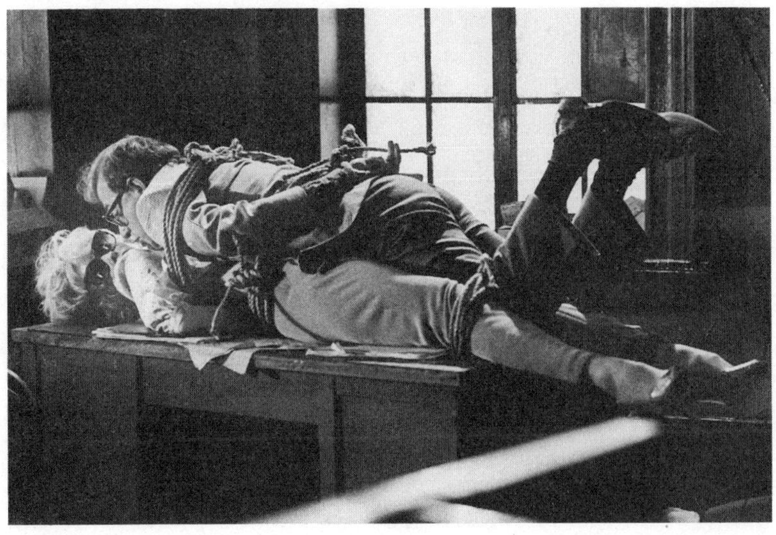

TINA *(Interrupting)* You were really quick on your feet to come up with that name so fast.

DANNY *(Sarcastically)* Oh, great. That's wonderful. Let me tell you something, darling. I was traumatized. I-I, well, my body went into shock when they, when they stuck that gun in you, and I— All I thought was they're gonna kill us, they're go-, I'm gonna be dead, and-and, Milton is coming to the Waldorf soon. You know what I'm saying?

The film cuts to a closer view of the couple. Danny and Tina's faces fill the screen. Their noses are almost touching; their lips almost meet.

TINA Listen, Danny. Listen.

DANNY *(Continuing)* And I'm . . . uh . . .

TINA *(Overlapping Danny)* Listen, they're gonna be back in a minute. We gotta do something.

DANNY So what do you . . . What? *(Looking out, trying to move)* I can't move a finger. I'm t-, I'm tied up here like a pig.

TINA *(Overlapping Danny, struggling with the ropes that bind them)* Maybe, if we just get out of these ropes.

DANNY I can't!

TINA *(Overlapping Danny, her voice at first indistinct, muttering)* . . . they just left one guy out there. There's two of us against him.

DANNY Yeah, but let me remind you, he's got an axe. The man has an axe. So there's, there's two of us. There'll be four of us in no time.

TINA *(Overlapping Danny)* Well, maybe we could sneak away.

DANNY No, I . . . *(Pauses)* You know, you know what I'm thinking, though? I used to handle . . . I used to handle an escape artist named Shandar . . . who could get out of ropes. But . . . *(Grunting, looking down at the offscreen ropes)* the problem is you gotta be standing up to . . . Even then, I'm not sure we could do it. *(Turning his head briefly)* Let me, let me ask you something. Do you think it's possible that we could . . . we could work our way off this table?

TINA Ah, I-I can hardly move.

DANNY *(Overlapping Tina, grunting)* Wait. Let's, try, try it with me. Try . . . *(Mumbles as they start to squirm)* I'm, I'm serious. Tr-try a little bit. Come on, come on. Give it a try.

TINA *(Squirming)* You're so heavy.

DANNY *(Grunting and squirming)* All right, all right. Just try. Just do what I'm telling you. Come on, come on! It'll happen. Move. Move! Okay, you all right?

TINA *(Grunting and squirming)* Yeah.

DANNY *(Squirming, his body and Tina's starting to slide off the desk)* Come on, try and pull. That's it. See? It's not so tough. Uh-huh, very good. Start, that's it. Try and slide down. That's it. *(Grunting as they begin to slide offscreen, as Tina grunts and squirms as well)* That's it. Very good. *(Offscreen, sliding off the table)* Slowly, that's it.

Tina, under Danny, slides offscreen as well. The desk is now empty, its top holding only a few pieces of office paraphernalia; cartons are piled up in the background under the windows. Danny's voice is heard as the film cuts to the couple bound together, sliding off the end of the desk into a standing position. Their hands are tied behind their backs.

DANNY *(Offscreen)* Slowly, that's it. Come on, now pull. Come on, hard. That's it, that's it. A little more. I think we got it. Thatta girl. *(Onscreen, standing with Tina at the edge of the desk)* That's right. Okay. *(Grunts)* You got it?

TINA Yeah.

DANNY Okay. All right. *(Panting)* All right, very good. Now . . . *(Panting)* I'm out of breath. All right, now, here's what Shandar, when Shandar was, was like this, what he would do is . . . *(Clears his throat)* he would wriggle.

TINA Wriggle?

DANNY Yeah. He would wriggle and what happens is the ropes gradually, eh, start to get some play in them. They start to get loose. That's what he, take my word for it. He would wriggle.

TINA *(Overlapping Danny)* Hmm?

DANNY *(Nodding)* Yeah.

TINA You sure?

DANNY Yeah, yeah. You jus— So, so you ready? Ready?

TINA Yeah.

DANNY *(Starting to wriggle along with Tina)* All right, now, now, all right, now start to wriggle. That's right. Wriggle. Yeah, see what I mean? That's it, that's a girl. Thrust, wriggle. That's it.

The film cuts to Tina's face, looking straight at Danny, whose back is to the camera. They both wriggle.

DANNY That's it.

TINA Hey, I'm wriggling.

DANNY That's it. Keep wrig— Oh, keep wriggling. That's very important. Are you wriggling?

TINA Uh-huh.

The film moves to Danny's face, looking past Tina, whose back is to the camera. He's wriggling his body, a half-smile on his face.

DANNY Oh, whooo.

TINA I'm wriggling.

DANNY *(Overlapping Tina)* That's good. That's good wriggling.

Tina pants.

DANNY Yes.

TINA *(Panting)* I don't want to . . . overwriggle.

DANNY *(Overlapping Tina)* No . . . no, but it's nice wriggling.

They move together, caught up in the now sensuous wriggling, as the film moves back to Tina's face. Her sunglasses fall off; her eyes are closed.

DANNY *(His back to the camera)* That's it. *(Grunting)* The ropes are starting to get loose.

They are now seen together, in profile, as they try to wriggle out of their ropes at the desk's edge. Danny's head is on Tina's shoulder.

DANNY *(Grunting, murmuring in concentration, then more distinctly)* Come on, it's happening. It's, come on, my han-, my hand's getting free. Keep wriggling. Don't stop now. Oh, I got it, I got it.

TINA Yeah?

DANNY *(Overlapping Tina)* I got it, yeah, yeah. Hold on. I got it. I got it.

TINA Yes?

DANNY *(Holding up his freed hands, grunting)* Yeah, yeah.

TINA Oh . . . *(Panting)* Great.

DANNY *(Struggling with the ropes that bind their torsos, wriggling)* Now, come on, keep wriggling, keep wriggling, darling. *(Grunting, pulling the ropes up over Tina's chest)* Don't . . .
Danny pulls the ropes over his head. He turns Tina around and starts to untie her hands.

TINA *(Panting)* Oh. Great.

DANNY *(Overlapping Tina's panting)* I told you, that's what Shandar did. He would wriggle and then the, then he'd get the, whole thing to happen. I saw it a million times.
The film cuts to the top of the warehouse stairwell. Tina and Danny peer around the doorway, then make their way cautiously down the stairs; Danny is in the lead. A slow Italian song begins playing in the background. The warehouse is dark.

They reach the bottom of the stairs; light filters through a background window. Danny points to the right and they turn offscreen in that direction—just as Pete is seen in the background, in silhouette, looking in from the outside through the window.

PETE *(Pounding on the window)* Hey, hey, hold it!
The slow, sensuous song becomes a fast "Agita" as the camera moves

right, in the direction Tina and Danny choose, past a doorway leading outside—where the couple, their backs to the camera, are hightailing it across the pier. Tina looks briefly behind her as they run. A large warehouse looms in the background.

The film cuts to Pete, in fast pursuit. He dashes around a truck, parked underneath a viaduct, towards the fleeing couple. A tree stands in the background.

Then it's back to Tina and Danny, running towards the camera under a series of covered viaducts. Pete follows them in the distance as they turn and race up some steps to a different warehouse. Parked trucks line the viaduct's walls; a sign is posted on one of the walls.

The film cuts to Pete, racing closer and closer to the camera. He holds a gun; he stops directly in front of the camera. He looks off in the direction they've gone and the film cuts inside the new warehouse. Light filters through an offscreen window, revealing a nearby stairway. Danny and Tina race noisily down the stairs, their feet seen from underneath the stairs, then, turning, they appear onscreen, racing down the stairs towards the camera, their shadows playing on the stairwell wall. They stop at the bottom, looking around. The music stops; the warehouse is dark.

DANNY *(Racing down the stairs)* Let's go. *(Looking around at the bottom)* Jesus, where the hell are we?

TINA *(Taking off her sunglasses, looking around)* God.

DANNY *(Walking farther into the warehouse, towards the camera)* What is this? This looks like some kind of a factory or something.

TINA *(Walking with Danny, farther into the gloom)* It looks like a warehouse.

DANNY Yeah. *(Turning around, panting)* Oh, you, you hear him? Is he, I think he's right behind us.

TINA *(Overlapping Danny, turning around)* I don't know. Yeah, he is.

DANNY Let's get out of here.

The film cuts to a different view of the warehouse, high up near the ceiling looking down at the expansive gloom. Parts of parade floats can be seen in the dark. Tina and Danny, far below, walk onscreen, talking; they stop near the looming floats. Their voices echo in the large room.

TINA *(Offscreen)* Jeez, it's so *(Onscreen)* dark.

DANNY All right, don't panic.

TINA *(Whispering)* Looks like a lot of parade floats and stuff.

DANNY Oh, perfect. There's a guy with a pistol running after us, we're stuck in the middle of the Macy's Day Parade. What the hell's—?

With a loud booming sound, the cavernous room is suddenly awash with bright light. It looks like an airplane hangar. A huge sailor head sits in the foreground; the Underdog balloon glares out in the back. Other pieces of parade-float paraphernalia are scattered around the warehouse among several helium trucks. Tina and Danny look very small.

TINA *(Overlapping Danny)* Do you see anyone?

DANNY No. What's going on here? Wh-where the . . .

TINA *(Interrupting Danny, looking around)* I don't know.

DANNY *(Continuing)* . . . hell are we?!

The film quickly cuts to the ground, to Pete running out between two floats, his pistol cocked. He fires—and the film cuts back to Danny and Tina, seen far away like sitting ducks, past a helium truck and some scaffolding. They start to run, their backs to the camera.

DANNY Jesus!

The film moves closer to the fleeing couple; they huddle behind a truck, its back reading: HELIUM/COMPRESSED GAS–NON-FLAMMABLE. *Pete fires off another shot; it hits the side of the truck. Helium gas starts spraying out with a loud hiss. Pete is seen in the background, running towards them; he is partially obscured by the escaping gas.*

The film cuts to a closer view of the running Pete; he stops, looking offscreen at Tina and Danny as the film moves to his point of view: the fleeing Danny and Tina, racing behind a partially assembled Doodlebug float, then out in the open again as another bullet hits the Doodlebug head and they race behind the safety of another helium truck.

Then it's back to Pete, a determined look on his face, a float in the background behind him. He raises his gun and fires off another shot.

The film cuts to the shot's destination: a pipe on the helium truck where the offscreen Tina and Danny are hiding. Gas spews out into the air with a loud hissing sound.

The scene shifts to a different view of the escaping gas, at the end of the damaged truck, and the clouds of gas billowing around the nearby floats. Pete rushes toward the damaged truck, partially obscured by the clouds of gas. He aims his gun at the offscreen Danny and Tina, fire in his eyes.

PETE *(His voice comically high-pitched from inhaling the helium)* Don't move or I'll blow your goddamned brains out!
The film moves to Danny and Tina, seen behind the truck's rigging. They look at the offscreen Pete through a cloud of helium.

DANNY *(Also in a silly, high-pitched voice)* Don't shoot. *(Gesturing)* Don't shoot. I'm just a beard, really. I'm just a b—

TINA *(Also in a high-pitched voice, interrupting and gesturing)* You're making a mistake. He's just a beard!
The film cuts back to Pete. He hasn't budged. He holds out his gun

and aims it at the offscreen couple. A giant hand and other partially seen floats are in the background.

PETE *(In his helium voice, looking at the offscreen Danny)* Don't tell me you're the beard, you goddamn little rat, you!
Pete pulls the trigger, but there are no more bullets. Grimacing, he starts to fill the barrel.

DANNY *(Offscreen, in his helium voice)* Run, Tina, run!
The film moves back to Danny and Tina. Danny grabs Tina's arm; they run past the rigging, then behind the truck, which is partially obscured by the billowing, hissing gas. They run behind the truck as they talk in their high-pitched munchkin voices. Their legs can be seen beneath the vehicle.

DANNY *(In his helium voice, his face offscreen)* He's out of bullets! *(Running behind the truck)* It's our chance. Tina, it's our chance! He's out of bullets!

TINA *(In her helium voice, her face offscreen, following Danny's lead)* All right, all right, I'm coming!

DANNY *(In his helium voice)* Come on!
Tina and Danny run out from behind the truck and race towards the warehouse wall, where there is a power switch near a ladder and some Dutch children floats. Tina turns around, looking at the offscreen Pete and muttering indistinctly in her high-pitched voice, as Danny reaches the switch, as another gunshot is heard, as the room is flooded in darkness. Only the spewing gas and parts of some floats can be seen.

PETE *(Offscreen, in his helium voice)* Goddamn, you little rat, you're never gonna get out of here! I'll find ya!
Pete fires a round of shots; they flash brightly in the darkness as the warehouse scene dissolves to a taxi, driving along at night. Danny sits wearily in the backseat; light reflected on his face rhythmically brightens and dims as the taxi moves along. Slow Italian music begins

to play as he turns his head to the right. The camera moves across the backseat to reveal his point of view: a dimly seen, then brightly seen, Tina, looking out the window, backlit by flickering headlights. She turns to her left and smiles at the offscreen Danny, then turns back to the window, reflective, her hand to her mouth.

The rhythmic light flickers on Tina's face as the film cuts to upper Park Avenue at night. Rows of cars drive down the dark street, their headlights glowing; the streetlamps are round, hazy orbs of light. Tina and Danny's taxi is among the cars. The slow, sensuous music continues; the taxi moves past the camera, driving towards its Waldorf-Astoria destination offscreen.

CUT TO:
INTERIOR. WALDORF-ASTORIA DRESSING ROOM—NIGHT.

The Waldorf nightclub manager, in tux and frilly shirt, is standing in the doorway of the bathroom, facing out into the dressing room. A bathroom mirror is partially seen behind him. He is framed by the open slatted door on one side, an open shower on the other.

MANAGER *(Gesturing and shouting, looking out at the offscreen dressing room)* I don't believe this! He's drunk. I've got a show in a half hour. I got a packed house, Danny! I need it right.
Lou is seen in the background, walking on, then offscreen, in the bathroom; he holds a cloth to his face. The camera moves away from the manager, past a friend who is with him, past a mirror reflecting the manager and his friend—to reveal Danny and Tina standing in the dressing room. Another mirror hangs on a wall above a dresser in the background. It reflects the gesturing manager and his friend.

MANAGER'S FRIEND *(Overlapping the manager)* He came in drunk.

DANNY *(Offscreen)* Don't panic. *(Onscreen as the camera moves over to him in the dressing room, stammering)* Don't panic. Let me, I'll deal with him.

Danny walks towards the bathroom, past the manager's friend, past the manager in the doorway. The manager's friend walks offscreen; the manager turns and follows Danny into the bathroom, where Lou is slouched in a chair. They are all seen through the doorway, the camera looking in on them.

MANAGER *(Overlapping Danny, gesturing and shouting)* I mean, what do we do?! Danny, you've got to do something!

DANNY *(Overlapping the manager, walking into the bathroom and gesturing)* Relax, will you? I can talk to him. *(To Lou)* Lou, Lou. *(To Teresa)* Yes, is Milton here yet?
Teresa, dressed up in a white stole, walks onscreen from another area of the bathroom. She flings a towel into the nearby shower and leans against it, her back to the camera.

TERESA. Yes. He came with Howard Cosell.
Everyone is talking at once. Pandemonium is in the air. A waiter walks through the doorway into the bathroom, carrying a tray of coffee. The manager's friend paces in front of the camera, on, then offscreen. He smokes a cigarette.

DANNY *(Overlapping Teresa and the manager, gesturing, his arm on Lou's shoulder)* Jesus, all right, relax, everybody.

MANAGER *(Overlapping Danny, gesturing to the waiter)* I ordered black coffee. Bring it here.

DANNY *(Overlapping the manager, to Lou)* You're gonna be o—

MANAGER *(Overlapping Danny, to the waiter)* Put it down.

DANNY *(Overlapping the manager, pointing towards the offscreen Tina)* Eh, eh, th-this is, this is Lou's wife, uh, Teresa.

MANAGER *(Overlapping Danny, reacting to the situation)* Wow.

DANNY *(Pointing to Teresa)* That's, uh, th-th-that's Tina M-Musante.

Teresa turns her head towards the offscreen Tina; she smiles briefly.

MANAGER *(Overlapping Danny, hitting himself in frustration)* Jeez.

The film cuts to Tina, walking towards the bathroom doorway. She is wearing her sunglasses. Teresa stands in the foreground, near the shower, looking in at the offscreen bathroom scene.

TINA Vitale.

MANAGER *(Offscreen, overlapping Tina)* Danny, you gotta do something.

DANNY *(Offscreen)* All right, relax.

MANAGER *(Offscreen, overlapping Danny)* He's got to go on in twenty minutes. I got a full house out there.

Tina and Teresa shake hands briefly in the doorway. They smile hello at each other. They both turn back to the offscreen bathroom drama; they react as the drama unfolds before them.

DANNY *(Offscreen)* Okay. *(To Lou)* Lou, Lou.

MANAGER *(Offscreen, clearing his throat)* Something's gotta happen.

DANNY *(Offscreen)* Okay, Lou, st— Now say the three S's, Lou. Lou, please, you gotta pull yourself together. You're gonna pull yourself together. Listen to me. You're gonna do a great show. So don't worry about it.

TINA *(Overlapping Danny, her hand to her mouth, to Teresa)* Is he gonna be okay?

TERESA *(Nodding, looking offscreen into the bathroom)* Danny'll get him sober. He's done it before.

DANNY *(Offscreen, overlapping Teresa)* Come on, Lou. Just relax.

Now come on, Lou, just relax. Uh, I need two aspirin, some tomato juice, and some Worcestershire sauce.
The manager walks past the two women in the doorway and leaves the dressing room.

WAITER *(Offscreen, repeating Danny's order)* Two aspirin and tomato juice . . .

DANNY *(offscreen)* Right. And some goat cheese and some chicken fat.

TINA *(To Teresa)* And that's gonna do it?

DANNY *(Offscreen, overlapping Tina, to Lou)* Just relax.
Lou grunts offscreen.

TERESA *(Overlapping Lou's grunts)* That's a Danny Rose formula. *(Shaking her head)* I still can't figure out how it works.

DANNY *(Offscreen, overlapping Teresa, to Lou)* Come on, relax. Do it. I promise you're gonna be okay tonight. My hand to God.
Teresa reacts, biting her lip. Tina crosses her arms in front of her chest as the film cuts to the Waldorf nightclub stage. Lou's show is in progress. He is seen across the backs and heads of the audience, lit by a spotlight; he is singing "My Bambina," his microphone in hand. An orchestra accompanies him.

As Lou sings, the film cuts to a table in the nightclub audience, where Teresa, Danny, Howard Cosell, and Milton Berle are seen, sitting and watching the offscreen show. Tina, sitting on the other side of Danny, is offscreen. The tabletop is littered with coffee cups. Teresa sits in the foreground, her back to the table. She turns briefly to Milton Berle, smiling. He's enjoying the show. Danny, sitting to the comedian's left, is only partially seen. He keeps one eye on Berle. Other patrons, sitting at their tables, surround the group.

The film moves back to Lou, to a closer view of him on the stage, still singing. The orchestra's drummer is seen behind him, in front of the background curtain.

As Lou continues "My Bambina," the film cuts to various people in the audience:

—*An older, elegant woman mesmerized by his voice. She sits in the foreground at her table, her body slightly turned towards the stage. She is beaming. Two men share her table; they sip their drinks. She reaches for hers.*
—*A younger, sophisticated, dark-haired woman, intently watching the offscreen Lou. She takes a sip of champagne and smiles. A tuxedoed man sits behind her at his table, turned towards the stage. A woman, faintly seen, is next to him.*

—Tina, in her sunglasses, sitting between Danny and another man. Milton Berle and the others are all offscreen. Tina turns briefly and smiles at Danny, then across the table. She looks back at the offscreen stage, enjoying the show. Danny, too, watches the stage; his mouth is open.

The film moves back to Lou, seen in the distance past the backs and heads of the audience. He finishes his song. The audience applauds enthusiastically as he takes his bows.

LOU Thank you. Thank you. Thank you.
The camera moves closer to him, up on the stage, his drummer behind him; another musician, on his other side, is partially seen.

LOU *(Into the microphone)* Love ya. This is what you get when you eat too much. *(Tapping his stomach)* Oo-da-too.
Lou begins singing "Agita," and the orchestra joins in with a flourish. A man in the audience cries out his approval. There are whistles and applause.

As Lou sings, the film cuts back to the Milton Berle table, amidst the other patrons. Teresa, Howard Cosell, and Milton Berle are all smiling. A nervous Danny turns to the comedian, who nods and mouths his approval. Grinning, Danny turns to the stage, then back to Milton Berle.

Lou continues to sing as the scene shifts to the stairs that lead into the nightclub area. Agent Sid Bacharach walks onscreen, pausing at the bottom of the stairs to look at the offscreen Lou. Two women walk down the stairs behind him, en route to their table from the lounge.

Then it's back to Lou, doing his classic number on the stage, the drummer behind him. The audience laughs and cheers appreciatively.

Lou tosses his microphone from hand to hand; the orchestra plays as the film cuts to Danny, Tina, and another man at their table. Milton Berle and the others are all offscreen. The three of them are watching the offscreen Lou; Tina smiles, putting her fingers to her lips.

The scene shifts to a closer view of Sid, leaning against the stairs and watching the offscreen stage intently. A man passes briefly in front of him. Lou's song is interrupted abruptly as the film cuts to:

INTERIOR. WALDORF-ASTORIA DRESSING ROOM—NIGHT.

Lou's dressing room is crowded with people. There's a constant din of conversation and good cheer. Lou stands in the foreground, his tie askew, greeting the surge of well-wishers. People mill about in the background, including Danny, Tina, and Milton Berle talking in a group. Jeanette, a fan and friend, walks into the room. The Waldorf nightclub manager is right behind her; another man ("first man") follows him in, his back to the camera.

JEANETTE *(Kissing Lou)* Lou, you were wonderfully superb. And my, "Chicago" is my favorite. *(Turns towards the crowd in the background)*

LOU *(To Jeanette)* I know my fans. Thanks, honey.

MANAGER *(Overlapping Lou, slapping him on the back)* What else would it be? You were terrific, Lou.

LOU *(Overlapping the owner, gesturing)* Oh, you guys. You were worried. *(Laughs)*

MANAGER *(Walking towards the crowd in the background)* It was fabulous.

FIRST MAN Ah, I wasn't worried at all. You were the greatest.

LOU *(Shaking his hand)* Thank you for coming. *(Slapping his back)* I don't forget my friends.

The first man walks towards the crowd in the background as another man, wearing a plaid tux, enters, his back to the camera.

SECOND MAN *(Overlapping Lou, shaking his hand and touching his shoulder)* Lou, Lou. Great show. I really enjoyed it.

LOU George, you don't miss an act, huh?

SECOND MAN *(Overlapping Lou, walking towards the back)* Really loved it.

Teresa leaves the background bustle with Bill and Diane, two family friends. She walks over to Lou. People pass back and forth in front of them, all around them.

LOU *(Kissing his wife)* How you doin', hon? You holdin' up all right? *(Nods and smiles at Diane)*

TERESA *(Nodding to Diane, then looking at Lou)* Oh, yeah. I'm g— Bill and Diane are gonna give me a lift home. I'm so tired.

DIANE *(Overlapping Teresa, smiling at them and exiting with Bill)* Good night.

LOU *(Overlapping Diane, to Teresa)* Are you?

TERESA *(Nodding)* And I have to take care of the sitter, too, you know.

LOU *(Gesturing)* I'm, I appreciate it because I gotta do some serious things with Danny. I gotta talk with Milton, the cigar man, you know and everything.

TERESA *(Overlapping Lou, walking offscreen)* Yeah, I know. Everything went okay. Yeah.

LOU *(Looking after her)* I'll be home about two, three hours.

TERESA *(Overlapping Lou, offscreen)* Terrific. Okay. *(To Danny)* Danny, make sure he gets home early.

BILL Lou.

LOU *(Overlapping, to Teresa)* Okay. *(To Bill, shaking his hand)* Thanks for coming!

Lou laughs, distracted, a framed mirror and lamp behind him. The sounds of the well-wishers are all around him.

EDDIE *(Offscreen)* Lou!

LOU *(Looking towards the left, towards the crowd in the room)* Eddie, *(Offscreen as he walks over to Eddie)* all right.

EDDIE *(Offscreen)* It was good to hear you.

The camera holds on the mirror and the nearby lamp for a beat, before the film cuts to:

The expansive, luxurious lobby of the Waldorf. Danny, Tina, and Lou are in the distance, walking through a glass door into the lobby, passing a group of people going the other way. Chandeliers dot the ceiling; a patterned carpet covers the floor; furniture and display cases line the walls. A man waits in the foreground. Danny, Tina, and Lou walk down the corridor, closer and closer to the camera. Danny and Lou do all the talking; Tina walks in silence between them.

DANNY Have I got a story for you. Wh— Lou, when I tell you what this woman and I have been through today! Wh-what, really, when, when you find out what you put me through today. Unbelievable!

LOU Danny, I gotta speak to you, and I gotta do it now while I'm still a little high.

DANNY *(To Tina)* He-he'll fall down when I tell him. *(To Lou)* Lou, I-I-I can't sleep home tonight, okay?

LOU I gotta get this off my chest. It's only right that Tina be here because she's part of it.

DANNY *(Reacting)* What? Wh-wh-wh-wh-what, wh-what?

LOU Well, come next week, I feel some changes gotta be made.

DANNY Yeah? Like what?

LOU *(Gesturing)* Like . . . Tina and I, y-you know, we're crazy about each other, and I feel I gotta say something to Terry about it.

DANNY *(Gesturing)* Well, you know, if that's what you guys decide on, that's what you want to do, you know? I mean, if you-you gotta do it you gotta do it. I just hope, you know, that you know what you're doing.

LOU *(Gesturing)* Well, we're sure about a lot of things. Tina and

I have been doing a lot of discussing. I feel for myself that . . . I gotta make a few changes.

DANNY *(Scratching his head)* Like what kind of changes?

LOU Like management.

Tina and Lou walk offscreen, past the camera—leaving a stunned Danny alone on the screen, his face close to the camera.

DANNY *(After a beat)* What do you mean, "management"? Like wh-wh-wh- . . . what do you mean, "management"?

LOU *(Offscreen)* Tina's really close to Sid Bacharach. You had to notice him there tonight . . .

Danny swallows as Lou pauses.

LOU He was there to see me.

DANNY Wh-wh-wh- . . . I don-, I don't understand. You . . . what is . . . you want to change management?

The film cuts to Tina and Lou, standing nearby in a darkened corridor. Tina looks down at the floor.

LOU *(Shaking his head and looking at the offscreen Danny)* Don't think it's not hard for me to say, but I gotta do what's right for my career.

The film moves back to Danny's stunned and hurt face, in the lobby . . .

DANNY *(Touching his temples, looking down)* Uhhh . . . what do you mean? Am I hear— I don't know. *(Looking up at the offscreen Lou)* I can't believe you're saying this.

. . . then back to Tina, her head still down, and Lou. She looks up briefly at Lou as he talks. She scratches her nose.

LOU *(Gesturing)* Danny . . . Sid can really move me. I mean, we've got this special rapport.

The film cuts back to Danny . . .

DANNY *(To Tina)* How do you know Sid? *(Pauses)* Have you been pushing him to, to, to leave me?

. . . then back to Tina and Lou.

TINA *(Gesturing)* Hey, leave me out of this. *(Walking in front of Lou and offscreen, leaving a sad-looking Lou alone in the corridor, looking offscreen at Danny)* All I know is he's a big talent and he's playing joints.

The film is back on Danny in the corridor, looking offscreen at Tina.

DANNY *(Reacting with disbelief)* Joints? What do you mean? He was lucky to get j— When I met him he was, he was still singing "Funiculi, Funicula."

Danny walks towards the camera and offscreen as the film cuts to the main lobby of the hotel. A man and a woman walk across the screen in the foreground, talking indistinctly. Behind them is a Greek-style mezzanine, with a center staircase, a marble statue, pillars, large murals, and potted plants. Doorways lead to other corridors. Stairs lead down to the mezzanine from the side. Danny, Tina, and Lou are heard over the scene; they soon appear onscreen, walking down the side stairs to the mezzanine.

TINA *(Offscreen)* Look, Danny, facts are facts.

DANNY *(Offscreen)* What are you talking about, "facts are facts"? *(Onscreen, walking down the side stairs)* What does that— Y-you know, this kid owes me his life!

A group of hotel guests walk onscreen, chattering indistinctly as the trio walks behind the pillars, across the mezzanine to the center staircase.

LOU *(Walking down the center staircase with Tina in the lead)* Will you leave her out of this! What's done is done.

DANNY *(Gesturing, walking down the center staircase)* I don't understand you, Lou. We've been through so much together.

LOU *(Gesturing)* That's your trouble, Danny. You make everything into a personal situation.

Tina, Lou, and Danny reach the bottom of the stairs in the main lobby. A couple stands nearby, talking by the stairs. The trio walks to the center of the lobby, in the middle of a large, round area rug, still in the midst of their emotional discussion. Other hotel guests mill about, passing in front of them, walking up and down the stairs and chattering indistinctly.

DANNY *(Gesturing)* I, of, of, of course I make it personal. That's the point. Well, that's our relationship. You can't put into a contract what I do with you. You know, it's— *(To Tina)* Look, all right, ah, can I, can I give you, may I give you one? My Uncle Meyer, the man sold apples.

LOU *(To Tina, overlapping Danny, his voice raised)* Say something, will you?! *(Gesturing)* You know I'm not verbal at all.

TINA *(Overlapping Lou, gesturing, her voice also raised)* What am I gonna say?! This is business between the two o' you. You gotta do what you gotta do, and Danny's gotta understand it. He's a big boy.

DANNY *(Gesturing, to Tina)* What are you talking about?! What are you telling him?

LOU *(Overlapping Danny, gesturing)* Danny, naturally if anything comes out of this, you know you're gonna be in for a taste.

DANNY *(After a beat, in disgust)* Shh . . .

He shoves past them, furious and hurt, hurrying down a nearby staircase and offscreen. Tina and Lou look after him.

LOU *(Calling out)* Danny, where're you going, Danny? Danny! Danny . . .

CUT TO:
INTERIOR. CARNEGIE DELI—NIGHT.

Danny is sitting alone at a table, his hand at his head. A lone cup of coffee sits in front of him, near the ketchup and the other condiments. Rows of empty tables are seen in the background. A few scattered customers are seen, chattering low and indistinctly over the scene. Danny rubs his forehead, staring into space. It is quiet for a beat.

DELI OWNER *(Offscreen)* Hey, how you doin', Danny? You hear about Barney Dunn? Couple of guys done a pretty good job on him, they beat him up pretty badly.
There is a pause. Danny looks up offscreen at the owner, rubbing his chin.

DANNY *(Gesturing, looking ill)* I thought he was on a cruise.
As the deli owner replies, the film cuts to the deli take-out counter. The owner, his face hidden by the high counter, is behind it, preparing some food. Other men work behind the counter as well. A raincoated customer walks onscreen to the counter; he picks up a bag of food and leaves as the owner talks. On the wall behind the counter is a menu with prices; beer bottles line the inside edge of the display case. A portion of the case is mirrored, reflecting the opposite wall's framed photograph and light fixture. The top of the counter is filled with stacks of plates and food.

DELI OWNER *(His face partially obscured by some food on the counter)* Naaa-aaw, naw, that was canceled. He's in the hospital now. It was pretty rough for a while. It was touch and go. But it-it-it's, but it's all right now. The cops got 'em. They got the guys that done the job on him.
The film cuts back to Danny at his table, looking at the offscreen owner, stunned.

DANNY *(After a beat)* Which hospital?

DELI OWNER *(Offscreen)* Roosevelt.

Danny, still stunned, turns away from the offscreen owner, looking off, then down at his table. He starts to stand up and the film cuts to:

The outside façade of Roosevelt Hospital in the dark. Electric lights above the entrance spell out the hospital's name. Spotlights play against the entrance, creating shadows and glimmers of light. "Agita," played at a melancholy speed, is heard in the background as the camera moves across the entrance to its large ground-level windows in the reception area. Danny is seen in the distance, through the windows, talking to a security guard who is sitting behind a long desk. Danny points towards the left; the guard nods. Gesturing and talking, Danny walks away, to the left. The camera, outside, follows him through the windows, past a sitting area with sofas and potted plants, as he turns a corner and walks down a corridor, his back to the camera. A large framed portrait hangs in the background, at the end of the corridor. Some branches on an outside tree hang down, over the windows.

With "Agita" slowly playing, the film moves to Barney's hospital room, the camera inside facing the doorway. A sink and mirror are seen in the foreground. Danny gingerly walks onscreen, walking from the corridor to the doorway. He peers inside, towards the camera, then slowly and cautiously makes his way in, past the sink, past the curtain partition, to Barney, all bandaged up, lying in his hospital bed. His bandaged arm lies across his chest; he is immobile. The wall behind Barney is bare; a long light fixture glows down.

DANNY *(Clearing his throat)* How you doing, Barney?

BARNEY Danny, wh-wh-what are you doing here?

DANNY *(Standing on the side of Barney's bed, looking down at him)* Well, *(Clears his throat)* I heard that, eh, that-that you got beat up. *(Gesturing)* So . . .

BARNEY *(Shaking his bandaged head)* I s-s-still don't know what happened.

DANNY *(Gesturing)* Barney, I want you to know if there's anything I can do, anything at all, you know what I mean? You worried about, you know, hospital bills? Anything at all, I'll take care of it.

BARNEY You wanna p-pay my hospital bills? D-Danny, are you sure *you're* okay?

DANNY *(Gesturing)* Really, Barney, anything at all, whatever you need.

Barney sighs deeply as the film cuts back outside, to the hospital's entrance, as seen from a different angle. The ROOSEVELT HOSPITAL *sign is seen again, over the hospital's covered drive-up entranceway. Lights from the reception area glare out from the ground-level windows into the gloomy night. It is raining. A man walks past the entrance as Danny walks out the glass doors. His shoulders are slumped. As the sounds of the melancholy "Agita" continue, he makes his way slowly towards the camera, across the driveway. He stops; the rain continues to fall. The wind blows, and the film cuts to:*

INTERIOR. CARNEGIE DELI—NIGHT.

The comics are still gathered at their table, which is littered with plates and cups, discussing Danny Rose. Corbett, Sandy, Will, and Jack face the camera. Morty, partially seen, sits across from Sandy. The sounds of cutlery and other customers are heard indistinctly in the background.

MORTY *(Gesturing)* I thought this was a funny story. It's terrible!

SANDY *(Gesturing, a cigarette in hand, to Morty)* So, what do you want me to do? It's not *my* life. *(Pauses, then changes the mood at the table as he continues his tale, looking at the others, smiling)* So *(Chuckling)* Lou leaves his wife and kids and he moves in with Tina.

The film cuts to a smoky nightclub. Lou's legs and a portion of his sequined jacket are seen on the raised stage in the foreground; his microphone wire dangles down. He's singing. Around him are the club's patrons, crowded at small tables, listening and moving their heads in time to the music. Waiters make their way through the crowded maze of people and tables; new patrons are led to tables. Tina and Sid are dimly seen at a background table, watching Lou.

SANDY'S VOICE-OVER Sid Bacharach's handlin' him. He's doin' all right.

LOU *(His face offscreen, overlapping singing)* "You may be king, you may possess / The world and all of its gold. / Ahh, gold won't bring you happiness . . . "
The film cuts to Tina and Sid at their table against the wall. Tina wears a white fur and her sunglasses. She smokes a cigarette. While Sid watches the offscreen Lou, she rubs her forehead. She looks out of sorts. Other patrons sit at surrounding tables.

LOU *(Offscreen, singing)* " . . . when you're growing old. / Ohh, the world, it's still the same / And you can never change it."

SID *(Over Lou's singing, which continues in the background, looking at Tina)* You okay? You seem a little down.

TINA *(Flicking a cigarette ash)* No, I-I have a headache.
A waiter walks over to their table; he puts a drink down in front of Tina. His back is to the camera; he is only partially seen.

TINA *(To the waiter)* What are you doing with this? I . . . I ordered a Courvoisier.

WAITER Gee, I'm awfully sorry. Didn't you order a Jack Daniel's?

TINA *(Overlapping the waiter, reacting)* Don't tell me what I ordered, I ordered a Courvoisier.

SID *(To Tina)* You did say Courvoisier.

TINA *(Waving her hand in frustration, then putting her empty glass on the waiter's tray)* Okay. All right. Let's not make a federal case out of it.

The waiter walks off. Tina sits glumly, still out of sorts. Sid looks at her, concerned. Lou continues singing with his band and the film cuts to:

INTERIOR. LOU AND TINA'S APARTMENT—NIGHT.

The apartment is dark, silent. The bedroom doorway is seen next to a portion of the living room wall with two hanging pictures. An end table holding a lamp sits against it.

LOU *(Offscreen)* Honey, what are you doing up?

TINA *(Offscreen)* I can't sleep.

A light is switched on in the bedroom, revealing Lou's legs on the bed. Also seen through the doorway are a portion of draped window, some pictures on the wall, and a chair in the corner of the room.

LOU *(Grunting, getting out of bed, his body framed by the doorway)* You know, it's four o'clock in the morning. *(Puts on his slippers)*

TINA *(Offscreen)* Yeah, I know. I had a bad dream.

LOU *(Walking through the bedroom into the living room, gesturing)* Well, what is this, like a thing or something? I mean this is going on every other night. *(Walking over to Tina, his back filling the screen)* Uh, eh, why don't you take a pill or something?

Tina is seen over Lou's shoulder, sitting at the kitchenette counter, flipping through a magazine. She is bathed in light from the kitchen.

TINA *(Flipping through her magazine)* Nah, no, I don't like pills.

The film cuts to a different view of Tina and Lou. He stands behind a glass-block wall, in profile, talking to Tina in the doorway of the kitchenette. She sits behind the kitchenette's counter, facing the cam-

era. Behind her are cabinets and appliances. The corner of the counter holds a lazy Susan filled with spices. Stools sit on the visible side of the counter, facing the camera and the rest of the offscreen living room. An open magazine is in front of Tina; she smokes a cigarette.

LOU *(Gesturing)* When I can't sleep, I take one of those Seconals, I go out like a baby.

TINA *(Gesturing, not looking up from her magazine)* I'm okay. I'm fine.

LOU *(Walking into the kitchenette, behind the counter next to Tina)* You're okay. Listen, *(Stuttering)* I got a great new idea. When I go to Atlantic City, *(Leaning over Tina and gesturing)* I'm gonna open, you know I'm gonna open up with that "You're Nobody Till Somebody Loves You," then I'm gonna go right into that "When You're Smiling"—

TINA *(Looking up from her magazine in annoyance, interrupting)* Lou, will you give me a break? *(Gesturing)* It's four in the morning.

LOU *(Gesturing)* You're not— Listen to me. This is important stuff.

TINA *(Overlapping Lou, going back to her magazine)* I'm listening.
The film cuts to a close view of Angelina's little dog, panting, sprawled out on Angelina's bed. Tina's voice is heard over the scene as the film moves to her face. She is sitting at the foot of the bed in Angelina's apartment. A standing assistant is partially seen next to Tina; she holds some dollar bills in her hand.

TINA *(Offscreen)* Angelina, I can't sleep. I— *(Onscreen)* I feel jumpy. I mean some, I don't know. *(Shaking her head)* I'm not myself.
The film cuts to Tina's point of view: Angelina, sitting up in her bed, looking at the offscreen Tina.

ANGELINA *(Holding up her hand dramatically)* I see bad dreams, deep dreams. *(Hitting her chest)* Bad conscience.

TINA *(Offscreen)* Yeah . . . A little while ago, I met some man. *(Onscreen as the film cuts back to her, sitting at the edge of the bed)* You know, I, I hardly spent any time with him. *(Shaking her head)* One day. We had an adventure.

ANGELINA *(Offscreen)* Yes. *(Onscreen as the film cuts to her in the bed, wagging her finger)* He makes you feel uneasy.

TINA *(Offscreen)* I did, I-I did him some, some little wrong, you know. *(Onscreen, the camera back on her face)* Just s-some, some small business matter. *(Touching her neck)* I-I didn't even know him very well. But, you know, when I had the chance to, *(Gesturing, shaking her head)* to say something, I, uh, I-I-I didn't, I didn't speak up.

The camera continues to cut back and forth between Angelina in her bed and Tina, sitting at its edge, the assistant at her side, as each one speaks to the other.

ANGELINA *(Wagging her finger)* I have a vision of you . . . standing before a large mirror. *(Holds her hands out wide)*

TINA *(Amazed)* I j— I had that dream last week. That was it, exactly my dream.

ANGELINA *(Gesturing dramatically)* What is it you're seeking there?

TINA *(Sighing, looking off for a beat as she thinks)* I want to rest easy again. I want to find myself. Um, *(Inhales deeply, shaking her head)* I want to wipe out my thoughts and forget this guy.

The film moves back, to a wider view of Angelina's bedroom. Seen through its glass-paned doors are Tina, her back to the camera, sitting at the edge of the bed, the assistant, standing nearby in purple—and Angelina, her hands to her forehead, her eyes closed, sitting up in her bed. A crucifix hangs above her on the wall; her little dog is sprawled out on the comforter.

ANGELINA *(Sighing)* I can't see clearly. *(Taking her hands away from her head, gesturing)* It-it-it's unclear. It's all unclear . . . *(Continues in Italian)*

CUT TO:
INTERIOR. TINA AND LOU'S BATHROOM—DAY.

Lou is taking a shower; he is in the stall, hidden by the shower curtain. Tina, wrapped in a terry robe with a towel-turban on her head, is standing by the steamed-up bathroom mirror, her back to the camera. Her face is seen in the misty mirror. The running water in the shower is loud.

LOU *(Offscreen)* And, ah, what's the, what's the matter with you lately? I mean, you're always so edgy.

TINA I don't want to go to California, okay? *(Applying some blush to her cheeks)* It gives me the creeps out there.

LOU *(Offscreen)* Honey, it's important you go to California with me.

TINA *(Rubbing some powder on her blush brush)* Well, then you go.
The shower stops. Lou sticks his shower-capped head out of the stall. As he talks to the nearby Tina, the camera slowly moves closer and closer to her reflection in the mirror, until only her reflected, sad face fills the screen.

LOU *(Gesturing with one hand, the other behind the shower curtain)* I mean, wh-what is it with you? I mean, lately, everything's going so nicely. My comeback's in full swing now, but, oh, you, you weren't happy in Vegas, you weren't happy in Atlantic City. You complained all the time. I thought you'd be happy.

TINA *(Looking down, fingering her brush, then applying more blush)* I'm moody. I, y-you knew I was moody when you met me.

LOU *(Offscreen)* I've had it with the moods. I mean, I gotta go to California, that's it. *(Pauses)* Hey, what's the matter?

TINA *(Looking down, sighing)* I don't know.

After a beat, she slides the mirror back, revealing a cluttered medicine cabinet. Her reflection disappears and the film cuts to the busy daytime sidewalk outside P. J. Clarke's in Manhattan. Tina, in scarf and sunglasses, stands near the entrance, looking around as she waits. People in all shapes and sizes walk up and down the sidewalk in front of her, oblivious, as the Carnegie Deli comedians' voices are heard.

SANDY'S VOICE-OVER Lou moves to L.A. Tina doesn't.

MORTY'S VOICE-OVER Uh-huh.

SANDY'S VOICE-OVER It's all over between them.

MORTY'S VOICE-OVER Yeah.

SANDY'S VOICE-OVER Guess who calls her for a date.

MORTY'S VOICE-OVER I have no idea.

Ray Webb suddenly bursts onscreen, running up to Tina. He puts his hands on her shoulders; she smiles. They looked pleased to see each other.

TINA *(To Ray)* Hi.

RAY *(To Tina)* Hi.

They continue their conversation in low and indistinct tones as the comedians speak over the scene, as the camera moves closer to them, past the crowds on the street. Pedestrians pass in front of the camera. As the comedians talk, a smiling Ray gestures to the bar's door. He opens it for Tina, his hand on her waist, and follows her inside.

SANDY'S VOICE-OVER Remember the shaving cream man from outer space?

MORTY'S VOICE-OVER The guy she met with Danny when they were lost in the reeds?

SANDY'S VOICE-OVER That's right. Well, now *they* start going out. But she's just as moody with him.

MORTY'S VOICE-OVER Naturally.

SANDY'S VOICE-OVER *(Overlapping Morty)* They fight. They argue.
As Sandy continues his tale, the film cuts to the sky over Central Park West. A giant inflated Snoopy balloon fills the screen. The sounds of cheering, squeals of delight, and chatter compete with the music from a marching band.

SANDY'S VOICE-OVER Then one morning, Thanksgiving morning, the two of them are on Central Park West. There's the parade.
The film cuts to a throng of excited spectators on the sidewalk, watching the offscreen Macy's Thanksgiving Day parade. Balloons dot the crowd of men, women, and children. The camera moves away from the throng to reveal the parade in full swing. A marching high school band in full regalia streams down the street, the students' feet in perfect unison. A Kermit the Frog balloon is seen in the background, behind the band. Trees line the park side of the street. People are packed on the sidewalks on both sides of the avenue.

Over the sounds of marching bands and enthusiastic spectators, the film cuts to a montage of the parade, a series of scenes showing:

—The giant Lionus balloon filling the screen.
—The giant Woody Woodpecker balloon moving in the sky.
—A marching group of white-clad majorettes, swinging their batons, and full-costumed clowns, marching backwards and acting silly.

Behind them, a giant turkey and a giant Bullwinkle the Moose follow, bobbing in the sky.

—*Sammy Davis, Jr., standing on top of a float, smiling and gesturing to the offscreen crowd. The branches of the Central Park trees are behind him, in the background.*

—*Tina and Ray standing on the sidewalk in the crowd. Ray is smiling, watching the band moving down the street; Tina is looking off in the opposite direction. He turns to her, smiling, then frowning as he notices her faraway look. The Superman balloon floats in the background.*

—*The Doodlebug float, weaving its way through the street. A woman sits on its grinning cartoon head, waving to the crowd.*

—*Milton Berle, dressed as Cinderella, complete with blonde wig, long white gown, and waving fan, standing on a float. Behind him is a giant clock, with* BULOVA *on its face. Next to him is a young boy dressed as a page. Milton Berle notices the camera.*

MILTON BERLE *(Mouthing his words, to the camera)* Hello. How are you? *(Nudging the waving page)* There's a camera over there. *(To the camera, waving)* Hello. I love you.

The film continues its montage of the parade, showing over the sounds of music and cheers:

—*An exotic-looking float surrounded by people marching in costume. The giant Underdog balloon floats in the background. Spectators line the sidewalks.*

—*Santa Claus standing with Big Bird on the top of a giant house float, a chimney sitting behind them. Santa Claus waves to the crowd.*

—*The giant Underdog balloon, filling the sky, floating across the screen.*

The film moves back to Ray and Tina, standing on the sidewalk among the other spectators. Tina is still looking off, lost in her own world. Ray turns and looks at her with annoyance. The partially seen parade continues on the street. The sounds of the bands and the crowds are heard in the background.

RAY *(Looking at Tina)* Now what's wrong?

TINA *(Shrugging her shoulders)* I don't know.

RAY *(Reacting angrily)* Jesus, Tina, what's wrong with you?!

Tina puts her hand to her face. She starts to cry.

RAY *(Gesturing, exasperated)* Look, w-, maybe, mayb-, maybe we should have a little heart-to-heart. Everything makes you cry. Maybe you should see a doctor. I don't know what to do with you.

TINA *(Overlapping Ray, turning around and waking away)* Excuse me.

RAY *(Looking after her)* Baby! Tina, what are you trying to pull here?

Ray goes offscreen after Tina, and the film cuts to Angelina's bedroom, as seen through the glass-paned door. The bed is empty, no one is in sight. Tina's and another woman's voices are heard over the empty room.

TINA *(Offscreen)* I got-, I gotta see Angelina right away.

WOMAN *(Offscreen)* I'm sorry, Angelina's not here.

TINA *(Offscreen)* She's not?

The film cuts to the open front door of the apartment, as seen through the glass-paned door. The camera is inside the bedroom, looking out. Tina stands in the doorway; an elderly woman holds the door open. The scene is bathed in shadow.

TINA Well, wh-wh-what time's she coming back? I-I need her advice.

WOMAN *(Gesturing)* Well, Angelina's having Thanksgiving with her grandchildren, and she won't be here until Monday.

TINA *(Overlapping the woman)* This is important.

WOMAN *(Gesturing)* Well, I can't help it if it's important. She won't be here until Monday. Please come Monday.

TINA *(Overlapping the woman, groaning and muttering, nodding her head in disappointment)* Yeah, okay.

CUT TO:
INTERIOR. DANNY'S APARTMENT—THANKSGIVING DAY.

The water glass virtuoso is playing a song in Danny's living room. She stands behind a long table lined with glasses; she moves her hands above their rims. She looks up towards the camera as she plays, smiling. A framed picture hangs behind her, on the wall. Barney and the blind xylophonist are heard over the scene, having a conversation offscreen. Herbie Jayson, holding a glass, walks through a doorway in the background. He walks in front of the water glass virtuoso to a makeshift bar on a table in the foreground. He puts down his glass as the film cuts to a wider view of the living room. Herbie is seen at the table bar, set up in the middle of the room. It's crowded with bottles, plates, and glasses. Barney, sipping a drink, stands by the window near the wall that's covered with framed photographs; he is talking to the blind xylophonist, who is seated on the couch. The bird lady sits in a nearby chair; she is feeding her parrot—who is dressed up in a party dress and hat.

HERBIE *(Gesturing to Barney, then to the table of drinks)* Hey.

BLIND XYLOPHONIST *(To Barney, who shakes his head at Herbie)* You know . . . *(Continues indistinctly)*

HERBIE *(Overlapping their conversation)* This is great. *(To the bird lady, reacting to the bird)* Hey, look, h— *(Chuckling)* Hey.
The film cuts to a closer view of the bird lady and her cutely dressed parrot sitting near a desk. She touches the bird's head and wing, murmuring. Barney, Herbie, and the blind xylophonist are heard over the scene, chattering indistinctly as the water glass music continues, as Danny's voice is heard and the film cuts to:

Danny, walking into the center of the room, his back to the camera. He turns around near the table, to his guests. He's holding a tray of turkey TV dinners.

DANNY *(Offscreen)* Okay, I got the *(Onscreen, walking into the room)* frozen turkeys.
Herbie grabs a plate from the table; the water glass virtuoso stops playing and walks over onscreen to the group. She picks up a napkin and some silverware. Everyone chatters at once, exclaiming their approval and enthusiasm indistinctly.

DANNY *(Overlapping the group, walking over to the window)* Here they are. All right, here we go. Here we go.

BARNEY *(Overlapping Danny, looking at the tray of food)* Thank you, Danny.

DANNY *(Overlapping Barney, taking the plate from Herbie and putting a dinner on it)* Give me a little room there. God love you. *(To Barney, handing him his dinner)* Here's a, here's your frozen turkey.

BARNEY *(Taking the plate, looking at it)* Ah, thank you. D-Da— Yeah, b-b-believe me, the frozen is just as g-g-good as the re-real.

DANNY *(To the blind xylophonist, handing him a dinner)* You got it?

BLIND XYLOPHONIST Uh-huh.

DANNY *(To Barney, as he turns towards the table, putting another dinner on a plate that Herbie's holding out)* Yeah? Yeah, and the frozens are much cheaper than the real ones, you know.

HERBIE *(Passing the dinner plate to the water glass virtuoso)* I think it's delicious.

BLIND XYLOPHONIST Can I help, please?

DANNY *(Turning to the blind xylophonist and gesturing)* No, no, no, no. Sit there, you'll fall over.

WATER GLASS VIRTUOSO *(Overlapping Danny)* And it smells so good! It really smells terrific. It really does.

Danny busily serves turkey dinners to Herbie, the bird lady, and himself. Everyone is talking at once, starting to eat and enjoying themselves. The bird lady gives her parrot a piece of food; she takes it away seconds later. The parrot looks around the room.

DANNY *(Overlapping the water glass virtuoso, to her)* Yeah, just dig in, dig in. Don't, don't hesitate.

WATER GLASS VIRTUOSO *(Overlapping Danny, exclaiming)* Really? Okay, yeah, that's terrific.

HERBIE *(Overlapping the water glass virtuoso, taking a fork from the table)* This is really great, you know.

BIRD LADY *(Overlapping Herbie, reaching out to him)* Can I have a fork, please? Can I have a fork?

DANNY *(To the water glass virtuoso, busily putting down his tray, squaring things away)* W-would you like a drink or something?

WATER GLASS VIRTUOSO Oh, I'd love it.

HERBIE *(To the water glass virtuoso, ready to pour her a drink)* Oh, here, let me do that.

DANNY *(Overlapping Herbie, gesturing with his pot holder)* Yeah? There's some Tab over here, and there's some club soda.

The telephone begins to ring over the chattering crowd.

WATER GLASS VIRTUOSO *(Overlapping Danny, picking up a glass)* A little Coke, a little Coke would be fine.

DANNY *(Overlapping the water glass virtuoso, pointing to Herbie)* You know, just . . . uh . . . give her some Coke. *(Walking away)* Excuse me just a second.

Danny wipes his hands on the pot holder and throws it down. He rushes towards the ringing phone in the foreground while Herbie pours some Coke from a can into the water glass virtuoso's glass.

WATER GLASS VIRTUOSO *(Overlapping Danny, to Herbie, watching as he pours)* Oh, that's fine.

Danny picks up the phone; the group behind him continues to chatter and eat.

DANNY *(Into the phone)* Hello? . . . Yeah, yeah, sure, we're, yeah, that's right. *(Turning to the party group)* Hey, it's the twins! It's the twins! They're—

WATER GLASS VIRTUOSO *(Interrupting Danny)* Wooo! Where were they?

Everyone in the room is excited, talking all at once, indistinctly.

DANNY *(Overlapping the group, turning back to the phone)* Yes, yes . . . Sure . . .

The door buzzer sounds. Danny picks up the phone and walks towards the offscreen door, past the camera. The group in the living room continues to chatter and laugh indistinctly.

DANNY *(Continuing, into the phone)* . . . sure, darling, sure. Yes, darling. An-and the new noses are *(His face offscreen, walking towards the door)* good? *(Offscreen, only the group in the living room on-camera)* . . . Yes, we're . . . sure.

An offscreen Danny opens his door—revealing Tina. A slow, sad version of "My Bambina" begins; the offscreen chattering becomes fainter. She stands there for a beat.

TINA *(Looking at the offscreen Danny)* I-I-I came to apologize.

The film cuts to Danny, at the door, impassive, staring silently. It moves back to Tina.

TINA You gonna ask me in?

DANNY *(Offscreen, into the phone)* Let me call you back. Ca-can I . . . Yeah . . . No, I'll get back to you. Let me call you, I'll call you back.
Danny hangs up the phone offscreen. Tina walks through the door, past Danny.

TINA *(Walking into the apartment)* Hope I'm not intruding.
Tina walks offscreen; Danny closes the door behind her. He looks off at Tina, his face grim, still silent. The camera moves back to Tina, standing in the foyer.

TINA *(After a beat)* I realize you hate me.

HERBIE *(Offscreen)* Danny, come on, bring her in, will you? The food's getting cold.

BARNEY *(Offscreen, overlapping Herbie)* Hey, D-D-Danny, who's your f-f-f-f-f-fr-, ah, your guest?
The camera moves back to Danny, still in shock, still at the door. He walks forward a few steps; he puts his hand on the wall.

DANNY *(To the offscreen Barney)* Oh, s-, nobody. I-it's nothing.
The camera moves back to Tina, looking offscreen at Danny . . .

TINA Was it your Uncle Sidney who said, "Acceptance, forgiveness, and love"?

. . . then moves to Danny near the door.

DANNY *(Shaking his head, looking down)* Look, I've had a bad year. I, you know, I . . . If things don't pick up for me, I'm gonna be selling storm windows soon.
The film cuts to Tina. She looks down, reacting to Danny's words, then up at him.

TINA I'd like to be friends.

DANNY *(Offscreen)* No, I don't think that would be such a great idea.

Tina stares blankly behind her sunglasses.

HERBIE *(Offscreen)* Hey, this is the . . .

The film cuts back to the living room at large, as seen from its back wall. Herbie is standing in front of the table, his back to the camera. Barney and the bird lady and her dressed-up parrot sit on the sofa. The water glass virtuoso is in a nearby chair. Everyone is eating their TV dinners and chattering at once. Tina and Danny are seen in the background, through the doorway, in the foyer.

HERBIE *(Continuing, onscreen)* . . . best Thanksgiving party we've had so far. *(Picking up a napkin from the table and walking over to the water glass virtuoso)* Here's you napkin, honey, you said you needed one. *(Walking back to the table, to the group)* This is absolutely the best Thanksgiving party. *(Walking offscreen to the window area, his face offscreen, to Danny)* Danny, this is marvelous.

Danny, his head down, looking sad, slowly walks away from the foyer into the living room. He makes his way to the table. Tina, in the background foyer, watches him through the doorway.

BARNEY *(Overlapping Herbie, to the approaching Danny)* Hey-ya, hey, D-D-Danny, who's your f-f-f-f-, ah guest?

The camera moves closer to Danny as he picks up his TV dinner and salts it, as the blind xylophonist walks past the camera, eating his food, as Tina turns around in the background and exits through the front door.

BLIND XYLOPHONIST *(Walking past the camera)* The cranberry sauce is dry.

HERBIE *(Offscreen to the blind xylophonist)* You're eating the mashed potatoes. *(Laughs)*

The camera continues to move closer and closer in on Danny's forlorn face, past Barney, past the water glass virtuoso, past the bird lady and her parrot. The blind xylophonist walks through the doorway in the background, his back to the camera. Danny picks up a bottle of beer, putting his plate down on the table. Barney walks over to him, holding his ventriloquist dummy. The others continue to chatter and laugh in the background. "My Bambina" continues.

BARNEY *(Offscreen, through the dummy)* Hey! What a spread! Hi, Gloria, wait a second, I'll be right with you. *(To Danny)* Hey, Danny, thanks *(Onscreen, standing next to Danny)* a lot for the invite. Boy, Thanksgiving sure rolls around fast.
Barney, still moving his dummy's mouth, walks offscreen behind Danny, who is opening up his bottle of beer. The music gets louder; Danny looks thoughtful, his face framed by the dark doorway.

The film cuts from Danny's face to the outside of his apartment building. A taxi and several other cars are lined up waiting for the light to change. People are bundled up. They cross the street; they walk down the sidewalk. It is snowing lightly. Danny comes out of his building in his shirt. He looks around, then starts to run down the sidewalk and across the street. He runs faster, past the Oyster Bar Restaurant, past other storefronts. Cars pass in front of him, obscuring him momentarily. The music swells as he runs past a hair salon, past a boarded-up building, past a grocery store. He continues to run; Tina is seen in front of him, walking slowly. He catches up to her, his arm going around her waist, in front of the . . . Carnegie Deli. She starts to pull away, he stops her. They talk. People and cars pass by. Danny takes Tina's arm. They walk off together back the way they came.

The music becomes softer. A few pedestrians walk by. Some cars, a truck, and a taxi drive past. People enter the deli. The snow continues to fall as the comics' voices are heard. As they laugh and talk, the CARNEGIE DELICATESSEN/RESTAURANT *sign flashes on and off.*

SANDY'S VOICE-OVER Well, that's my Danny Rose story.

CORBETT'S VOICE-OVER Unbelievable.

HOWARD'S VOICE-OVER Fantastic.

SANDY'S VOICE-OVER The man is a living legend. Do you know that only six months ago, they gave him the single greatest honor you can get in the Broadway area?

HOWARD'S VOICE-OVER Why? What's that?

SANDY'S VOICE-OVER Look at the menu. At this very delicatessen, they named a sandwich after him. The Danny Rose special.

MORTY'S VOICE-OVER Oh, sure. Probably a cream cheese on a bagel with marinara sauce.

The film fades to black. White credits appear on the black screen as the comics continue to talk and laugh and remember Danny Rose.

HOWARD'S VOICE-OVER He deserves it, he deserves it.

WILL'S VOICE-OVER Yeah.

JACKIE'S VOICE-OVER No.

SANDY'S VOICE-OVER Did you ever go to one of his Thanksgiving parties?

JACK'S VOICE-OVER Once.

SANDY'S VOICE-OVER Anybody go? Did you go?

HOWARD'S VOICE-OVER One, one time.

WILL'S VOICE-OVER I went, yes.

JACK'S VOICE-OVER Yeah, yeah, where they, where they have the frozen turkey, right?

HOWARD'S VOICE-OVER Yes. Sorry.

CORBETT'S VOICE-OVER Economical, but a lot of laughs, lot of laughs, lot of laughs.

WILL'S VOICE-OVER Cranberry sauce made like a rocket.

HOWARD'S VOICE-OVER You have to dethaw the corn. *(Laughs)*

CORBETT'S VOICE-OVER Ah, it was incredible.

MORTY'S VOICE-OVER Listen.

ONE OF THE COMICS' VOICE-OVER What?

JACKIE'S VOICE-OVER Nice . . . *(Trails off)*

MORTY'S VOICE-OVER Excuse me. Before we go any further . . .

SANDY'S VOICE-OVER Huh?

MORTY'S VOICE-OVER . . . may I ask you a favor?

SANDY'S VOICE-OVER Sir.

MORTY'S VOICE-OVER Can we go home now? I'm tired.

SANDY'S VOICE-OVER Oh, what are you talking about?

WILL'S VOICE-OVER We're having laughs. What a time to go home.

SANDY'S VOICE-OVER I haven't seen you in a hundred and ten years. Stay.

MORTY'S VOICE-OVER Let's go home. Let me tell you here, I have to go to Atlantic City tomorrow.

CORBETT'S VOICE-OVER I'll get the check. I'll take care of it.

HOWARD'S VOICE-OVER Hold it.

ONE OF THE COMICS' VOICE-OVER Oh, really?!

JACKIE'S VOICE-OVER Yeah, yeah . . . *(Trails off)*

ONE OF THE COMICS' VOICE-OVER Whoops.

SANDY'S VOICE-OVER Oh, a national holiday. Corbett has the check. My, my.

HOWARD'S VOICE-OVER Maybe you could get a discount.

CORBETT'S VOICE-OVER Oh, but for these kinds of laughs, I figure it's worth the price.

MORTY'S VOICE-OVER Well, we'll do it again tomorrow.

As the remaining credits pop on and off the screen, "Agita" begins to play, changing midway through the credits to "Funiculi, Funicula."

Cast Featured

The Comics

CORBETT MONICA
HOWARD STORM
MORTY GUNTY
WILL JORDAN
JACKIE GAYLE
JACK ROLLINS
SANDY BARON

PAUL GRECO
FRANK RENZULLI
OLGA BARBUTO
EDWIN BORDO
PETER CASTELLOTTI
CRAIG VANDENBURGH
HERB REYNOLDS
GERALD SCHOENFELD
SANDY RICHMAN
GINA DEANGELIS
MILTON BERLE

Music Supervisor
DICK HYMAN

"Agita" & "My Bambina" Written and Performed by
NICK APOLLO FORTE

Production Manager
FREDRIC B. BLANKFEIN

First Assistant Director
THOMAS REILLY

Second Assistant Director
JAMES CHORY

Unit Production Manager
EZRA SWERDLOW

Location Coordinator
TIMOTHY MARSHALL BOURNE

Additional Second Assistant Directors
LES BANDA
JONATHAN FILLEY

Set Director	LES BLOOM
Chief Set Director	DAVE WEINMAN
Set Dresser	KEVIN McCARTHY
Master Scenic Artist	JAMES SORICE
Production Coordinator	HELEN ROBIN
Script Supervisor	KAY CHAPIN
Production Associate	GAIL SICILIA
Camera Operator	DICK MINGALONE
Assistant Cameraman	DOUGLAS C. HART
Second Assistant Cameraman	BAB PAONE
Still Photographer	BRIAN HAMILL
Production Sound Mixer	JAMES SABAT
Boom Man	LOUIS SABAT
Sound Recordist	FRANK GRAZIADEI
Accordion Soloist	DOMINIC CORTESE
Re-Recording Mixer	RICHARD DIOR TRANS/AUDIO INC.
Music Recording Engineer	ROY B. YOKELSON NATIONAL RECORDING STUDIOS, INC.
Key Grip	BOB WARD

Dolly Grip	RONALD BURKE
Construction Grip	ARNE OLSEN
Gaffer	RAY QUINLAN
Best Boy	JAMES FITZPATRICK
Property Master	JAMES MAZZOLA
Property Man	KENNETH VOGT
Makeup Design	FERN BUCHNER
Hair Design	ROMAINE GREENE
Assistant to Mr. Kurland	TOM McKINLEY
Men's Wardrobe Supervisor	BILL CHRISTIANS
Woman's Wardrobe Supervisor	PATRICIA EIBEN
Assistant Production Coordinator	TODD MICHAEL THALER
Assistant to Mr. Allan	JANE MARTIN
Art Department Coordinator	JOAN LOPATE
Casting Associate	PAULA HEROLD
Extras Casting	NAVARRO BERTONI CASTING
Sound Effects	HASTINGS SOUND EDITORIAL, INC.
Supervising Sound Editor	DON SABLE
Assistant Sound Editor	LYNN SABLE
Apprentice Sound Editor	NEIL WENGER
Assistant Film Editors	JEFFREY STERN
	RICHARD NORD
Apprentice Film Editor	A. DEAN BELL
Transportation Captain	WILLIAM CURRY
DGA Trainee	CARL KABAT
Studio Manager	JAMES GREENHUT
Production Staff	JAMES A. DAVIS
	JOSEPH PIERSON
	NICHOLAS BERNSTEIN
	LEE GOTTSEGEN
	TOM SWERDLOW
Location Auditor	JOSEPH HARTWICK
Assistant Location Auditor	PETER LOMBARDI
Production Accountant	AMY LUBCHANSKY

Insurance	ALBERT G. RUBEN INSURANCE CO., INC.
Dailies Processing	DU ART LABORATORIES
Release Prints	DELUXE LABORATORIES
Optical Effects	CINOPTICALS
Titles	THE OPTICAL HOUSE N.Y.
Negative Matching	J.G. FILMS
Projectionist	CARL TURNQUEST

The Producers Gratefully Acknowledge and Wish
To Thank the Following for Their Assistance:
Lenses and Panaflex® Cameras by Panavision®
Charles Ross, Inc.
General Camera Corp.
Empire Custom Coach for Constructing
Automobile Rig
Messmore & Damon, Inc.
Variety Scenic Studios

And Also Thank:
Macy's Thanksgiving Day Parade
Mayor's Office of Film, Theater and Broadcasting
The New York State Office of
Motion Picture and Television Development
The New Jersey Motion Picture
and Television Commission

The Cast

WOODY ALLEN	*Danny Rose*
MIA FARROW	*Tina Vitale*
NICK APOLLO FORTE	*Lou Canova*
SANDY BARON	*Himself*
CORBETT MONICA	*Himself*
JACKIE GAYLE	*Himself*
MORTY GUNTY	*Himself*
WILL JORDAN	*Himself*

HOWARD STORM	*Himself*
JACK ROLLINS	*Himself*
MILTON BERLE	*Himself*
CRAIG VANDENBURGH	*Ray Webb*
HERB REYNOLDS	*Barney Dunn*
PAUL GRECO	*Vito Rispoli*
FRANK RENZULLI	*Joe Rispoli*
EDWIN BORDO	*Johnny Rispoli*
GINA DEANGELIS	*Johnny's Mother*
PETER CASTELLOTTI	*Hood at Warehouse*
SANDY RICHMAN	*Teresa*
GERALD SCHOENFELD	*Sid Bacharach*
OLGA BARBATO	*Angelina*
DAVID KISSELL	*Phil Chomsky*
GLORIA PARKER	*Water Glass Virtuoso*
BOB & ETTA ROLLINS	*Balloon Act*
BOB WEIL	*Herbie Jayson*
DAVID KIESERMAN	*Ralph, Club Owner*
MARK HARDWICK	*Blind Xylophonist*
ALBA BALLARD	*Bird Lady*
MAURICE SHROG	*Hypnotist*
BELLE BERGER	*Lady in Trance*
HERSCHEL ROSEN	*Lady's Husband*
JOE FRANKLIN	*Himself*
CECILIA AMERLING	*Fan in Dressing Room*
MAGGIE RANONE	*Lou's Daughter*
CHARLES D'AMODIO	*Lou's Son*
JOIE GALLO	*Angelina's Assistant*
CARL PISTILLI	*Tommy's Brother*
LUCY IACONO	*Tommy's Mother*
JULIA BARBUTO	*Tropical Fish Lady*
NICHOLAS PANTANO	*Greeter at Party*
ROCCO PANTANO	*Greeter at Party*
TONY TURCA	*Rocco*

GILDA TORTERELLO	*Annie*
RONALD MACCONE	*Vincent*
ANTOINETTE RAFFONE	*Vincent's Wife*
MICHAEL BADALUCCO	*Money Ripper*
RICHARD LANZANO	*Money Ripper*
DOM MATTEO	*Carmine*
CAMILLE SAVIOLA	*Lady at Party*
SHEILA BOND	*Lady at Party*
BETTY ROSOTTI	*Lady at Party*
HOWARD COSELL	*Himself*
JOHN DOUMANIAN	*Waldorf Manager*
GARY REYNOLDS	*Manager's Friend*
DIANE ZOLTEN	*Fan at Waldorf*
WILLIAM PAULSON	*Fan at Waldorf*
GEORGE AXLER	*Fan at Waldorf*
LEO STEINER	*Deli Owner*

The story, all names, characters and incidents portrayed in this production are fictitious. No identification with actual persons is intended or should be inferred.

This motion picture is protected under the laws of the United States and other countries and its unauthorized distribution or exhibition may result in severe liability and criminal prosecution.

(emblem) (I.A.T.S.E. emblem)

MOTION PICTURE ASSOCIATION OF AMERICA
Approved No. 26911

AN ORION PICTURES Release

THE PURPLE ROSE OF CAIRO

The Orion logo, a circle of stars in a starry sky, appears on the screen, followed by the official AN ORION PICTURES RELEASE. *The screen goes black-and-white, credits pop on and off. All the while, Fred Astaire sings "Cheek to Cheek" in the background.*

FRED ASTAIRE'S VOICE-OVER *(Singing)* "Heaven, I'm in heaven / And my heart beats so that I can hardly speak. / And I seem to find the happiness I seek / When we're out together dancing cheek to cheek . . ."

A
Jack Rollins and Charles H. Joffe
Production

THE PURPLE ROSE OF CAIRO

Starring

MIA FARROW

JEFF DANIELS

DANNY AIELLO

With

DIANNE WIEST
VAN JOHNSON
ZOE CALDWELL
JOHN WOOD
STEPHANIE FARROW
ALEXANDER H. COHEN
CAMILLE SAVIOLA
KAREN AKERS
MILO O'SHEA
DEBORAH RUSH
IRVING METZMAN
JOHN ROTHMAN
MICHAEL TUCKER
ANNIE JOE EDWARDS
PETER McROBBIE
JULIANA DONALD

and

EDWARD HERRMANN

Associate Producers
MICHAEL PEYSER
GAIL SICILIA

Casting
JULIET TAYLOR

Original Music By
DICK HYMAN

Editor
SUSAN E. MORSE

Costume Designer
JEFFREY KURLAND

Production Designer
STUART WURTZEL

Director of Photography
GORDON WILLIS, A.S.C.

Executive Producer
CHARLES H. JOFFE

Produced by
ROBERT GREENHUT

Written and Directed by
WOODY ALLEN

While Fred Astaire continues singing in the background, the credits fade out, replaced by a large, old-fashioned movie poster, a montage of drawn faces and scenes: In the shadows, to the left of an elongated black shape, is a man wearing a pith helmet; next to his face is the Sphinx, complete with a palm tree. The camera moves past the Egyptian scene, past the black shape, to a drawing of two men in tuxedos.

One holds a champagne glass. Behind them is an elegant car, a hint of city glamour parked next to a streetlamp in front of a faint city skyline. The camera next moves up the elongated black shape to reveal an oversize sophisticated woman; the black shape is her long slinky dress. Above her sleek bobbed hairdo is the movie's title, THE PURPLE ROSE OF CAIRO. *Parts of the movie credits are seen between the drawings, including:*

WITH
GIL SHEPHERD
BEATRICE KELLY
SIDNEY OLIVER
KATE PAYSON

As Fred Astaire croons in the background, the film cuts to Cecilia's face, staring dreamily at the now offscreen movie poster. Behind her is a parked car in the street; pedestrians pass on the sidewalk. As she gazes, lost in her own world, one gloved hand to her lips, a loud clunking sound is heard; the song abruptly stops. Cecilia, startled, looks down.

The camera moves back, revealing the front of the Jewel Theater with its marquee. A ladder is leaning against the marquee; a man is putting in the letters of its newest attraction: THE PURPLE ROSE OF CAIRO. *The theater manager walks over to Cecilia, picking up the letter that "clunked" and dropped. Cars and pedestrians loudly pass by on the street.*

THEATER MANAGER *(Picking up the dropped letter, to Cecilia)* Oh, Cecilia, be careful. Are you all right?

CECILIA *(Walking away, down the street)* Yes.

THEATER MANAGER *(Calling after her)* You're gonna like this one. It's better than last week, more romantic.

CUT TO:
INTERIOR. DINER—DAY.

A woman's face, in glasses and cloche hat, fills the screen. The sounds of clattering dishes and conversation are dimly heard.

WOMAN *(Impatiently, looking annoyed)* Miss, I wanted oatmeal before my scrambled eggs.
The camera cuts to a larger view. The woman is sitting in a booth. Cecilia, in a waitress uniform, picks up the plate of scrambled eggs, scurrying away as she apologizes. She walks past other diners, a few sitting at the counter, to the kitchen side of the counter, where Jane, also in a waitress uniform, is busy wiping its top. Cecilia begins dishing some oatmeal from a large pot into a bowl. The hum of the customers continues; the diner is busy. The diner boss cooks at a grill in the background.

CECILIA Oh, sorry, I'll get it right away, sorry.

MAN *(Offscreen)* I get cereal too . . . and a doughnut.

CECILIA *(Overlapping)* Oh . . . cereal and a doughnut, right. *(To Jane)* Listen, there's a new movie at the Jewel starting tonight.

JANE *(Shaking her head, wiping the counter)* I didn't even get to see last week's.

CECILIA *(Turning to look at Jane, still spooning her oatmeal)* Oh, you missed it? It was wonderful! I love Jane Froman, and James Melton plays— First he's a hotel porter and then he becomes a radio singer and then he becomes an opera singer. The music was just beautiful. *(Places the full bowl on the counter)*
While Cecilia talks and spoons, Jane is busy pouring coffee, bending over Cecilia's back to get a plate. The two continue to chatter as they fill the customers' orders, retrieving plates, dishing out food, placing doughnuts from a tray onto individual plates.

JANE *(Giving a counter customer some utensils)* You know the one that I like, is-is *OK America.*

CECILIA *(Holding a doughnut, enthusiastically)* Oh, yeah, I saw that twice. That was *great*! When she threatens to kill Lew Ayres, and the—

JANE *(Interrupting, scraping a plate)* I love Lew Ayres's looks. Do you think he's married?

CECILIA Is he mar— Are you crazy? *(Wiping her hands on her apron)* Yes, he's married to Ginger Rogers. God. They got married on a boat off the island of Catalina. *(Dishing out another bowl of oatmeal, while Jane wipes the counter)* They live in Beverly Hills and sometimes holiday in Spain. He used to be married to Lola Lane, but Ginger's better for him. *(Shaking her head)* She's so lovely.

MAN *(Offscreen, overlapping)* Where's my toast?

CECILIA *(Turning, to offscreen man)* Oh, Coming right up, one second. *(Turning off the stove)* Ginger used to be married to Jack Col—

DINER BOSS *(Offscreen, interrupting)* Let's go, girls. Let's go, Cecilia.

The owner, a short, portly man in an apron, squeezes past the two women.

CECILIA *(Overlapping, picking up some toast)* Sorry.

DINER BOSS *(To Jane as he passes her)* Your sister is slow.

JANE *(Stacking dishes below the counter, looking up at her boss)* But she's still learning.

DINER BOSS *(Picking up a tray of egg cartons near the stove)* Ladies, there's a depression on. *(Squeezing past the women again, going back to his grill)* There are a lot of other people who would like this job if you can't handle it.

CECILIA *(Turning to look at his retreating back)* No, I can handle it. It's okay. *(To Jane, who walks past Cecilia around the counter)* Ginger used to be married to Jack Culpepper, *(Balancing a bowl and a plate while trying to butter a piece of toast)* who I think took out Ruth Chatterton before she married George—Oh, I—

Cecilia stops in midstream as a plate crashes to the floor. She looks down in dismay.

DINER BOSS *(Offscreen)* Look, that's the second one this week.

CECILIA *(Shaking her head, overlapping the boss)* I'm sorry. *(Bending down, offscreen)* I'll pick it all up.

DINER BOSS *(Offscreen, over the now empty counter)* Come on, Cecilia, shape up.

Light jazz begins to play as the film cuts to the outside of a factory, its dismal brown walls contrasting with the bright snow on the ground. A stack of lumber leans on the factory wall. Three men, in coats and caps, are seen in the distance pitching pennies against the wall. Near them is a makeshift coal heater. As they talk, engrossed in their game, the film moves in closer.

PENNY PITCHER #1 All right now, Monk. Start pitching pennies.

Monk, a burly man in a cap, pitches his pennies.

PENNY PITCHER #1 *(Reacting)* Ohhh!

Monk walks over to the wall to retrieve his pennies. He kneels down.

PENNY PITCHER #2 *(Offscreen)* Hey, Monk. Here comes your wife.

Monk looks up, at the offscreen camera, as the film cuts to his point of view: Cecilia, carrying a bundle of laundry. She looks tired as she watches the offscreen Monk.

MONK *(Walking over to Cecilia, his arms outstretched)* Boy, am I glad to see you. You got any dough?

CECILIA *(Offscreen)* Oh, tips weren't so good *(Onscreen, walking up to Monk)* today.

MONK Come on, give me something. I'm busted. *(Takes the bundle of laundry from Cecilia)*

CECILIA *(Rummaging through her purse)* Hmm. I-I hear there's some jobs opening up over at the ice factory.

MONK *(Shaking his head, pointing to the air)* No, there's nothin'. I was there.

CECILIA Yeah?

MONK Yeah, I was there. All right?

Cecilia continues to rummage in her bag while Monk, impatient, looks back at his friends, who can be heard playing indistinctly in the background.

CECILIA Harriet Rufus says all you guys do all day is just pitch pennies and-and make passes at the girls who walk by.

MONK *(Chuckling, looking around)* Well, Harriet Rufus is a douche bag.

CECILIA *(Putting some change in Monk's outstretched palm)* Listen, I-I-I got to save the rest for groceries and stuff, okay?

MONK *(Overlapping, handing the bundle back to Cecilia)* Yeah, okay, yeah, right. *(Checking out the bag as he puts the change in his pocket)* Ya got it? *(Taking Cecilia's arm and moving her away)* What are you doin' here?

CECILIA *(Looking up at Monk as they walk)* Oh, you want to go to the movies tonight? There's-there's an early show.

MONK *(Shaking his head)* I can't, I can't.

CECILIA *(Overlapping)* How come?

MONK *(Gesturing)* Well, the guys are coming over tonight.

CECILIA Again?

MONK *(Gesturing, moving slightly away)* What, ya don't like it?

CECILIA *(Looking down)* Well, all you, all you do is . . . drink and play dice *(Gesturing)* and . . . I-I wind up getting smacked.

MONK *(Pausing for a beat, gesturing)* Well, I got to get even, don't I? I owe everybody in town.

They stop walking and face each other. As Cecilia speaks, Monk looks away, sighing and putting his hands in his pockets. The penny pitchers are seen playing in the background.

CECILIA You're never home anymore except to play dice and cards. Meanwhile, I gotta, I gotta take in extra laundry after work to pay the rent.

MONK *(Getting louder, defensively, gesturing)* Well, what do you want? Did I close the factory?

CECILIA *(Sighing)* You didn't used to be like this, Monk.

MONK *(Gesturing)* Well, I got a lot on my mind.

PENNY PITCHER #1 *(In background)* Pick 'em up.

MONK *(Gesturing)* You think I like scratching around for work? *(Looking around)* Livin' like a bum the last two years?

CECILIA *(Gesturing, looking down)* I don't know how much longer I can go on like this, you know?

MONK *(Overlapping, sighing)* Listen, the country will get back working again. Things are bound to get better. *(Taking Cecilia's hand from the bundle)* I promise.

CECILIA *(Overlapping)* Yeah.

MONK *(Holding Cecilia's hand in both of his)* You know I'm crazy about you, huh?

CECILIA You never pay any attention to me anymore. *(Looking intensely at Monk as he sighs and glances away, removing his hands and thrusting them in his pockets)* That's why I thought if-if we could go to the movies tonight, you know, you could forget your troubles a little.

MONK *(Overlapping)* Yeah, yeah, forget my troubles. *(Gesturing emphatically)* Cecilia, you like sitting through that junk, okay? I'm gonna shoot crap, okay?

CECILIA *(Sighing)* Tch.

MONK *(Starting to move away)* Go to the movie by yourself.

CECILIA *(Turning to look at Monk)* You make passes at the girls who go by?

MONK *(Overlapping, loudly)* Hey, look, you're not my boss. And don't give me that look. *(Pointing at Cecilia)* You'd think I was a criminal. *(Gesturing)* Come on, give us a hug, just one, come on. *(Hugging the pouting Cecilia, patting her back)* All right? Good. And don't come home late. *(Moving away, releasing Cecilia's hand as she walks away)* I worry. All right? *(To the offscreen Cecilia, waving and smiling)* See you later? *(To the penny pitchers, as he turns and starts to run towards them, clapping his hands)* Let's go.

Upbeat jazz begins to play as the movie cuts to the outside of the Jewel Theater. It's night and the marquee is brightly lit. Inside a border of moving lights is the Jewel's attraction: THE PURPLE ROSE OF CAIRO / R. TALMADGE / RAYBURN / MORGAN. *People mill about, buying tickets and standing underneath the marquee. Some cars pass by in the street as the film cuts to the window of the ticket booth, as seen from its interior. A man wearing a fedora and glasses stands in front of the window. His head and shoulders fill the screen.*

MAN Two, please.

He takes his tickets and leaves as a woman behind him steps up to the window. She wears bright red lipstick.

WOMAN Two.

Cecilia is next. She approaches the window and leans over.

CECILIA Just one tonight, please, Doris. *(Taking her ticket)* Thank you.

CUT TO:
INTERIOR. MOVIE THEATER LOBBY—NIGHT.

Moviegoers are seen handing their tickets to an offscreen usher as they walk into the main lobby. Cecilia opens the lobby doors from the outside and joins the line. She is beaming.

CECILIA *(Handing the usher her ticket)* Evening, Mr. Ruskin.

The camera follows Cecilia as she walks past the now onscreen usher and he tears her ticket and hands her the stub. She walks through the crowded lobby to the concession stand. She buys a box of popcorn from the woman behind the counter, then walks through the swinging doors into the auditorium. The jazz music continues; people walk past the camera.

The film moves inside the auditorium. The house lights are still on. The theater is full. People sit chatting in their seats, getting settled; one man stands up and takes off his coat. Cecilia is one of the crowd, walking down the aisle and taking a seat. The jazz stops, and for a moment, only the soft buzz of conversation is heard. As Cecilia settles in her seat, the house lights dim, the light from the projectionist's booth shines down on the theater, and the music from the movie begins.

The film shifts to the movie screen, as seen over the heads of the audience. The screen shows the RKO logo—an antenna on top of a globe—bearing the legend AN RKO RADIO PICTURE. *This fades into a title credit—black script on a plain background. The camera moves in closer to the movie screen so it can be read:* THE PURPLE ROSE OF CAIRO. *It looks like a large calling card; a hand picks it up to reveal another underneath:* STARRING ROBERT TALMADGE / ANNA RAYBURN / TODD MORGAN.

The film cuts quickly to Cecilia, who is absorbed in the offscreen movie, sitting among the other patrons, as her image dissolves to the movie screen. The Purple Rose of Cairo, *seen over the heads of the audience, is in progress. The movie music becomes an exotic Egyptian tune, played in the background. On the black-and-white screen, Henry, a sophisticated playboy/writer, sits on a piano bench in a penthouse living room. His arms are draped on a white piano. He wears a tuxedo and smokes a cigarette. The music stops as he speaks his lines.*

HENRY *(Looking offscreen)* Jason, I'm bored. *(Exhaling, looking out at the camera)* I'm bored with cocktail parties and opening nights.

The film cuts closer to the movie in progress so that only The Purple Rose of Cairo *fills the screen. The audience is no longer seen.*

HENRY I'm bored with evenings at the opera and weekends at the races.

JASON *(Offscreen)* A few days in . . .

As Jason begins to speak, the movie screen cuts to him behind an Art Deco bar. A jovial man, he too wears a tuxedo as he takes two glasses of champagne and carries them over to Henry. He passes some Art Deco objets d'art on pedestals, a spiral staircase, and floor-to-ceiling windows offering a magnificent view of the Manhattan skyline at night. Henry, gracefully sprawled at the piano, is in front of glass doors leading to the terrace. Jason continues to speak as he walks over to Henry, handing him a glass of champagne.

JASON *(Continuing onscreen)* . . . Paris might be just the thing to get the creative juices flowing again. I can have George cable the Ritz for the usual suite.

HENRY *(Taking the glass of champagne)* I'm not talking about Paris. I'm talking about someplace completely different.

The film cuts back to the audience in color. People are engrossed in the offscreen movie; a man nibbles popcorn.

HENRY *(Offscreen)* Like Morocco, or Egypt.

RITA *(Offscreen)* Ooo . . .

The film cuts back to The Purple Rose of Cairo *in black-and-white. Henry is still at the piano; Jason still stands nearby. As the offscreen Rita continues to talk, Henry takes a sip of champagne; he looks offscreen at her.*

RITA *(Offscreen)* . . . ooh. A boat trip down the Nile.

The camera shows Rita, a blonde-on-blonde in a slinky dress, as she walks past the objets d'art and the spiral staircase towards the two men.

RITA *(Onscreen)* Sounds so romantic. *(Moving her hands in an angular Egyptian walk)* I've got just the dress to wear to the Pyramids.

The movie audience laughs offscreen as Rita stops at a white couch in the foreground. She daintily picks up a cigarette from a holder on the coffee table and turns her head towards Henry and Jason.

HENRY *(Overlapping the audience's laughter, putting his champagne glass on the piano and walking over to Rita, Jason following behind him)* Hey, we could leave next week. Spend a couple of weeks there. *(Gesturing and smoking)* Maybe stop in Casablanca or Tangiers as long as we're hopping around and still be back in time for the opening of my new play.

RITA *(Smoking her cigarette)* Ooooh.

JASON *(Holding his champagne glass)* To Cairo and Morocco and Tangiers . . .

The film cuts to the audience in color, to Cecilia looking up at the offscreen movie, totally absorbed.

JASON *(Offscreen)* . . . to all the exotic and romantic places in the world.

As the offscreen movie continues, Cecilia's face dissolves to other moviegoers in the audience. A couple, engrossed in the movie, are smiling; the woman mouths her approval as she stares at the offscreen action. The man touches her arm. The exotic music of the Purple Rose of Cairo *soundtrack begins.*

HENRY *(Offscreen)* Hey, there's another room in here.

The film next shows the black-and-white screen and the full-color backs of the audience in the theater. The moviegoers are looking up at the

screen, which now shows Henry, Jason, and an extravagantly dressed Rita in a pyramid. Henry holds up a flashlight; he holds Rita's hand. Part of an Egyptian statue is seen; hieroglyphics cover the walls.

RITA *(Looking at the walls around her)* Oh, isn't it divine? Everything's so perfectly preserved.

JASON *(Looking around)* It's quite lovely. I just don't want to suddenly feel a bandaged hand around my throat.
The audience laughs as the black-and-white screen cuts to a different area of the pyramid wall—where Tom Baxter, in pith helmet and khaki, walks through a narrow doorway. He holds up a lantern. Rita, now offscreen, gasps loudly.

TOM Hi there. Who are you?
The film cuts to Cecilia in the audience, eating her popcorn and watching the offscreen action with eyes wide.

HENRY *(Offscreen)* Oh. We're sightseeing. We thought we were alone.

JASON *(Offscreen)* You gave me quite a start.
The film cuts back to The Purple Rose of Cairo. *The black-and-white movie fills the screen.*

TOM Oh, I'm awfully sorry. *(Walking over to the trio)* Tom Baxter—explorer, adventurer. I'm doing a little archeological work.

RITA A real-life explorer.

TOM I've come in search of the purple rose of Cairo. *(Gesturing)* It's an old legend that's fascinated me for years.
The film cuts to the audience in color, looking up at the offscreen movie. A man smokes a cigarette as he watches, the smoke momentarily hiding his face.

TOM *(Offscreen)* A pharaoh had a rose painted purple for his queen, and now the story says . . .
The film moves back to the black-and-white Purple Rose of Cairo.

TOM *(Continuing, onscreen)* . . . purple roses grow wild at her tomb.

RITA *(Reacting)* How romantic.

TOM And you?

HENRY Ah, we're going back to New York tomorrow. *(Nodding)* It's been a refreshing two weeks.

JASON *(Gesturing)* Say, we could bring him back to New York to meet the Countess. She *loves* anything in a pith helmet.

HENRY Right.
The offscreen movie audience laughs, reacting.

TOM I *will* say it's tempting.

HENRY Oh, then it's settled. You can explain to us what we've been looking at for the last two weeks, and we can take you nightclubbing.

TOM *(Shaking his head)* It's so impulsive but . . . I'll come. *(Laughing)* Why not? I mean, what's life without a little risk-taking?

Upbeat, swinging music begins in the Purple Rose of Cairo *soundtrack as the film cuts back to Cecilia in color, in the audience, eating her popcorn almost automatically as she stares at the offscreen movie.*

TOM *(Offscreen)* Who knows? A fortune-teller predicted I'd fall in love in New York.

Cecilia's face dissolves to the face of a trumpet player blowing his horn in black-and-white: We are viewing a later scene in The Purple Rose of Cairo. *As the trumpet player, accompanied by a big-band sound, plays on, the black-and-white movie cuts to the entrance of a restaurant/nightclub. Jason, Rita, Henry, a friend of Henry's named Larry, the Countess, and Tom are gathered around the mustachioed maitre d', Arturo. All are in formal dress except Tom; he still wears his pith helmet.*

JASON Table for six, please, Arturo.

ARTURO Six, sir.

Arturo leads the group through the crowded club. A glamorous crowd sits at surrounding tables; some people are dancing to the big-band sound. The sounds of people enjoying themselves are heard over the band, which is seen playing in the background. Potted palms line the walls.

The film quickly cuts to Cecilia watching the offscreen movie. She chews some popcorn; she is mesmerized by the screen.

As Cecilia stares at the screen, the film cuts back to the movie in progress. The group is sitting down at a round table near a railing.

As they settle down in their chairs, smiling and chatting indistinctly, the music stops. The group begins to applaud as the offscreen band-leader begins an introduction.

BANDLEADER *(Offscreen)* Now, ladies and gentlemen, the Copacabana is proud to present . . .
The movie cuts to the bandleader, a chubby man in a white tuxedo, in front of his band.

BANDLEADER *(Continuing)* . . . Miss Kitty Haynes!
The bandleader turns to his band and starts to conduct the next number. Applause is heard as the glamorous, dark-haired Kitty Haynes walks out on the floor in front of the band. She stops by the bandleader and, looking out at the offscreen patrons, begins to sing. She wears black over-the-elbow gloves and a floor-length dress.

KITTY *(Singing)* "Ours could be a different sort of love affair / Those busybodies couldn't help but stare. / Still we wouldn't care, dear. / Let's just take the dare, dear."
While Kitty sings, the screen cuts to the group's table. A waiter passes in front of the camera; an engrossed Tom stares at the offscreen Kitty. Henry and Rita have a private conversation while they watch the offscreen singer.

RITA *(Reacting to the singing)* Mmmmm.

HENRY *(Aside, to Rita, as he hands her a cigarette)* I think our poetic little archeologist is about to make a discovery.

RITA Well, ain't life swell. *(Looking across the table as Henry lights his cigarette and laughs)* Hey, open the champagne. I feel like getting plushed to the scuppers.
Henry lights Rita's cigarette as the movie audience laughs, reacting. The film cuts to a view of the black-and-white screen with the movie audience, in color, in the theater, watching the screen. Kitty, in the black-and-white movie, is back on the screen at center stage.

KITTY *(Singing, continuing)* "Let's take it one day at a time / And who cares just how it turns out."

CUT TO:
INTERIOR. DINER—DAY.

Cecilia is staring off into space behind the counter. She dreamily dries a solitary dish. Her boss can be partially seen on the screen, working at the grill. The sounds of chattering customers and clattering dishes can be heard.

MAN *(Offscreen, over the indistinct diner sounds)* Ah, check please . . . Ah, miss, could I have the check, please?

DINER BOSS *(Angrily, walking over to Cecilia and gesturing)* Come on, the man wants his check.

CECILIA *(After a beat)* Oh, sorry. *(Fumbling in her pocket for the check, then handing it to the offscreen customer)* Sorry.
Cecilia walks away, down the counter, past another customer sipping some coffee. She stops near Jane, still drying her dish, still in a dreamy state.

JANE *(Busily clearing the counter)* So what were you thinking about?

CECILIA Oh, a penthouse, the desert . . .

JANE *(Shaking her head)* Oh, God.

CECILIA *(Continuing, stacking the dish on a shelf above the stove)* . . . kissing on a dance floor.

JANE *(Smiling as she scrapes a plate)* So you did go to the movies last night after all.

CECILIA *(Fingering the towel she was using)* The people were so beautiful. *(Shaking her head)* They, they spoke so cleverly and they do such romantic things.

JANE *(Overlapping)* Really?

CECILIA *(Moving closer to Jane, gesturing)* Listen, well I mean, the one they've got playing Tom Baxter, he was so cute.

JANE *(Overlapping, as a customer walks past the camera)* Ah, I'm sorry I missed it.

CECILIA *(Looking quickly around her, then back at Jane, touching her arm)* Hey, you want to go to the movies after work?

JANE *(Overlapping)* Yes, I'd love to.

CECILIA *(Nodding)* I'd love to see it again. Let's go then.

DINER BOSS *(Offscreen, overlapping the women)* Come on, what is this, a social club? *(Walking onscreen to Jane and Cecilia, who puts the towel on her neck, letting him pass)* I got a sink full of dirty dishes. Come on, girls, *(Walking past them offscreen, impatiently)* come on.

Jane and Cecilia, looking down, get busy, picking up the dirty dishes on the counter. The film cuts to the outside of the Jewel Theater. Jane and Cecilia are at the ticket booth buying their tickets.

CECILIA *(To the ticket booth clerk, indistinctly)* Thanks a lot.

They walk into the theater. It's still daylight. Some cars are parked on the street; a few cars and pedestrians pass. Light music plays in the background.

The film cuts to the inside of the movie theater. Jane and Cecilia are in their seats, eating popcorn and watching The Purple Rose of Cairo, *which is in progress.*

TOM *(Offscreen)* Well, I am *impressed*!

The film cuts to the black-and-white movie screen. Tom, in his pith helmet and khakis, his hands on his hips, is looking around the penthouse living room, impressed.

TOM *(Onscreen)* I really am. You have yourself quite a place here. *(Walking down into the center of the room, the spectacular view partially seen behind him)* You know, I still can't get over the fact that twenty-four hours ago I was in an Egyptian tomb, I didn't know any of you wonderful people, and here I am now. *(Shaking his head in wonderment)* I'm on the verge of a madcap Manhattan weekend.
The camera cuts to Jason at the bar, mixing a pitcher of martinis.

JASON *(To the offscreen Tom)* I hope you like your martinis very dry.
The camera cuts back to Tom.

TOM *(To the offscreen Jason)* Oh, no, no thanks. Uh . . . I think I'll wait for that glass of champagne at the Copacabana. *(Nods emphatically)*

CUT TO:
INTERIOR. CECILIA'S APARTMENT—NIGHT.

A curtained front door fills the screen. Cecilia's silhouette is seen as she turns a key in the lock, then walks inside. A wall lamp is seen in the hallway beyond the door. The apartment itself is dark. There is no music.

CECILIA *(Closing the door behind her)* I'm home, Monk.
Cecilia walks through the dark living room, past a wall shelf holding bric-a-brac, as the camera moves to Monk, half-hidden by the bedroom door, talking to his offscreen wife.

MONK *(Buttoning his shirt)* What are you doing home so early? I thought I said you can go to the movies.
The camera moves back to Cecilia, standing in the darkened room.

CECILIA *(Nodding)* Yeah, I did.
The camera moves back to Monk at the bedroom door as high-pitched laughter is heard—quickly followed by its source: a heavy, blowsy-looking woman named Olga. Still laughing, she moves up behind

Monk, grabbing his arm. She holds a glass of whiskey. Monk, in turn, leans up against the door. They are both doubled over with laughter.

OLGA *(Laughing)* I better go.

Olga, laughing, stumbles into the living room towards Cecilia. She drinks from her glass as she walks.

MONK *(Laughing)* No, don't, stay. *(Offscreen as the camera follows Olga)* This is Cecilia.

Without skipping a beat, Monk walks over to Olga and Cecilia. Without a word, Cecilia walks past Monk and Olga into the offscreen bedroom. Monk holds a deck of cards.

MONK *(Continuing, turning as Cecilia walks off)* Ah, this is, uh, my friend, Olga. Olga's an acrobat. *(Laughs hysterically)*

OLGA *(Overlapping Monk, laughing, gesturing and drinking)* I am not. *(Grunting, picking up her coat from the sofa)* I have to go home.

MONK *(Fanning out the deck of cards)* Oh, no, c'mon, c'mon, I was going to tell your fortune here.

OLGA *(Walking towards the door)* No . . . you're drunk.

MONK *(Following the now offscreen Olga)* Uh, what do you mean drunk? I'm not drunk.

OLGA *(Offscreen, starting to close the front door behind her)* Drunk, drunk.

MONK *(Pointing towards the bedroom)* C'mon, don't worry about her. *(Gesturing)* She's my ball and chain, or she tries to be. *(Standing at the door, opening it wider as he yells down the stairwell to Olga)* Olga, Olga, where the hell are you going? *(Rushing to the couch to pick up his coat)* Hey, Olga, c'mon, I want to show you a card trick.

Olga's hysterical laughter is heard as Monk races down the offscreen stairwell after her.

MONK *(Offscreen)* Olga!

Their laughter echoes up from below; their feet are heard clumping down the stairs. The front door is wide open and a slow-moving Cecilia is seen walking over to it. She closes the door and stands there for a beat, her back to the camera. Tommy Dorsey–like music begins to play and the scene dissolves to an open suitcase on the bed. Cecilia's hands are seen furiously packing. She punches her clothes down flat. The music continues as the film cuts to the front door in the living room. Monk enters, shutting the door behind him. He takes off his coat, looking in the direction of the bedroom. He wears a cap; he has a tentative look on his face.

MONK *(Flinging his coat down and walking into the kitchen area)* Is there any more of that meat loaf left? *(Bending down to look in the refrigerator)* That, uh, stuff you made yesterday was delicious.

The camera moves back to Cecilia, seen through the doorway from Monk's point of view. She is still furiously packing the suitcase on the bed.

MONK *(Offscreen)* What's going on?

CECILIA *(Breathlessly)* I'm moving out.

Cecilia strides through the doorway into the living room, passing Monk in the kitchen before moving offscreen. The sound of a drawer opening and closing is heard. She strides back, past Monk, as he talks to her offscreen figure. He is framed by a doorway and a wall lamp. The sound of another drawer is heard.

MONK *(Gesturing, fumbling with the cap now in his hands)* Now what are you talking about? What's wrong? . . . What? Because of before? *(Walking over to the offscreen Cecilia, gesturing)* Because of Olga, is that it? Because that would be funny. That would be ridiculous. *(Laughing)* I mean, if it's because of Olga, you'd be making a bigger fool out of yourself than you usually are.

CECILIA *(Pushing past Monk, her arms full)* Pardon me.

Cecilia walks back to the bedroom, her back to Monk as she continues to pack. The bedroom is well lit, contrasting with the dark living room where Monk stands.

MONK *(Turning to talk to Cecilia through the doorway, gesturing, partially offscreen)* She's Joe Caruso's sister. And I was just showin' her a card trick.

CECILIA *(Walking back into the living room, glancing at Monk)* Your undershirt's on backwards.

Cecilia strides into the bathroom; the camera follows her as she disappears into the bright room. Monk walks onscreen as he continues to plead his case. He stands in the dark near the bathroom doorway.

MONK *(Offscreen)* I put it on that way *(Onscreen)* this morning. Now listen, Cecilia, you're making a mistake. *(Gesturing, still holding his cap)* All right, I'm sorry. I was drinking. You know how I get when I drink, sweetheart. You think it means I don't love you?

CECILIA *(Striding out of the bathroom, pushing past Monk once again; her arms full of bathroom supplies)* Move.

MONK *(Following Cecilia)* You can't leave. I need you. *(Standing in the doorway of the bedroom as Cecilia, her back to him, puts on a hat in front of a mirror)* And, and you know I love you. Now look, I made a mistake.

CECILIA *(Turning from the mirror to look at Monk, crying)* You don't love me.

MONK Now, baby, c'mon.

CECILIA *(Reacting, crying, her voice raised)* You don't. You treat me bad and you beat up on me. *(Walks out of the room once again, past Monk)*

MONK *(To the offscreen Cecilia, gesturing)* Look, I hit you when you get out of line, and I never just hit you, I always warn you first *(Pointing)* and then if you don't shape up you get whacked.

The camera moves to the front door, where Cecilia is tearfully struggling to get into her coat.

CECILIA I'm leavin'.

MONK *(Offscreen)* Now listen, Cecilia. I don't know who's *(Walking onscreen to Cecilia)* fillin' your head full of these crazy notions, but I've had enough.

Monk strides into the kitchen, his pleading tone suddenly turning to anger. He sits down at the kitchen table and yells at the now offscreen Cecilia without missing a beat.

MONK *(Continuing, shoving his hat across the table)* I want supper. *(Smoothing his hair)* Get my meat loaf!

CECILIA *(Offscreen)* Huh-uh. *(Rushes past him once again)*

MONK *(Standing up from the table, his conciliatory tone back)* C'mon, Cecilia, you know I can't live without you. *(Walking to the bedroom, where Cecilia is closing her suitcase, gesturing)* I'm like a little kid when it comes to you.

CECILIA *(Angrily, turning to glance at Monk)* That's just tough.

Cecilia walks offscreen briefly to a bedroom closet, returning to tie her suitcase closed. She ignores Monk, her back to him as he continues to plead.

MONK *(Gesturing frantically)* Look, I'm sorry. I mean, I'm really sorry. Can't I be sorry? I drink, I get crazy. It's not me, it's the whiskey.

CECILIA *(Grabbing her suitcase and pushing past Monk in the doorway, crying)* I'm going, Monk, I'm going.

MONK *(Turning towards the now offscreen Cecilia)* Ah, Jesus Christ, I can't reason with you. *(Gesturing)* All right, go ahead. Let's see how far you get. Go on, go on, you won't last. You see how it is out in the real world. *(Angrily, as he hears the door close)* Go on, you'll come back. *(Walking to the front door)* You're just bluff. You're all phoney. *(Opening the door and yelling down the stairwell)* You'll be back!

The sound of the closing apartment house door at the bottom of the stairwell is heard. Monk ignores it.

MONK It may take a week, it may take an hour, but you'll be back!

Monk slams the front door shut with a vengeance and the film cuts to:

EXTERIOR. STREET—NIGHT.

A panoramic view of a desolate, dark main street is seen on the screen. A solitary car is parked by the side of the road; streetlamps line the empty sidewalks. The glint of Cecilia's suitcase is barely seen as she walks down the street. Upbeat jazz begins to play as the camera cuts closer to the equally desolate Cecilia. She clutches her coat at her neck. The wind blows her hair as she suddenly stops and looks straight ahead.

The film cuts to her point of view: the Jewel Theater. It, too, is as deserted as the street. Even without its bright marquee lights, the attraction, in bold black letters, can be seen: THE PURPLE ROSE OF CAIRO. *After a beat, the camera moves back to Cecilia, the wind still blowing her hair. She starts to walk again, her head down, her mind elsewhere.*

The scene dissolves to a neon sign in a window: TAVERN. *The sounds of the busy bar, its laughter and conversational hum, can be heard over the jazz. Bar patrons can be faintly seen through the blinds of the window as the film moves back to the desolate main street. Cecilia is slowly walking down the sidewalk, still carrying her suitcase and clutching her coat. Emma, a prostitute, walks partially onscreen. Her face in profile fills the left side of the screen. Cecilia is in darkness behind her.*

EMMA *(Looking into the offscreen bar window)* Oh, jeez, look at all those guys. *(Turning to her companion)* C'mon, honey, we're gonna make a buck.

The two women walk past the camera into the offscreen bar. Cecilia stands behind them, clutching her suitcase and the neck of her coat. She doesn't move. After a beat, the jazz playing louder, Cecilia slowly turns around and walks back the way she came, her retreating figure fading in the darkness.

CUT TO:
INTERIOR. CECILIA'S APARTMENT—NIGHT.

Cecilia's silhouette can be seen at the curtained front door as she unlocks it; picking up her suitcase, she enters the darkened apartment. The jazz plays on. She closes the door and walks heavily into the living room. The music fades as loud snoring takes its place. Cecilia stops in the middle of the room, the suitcase in her hand.

CUT TO:
INTERIOR. DINER—DAY.

A proper-looking woman sitting in a booth fills the screen. She wears a hat and coat. Customers and clinking dishes can be heard in the background.

WOMAN I ordered bacon and tomato. *(Frowning)* You brought me ham and Swiss.

The camera shifts to Cecilia, standing at the booth, her back to the camera. A man sits in the booth opposite the woman. A fedora hangs on a nearby peg.

CECILIA *(Taking away the plate)* I-I'll-I'll get it right away, ma'am.

Cecilia scurries from the booth—and almost bumps into Jane in the aisle. The diner is crowded.

JANE *(Excitedly, gesturing, a towel in her hand)* Cecilia, I want you to meet somebody.

CECILIA *(Overlapping)* Who?

JANE *(Gesturing)* Well, remember I told you I was going to keep my eyes open for eligible men?

CECILIA *(Resisting)* Oh, c'mon.

JANE *(Pulling Cecilia over to a booth)* C'mon, just keep an open mind.

CECILIA *(Sighing)* Tch.

JANE *(To a solitary man sitting in a booth, his back to the camera)* This is my sister, Cecilia. *(To Cecilia, gesturing)* This is Mister . . .
The camera shifts to the man in the booth. His beaming, round face fills the screen over the backs of the women. He wears a bow tie.

JANE *(Offscreen)* . . . Teddy Ashcroft.

CECILIA *(Nodding her head, her back to the camera)* How do you do?

TEDDY *(Smiling)* Charmed.
The film cuts to Jane and Cecilia, looking down at the now offscreen Teddy.

JANE *(Touching the arm of a forced-smiling Cecilia)* Teddy's an exterminator.

TEDDY *(Smiling, the camera back on his face)* Right. Merson's Pest Control. My specialty are mice and silverfish.

CECILIA *(Nodding, looking uncomfortable but trying hard, as the camera moves back to the women)* I'm pleased to meet you.

TEDDY *(Offscreen)* Nice to meet you.

MALE CUSTOMER *(Offscreen, yelling)* Waitress, *please*, my hamburger!

CECILIA *(Overlapping the customer, turning her head)* I'm coming.

ANOTHER MALE CUSTOMER *(Offscreen)* Can we have a check?

CECILIA *(Turning around towards the voice)* I'll be right there. *(Dropping a plate, reacting to its crash)* Oh . . . Oh . . .

DINER BOSS *(Offscreen)* That's it.

The film cuts to the diner boss—looking very grim. He stands by the grill.

DINER BOSS *(To the offscreen Cecilia)* That's it, Cecilia, you're fired. Get out!

Cecilia reacts. She and Jane stand in front of the diner's Venetian blind windows, looking at the offscreen boss.

CECILIA *(Pleading)* But I-I-I'll pay for it. I'll be more careful.

DINER BOSS *(Offscreen)* Out. *(Onscreen, not moving from his grill)* Out. Take off your apron, go home. You're fired!

JANE *(Looking at her offscreen boss as the film cuts back to her and Jane)* If she goes, then I go too.

DINER BOSS *(Looking at the offscreen women, the camera on his set face)* That's fine with me.

The camera shifts back to Jane and Cecilia.

CECILIA *(Shaking her head, looking at Jane)* She doesn't mean that. No, you've got kids. *(To the offscreen boss)* No, she doesn't mean that.

DINER BOSS *(Not moving from his grill as the film cuts back to him)* Then tell her to mind her own business. You're fired.

The film cuts to a very distraught Cecilia walking down the sidewalk near the Jewel Theater. Her arms are crossed over her chest. She passes under the marquee, crying. The street sounds of cars and passersby are heard in the background. An organ-grinder plays faintly. She abruptly stops walking, framed by the marquee she's just passed under. In bold letters, it says: NOW PLAYING: THE PURPLE ROSE OF CAIRO.

CUT TO:
INTERIOR. MOVIE THEATER—DAY.

A few patrons sit in the darkened theater. Over the backs of their heads, the black-and-white movie screen is seen. The Purple Rose of Cairo *is in progress. The penthouse foyer is empty for a beat before Rita, Henry, Jason, and Tom (in his pith helmet) walk onscreen, laden with suitcases. Henry and Rita continue into the living room offscreen, while Jason puts down the luggage. Tom stands nearby in the foyer, looking around. Lilting movie music is heard.*

HENRY *(Offscreen)* Ah, back from *(Onscreen, walking towards the living room)* Egypt. From the Bedouins to Broadway.

JASON *(Putting down his suitcases)* Even though I'm not a religious man, I hereby vow never to fly over the Atlantic in bumpy weather, and never to look at another camel. *(Walking over to the bar, holding his stomach)* Drinks anyone? *(Claps his hands in anticipation)*

The film cuts to a close-up of a row of seats in the theater, in color. Cecilia, her eye makeup smeared from crying, moves onscreen, settling into a seat. She holds a box of popcorn. She wipes her eyes with a tissue; she blows her nose, looking at the screen.

RITA *(Offscreen)* Boy, I can't wait to get out of these clothes and hit some of the night spots.

HENRY *(Offscreen)* Well, children, let's not waste any time. The floor show at the Copacabana starts in ten minutes, and we're meeting the Countess and Larry Wilde.

The film cuts back to the black-and-white screen as seen over the full-color backs of the theater audience. Tom, in his safari outfit, is looking around him; it's a scene we've seen before.

TOM *(Looking around the penthouse, his hands on his hips)* Well, I am *impressed*! I really am. You have yourself quite a place here. *(Walking down the few stairs to the living room, the Manhattan view behind him)* You know, I still can't get over the fact that twenty-four hours ago I was in an Egyptian tomb, I didn't know any of you wonderful people, and here I am now—I'm on the verge of a madcap Manhattan weekend.

JASON *(Stirring a pitcher of martinis by the bar, as before)* I hope you like your martinis very dry.

The film moves back to Cecilia, watching the offscreen movie, sniffling, still crying.

TOM *(Offscreen)* Oh, no, no thanks. Uh . . . I think I'll wait for that glass of champagne at the Copacabana.

Cecilia's tearstained face dissolves to the black-and-white movie. Another viewing of the movie has begun. The title credits we've seen before fill the screen. The exotic title music plays in the background. First, in script on a large calling card, is THE PURPLE ROSE OF CAIRO. *A hand removes the card, revealing a second one, saying, in script:* STARRING ROBERT TALMADGE / ANNA RAYBURN / TODD MORGAN. *The card dissolves to the black-and-white screen as seen over the full-color backs of the theater audience. Delilah, a large black maid in a uniform, is fluffing up some pillows in the bedroom of the penthouse. The exotic music stops.*

DELILAH *(Looking at the offscreen Rita)* Miss Rita, something on your mind? *(Fluffing a pillow and putting it back on the bed)* 'Cause you ain't been yourself since you come back from them Pyramids.

The camera moves back, revealing a languid Rita reclining on a divan. She's polishing her nails, her back to Delilah.

RITA No, it's nothing really. I'll be okay.

The film cuts closer to The Purple Rose of Cairo. *The black-and-white movie fills the screen. The bedroom is clearly seen now, with its satin quilted headboard and double bed, its delicate lamp and end table, its frilly curtains and cut fresh flowers.*

DELILAH *(Smoothing the sheets on the bed)* I don't suspect it has anything to do with that explorer fella, Mr. Tom Baxter.

RITA *(Polishing her nails, slurring her words)* Now, why would you say that?

DELILAH *(Gesturing)* The way he speaks, all romantic-like.

RITA *(Putting the polish brush in the bottle, smiling)* Yeah . . . *(Drying her nails in the air, blowing on them)* C'mon, Delilah, draw my bath.

DELILAH *(Walking in front of the bed, talking to Rita's reclining back)* Yes, ma'am. Now will you be wanting the big bubbles, or the asses' milk?

The bedroom scene dissolves to yet another viewing of the title credits, this time listing several members of The Purple Rose of Cairo *production team in small script. While the exotic movie music plays, a hand removes this card, revealing another with* PRODUCED BY RAOUL HIRSCH *written in script.*

The film cuts to Cecilia, in color, sitting in the audience. She is enraptured by the movie; she is no longer crying. Upbeat movie music plays.

RITA *(Offscreen)* Boy . . .

Cecilia's face dissolves to the black-and-white movie screen as seen over the full-color backs and heads of the theater audience. Rita is on the screen, swathed in fur and a traveling suit. She stands in the penthouse living room, the magnificent Manhattan view behind her. We've heard the scene before, though we haven't seen it on the screen. The group has just returned from Egypt.

RITA *(Onscreen, continuing)* I can't wait to get out of these clothes and hit some of the night spots.

Henry is next seen on the black-and-white screen. He stands in a different area of the living room, lighting a cigarette with a table lighter.

HENRY *(Putting the lighter down on the table)* Well, children, let's not waste any time. *(Walking towards the foyer, a cigarette in hand)* The floor show at the Copacabana starts in ten minutes *(Turning back to look at the others offscreen)* and we're meeting the Countess and Larry Wilde.

The movie cuts to the foyer, where Tom, in his pith helmet and khakis, stands looking around the penthouse, his hands on his hips—a replay of the scene we've seen twice before.

TOM *(Looking around)* Well, I am *very* impressed! I really am. You have yourself quite a place here. *(Walking down the few stairs to the living room, the Manhattan view behind him).* You know, I still can't get over the fact that twenty-four hours ago I was in an Egyptian tomb, I didn't know any of you wonderful people . . . *(Stops for a beat, looking out at the offscreen audience)*

The film cuts to the audience, in color, to Cecilia sitting in her row. She's been watching the movie, her cheek leaning on her hand. When Tom pauses, she sits up, startled. Other patrons sit watching the movie in scattered seats. The upbeat music continues.

TOM *(Offscreen)* . . . and here I am now—I'm on the verge of a madcap . . . Manhattan . . . weekend . . .

As Tom's offscreen voice trails off, Cecilia reacts, looking around the audience, moving about in her seat. The film cuts to Tom on the black-and-white movie screen—as seen over the full-color heads and backs of the theater audience.

TOM *(Shaking his head, looking out at the offscreen Cecilia)* My God, you must really love this picture.
The film cuts back to the audience, to Cecilia in her row, surrounded by other scattered patrons.

CECILIA *(Pointing to herself, looking at the offscreen Tom)* Me?
A woman a few rows in front of Cecilia turns around to look at her.

TOM *(Offscreen)* You've been here . . .
The film is back on the larger-than-life Tom on the black-and-white screen—as seen over the full-color backs of the audience.

TOM . . . all day and I've seen you here twice before.
The film moves back to a closer shot of Cecilia, sitting in her seat, incredulous.

CECILIA *(Pointing to herself, looking up at the screen)* You mean me?
The film moves back to a closer shot of Tom on the black-and-white screen.

TOM *(Looking down at the offscreen Cecilia)* Yes, you-you-you've— This is the fifth time you're seeing this.
The camera shifts to a close-up of Rita on the black-and-white screen.

RITA *(Whispering, reacting)* Henry, come here . . . quickly!
The movie cuts back to the close-up of the larger-than-life Tom.

TOM I gotta speak to you.
He begins to leave the black-and-white screen. The audience, reacting, begins to gasp. The film cuts to a shocked Cecilia, immobilized in her seat. As the other patrons cry out in the background, the film quickly cuts back to Tom. He actually walks off of the black-and-white movie screen, turning into living color as he enters the theater.

The film cuts to a woman in a hat, sitting in the last row of the theater. She screams and falls over in a faint as the scene shifts back to the screen—as seen over the backs and heads of the audience. Tom, in color, jumps off the stage and begins to walk up the center aisle. The black-and-white movie screen is empty where Tom was standing. Henry, on the black-and-white screen, walks over to its edge, to the spot where Tom was standing. He looks out at the audience. Rita follows close behind. The audience, in color, is in an uproar.

HENRY Listen, old sport, you're on the wrong side.

RITA Tom, get back here; we're in the middle of a story!

TOM *(Overlapping Rita, gesturing and turning his head back as he walks)* Leave me alone. I want to have a look around. You go on without me.

Tom, in his pith helmet, walks over to Cecilia's row. He bends down to talk to her. His face fills the screen. The audience continues to screech. The offscreen movie actors continue to appeal to him. The upbeat music plays on. Tom ignores them all.

JASON *(Offscreen)* We can't continue with the story!

TOM *(To the offscreen Cecilia)* Who are you?

The camera cuts to Cecilia's incredulous face, looking up at the offscreen Tom.

CECILIA C-C-Cecilia.

The film cuts to a terrified usherette in uniform, standing in the aisle, waving a flashlight. The audience continues to react.

USHERETTE I'll go get the manager!

She turns around and starts to run back up the aisle to the doors as the camera moves back to Tom, leaning over some empty seats as before, talking to Cecilia.

TOM *(Taking Cecilia's hand and pulling her up from her seat)* Let's get out of here and go somewhere where we can talk.

CECILIA *(Reacting, letting herself be pulled up)* But . . . you're in the movie!

TOM *(Running with Cecilia down the aisle and around the first row, the black-and-white legs of his fellow actors seen on the partially shown movie screen)* Wrong, Cecilia, I'm free! After two thousand performances of the same monotonous routine, I'm free!
Hand in hand they run through a curtained side exit as the film cuts to the black-and-white screen. An agitated Henry is shouting. Rita stands at the edge of the black-and-white screen, looking down at the offscreen fleeing Tom.

HENRY *(Walking over to Jason in the background by the windowed view)* Call Father Donnelly.

RITA Tom! *(Presses her face and hands against the invisible black-and-white movie screen, as if against glass; she cannot get out)*

CUT TO:
EXTERIOR. REAR OF THEATER—DAY.

Cecilia and Tom emerge into the daylight from the theater's rear door. They are seen in the background, at the end of a short alley. A drugstore front is partially seen in the foreground, at the opening of the alley. A few people pass by the camera, past the drugstore on the sidewalk, momentarily obscuring the couple. Moving cars are reflected in the drugstore's window. As the couple talk, they run up the alley, closer and closer to the camera. Fast-paced jazz music begins to play.

CECILIA *(Breathlessly, reacting, her hand on her hat)* I don't understand. What's going on? Who are you?

TOM *(In an excited voice, pulling Cecilia along)* Who am I? You've seen the movie five times. I'm Tom Baxter, poet, adventurer, explorer, of the Chicago Baxters.
They stop at the end of the alley. Tom holds on to the drugstore's side wall, looking both ways in an excited state. More pedestrians pass by, oblivious.

CECILIA *(Breathlessly)* Well, yes, I know you're Tom Baxter. You wind up with Kitty Haynes, the nightclub singer, but still, I don't—

TOM *(Looking at Cecilia, interrupting her as he lets go of Cecilia's hands, putting his in his pockets)* Not anymore I don't have to.

CECILIA *(Buttoning her coat, looking at Tom, reacting)* What do you mean?

TOM *(Gesturing)* Well, I'm out before the wedding. I'm free.

CECILIA Don't you have to marry her?

TOM *(Gesturing at the theater's side wall)* Not while I'm here and she's up there.

CECILIA *(Fingering her pocketbook strap, reacting)* Don't you want to? She's so beautiful.

TOM *(Nodding)* She's not for me. She's too bony.

Tom grabs Cecilia's hand anew and starts to run back up the alley.

CECILIA *(Holding on to her hat as Tom pulls her along)* Kitty Haynes, the nightclub singer, is bony?

TOM *(Stopping in the background, at the other end of the alley)* I need a place to hide! *(Looking at Cecilia, then dropping her hand)* Look, I'm never going back, now that I've met you.

CECILIA *(Looking around)* A place to hide? A place to hide?

Cecilia takes the lead, Tom close behind, as they dash out of sight. The film cuts to the inside of the theater, where the manager and the usherette walk onscreen at the rear of the theater, the doors behind them.

THEATER MANAGER *(Looking at the off-camera movie screen)* What's happening? What's going on?

The camera cuts to the black-and-white screen—as seen over the backs and heads of the audience. Rita, Jason, and Henry stand in the penthouse living room, near the front of the screen, looking out at the offscreen manager.

JASON *(Gesturing)* Tom's *left*. He just walked right out.

The film cuts closer to the black-and-white actors. The black-and-white movie fills the screen.

HENRY *(Gesturing, looking offscreen at the theater manager)* I don't know how he did it. I can't get out.

JASON It's absolutely . . . *(Continues to mutter indistinctly, putting his hands in his pockets as he turns away)*

RITA *(Pointing and shouting at the offscreen manager)* This is just disgusting. I am an heiress and I don't have to put up with this!

While Henry and Jason mutter angrily to each other, the camera moves back to the theater manager, in color, standing next to the shocked usherette.

THEATER MANAGER *(Looking at the offscreen black-and-white actors)* He left the picture? Oh, my gosh. Well, don't-don't panic. *(Touching his mouth)* Just stay up there and keep calm. *(Starts running up the aisle, the usherette following)*

The film cuts back to the action on the black-and-white movie screen.

HENRY *(Looking at the offscreen manager, uncrossing his arms)* Keep calm? Are you crazy? *(Continues to mutter agitatedly)*

JASON *(Muttering, overlapping Henry, at first indistinctly)* What do you mean, "Keep calm"?

Father Donnelly suddenly appears on the black-and-white screen, in front of the others, his back to the camera.

FATHER DONNELLY *(To Rita, Henry, and Jason, over their angry mutterings)* Somebody call for a priest?

HENRY *(Looking at the Father, while Jason, also looking at the Father, continues to mutter)* Thank God you're here.

FATHER DONNELLY *(Turning his head to face the camera)* Wait a minute, this is the second reel.

JASON *(Gesturing)* That's the point.

FATHER DONNELLY *(Shaking his head, confused)* I'm not on till later.

Father Donnelly walks offscreen.

JASON *(Calls after him, gesturing)* Tom's gone.

The three actors start talking all at once as the film cuts back to the theater manager, in color, standing in the aisle and looking up at the offscreen black-and-white screen. His profile almost fills the frame.

THEATER MANAGER Can't you go on? There's an audience.

The film cuts to a large man in an aisle seat, eating popcorn and watching the offscreen action.

RITA *(Offscreen)* How? Tom was the linchpin of the story.

The film cuts to another section of the audience, to a man and a woman sitting and enjoying the offscreen spectacle. They grin broadly.

HENRY *(Offscreen)* That's right!

JASON *(Offscreen)* Whoever you are . . .

The film moves back to the black-and-white screen. Henry, his arms crossed, and Rita, looking annoyed, stand on either side of Jason. They look out at the offscreen manager. A portion of Father Donnelly's suit is seen in the foreground.

JASON *(Continuing, gesturing, walking forward to the edge of the screen)* . . . you see, sir, although this is basically my story, Tom moves the exposition along.

HENRY *(Overlapping Jason, walking over to him)* What do you mean, your story? It's not your story, *(Pushing Jason away, gesturing to himself as he addresses the offscreen manager)* it's the story of a man's quest for self-fulfillment.

JASON *(Overlapping Henry, gesturing, looking at the offscreen manager)* He lays out the facts. It's the story of a complex, tortured soul.

HENRY *(Overlapping Jason, looking up at him)* Oh, stop that—

RITA *(Interrupting Henry, joining the two men at the edge of the screen, gesturing)* They don't know what they're talking about. It's the story of the effect of money on true romance . . .

The three actors begin talking all at once.

JASON *(Overlapping, looking at Rita, then Henry)* I don't think money comes into it.

HENRY *(Overlapping, pushing Jason to talk to Rita)* Money? That doesn't have a thing . . . oh, *(Pointing to himself)* it's . . . I'm the one who marries royalty.

RITA *(Overlapping, gesturing, pushing Jason as she moves her hand, talking to the offscreen manager)* . . . my upbringing, my wealth, my private schools.

HENRY *(Overlapping, looking at Rita)* I'm the one—a humble kid—

RITA *(Overlapping, shaking her head, looking at Henry)* Nobody cares . . .

Jason, muttering, turns around, looking from one to the other.

HENRY What do you mean, they don't care?

RITA *(Overlapping, to Henry)* They wouldn't sell a ticket if it were your story.

HENRY *(Overlapping, to Rita)* I'm a humble kid from a small town who marries the sister of a count—

JASON *(Overlapping, to Henry, his back to the camera)* The Countess's sister is about as far away from royalty as you can get.

HENRY *(Overlapping, to Jason)* Well, I—

RITA *(Overlapping)* Ohh . . .

While the trio continue to argue, their voices raised, the film cuts to the theater manager, in color, trying to talk over the offscreen black-and-white actors. The usherette stands next to him, backlit by the projector's light.

THEATER MANAGER *(Overlapping)* Stop arguing.

RITA *(Offscreen, loudly)* And do what?

USHERETTE *(Aside, to the manager, clutching her flashlight)* Maybe you should just turn the projector off.

The film cuts back to the black-and-white screen. The group is still huddled together; Father Donnelly has joined them.

HENRY *(His eyes wide in horror, holding his hands out)* No! No! Don't turn the projector off! No! No . . . it gets black and we disappear.

JASON *(Looking weary, turning around to face the offscreen audience as he mutters indistinctly)* Calm down . . .

The group begins to talk all at once again. Rita mutters, looking at the offscreen manager. Jason pats Henry's shoulder. Father Donnelly reaches over Rita and Jason to pat Henry as well, offering soothing words.

FATHER DONNELLY *(Overlapping, gesturing)* Easy. Easy. Easy. Easy. Take it easy. Easy, my son. We're all in this together.

HENRY *(Loudly, to the offscreen manager)* Yes, but you don't understand what it's like to disappear and to be nothing . . . *(Pauses with emotion, gesturing)* to be annihilated.

The film cuts to the audience, in color, to a thin young man in a suit, eating popcorn and watching the offscreen action. Other patrons are seated here and there.

HENRY *(Offscreen)* So don't . . . turn the projector off.

The film cuts back to the black-and-white screen. The group is no longer gathered at the front of the screen. Rita moves offscreen as Delilah enters from a doorway near the piano. Father Donnelly, his back to the camera, looks at her. Henry is seated in a chair near the couch.

DELILAH Miss Rita, your bath is ready.

JASON *(Walking onscreen to Delilah, carrying some drinks)* Not *now*, dear.

DELILAH Well, what's going on?

JASON *(Overlapping Delilah, motioning her towards the couch)* Come in and sit down, Delilah.

HENRY *(Overlapping, leaning forward in his chair momentarily)* Be quiet, Delilah.

DELILAH *(Pointing at Father Donnelly as she's led to the couch)* Well, what's he doing here?

JASON *(Overlapping Delilah, handing her a glass)* Have a martini.

DELILAH He's not supposed to be here till reel six.

HENRY *(Overlapping, gesturing)* We know that, Delilah.

JASON *(Overlapping, gesturing)* I'll explain it to you, now just sit down.

DELILAH *(Overlapping, flopping down on the couch)* What the hell is going on? Is somebody trying to hustle me?

HENRY *(Gesturing, with impatience)* They're not trying to hustle you.

CUT TO:
EXTERIOR. AMUSEMENT PARK—DAY.

A huge Ferris wheel is seen in a deserted amusement park. The surrounding trees are bare; an empty pagoda sits in the background. Not a soul is near; soft music plays in the background.

TOM *(Offscreen)* Hey, I know what this is, it's an amusement park!

CECILIA *(Offscreen)* Yeah, it's usually pretty dead around here till summer.
Tom and Cecilia walk onscreen, near the Ferris wheel.

TOM *(Turning to Cecilia)* I know exactly what an amusement park is, and what goes on, I do! *(Hits the base of the wheel enthusiastically)*

CECILIA *(Giggling)* Well, good.

TOM *(Laughing)* It's written into my character.
The camera moves closer to the couple as Tom climbs up the base, standing by one of its seats.

TOM *(Turning to look at Cecilia)* Remember I invite Kitty to Luna Park but she prefers just to stay home and talk?

CECILIA *(Nodding)* Oh, yes.

TOM *(Laughing)* So it's in me! Oh, the— Too bad nothing's open. *(Climbing off the base)* I'm starved!

CECILIA Oh, you are?

TOM *(Gesturing)* Well, yeah, I, uh, left the movie before the Copacabana scene. So that's when I usually eat.

CECILIA *(Fumbling in her purse)* Oh, wha-wait a minute, what am I thinking? Look, here, *(Holding out a bag of popcorn)* I've got a whole bag of popcorn . . .

TOM *(Overlapping, in a whisper, looking around in wonder)* Wow!

CECILIA . . . You can have that.

TOM *(Taking the bag)* Oh! *(Whispering again)* Wow!

CECILIA *(Reaching into her purse)* Also, I-I have a Milky Way bar you . . . you might . . .

TOM *(Overlapping, opening the bag, distracted)* No, that's . . . Popcorn is . . .

CECILIA You might want it later.

TOM *(Eating his popcorn)* Oh, boy, well, that's what . . . So that's what popcorn *(Chuckles as Cecilia nods)* tastes like. I've been watching people eat it for all those performances. When they rattle those bags, though, *(Begins walking, Cecilia at his side)* that's, uh . . .

CECILIA *(Interrupting, strolling with Tom around the Ferris wheel)* That's not . . . ?

TOM *(Overlapping, continuing, as he looks around, caught up in everything)* . . . kind of annoying.

CECILIA I still— I still don't understand what's going on.

TOM *(Touching Cecilia's arm)* I wanted to meet you. *(Eating his popcorn)* Don't tell me you didn't see me looking at you at, just, out of the corner of my eye. *(Gesturing)* When Kitty Haynes was doing her nightclub number?

CECILIA *(Gesturing)* Oh, wait a minute, I did, I di— I remember seeing you kind of— You were looking off to the side, somehow, but uh . . .

The two stop walking. They look at each other. Behind them is the Ferris wheel.

TOM *(Nodding, nibbling on the popcorn)* Sure.

CECILIA *(Continuing, shaking her head)* . . . I never thought it was to me.

TOM Yeah, that— Wh-when we take the drive to that little country inn? *(Nodding)* When I propose to Kitty? I was looking at you.

CECILIA *(Overlapping, shaking her head)* Oh, no, Kitty looked so beautiful in that black dress. I kn—

TOM *(Interrupting, shaking his head)* Oh, no, she's nothing compared to you.

CECILIA *(Modestly, shaking her head)* What are you talking about? N— I'm nothing.

TOM Like hell you are. *(Dropping his arms to his side)* You're fetching.

CECILIA Fetching?

TOM Fetching. *Gesturing with his popcorn bag)* Dad liked to use that word about Mom, back in Chicago. "Min," he'd say, "you're rather fetching."
Cecilia laughs. The soft piano music plays on.

TOM Dad was a card. *(Looking down at some popcorn in his hand)* I never met him. He died before the movie begins.

CECILIA Well, I have to confess, *(Nodding her head)* my-my eye did always go to you up, up on the screen.

TOM *(Swallowing some popcorn)* Really?

CECILIA Really.

TOM *(Gesturing)* Even when I'm around Detective Simms and Henry Adams, the playboy?

CECILIA *(Waving her arm and shaking her head)* Oh, yes, e-even though you're not the main character, you're the one you look at.

TOM *(Reacting, turning away as he eats his popcorn)* You don't— You don't think I'm the main character?

CECILIA *(Following Tom as they begin walking anew)* Oh, I, well, I didn't mean it that way. No, I . . . I think you're positively essential. *(Walking out of the fenced-in Ferris wheel area with Tom)* In fact, every time I saw the movie, I kept thinking, Tom Baxter's so handsome.

Tom laughs as they walk away from the camera, as their images dissolve to another scene at the amusement park. It is dusk; Tom is in a pavilion, hanging by his hands from the rafters, dangling his legs. The fading sun comes through the latticework; the soft romantic music plays on. He jumps down as the film cuts to Cecilia in her hat and brown coat, perched on a wooden bench in the pavilion. She is framed by the fading sun and the elaborate grillwork outside the amusement park.

CECILIA *(Looking at the offscreen Tom)* Shouldn't you be getting back?

The camera cuts back to Tom, barely seen in the dusk, jumping over rows of wooden tables and benches.

TOM I want to live. I want to be free to make my own choices.

CECILIA *(Offscreen)* Right now, the . . .

The camera moves back to Cecilia, sitting at her bench.

CECILIA *(Continuing, shaking her head)* . . . country's not in such great shape.

The camera is back on Tom, standing on a tabletop in his pith helmet and khakis.

TOM *(Looking at the offscreen Cecilia)* What do you mean?

CECILIA *(Offscreen)* Well, we're in the middle of a depression. Everybody's very poor.

TOM I got plenty. *(Taking a wad of bills from his pocket)* Look at this!

Tom laughs, holding out the money, as he jumps off the table and walks over to Cecilia. She is speaking as Tom approaches her at her bench. They are both obscured by the fading lights. Behind them are some spots of color—posters painted with the brand name Carter's. They look at each other; the romantic music plays on.

CECILIA *(Offscreen)* But . . . but . . . they need you. *(Onscreen)* The story doesn't work without you.

TOM Cecilia, I'm in love with you.

CECILIA *(After a beat)* I'm married.

TOM Happily?

CECILIA *(Getting up from the bench)* I sh— I really should get back home. I have to cook dinner.

TOM Slip away from your husband tonight. Meet me here. I'll wait for you. I want to learn about the real world with you.

CECILIA I can't.

TOM Well, look at it this way. *(Gesturing)* How many times is a man so taken with a woman that he walks off the screen to get her?

The camera cuts to a close-up of Cecilia's awestruck face. The music builds for a beat and the film cuts to the black-and-white movie screen. The music ends.

Delilah sits on the couch as before, drinking her martini. On the other end sits Jason, fidgeting with a pillow on his lap, his legs crossed. Rita sits at the white baby grand piano in the background, her cheek resting on her hand. Father Donnelly is standing in the corner, reading a Bible. Henry, pacing and sipping a drink, walks across the room as he talks, off, then on, then offscreen again.

HENRY *(Offscreen)* Okay, okay, let's not panic. *(Onscreen)* We're all adults.

JASON *(Gesturing, uncrossing his legs)* I'm bored with sitting around! I'm a dramatic character, I need forward motion!

FATHER DONNELLY *(Pointing offscreen)* Here comes the Countess and Larry.

COUNTESS *(Walking on screen, in tiara and evening wrap)* Where is everybody? *(Looking around)* Weren't we meeting at the Copacabana?

HENRY *(Offscreen)* Tom's gone.

COUNTESS *(Turning her head)* What?!

HENRY *(Offscreen)* He left the film.

Larry Wilde enters the room, in tails, holding a martini glass. On the couch in the background, Jason sips his drink.

LARRY What?!

RITA The bum walked out on us.

COUNTESS *(Gesturing at Larry)* But-but . . . but-but the Copa is where the two of us meet. I'm trying to get him to marry me.

LARRY *(Gesturing)* Forget it. I'm tired of marrying you every night anyway. We never even get to the bedroom.

COUNTESS *(Looking straight at the camera)* Where did Tom go?

RITA *(Shaking her head)* Into the real world.

HENRY *(Offscreen)* That two-bit minor character *(Onscreen as he paces across the room)* leaves and we're stuck. *(Paces offscreen again)*

LARRY *(Walking up to the edge of the screen, looking out at the audience)* I wonder what it's like out there?

COUNTESS *(Walking up next to Larry, looking out at the offscreen audience)* They don't look like they're having too much fun to me.

The film cuts to the movie theater audience, in color. The seats are half-full; people are scattered sporadically.

MAN IN AUDIENCE *(Standing up)* Hey, what the hell kind of movie is this?

WOMAN IN AUDIENCE *(Shouting)* The paper said it was a romance, set all over the world!

The others in the audience turn their heads at the commotion in the theater as the film cuts back to the black-and-white screen. The Countess still stands at the edge of the screen, looking out with disdain.

JASON *(Jumping up from the couch, shouting at the offscreen audience)* Look, don't tell us your sad stories. You think we like this?
The film cuts back to the audience, in color. A woman wearing glasses and a hat, looking up at the screen, reacts, gesturing. Other people sit nearby, talking angrily among themselves.

WOMAN WITH HAT *(Pointing at the offscreen movie)* Look at this. They sit around and talk, no action? *(Turning to look at the other patrons)* Nothing happens?
The camera cuts to the rear of the theater, where an elderly couple sits, indignant. A younger woman sits in front of them. They look up at the offscreen action.

ELDERLY WOMAN *(Nodding, loudly)* I want my money back. This is outrageous!

YOUNGER WOMAN *(Turning around)* Shh.

COUNTESS *(Offscreen)* Why don't you . . .
As the Countess begins to speak, the film cuts to the black-and-white screen. The Countess's face fills most of the screen; Jason is standing in the background.

COUNTESS *(Looking out at the offscreen elderly woman, continuing)* . . . stop yapping? We've got problems of our own.
The film cuts back to the audience, in color, to the elderly couple.

ELDERLY MAN *(Indignant)* You can't talk to my wife like that. Who do you think you are?
The camera is back on the Countess's black-and-white face on the movie screen. Jason stands in the background; Delilah can be seen on the couch.

COUNTESS *(Looking down her nose at the offscreen elderly man)* I'm a genuine Countess with a lot of dough, and if that's your wife, she's a tub of guts.

The offscreen audience applauds and cheers. A few whistles are heard as the film cuts to Cecilia's apartment. Monk is sitting at the kitchen table eating a bowl of spaghetti and some bread. A beer bottle sits next to him. The sound of breaking glass is heard, along with Cecilia's offscreen groan.

MONK *(Turning, to the offscreen Cecilia)* Hey, what are you so nervous about?

The camera moves to the bedroom doorway. Cecilia, in a bright red print robe, is bending down, picking up the broken glass from the floor near the dresser. The corner of the bed is seen; a mirror hangs above the dresser.

CECILIA *(Turning in the offscreen Monk's direction, straightening up)* Me? Oh, I-I'm not.

Cecilia puts the broken glass on the dresser top. She dusts off her hands, then smooths her hair and face in the mirror while Monk talks on.

MONK *(Offscreen)* There's too much pepper in the sauce. I told you to go easy on the pepper.

CECILIA *(Nervously, walking over to the doorway, pulling at her belt)* Hey, Monk? Are you, uh . . . I guess you-you and the guys are probably going out again tonight, huh?

The film cuts back to Monk at the kitchen table, still eating. The refrigerator stands in the background.

MONK No, I'm not. My back is acting up again. *(Burps)* You gotta give me one of your special rubdowns. I bought linament.

CECILIA *(Offscreen)* Oh, no.

MONK What?

The film cuts back to Cecilia in the doorway.

CECILIA *(Gesturing, shaking her head)* Well, I-I can't.

The camera moves back to Monk, reacting. He puts down his fork, wipes his hands on his napkin, and stands up, walking towards the offscreen Cecilia.

MONK *(After a beat)* What do you mean, you can't?

The camera moves back to Cecilia in the doorway, talking and fidgeting. Monk walks onscreen, facing her; only his shoulder and back are seen.

CECILIA *(Shaking her head)* I-I-di— *(Hitting her forehead with her hand)* I'm sorry, I didn't, I didn't mean I can't, I mean, I-I-I-I-I made some plans, I . . .

MONK You made plans?

CECILIA *(Gesturing)* Well, um, I, I-I did, I-I-I said I'd-I'd babysit tonight. I'd-I-I you know *(Looking at her hands)* I ran into Mrs. Lorenzo and-d-and in the rest— . . . in, I'm saying in the restaurant, *(Gesturing)* in the street today . . .

The film cuts to Monk's unmoving face, listening, while Cecilia continues to talk offscreen.

CECILIA *(Offscreen, continuing)* . . . and she-she has some, you know, I don't know, some like . . . I think it was a uh, uh, k-social club meeting or something she wanted to go to, 'n' . . .

The film cuts back to Cecilia, standing in the doorway; Monk's back is to the camera.

CECILIA *(Shaking her head)* Yeah, I-I-I, it won't be too long. *(Rubs her arm)*

MONK *(Walking offscreen)* Yeah, well, I think it's a great idea.

CECILIA *(Nodding, looking after him)* Yeah? Good. *(Turns and walks back into the bedroom)*

MONK *(Walking back onscreen, into the bedroom)* Yeah, because we can use every penny.

CECILIA *(Combing her hair in the mirror, with relief)* Yeah.

MONK *(Moving offscreen in the bedroom, behind the door)* All right, so what am I going to do about my back? *(Lights a cigarette off-screen)*

CECILIA *(Walking over to Monk, still combing her hair)* Oh well, don't worry. You know, I can do some now and I'll-I'll do some when I come in, 'n' you, you shouldn't move *(Walking offscreen through the doorway)* around too much, just kinda take it easy.

MONK *(Walking to the doorway, looking at his offscreen wife, smoking)* Well, if you're gonna go babysitting, get paid in cash.

CECILIA *(Offscreen)* I will.

MONK *(Gesturing with the cigarette in his hand)* Don't let her owe you. *(Puts his hands on his hips, the cigarette in his mouth)*

CECILIA *(Offscreen)* Okay.

CUT TO:
EXTERIOR. MOVIE THEATER—NIGHT.

The front of the Jewel Theater is all lit up, the marquee proclaiming THE PURPLE ROSE OF CAIRO / R TALMADGE / RAYBURN / MORGAN. *A huge crowd is milling about under the marquee, overflowing the sidewalk and street. A policeman stands out front blowing a whistle, motioning cars to move along on the street. Upbeat jazz begins to play.*

The film cuts to a reporter, in trenchcoat and fedora, standing in front of some "Coming Soon" movie posters outside the theater. His camera and flash unit are covering his face. A few people mill about in the background.

CAMERA REPORTER *(Taking a picture)* It's a miracle, a complete miracle!
The flash goes off—in the faces of a couple walking outside through the

glass doors of the theater as the film cuts to the reporter's point of view. They walk to the nearby manager, standing outside, the usherette at his side. The reporter scurries onscreen in the background, the camera still to his face, aimed out at the group. Crowds of people mill about; it's very noisy. The music continues.

WOMAN *(Without looking at the manager)* We want our money back! *(Stalks off)*

MAN I don't pay to watch those *(Angrily, to the manager)* socialites sitting around up there and staring back at us, making nasty remarks. *(Walks offscreen in the same direction as the woman)*

THEATER MANAGER *(To the usherette)* Is that what they're doing now?

USHERETTE *(Gesturing, the flashlight in her hand)* Well, the last time I looked, the priest had a deck of cards and the men were playing pinochle.

THEATER MANAGER *(Overlapping, reacting, shaking his head)* Oh . . . oh . . .

The reporter circles the manager and the usherette, snapping a picture, as another reporter holding a notepad walks over to them. People continue to mill about, walking past the group, past the camera.

NOTEPAD REPORTER How did this first happen?

THEATER MANAGER *(Ignoring the reporter, muttering, then to the usherette)* Iris, go inside and see what's happening.

The usherette nods and walks through the glass doors into the theater.

CAMERA REPORTER *(Overlapping the manager, to the notepad reporter)* Well, it's probably all the electrical storms we had this evening. The air is charged.

THEATER MANAGER *(Turning to the reporters as one jots in his pad, the other snapping pictures)* Look, fellas, I depend on the Jewel, I got personal expenses, I've got no substitute picture to put in here.

The film cuts to a man in a hat standing outside the glass ticket booth. The woman inside, with bobbed hair, is filing her nails, ignoring him.

MAN IN CAP I want my money back! This is a swindle!

The film next cuts to the glass doors of the theater. A man is directing his dazed wife outside, his hands on her shoulders.

MAN *(Looking out at the camera, at the offscreen reporters)* There's no story. Mrs. Lupus likes a story.

The camera moves back to the notepad reporter in close-up, still deep in discussion with the camera reporter and the manager.

NOTEPAD REPORTER *(To the offscreen manager)* I still think you should turn the projector off and shut down. This could be the work of Reds, or anarchists.

As he finishes his speech, the camera moves past him, revealing the other reporter in close-up. In the background, people continue to pass by. Lights flicker on the reporter's face.

CAMERA REPORTER *(To the offscreen notepad reporter)* You can't do that. If he turns off the projector, you're liable to strand this-this Tom Baxter out in the world someplace. You want an extra guy running around?
A woman in a busy hat runs out the glass doors towards the reporters. She holds a bag of popcorn. The camera reporter puts a new flashbulb in his camera.

WOMAN *(To the reporters)* I saw the movie just last week. This is not what happens!

NOTEPAD REPORTER Where is the Tom Baxter character?

THEATER MANAGER *(Overlapping, to the woman)* Wh— . . . ah . . . you'll get your money back.

WOMAN *(Gesturing)* I want what happened in the movie last week to happen this week, *(Shaking her head, looking at the men)* otherwise what's life all about anyway?
The film cuts to a couple sitting in the backseat of a parked car, talking to the offscreen manager through the open window. A woman sits in the driver's seat. People pass by, lights flicker on their faces.

WOMAN IN BACKSEAT Can't we just go in and take a look? We don't want to stay long.
The camera moves back to the theater manager, standing with the reporters and the popcorn-carrying woman.

THEATER MANAGER *(To the woman in the parked car, shouting)* If you want to see it, you have to pay admission!
The reporters begin barraging the manager with indistinct questions. People continue to walk out the glass doors, milling about and passing by on the sidewalk. Things are at a fever pitch. A car horn blares; the policeman continues to motion cars along. Lights continue to flicker on the crowd; the upbeat music plays on.

POLICEMAN *(Shouting)* Okay, keep moving, folks!

CUT TO:
INTERIOR. MOVIE THEATER—NIGHT.

The black-and-white movie suddenly fills the screen. Larry, in the penthouse living room, looks out at the offscreen audience. Chattering is heard from the audience, low and indistinct—as well as from the offscreen movie actors.

LARRY Any word about Tom Baxter?
The film cuts to Larry's point of view: the usherette, in color, standing in the aisle, holding her flashlight. People sit in their seats on both sides.

USHERETTE *(Looking up at the screen, loudly)* Nothing yet.
The film cuts back to the black-and-white movie screen. Larry stands to the side, still looking out at the audience. Behind him, Rita, Jason, the Countess, Henry, Delilah, Father Donnelly, and a previously unseen character, the Communist, in coat and jacket, are gathered around the coffee table. They are playing pinochle and smoking cigarettes.

JASON *(Glancing up at the offscreen audience)* Then what are you people *doing* here? We can't continue the story till Tom gets back.
The film cuts to the audience, in color, to a middle-aged couple sitting in their seats, watching the action on the screen. Other patrons are seen in the background.

HUSBAND *(Pointing)* Oh, we don't mind observing you at all. *(Smiles)*

WIFE Yes, my husband is a student of the human personality. *(Smiles)*
The camera is back on the black-and-white screen. Rita, her legs crossed, smoking a cigarette, turns from the game and looks offscreen at the couple.

RITA Oh, yeah? Well, we're not human.

The audience chuckles appreciatively as the film cuts back to the middle-aged couple, in color.

WIFE *(Looking up at the screen)* It doesn't matter to Harold. He has trouble with humans.

HUSBAND *(Turning to his wife, pointing at himself)* I have trouble? What, do have trouble with the real people?

WIFE *(To her husband)* Oh, I suppose you behave perfectly with Donald? *(To the offscreen movie actors)* He won't speak to my own son-in-law.

HUSBAND *(Pointing to himself, to his wife)* I won't speak? *(Gesturing, to the offscreen actors)* The kid is quiet. He never makes conversation.

WIFE *(Turning to her husband, reacting)* He has to be drawn out.

HUSBAND I don't like to draw people out. *(Sighs)*

WIFE *(To the offscreen movie actors)* That's what I said. He has trouble with live humans.

CUT TO:
INTERIOR. THEATER MANAGER'S OFFICE—NIGHT.

The frazzled theater manager, standing by his desk, is talking on the phone. The desk is cluttered with papers and pens. A calendar and other paraphernalia hang on the wall. In the background, in the offscreen lobby and front entrance, disgruntled moviegoers are heard. Police whistles blow; the murmur of the outside crowd is low and continuous.

THEATER MANAGER *(Into the phone, nodding)* Yes, yes, RKO!

MALE MOVIEGOER *(Offscreen)* I want my money back!

THEATER MANAGER *(Into the phone, overlapping the offscreen patrons)* I want to speak to Mr. Raoul Hirsch. *(Nodding, walking over to the percolator)* Yes—Mr. Hirsch. *(Pouring himself a cup of coffee)* He's the producer of *The Purple Rose of Cairo*, yes . . . No, he's not.

POLICEMAN *(Offscreen, overlapping)* Sir . . .

THEATER MANAGER *(Into the phone, continuing, overlapping as he sets his coffee cup down on the desk)* Just tell him I have a theater in New Jersey and there's a crisis with his film. *(Retrieves a napkin from his desk to wipe up a coffee spill)*

The film cuts to Raoul Hirsch's Hollywood office, a spacious, sleek room with a large window and potted plants. Raoul Hirsch sits at a large desk, facing the camera, talking on the phone. A man sits nearby, discussing some papers with a press agent standing in front of him. The crossed legs of a lawyer are partially seen in the background; he's swinging his leg. A secretary walks offscreen across the room as the scene opens.

HIRSCH *(Into the phone, with a slight accent)* Yes, this is Mr. Hirsch. What's the problem? . . . What?

The camera cuts back to the theater manager talking on the phone near his desk. In the background, a policeman, his back to the camera, lights a cigarette and pours himself a cup of coffee.

THEATER MANAGER *(Into the phone)* They're all just sitting around up there on the screen. *(Stuttering)* Rita, the Countess, Larry Wilde, the playboy. I, *(Grunts)* but, people are demanding their money back. The theater is nine-tenths empty.

A reporter moves onscreen, directly in front of the theater manager, his back to the camera. He holds a camera to his face—the flash goes off. Without missing a beat, the theater manager turns and taps the policeman on the back.

POLICEMAN *(Turning, to the reporter)* Come on, talk a walk, will you? *(Grabs and pulls the protesting reporter away offscreen)*

THEATER MANAGER *(Into the phone, overlapping the policeman and the murmuring reporter)* Look, *(Grunting)* he just walked out!

POLICEMAN *(Overlapping)* Come on! *(Continuing indistinctly offscreen, slamming an offscreen door)*

THEATER MANAGER *(Into the phone, continuing)* Baxter! The Communist is screaming. The priest in reel five is in reel two!
The film cuts back to Hirsch's Hollywood office, to a closer view of the desk area. The press agent, his back to the camera, stands in front of the desk, talking to the seated man. Hirsch, shaking his head, is on the phone—holding his hand over the receiver as the executives talk among themselves. A figurine sits on the corner of the desk.

SEATED EXECUTIVE *(Gesturing)* How can he come off the screen? It's impossible. It's never happened before in history.
The camera moves to the seated lawyer, only partially seen before. Framed photographs hang on the wall behind him.

LAWYER *(Leaning forward)* Just because a thing never happened before doesn't mean it can't happen for a first time.
The camera moves to the press agent, now standing at the bar pouring a drink, still holding his papers. A framed mural fills the wall behind the bar.

PRESS AGENT *(Gesturing with his glass and the bottle of liquor)* That's all you'll need. Hundreds of Tom Baxters, on the loose, runnin' around. *(Pours his drink)*
The camera cuts to Hirsch, hanging up the phone, a look of dismay on his face.

HIRSCH *(Grimacing skeptically)* Hundreds?

LAWYER *(Offscreen)* As your . . .
The camera moves back to the lawyer, getting up from his armchair. The press agent, his head turned to the lawyer, is seen in the background by the bar. He nods his head as the lawyer presents his case.

LAWYER *(Walking over to the offscreen Hirsch)* As your lawyer, I advise you to get control of it fast. A character from one of your productions on the loose? Who knows what he's capable of? Robbery, murder. *(Gesturing)* I see lawsuits.

SEATED EXECUTIVE *(Offscreen, in a clipped voice)* I'd *(Onscreen as the camera cuts to him in his chair)* charter a plane right away, and *(Gesturing, a cigarette in his hand)* I'd get down there fast.
The camera moves back to Hirsch, his face turned to the executive. Without missing a beat, without looking, he reaches for the phone.

HIRSCH *(Into the phone)* Get me Gil Shepherd.

CUT TO:
EXTERIOR. SUPPER CLUB—NIGHT.

A rambling one-time mansion is seen on the screen, its parking area crowded with cars. A blue neon sign over the entrance reads DINE AND DANCE. *The windows are lit up. The laughter and chatter of the club patrons are heard over a big-band sound playing in the background.*

The film cuts inside, to a dancing Cecilia and Tom. They smile into each other's eyes; Tom wears his pith helmet and khakis. Other couples dance in the background; dark wood doors and small lamps line the walls behind them. The din of conversation and laughter and clattering dishes is heard over the big-band sound. A male patron walks across the dance floor as Cecilia and Tom talk and slowly spin around.

CECILIA *(Smiling)* Sorry I'm not too light on my feet. *(Chuckles)*

TOM *(Overlapping)* Oh, no, you're a feather in my arms.

CECILIA *(Overlapping)* Oh, *(Chuckling)* Monk never took me dancing. I, not even, n-not even when we first met. Not even if I *begged* him.

TOM Really? So it's, so it's been bad for you. *(Sighs)*

CECILIA Oh, *(Looking down)* it-it's *(Shaking her head)* it's been hard for everyone. You know, living in the world with, with no jobs and, and wars. You, you probably never even heard of the Great War.

TOM *(Shaking his head)* No, I'm sorry. I missed it.

CECILIA Yeah, well *(Shaking her head)* y-you, people, people get old and, and sick and, and never find true love.

TOM *(Sighing)* Well, you know, where I come from, people, they don't disappoint. They're consistent. They're always reliable.

CECILIA Y-you don't find that kind in real life.

TOM You have.

They look at each other for a beat as the film abruptly cuts to a panoramic view of the back of a Hollywood mansion, lit up at night. A large, blue swimming pool reflects the light from its windows. Palm trees frame the three-storey house. The romantic big-band music has turned to upbeat jazz; the sounds of a party in progress are heard in the background. Through the windows, guests can faintly be seen milling about.

The film moves inside, to a large reception room. The camera looks down on the crowd, at the people milling about in clusters, walking and gathering on the stone staircase. Waiters in uniform weave their way through the guests; they hold silver trays of hor d'oeuvres. The men and women wear hats; some of the women wear flowery dresses. Potted plants line an alcove; a decorative armchair and a lamp sit against the wall. The din of conversation is heard over the upbeat jazz as the film cuts to a close-up of one of the guests, a suited woman in hat and veil. She is a Variety *reporter, flipping through a notebook, talking to an offscreen Gil Shepherd. Guests mill about in the background.*

VARIETY REPORTER *(Ready to write in her notebook, her pencil poised)* Is it true they'rc talking to you about the life of Lindbergh?

GIL *(Offscreen)* It's nearly set, but don't print it till it's firm.

VARIETY REPORTER *(Stopping her note-taking, smiling)* You were great in *The Purple Rose of Cairo.*
The camera cuts to Gil Shepherd—the actor who plays Tom Baxter. He wears a white suit; his hair is slicked back. The reporter's back is to the camera.

GIL Thanks, I was, uh . . . *(Pauses, smiling in a self-satisfied manner)* Did you know I was singled out by all the East Coast critics? Mm-hm. *(Inhaling) The New York Times* said that I was, *(Pauses, gesturing)* I had almost too smoldering a quality to just play comedy.

VARIETY REPORTER Would you play Lindbergh the way you played Tom Baxter?

GIL Would I play . . . ? *(Shaking his head)* No, of course not. Tom was kind of a change of pace for me. *(Looking past the reporter)* He was—from my earlier roles. *(Sighing)* I played Tom Baxter with a kind of poetic, idealistic quality that, uh *(Inhaling and gesturing)* just . . . Lindbergh was a loner. He was . . . just self-reliant. I'd have to work it out with my dialogue coach. He's a, he's a genius. He'll—

GIL'S AGENT *(Offscreen, interrupting)* Gil, *(Onscreen, walking up to Gil)* can I see you for a minute? Alone, please?

GIL Uh . . . *(Looks at the reporter)*

GIL'S AGENT *(Overlapping, to the reporter)* Excuse me, I'm sorry.

GIL *(Overlapping, walking away with his agent)* . . . sure.

GIL'S AGENT *(Pulling Gil away, past several milling guests)* Here, now right over here. *(Stopping at a private corner, near some plants)* Uh . . .

GIL *(Overlapping)* What's up?

GIL'S AGENT *(Grabbing Gil's arm)* Tom Baxter's come down off the screen and he's running around New Jersey.

GIL What are you talking about?

GIL'S AGENT *(Overlapping, in a stage whisper)* I just spoke to Raoul Hirsch. Nobody knows how it happened, but he's done it.

GIL How could he do that? It's not physically possible for—

GIL'S AGENT *(Looking off for a moment, nodding)* In New Jersey, anything can happen.

GIL *(Gesturing, oblivious to the guests who pass by on the balcony above them and in the reception hall)* But I created the character.

GIL'S AGENT That's my point! *(Looks around nervously)* As your agent, I would hate to see anything happen to your career now that it's starting to move.

GIL What, like, like, like what?

GIL'S AGENT Who knows? There's a double of you on the loose! What's he up to? Is he robbing banks? Is he raping broads?

GIL But is he?!

GIL'S AGENT *(Looking around for a moment)* Who knows? *(Gesturing dramatically)* Look, the last thing we need is for you to get a repu—

GIL *(Interrupting, whispering as a couple walks by)* Shhhh.
Gil rubs the back of his neck, waiting for the couple to walk past offscreen. Gil's agent looks around, waiting for them to exit.

GIL'S AGENT *(After a beat)* The last thing we need is for you to get a reputation as somehow difficult.

GIL *(Outraged)* But I'm not, it's not my fault!

GIL'S AGENT *(Overlapping)* Raoul Hirsch already said, if you can't control your own creation *(Pointing at Gil)* nobody's going to risk a picture on you.

GIL *(Flailing his arms)* Oh, my God! There g— I mean, you know, I worked so hard to make him real.

GIL'S AGENT *(Overlapping, nodding his head)* Yeah, well, maybe you overdid it.
Gil's agent takes a puff of a cigarette; he looks around. A waiter passes in front of the camera.

GIL Jeez, I'll sue my dialogue coach, that louse. *(Groans, his hand to his mouth)*

GIL'S AGENT *(Overlapping Gil's groan, gesturing)* Look, I'm s— You've got to fly down there and check into this, quick.
Gil sighs deeply.

GIL'S AGENT *(Gesturing)* Right now it's only one movie house, but who knows?

GIL *(Shaking his head)* I can't, oh, I'm, I'm afraid to fly.

GIL'S AGENT Gil, this is the scandal of all time. You know what happened to Fatty Arbuckle's career?

GIL *(After a beat, holding up his hand)* I'll fly. I'll fly.

GIL'S AGENT Good.
They both look around; Gil's agent takes another puff of his cigarette. A man passes in front of the camera, his back to them; the film cuts to:

INTERIOR. SUPPER CLUB—NIGHT.

Tom and Cecilia are sitting at a dark, romantic table. They hold their champagne glasses up to each other's mouths. A lamp sits on the wainscotted wall near their table. A waiter passes by. The clatter and laughter of the other patrons are heard in the background; the big-band music begins to play.

TOM *(Sipping from Cecilia's glass)* This is how they drink champagne in Cairo.

CECILIA *(Sipping from Tom's glass, sniffing)* I never had champagne before. I fee— *(Gesturing)* It makes me feel silly.

TOM *(Smiling)* It's supposed to.

CECILIA *(Laughing, touching her forehead)* Yeah.
Tom also begins to laugh as a waiter, his back to the camera, walks over to their table, obscuring Tom for a moment.

WAITER *(Overlapping their laughter, putting the check on the table)* The check, as you requested, sir.

TOM Ah! *(Lightly hits the tabletop, then reaches into his pocket for his wallet)*

CECILIA *(Gasping, looking at the check and reacting)* It's so much!
The camera cuts to a different view of the table. The waiter is now seen at Tom's side. Cecilia's back is to the camera. Tom, smiling, takes some bills from his wallet. The waiter's hands are clasped in front of him.

TOM *(With nonchalance, wetting his finger as he counts out the bills)* Oh . . .

WAITER I, I hope you found it to your liking, sir.

TOM It was superb.

CECILIA *(Overlapping)* Oh, it was, it was wonderful.

TOM *(Overlapping)* My compliments to the chef. *(Counting out a few more bills and handing them to the waiter)* And, uh, keep twenty percent for yourself. *(Holding his hand up)* No— *(Pauses, looking at Cecilia and smiling)* Make that thirty percent.

WAITER *(Looking at the money)* Yes, quite amusing.

TOM *(Smiling, glancing at the waiter)* What is?

WAITER Th-the fake money.

TOM Fake money?

The camera cuts to a close-up of Cecilia's puzzled face.

WAITER *(Offscreen)* Is it, uh, play money, sir, or stage money?

The camera moves back to Tom and the waiter standing at his side. Tom reacts, looking at Cecilia, then up at the waiter—who is holding the money and looking intently at Tom.

TOM *(Gesturing, with impatience)* Keep thirty percent for yourself, and stop looking so serious.

WAITER *(After a beat, picking up the check from the table)* I'll get the maitre d'.

The camera moves to a close-up of Cecilia's face as the waiter walks off. As the big-band music continues, the film cuts back and forth from Cecilia to Tom as they discuss their situation.

CECILIA *(Panic-stricken)* Tom, that's not real money!

TOM Well, what do, wha-what do you mean it's not real money? *(Sighs, then in stunned realization:)* Oh, my God, it's n— *(Sighing)* Do y—, uh, do you have any money?

CECILIA *(Gasping)* No. What are we going to do?

TOM W-just, we're going to have to make a run for it.

CECILIA *(Shaking her head)* No, I can't run. My ankles are bad from waitressing.

TOM *(Starting to rise from his seat, in a stage whisper)* Just— Get up. Follow me.

The film cuts to a wider view of the supper club dining room. Patrons sit at their tables, chatting and eating; a man pours champagne for his companion. Lights illuminate the tables; the walls are wainscotted halfway up in an arch design. Across the width of the room, past the other patrons, are Tom and Cecilia—getting up from their table. Tom nonchalantly takes off his pith helmet and stretches; he waves at some diners as he and Cecilia stroll to the nearby entranceway—an arch bordered in wood. As soon as they enter the lobby, they start to run. A chandelier hangs in the lobby; a waiter leans against its wall. A waiter in the dining room walks past the camera. The big-band music changes to fast-paced jazz.

A man walks onscreen in the lobby, waving to Tom and Cecilia's retreating figures as the film cuts to outside the supper club. Tom and Cecilia are running down the front entrance's awninged steps. The blue neon DINE AND DANCE *sign glows in the dark. They run into the parking area.*

TOM Quick, get in the car.

The film cuts to the windshield and front of an empty car—as Tom stumbles into the driver's seat. He slams the door closed. Cecilia jumps in on the passenger side and closes her door.

CECILIA *(Frantically)* Tom, this is not our car! We don't have a car! We came by foot.

TOM *(Holding on to the steering wheel)* It doesn't go.

CECILIA *(Shaking her head)* Well, 'c-c-course it doesn't go. There's no key.

TOM I just, hey, I don't understand. This is how I always go in the movie.

CECILIA *(Holding her face)* Oh, Tom, this is real life! They don't start without a key!

TOM *(Looking at Cecilia)* They don't?

CECILIA No!

TOM Let's go.

MAITRE D' *(Offscreen)* Hey, you two, get back here!

Tom and Cecilia open their doors almost simultaneously as the film cuts back to the entrance of the supper club. The maitre d' runs down the steps, the waiter fast at his heels. They stop at the bottom of the steps, under the awning, and facing the camera, they yell at the offscreen people. Another man walks out the door and stands at the top of the steps. The action jazz music continues.

WAITER They're leavin'.

MAITRE D' *(Shaking his fist, yelling as the waiter mutters indistinctly next to him)* You can't run out on these checks. *(To the waiter)* They're a couple of deadbeats. *(Yelling)* Get back here, right now!

WAITER *(Overlapping, yelling)* Hey!

The music stops and the film cuts to the deserted amusement park, to the silent Ferris wheel looking golden in the moonlight. Crickets are heard in the background and the film cuts to:

The darkened carousel, enclosed in a huge pavilion. As Cecilia and Tom talk offscreen, the camera pans across the shadowy horses, chariots, and carved animals.

TOM *(Offscreen)* I'm sorry about the money. I had no idea.

CECILIA *(Offscreen)* Oh, that's okay. *(Chuckling)* It's, it's not going to be so easy to get along without it in this world.

TOM *(Offscreen)* Oh, I guess I have to get a job. *(Sighs)*

The camera stops as it comes to the couple, who are sitting in a chariot. Tom's arm is around Cecilia's shoulders. They look at each other, illuminated by the moonlight.

CECILIA *(Inhaling)* But that's not going to be so easy, either. Right now, the whole country's out of work.

TOM Well, then we'll live on love. We'll have to make some concessions, but so what? We'll have each other.

CECILIA That's movie talk.

The camera moves closer and closer to their faces. Romantic piano music begins to play.

TOM *(Looking softly at Cecilia)* You look so beautiful in this light.

CECILIA *(Looking into Tom's eyes)* But you're not real.

Tom looks at Cecilia, then kisses her.

TOM *(Breaking the kiss, sighing)* Was that real enough for you?

CECILIA *(Sighing)* You, you kiss perfectly. It's what I dreamed kissing would be like.

TOM Come away with me to Cairo.

CECILIA Cairo?

TOM We'll live in the desert. It will, oh, and the blue-gold light of sunset falling over your hair and the—

CECILIA *(Interrupting, sighing, putting her hand on her face)* Look, I-I'm sorry. I'm a little tipsy. I, uh-oh-oh, from the champa—

Tom interrupts Cecilia with another kiss, his hand cradling her neck. The kiss becomes a lingering embrace.

TOM *(Breaking the kiss, looking around)* Where's the fade-out?

CECILIA *(Touching her hat, confused)* What? Uh . . .

TOM *(Overlapping, looking out at the offscreen camera)* Always when the kissing gets hot and heavy, just before the, the lovemaking, there's a, *(Turning his head, looking all around)* there's a fade-out.

CECILIA *(Sighing)* Oh, then what?

TOM Then . . . then we're making love in some private, perfect place. *(Chuckles and sighs)*

CECILIA *(Sighing)* Oh, that, that's not how it happens here.

TOM It's . . . *(Looking at Cecilia)* What, there's no fade-out?

CECILIA No . . . *(Shaking her head)* but when you kissed me, I felt like my heart faded out, and *(Nodding her head)* I-I closed my eyes and I . . . I was in some, some private place.

TOM How fascinating. You make, you make love without fading out?

CECILIA *(Chuckling)* Yes.

TOM *(Sighing)* Well, I can't wait to see this. *(Begins to kiss Cecilia again)*

CECILIA *(Inhaling, moving her head away)* Well, look . . . *(Sighing)* Listen, I, I can— I'm not that kind of girl. I'm, uh, I'm married.

TOM Cecilia, it's clear how miserable you are with your husband. And if he hits you again, you tell me.
Cecilia sighs, her head down. The piano music plays on.

TOM *(Overlapping Cecilia's sigh)* I'd be forced to knock his teeth out.

CECILIA *(Shaking her head)* I don't think that would be such a good idea. He's big.

TOM Tch, well, I'm sorry. It's written into my character to do it, so I do it.

CECILIA *(After a beat)* Listen, *(Nodding her head)* I . . . I-I-I think I better go home now. It's, it's late.

TOM *(Overlapping)* Okay.

CECILIA It's-it's been a whirlwind of a day. Don't you think?

TOM *(Nodding)* Yeah.

CECILIA What are you gonna do?

TOM *(Inhales)* Um, I'll just, I'll sleep here at the carousel . . .

CECILIA *(Sighing, overlapping, nodding her head)* Oh.

TOM *(Overlapping)* . . . and walk around . . . drink in the night air . . . enjoy my freedom . . . and dream of you.
Tom is silent for a beat, looking at Cecilia, as they embrace. The music finishes, the kiss lingers, and the film cuts to:

INTERIOR. CECILIA'S APARTMENT—DAY.

Monk is in the bathroom, looking in a mirror as he shaves with a straight razor. Shaving cream is on his cheeks and under his nose. The open doorway is reflected in the mirror. A bathroom light on the wall is lit.

MONK *(Shaving, to the offscreen Cecilia)* You got in late last night.

CECILIA *(Offscreen)* Oh, yeah, you were out like a light.

MONK I took a hot bath to relax me. *(Turning towards the camera, towards the open doorway)* You want to get me a cup of coffee? *(Turns back to the mirror, shaving)*
The film cuts to the bedroom, as seen through its doorway. Cecilia, in her robe, is making the bed, a pillow in her hand.

CECILIA *(Dropping the pillow back on the bed, quickly leaving the room to do Monk's bidding)* Oh, yeah, sure.
The camera follows Cecilia as she walks through the living room into the dark kitchen, as the offscreen Monk continues to talk to her.

MONK *(Offscreen)* There was some big deal going on over at the movie house. A big crowd when I went to buy cigarettes.

CECILIA *(Picking up a cup at the sink)* Yeah?

MONK *(Offscreen)* Yeah, I couldn't get the story straight. There's some guy who ran out the side exit with a customer.

CECILIA *(Pouring some perked coffee into the cup from an offscreen stove)* Who?

Monk walks out of the bathroom onscreen into the hall. He's only partially shaved, the razor in his hand. He leans against the hallway wall as he continues to talk. Cecilia can be seen in the kitchen, the wall separating her from Monk.

MONK Oh, a woman, a guy, uh, an actor. *(Feeling his face)* I don't know what the hell the cop was talking about. He didn't know.

CECILIA *(Walking out of the kitchen, holding Monk's cup)* W-well, di-di-did, they don't know who the woman was? *(Hands Monk his cup)*

MONK Some woman, dragged out in the dark. *(Gesturing with the razor in hand)* They got those real Geronimos at the movie houses. *(Leaning forward to Cecilia, gesturing)* See, that's why I don't like you staying out so late at night. *(Takes a sip of coffee)*

CECILIA *(Shrugging, gesturing)* I know. I-I-I-I couldn't help it.

Cecilia turns and walks back to the kitchen as she talks, her hands fidgety. The camera follows her, leaving Monk in the hall. She starts to putter, cleaning off the table. The kitchen is cluttered; there are dishes in the sink. The shade is down on the window over the sink.

CECILIA *(Continuing)* The Lorenzos didn't get back till late. I-I couldn't leave.

MONK *(Offscreen)* Well, I hope you got paid overtime.

CECILIA *(Wiping the table)* Oh, sure.

MONK *(Walking onscreen, into the kitchen)* Oh, good, good. *(Holding his hand out)* Let's have it.

CECILIA *(Shaking her head, gesturing with one hand holding a napkin, the other a dish)* They, uh, they, I, they didn't have any cash. I-I'll have to come back for it later today. *(Looking down at the table, clearing it, her back to Monk)*

MONK Cecilia, I told you to get paid, uh, in cash, didn't I?

CECILIA *(Scraping a plate, her head down)* Well, I know, but, uh, they . . . all they had was, was, was big bills, and, um, you know, I was getting late, so I thought I better leave.

MONK *(Overlapping, gesturing, the razor and cup in his hand)* Yeah, well, they're going to fork it over today, right?

CECILIA *(Nodding, her head still down, her back to Monk)* Oh, they, yeah, they will.

MONK *(Overlapping)* Yeah, yeah, sure. *(Gesturing)* Leave something to you, you can bet you're going to get fouled up.
Monk leaves the kitchen. Cecilia looks up as he exits. She walks away from the table, towards the camera, looking worried, rubbing her face with her hand. Upbeat jazz begins to play as the film cuts to the Jewel Theater, as seen from the street. It is daytime; several limousines are parked outside. Under the marquee, a policeman stands talking and gesturing to two passersby. Factories and other buildings can be seen farther down the street. The sidewalk is dotted with telephone poles. A barking dog is faintly heard over the music, as the film cuts to:

INTERIOR. MOVIE THEATER—DAY.

Raoul Hirsch's face fills the screen. He stands in the aisle of the empty theater, looking at the off-camera movie screen.

HIRSCH *(Shouting)* You have no idea where he went?
The film cuts to a wider view of the theater. The black-and-white

movie screen is seen over the full-color backs of Hirsch and his entourage. They are all standing, including Gil Shepherd. Cigarette smoke curls up in the illumination from the screen—which shows Rita, Henry, the Countess, and Jason in the penthouse living room, looking out at Hirsch and company. Another character, indistinct on the screen, paces in the background.

HENRY Mr. Hirsch, this is awful for us.

COUNTESS *(Muttering)* It sure is.

JASON *(Overlapping)* Really difficult.

The film moves back to Hirsch and company in color. Gil and the press agent stand on either side of the producer. The lawyer sits on the armrest of an aisle seat. The theater manager and the usherette stand behind the group. The light from the projection booth glares out over the scene. While Hirsch and company have a rapid-fire discussion, the offscreen movie characters chatter continuously, indistinctly, in the background.

GIL *(Looking up at the off-camera movie screen, gesturing)* Think of me, my reputation, my career!

LAWYER *(Gesturing, his face obscured by the projector's light)* First thing we've gotta do, is we gotta keep it contained.

GIL *(Nodding)* Yeah.

THEATER MANAGER The word's out already.

LAWYER *(Overlapping)* We gotta keep the crisis local.

THEATER MANAGER *(To the lawyer)* I know the two reporters in town. They're old friends. Maybe I could talk to them.

PRESS AGENT *(Overlapping)* Fine, a couple of bucks spread around town will buy us some time. Don't worry about a thing. We're . . .

GIL *(Overlapping, nodding vigorously)* Great, great.

The scene shifts back to the black-and-white movie screen, as seen over the backs of Hirsch and company. The characters are all gathered at the edge of the screen, joining the discussion.

PRESS AGENT *(Continuing)* . . . all . . .

HENRY *(Overlapping, gesturing on the black-and-white screen)* I mean, we-we're-we're all so lost.

HIRSCH *(His back to the camera, looking up at the screen)* I know it's rough. I just want the whole cast to know how much I appreciate your staying up there on the screen.

The film moves back to Hirsch et al., in color, now seen in profile in a side view. Gil, a long scarf flung around his neck, a pair of gloves in his hand, leans over to Hirsch. The illumination from the action on the off-camera movie screen flickers on their faces.

GIL *(Gesturing, to Hirsch)* I, I hope you're not going to hold this against me, R.H.

HIRSCH *(Turning to look at Gil)* You created the part of Tom Baxter, Gil. The facts are undeniable.

As Hirsch speaks, the film cuts back to the black-and-white movie screen; it fills the screen. Henry stands to the left, near the edge of the screen, sipping a drink. Rita, too, is at the edge of the screen, on the right; she holds her hand up. Larry is sitting on the sofa, a cigar in his hand. Delilah is seen sitting on the piano bench in the background.

LARRY *(Shouting, jumping up from the sofa)* I want to go too. I want to be free! I want out!

The film moves back to Hirsch and company, in color. They're all looking up at the offscreen movie characters.

HIRSCH *(Pointing to the screen)* I'm warning you, that's Communist talk!

THEATER MANAGER *(His face obscured by the projector's light)* We're

gonna have to pull the film out of the theater and you're gonna have to make good my receipts.
The group, reacting, turns to look at him as the film cuts back to the black-and-white screen. The Countess and Jason have joined Rita and Henry at the edge of the screen.

COUNTESS You mean, you're thinking of pulling the film because a minor character is missing?
The film cuts back to a closer view of Hirsch, Gil standing at his side. They both look up at the off-camera movie screen. Cigarette smoke from the offscreen lawyer billows up in the background.

GIL *(Indignant)* A minor character?! *(To Hirsch)* Would you listen to her? *(To the offscreen Countess)* You know, he may not have the most lines, but the plot turns on Baxter. I, I deliberately played him with a cheerful bravado.
The film cuts back to the black-and-white movie screen.

COUNTESS Who cares how you played him? He's minor.

HENRY *(Nodding slightly)* That's right.
Back to Gil and Hirsch, in color, in the aisle.

GIL *(Looking around, agitated)* I would just like to get my hands on him. Right when my career was taking off.
Back to the black-and-white movie screen, to a closer view of Rita. Larry, quiet now, sits on the sofa in the background. Only Henry's shoulder is seen.

RITA He could be raping that woman he abducted.

GIL *(Offscreen)* And he's . . .
As Gil begins to speak, the film cuts back to Hirsch and company, seen in their entirety.

GIL *(Onscreen, continuing, gesturing)* . . . got my fingerprints, my exact prints!
The film goes back to the black-and-white screen, to a closer view of the Countess, standing between a partially seen Jason and Henry.

COUNTESS You know what they get for rape in a small town, especially by a man in a pith helmet?

The film goes back to the theater, in color. Gil turns and runs up the aisle offscreen. The others glance at him, then turn back to the ensemble on the off-camera movie screen.

LAWYER *(Fidgeting on his armrest seat)* If this is the start of a new trend, our industry's as good as dead.

PRESS AGENT *(Gesturing)* The real ones want their lives fiction, and the fictional ones want their lives real.

HIRSCH *(Nodding, turning to the theater manager)* Does anybody know who that woman was?

THEATER MANAGER No. It was all so crazy, nobody noticed.

CUT TO:
INTERIOR. DRUGSTORE NEAR THE JEWEL THEATER—DAY.

The drugstore counter is busy; the stools are all taken. A woman sips her coffee; there is indistinct background clatter. Doughnuts are stacked on a plate on the counter. Cecilia is seen standing by the storefront window, talking to the man behind the counter; he wipes a glass with a towel.

Cars pass by on the street outside the window; parked cars line the sidewalk. A rack of magazines stands on the wall near Cecilia.

CECILIA *(To the counterman)* Just two doughnuts and a container of coffee to go, please.

The counterman, nodding, goes off to fill the order. Cecilia rummages in her pocketbook for money as the camera slowly moves away from her, past the customers on their stools, past the store's windowed door, complete with a hanging sign advertising pie. A woman enters, closing the door behind her, as the camera continues to pan across the store. Gil's voice is heard as the camera moves past some empty tables, holding napkin dispensers and salt and pepper shakers, past another magazine rack, past another storefront window. Cars and people pass by outside as the camera stops at a phone booth—where Gil is slouched over, talking on the phone. A young woman eats at a table near the booth.

GIL *(Offscreen, into the phone)* Right now, it's chaos . . . Well, how can rumors be circulating at the Brown Derby? It just happened! . . . Well, squash it, Herbie, I got a *(Onscreen)* career on the line . . . Look, I'll call you the minute I hear.
Gil hangs up and walks out of the booth, a disgusted look on his face. He goes to the store's door—just as Cecilia, holding her take-out bag, reaches for the doorknob. She looks at Gil; she gasps.

GIL *(Overlapping Cecilia's gasp)* Oh, excuse me.

CECILIA *(Astonished)* What are you *doing* here?!

GIL *(Gesturing, patting his pockets)* I'm, I'm sorry. I don't have a pencil, or I'd give you an autograph. *(Chuckles)*

CECILIA *(Overlapping)* Where, where'd, where did you get those clothes?

GIL *(Looking down at himself)* Pardon me?

CECILIA Those clothes, where did you get them?

GIL Uh, a little store on Sunset and Vine. *(Chuckles)*

CECILIA *(Overlapping)* What are you talking about?

GIL *(Chuckling)* What are, what are you talking about?

DRUGSTORE CUSTOMER *(Walking between them, out the door)* Excuse me.

CECILIA *(Handing Gil the take-out bag)* I, I, I just bought you these. Two dough-doughnuts.

GIL *(Overlapping)* For me?

CECILIA Yeah. A container of coffee.

GIL *(Overlapping, taking the bag)* Well, thank you very much. It, uh, I hope you enjoy my next movie. *(Starts to open the door, smiling)*

CECILIA But, do you, I-I thought you were going to stay hidden at the park.

GIL *(His hand on the doorknob)* What park?

CECILIA *(Puzzled)* Tom, what's the matter with you? You're acting so peculiar.

GIL *(Overlapping, touching his face)* Tom, no, no. I'm— *(Breaks off, suddenly understanding, taking Cecilia's arm)* Wait a minute! Come 'ere.

Gil opens the door and practically pushes Cecilia out, following close behind.

CECILIA What, what's come over you?

The film cuts outside as they stumble through the door and down its few steps. They begin to rush down the sidewalk, Gil still holding on to Cecilia's arm, passing several storefronts, passing several pedestrians walking the other way.

GIL *(Pointing to himself)* I'm not Tom. I'm Gil Shepherd. I play Tom.

CECILIA *(Putting her hand to her mouth)* What?

GIL How do you know Tom?

CECILIA You're Gi— You're— *(Amazed)* Oh, my God!

GIL *(Overlapping, breathlessly)* Yeah.

CECILIA I don't believe it! You're Gil She— *(Gasps)* I've seen you in lots of movies!

Gil pulls Cecilia into a covered alleyway, letting go of her arm. Cecilia is against the wall; Gil stands in front of her.

GIL *(Breathlessly)* Look, where's Tom?

CECILIA *(Overlapping, gasping)* Oh! *(Gesturing, grinning and reacting) Broadway Bachelors*, right? Right?

GIL *(Overlapping, nodding)* Ye—, yeah, yeah, well, you know . . .

CECILIA *(Overlapping, squealing)* *Honeymoon in Haiti? Honeymoon in Haiti?*

GIL *(Overlapping, nodding)* Done about six.

CECILIA *(Squealing)* You were a scream.

GIL *(Grinning, slowly)* Well, thank you.

Cecilia continues to gasp and squeal loudly. The camera moves from Gil to Cecilia as they talk.

GIL *(Laughing)* Thank you very much. That's . . . *(Laughing)* I try to do one, you know, just to keep . . . *(Pauses, touching Cecilia's arm)* You, wha— Uh, wh-where-where's Tom?

CECILIA Why?

GIL Well, he's my character. I created him.

The camera stays on Cecilia's glowing, excited face. She continues to gasp; she bites her gloved fingers.

CECILIA Well, didn't the man who wrote the movie do that?

GIL *(Offscreen)* Yes, technically. *(Coughing)* But I made him live. I fleshed him out.

CECILIA *(Gasping)* But you did, *(Waving her arms)* you did a wonderful job. He's adorable.

The film moves back to Gil's pleased face. It continues to cut back and forth, from face to face, as they continue their animated conversation in the alleyway.

GIL *(Grinning)* Thank you very much. *(Laughs, then after a beat, sighs)* What's your name?

CECILIA *(Smiling)* Cecilia.

GIL *(Offscreen, the camera still on Cecilia)* Cecilia.

CECILIA *(Overlapping)* Uh-huh. *(Gasps, almost swooning)*

GIL *(Offscreen, the camera still on Cecilia)* Where is he?

CECILIA *(Suddenly serious)* Why?

GIL Has he done anything wrong?

CECILIA *(Offscreen, the camera still on Gil)* Wrong, like what?

GIL Has he stolen anything or attacked any females? You?

CECILIA *(Shaking her head)* No, gosh, no, no, he's as sweet as can be.

GIL *(Shrugging)* Well, I played him sweet. *(Smiling)* I was well reviewed.

CECILIA *(Offscreen, gasping, the camera still on Gil)* Well, it comes across.

GIL *(Sighing with relief)* Good . . . Look, I gotta speak to him. *The camera moves back; both Cecilia and Gil are now seen on the screen, standing in the alleyway.*

CECILIA You're not upset with him?

GIL Well, a little, yes, but I know if I spoke to him, we could straighten everything out.

CECILIA Oh, I . . . I don't know.

GIL Please, I have a right.

CECILIA W-well, y-y-you-you, it has to be secret. *(Gesturing)* He doesn't want to have to go back into the movie.

GIL *(Dismayed)* He doesn't?

CECILIA *(Shaking her head)* No, he-he-he-he loves being free. He's having the time of his life.

GIL *(Sighing)* Oh, my God. *(Gesturing)* Would you take me to him? Trust me . . . *please.*

Old-fashioned jazz begins to play as the film cuts to the outside of the factory where Monk and his cronies are pitching pennies against the wall exactly as they did earlier in the film. Their laughter and chatter can be indistinctly heard over the music as the film cuts to a closer view of the group. Monk's leaning forward, poised to pitch his pennies, a cigarette dangling from his mouth. The other men are lined up in a row behind him, watching and leaning forward as well. A man stands next to a burning trash can in the background. Monk makes his pitch.

MONK *(Tossing his penny)* Ho!

Monk saunters away from the group, the camera following as he moves to the wall, looking down at his penny.

PENNY PITCHER #1 *(Offscreen)* Monk, *(Onscreen, walking over to Monk)* somebody saw your wife last night at the Dine and Dance joint.

MONK *(Standing next to penny pitcher #1, his back to the camera)* Oh, sure, she's there every night with the Rockefellers. *(Pointing at the offscreen pitchers)*

PENNY PITCHER #1 *(Looking at Monk)* Uh, she was with this crazy-looking guy wearing an explorer's hat and breeches.

MONK *(Overlapping, to the other offscreen penny pitchers)* Come on.

One of the pitchers walks onscreen briefly, to the wall and back offscreen, as he picks up the tossed pennies.

MONK *(To penny pitcher #1, after a beat)* Breeches? You know, you're nuts. *(Leaning over to penny pitcher #1)* She was babysittin'.

PENNY PITCHER #1 *(To Monk)* Right. I guess you know it all. *(After a beat, to the other penny pitchers)* All right, who's next?

While the penny pitchers continue their game in the background, Monk turns and walks away, towards the camera. He scratches his ear; he looks off, at the camera, reflecting, and the film cuts to:

INTERIOR. MERRY-GO-ROUND—DAY.

Cecilia, framed in the daylight outside, enters the darker pavilion through the doorway, hesitantly looking around. She holds the take-out bag. A colorful, carved carousel piece hangs on the wall nearby.

CECILIA Tom? Tom?

The film cuts to the deeper shadows of the pavilion; light is reflected off the merry-go-round poles as Tom, in his pith helmet, steps out onscreen. The faint outlines of the carousel can be seen.

TOM *(Grinning)* Cecilia. I dreamed of us in Cairo. We . . .

The camera moves back to Cecilia, in the doorway. The jazz stops playing.

CECILIA *(Overlapping, interrupting)* Tom. Tom . . . eh, *(Pointing behind her as Gil walks through the doorway)* I-I brought, eh, I brought Gil Shepherd.

GIL *(Overlapping, pulling off his gloves)* Gil, Gil Shepherd. I play you in the movie.

The camera moves from Tom, in the shadows, to Gil and Cecilia, standing by the doorway, as each one talks.

TOM You do?

GIL How dare you run away!

TOM *(Shrugging slightly)* This is disconcerting.

Gil begins an angry-sounding chortle as the camera moves back, revealing the three of them in their positions. Gil and Tom are facing each other; Cecilia hovers in the background.

GIL *(Rushing over to Tom)* Oh, I'll show you the meaning of disconcerting. *(Grabbing Tom's lapels, shouting)* I'm trying to build a career!

TOM Yeah, well, I don't want to be in the film anymore. *(Pushing Gil away, offscreen)* I'm in love with Cecilia.

CECILIA *(Offscreen)* Mr. Shepherd, *(Onscreen as the camera moves to her face)* you said you weren't angry.

GIL *(Offscreen)* You *(Onscreen as the camera moves back to the two men, Tom smoothing down his safari jacket)* can't do this to me. It's my best role. I've been critically acclaimed for this. *(Gesturing)* It's my very—

TOM *(Interrupting, jerking down his jacket)* I'd say, it's because of the way I do it.

GIL No, no, no, because of the way I do it. I'm doing it, not you. *(Turning to look at the offscreen Cecilia, gesturing)* It, it, it, it's me, not him. I mean, isn't that obvious?

TOM *(Pointing to himself)* Well, then, how do you explain that here I am? *(Crosses his arms on his chest)*

GIL *(Putting his hands on his hips)* Well, because I took you from the printed page, and I made you live. *(Gesturing)* I fleshed you out, just like—

TOM *(Interrupting, shrugging)* So, I'm living.

GIL Yes, but for the screen only, please. *(Gesturing)* And as soon—

TOM *(Interrupting)* I want my freedom. *(Hits his chest with emotion)*

GIL I don't want another one of me running around the world. *(Turning to the offscreen Cecilia)* I mean, I can just imagine what he's been up—

TOM *(Interrupting)* Why? *(Gesturing)* Are you, are you afraid I'll embarrass you?

GIL Yes. *(Nodding his head)* Frankly I am afraid—

TOM *(Interrupting, gesturing)* But, y-y-you created me.

GIL All right, look— *(Sighing)* I'm, be reasonable here. *(Gesturing)* I'm starting to build a career. Is life up on the screen so terrible that you—

TOM *(Interrupting, gesturing)* I wanted to be with Cecilia. I'm in love with her.
Gil flings his arms up in the air and, turning, walks back to Cecilia.

GIL *(Pointing behind him, to the offscreen Tom)* Will you tell him to go back? Tell him you, tell him that you don't love him. *(Gesturing, looking behind him, turning back and forth from Cecilia to the offscreen Tom)* Tell him you *can't* love him. He's *(Laughing)* fictional! You want to waste your time with a fictional character? I mean, you're a sweet girl. You deserve an actual human.

CECILIA B-but Tom's perfect!

GIL *(Gesturing)* Yeah, uh, but he's not real. What good is "perfect" if the man's not real?!
The camera moves back to Tom's face, following him as he walks over to Gil and Cecilia by the doorway.

TOM *(Shrugging)* I can learn to be real. *(Standing by the others, his back to the camera)* It's easy. You know, there's nothing to it. Uh, being real comes very naturally to me.
The film cuts to a different view of the three of them, to Tom and Gil as seen over Cecilia's back and shoulders.

GIL *(Interrupting, turning to Tom and gesturing)* Can't learn to be real. It's like learning to be a midget. It's not a thing you can learn. Some of us are real, some are not.

TOM *(To Gil, nodding, as he looks at Cecilia)* I say I can do it.

GIL *(Turning away, the camera following him as he stands near Cecilia)* I'm not going to stay here and argue with you. I'm gonna go back to town. *(Pulling on his gloves)* I'm gonna call my attorney, the Actors' Union. *(Glaring at Tom, whose back is to the camera)* I won't take this lying down . . . nor will Raoul Hirsch, nor the police, nor the FBI!

CUT TO:
INTERIOR. THEATER MANAGER'S OFFICE—NIGHT.

Hirsch and some of his entourage are crowded in the cramped office. Hirsch sits behind the cluttered desk, almost dwarfed by the stacks of paper and paraphernalia. The lawyer sits on the edge of the desk, talking into the telephone. Hirsch, immobile, watches him. His partially seen girlfriend sits in a nearby chair, her back to the camera. She smokes a cigarette. While the lawyer talks, a man in shirt-sleeves and suspenders walks onscreen, putting a cup of coffee down in front of Hirsch. He offers some to the woman, then puts her cup down on the edge of the desk. When Hirsch puts a cigarette in his mouth, his eyes never leaving the lawyer on the phone, the shirt-sleeved man quickly lights it.

LAWYER *(Into the phone)* Yes, yes, we found him . . . Gil Shepherd found him, but he refuses to get back on the screen. *(Looking over at Hirsch, who nods his head)* R.H. is very upset . . . No, no, we-we can't force him. *(Gesturing)* It's not a crime. We need a plan . . . Yeah, the press is on our side.
Without missing a beat, the lawyer turns to the shirt-sleeved man, who gestures that everything has been taken care of. The lawyer nods, still talking on the phone.

LAWYER *(Continuing, into phone)* It took a few bucks, but they're going to keep it quiet for now. Ah . . . What? Really?! *(Putting his hand on the receiver and standing up, to Hirsch)* The Tom Baxter character in a movie house in Chicago has been forgetting his lines. He just got a call from the manager.

HIRSCH *(Pausing, shaking his head)* If anybody wants me, I'll be in the bathroom . . . on the floor, weeping.

Hirsch starts to get up, his cigarette in hand, as upbeat jazz begins anew, as the film cuts to:

EXTERIOR. SUSPENSION BRIDGE—DAY.

The walkway of the bridge is empty. Apartments and other buildings can be seen in the background. The sky is gray. Cecilia and Tom's voices can be heard as they slowly walk onscreen, along the walkway. They continue to talk, walking across the screen, the camera moving with them, as a man strolls by, going in the opposite direction; he looks back at the oblivious Tom, reacting to his safari clothes.

CECILIA *(Offscreen)* I mean, you do, ar-aren't you at all *(Onscreen)* even worried? Well, what about Raoul Hirsch and what, the FBI?

TOM No, Cecilia, if I can be with you, I'm never going back.

CECILIA But I, you know . . . *(Trails off, murmuring)*

TOM *(Interrupting, gesturing)* No more buts. I said I was going to learn about the real world with you. Show me.
The film cuts to the blue doorway of the Salvation Army's red-brick building. Upbeat jazz plays over the soundless action. Under a hanging lamp is the Salvation Army's logo and a sign reading SOUP KITCHEN. *The screen moves to the brick wall with its partially seen windows outside the building. A group of bums sit along the sidewalk, leaning against the wall; others slouch on the stairs leading to the doorway. Cecilia and Tom walk onscreen, along the sidewalk. As the couple passes by, the bums stand up in turn and start to follow them, pointing to Tom's safari suit and pith helmet. A woman and a child are among the group. Tom's causing quite a stir; the upbeat jazz goes on.*

Tom turns and looks at the crowd; he stops by a bum sitting on the stairs. He points to him, talking to Cecilia, then puts his hands on his hips indignantly. He then reaches into his pockets, takes out some play money, and gives it to the bum—who hasn't moved, his hand on his chest. Cecilia, reacting, embarrassed, turns away. She begins to walk down the sidewalk; Tom pats the bum on the shoulder, then joins up with Cecilia. A bum on the stairs mouths a plea to give him some money, too. The group is excited.

As they walk past the stairs, a bum reaches down to get some money, too. Tom, not comprehending, reaches up and shakes his hand. Cecilia grabs Tom's arm and pulls him away. Meanwhile, the bum he just gave the money to stands up. He looks at the play money, reacting. He looks after Tom and Cecilia, now walking offscreen, then, disgusted, he wads the money up and throws it on the ground. The bum on the stairs who was asking for money leans over, shaking his head in disbelief. They mouth their amazement as the film cuts to:

The front of a blue-painted shoe repair shop, its storefront window displaying a red sign reading O'SULLIVAN'S. *A very pregnant woman, holding her small son's hand, walks out the door and down its few stairs. She carries a pair of shoes in her other hand; she chatters with her son as they walk around the corner—passing Tom and Cecilia, who are coming down the sidewalk in the opposite direction. Cecilia almost bumps into them; she moves out of the way. Tom reacts, stopping and pointing to the now offscreen woman. He pantomimes her large stomach. Cecilia, gesturing, explains what pregnancy is. Tom continues to react in disbelief. Astounded, he shakes his head and puts his hands on his hips. A barbershop sign, with a large arrow, is painted on the wall behind them. The music plays on as the film cuts to:*

A large polished wooden crucifix hanging on a brick wall. A partially seen stained-glass window sits above it; below is a wooden altar. As Tom and Cecilia talk over the screen, the camera moves down the crucifix to the altar, which they are standing in front of. A few candles burn in the background; the upbeat jazz stops.

TOM *(Offscreen)* It's beautiful. But I'm not sure exactly what it is.

CECILIA *(Offscreen)* Oh, di— This is a church. You, uh, you do believe in God, don't you?

TOM *(Onscreen, looking at the altar)* Meaning . . . ? *(Inhales)*

CECILIA *(Inhaling, onscreen, looking at Tom)* Mm, uh, the, the reason for everything. *(Shaking her head)* The, the world, uh, the universe.

TOM *(Nodding his head, briefly turning to look at Cecilia)* Oh, I think I know what you mean—the two men who wrote, uh, *The Purple Rose of Cairo. (Gesturing, looking at the altar)* Irving Sachs and R. H. Levine, the writers who collaborate on films.

CECILIA *(Overlapping, shaking her head, looking at Tom)* Tch, no, no, I'm talking about something much bigger than that. No, think for a minute. *(Gesturing)* A reason for everything. Eh, otherwise, i-i-it-it'd be like a movie with no point, and no happy ending.

MONK *(Offscreen)* So *there* you are.

The film cuts to the back of the church, across the rows of pews; Monk slowly walks in from a side entrance, his hands in his pockets. He walks past a row of church windows, then slowly down a center aisle. His footsteps are loud in the quiet church.

MONK *(Onscreen, looking out at the offscreen couple)* I'm looking for you.

CECILIA *(Offscreen)* Monk, I, uh . . .

The camera moves back to Cecilia and Tom at the altar. A flustered Cecilia looks out at her offscreen husband.

CECILIA *(Gesturing to the offscreen Monk)* Th-this, this is my husband. *(Gesturing to Tom)* Th-this is Tom Baxter.

TOM *(Looking at the offscreen Monk)* Adventurer, explorer, the Chicago Baxters. I'm charmed to meet you. *(Smiles)*

The film is back on Monk, walking down the center aisle, coming slowly towards the offscreen couple.

MONK *(In a monotone)* So you wear the britches.

CECILIA *(Offscreen)* What did you want to talk to me about?

MONK *(Shrugging)* I heard you were out on the town last night.
The film cuts back to Tom and Cecilia, watching the approaching offscreen Monk. A portion of stained-glass window is seen in the background.

CECILIA *(Shaking her head)* Yea, I'm sor— I, I admit I didn't tell the truth about that, *(Gesturing)* but things have been so strange the last twenty-four hours. . . .
Monk interrupts, barging onscreen as he grabs Cecilia and shakes her violently.

MONK *(Screaming)* You know what I told you I'd do to you if you ever lied to me?!

CECILIA *(Overlapping)* Monk, don't hit me!

TOM *(Overlapping, pushing Monk away from Cecilia)* Obvious-obviously your marriage has come to an impasse, sir.

MONK *(To Tom)* And you keep out of this.
Monk suddenly goes for Tom, violently pushing him to the floor. Monk's ready to go in for the punch when Cecilia runs over to him, gasping. She pulls at his arm; he grabs her arm, hard.

CECILIA *(Gasping)* Monk, let's just talk.

MONK *(Overlapping, holding on to Cecilia's arm)* No, you're coming home with me!

CECILIA *(Overlapping, reacting)* Can't we talk?
Tom gets up from the floor, pushing Monk and Cecilia apart.

TOM *(To Monk, his hand keeping Monk at bay)* Perhaps you don't understand, sir, but I'm in love with your wife. *(Pulls down his jacket)*

MONK Close your yap, jackass. *(To Cecilia)* Now let's go. *(Grabbing Cecilia's arm)* You're in for a lesson you won't for—

TOM *(Interrupting, pulling Monk away from Cecilia)* You're failing to understand, sir. *(Standing in front of Cecilia, protecting her)* She's not coming with you.

MONK Oh, she's not, huh?
Monk, breathing hard, makes a lunge for Cecilia.

TOM *(Overlapping)* No, you take your hands off. *(Pushing Monk back)* No man will hit the woman I love, nor any woman—

MONK *(Interrupting, grabbing Tom by his lapels and flinging him to the floor)* Beat it!
Cecilia gasps. Monk goes in for the kill.

MONK *(Screaming at the prostrate Tom)* Beat it! I'm gonna take you apart!

CECILIA *(Overlapping, screaming, running up to Monk)* Stop it! He's got a terrible temper.

MONK *(Turning to Cecilia, violently shaking her)* And you . . . *(Pushing her away)* Go home.
Fast-paced jazz begins to play over the action, as Tom gets up behind Monk and grabs him from behind.

TOM *(Getting Monk by surprise)* Sorry, it's written into my character—courage.
The camera cuts to a view of Cecilia's face. She looks frantic. She holds her hat with her hand.

CECILIA *(Gasping)* Stop it!
The camera's back on the action at the altar. Tom and Monk are in a

face-off, their fists raised, ready to strike. Monk hits Tom first, getting him in the jaw; Tom gets him back—twice to the jaw.

The fast-paced music plays on as the film cuts first to a closer view of Tom, his fists raised, fire in his eyes, then to a view of Monk—equally determined to deck his opponent.

MONK *(Breathing hard, his fist raised)* Come on.
The film cuts back to the watching Cecilia . . .

CECILIA Stop it! What are you doing?!

. . . then back to the action at the altar—in full swing. Monk takes a swipe at Tom. He ducks it—by rolling away on the floor, his helmet falling off. Monk comes in for another swing. Once again, Tom ducks it, moving under Monk's arm. He puts his helmet back on, adjusting it, ready for more.

MONK *(Grunting and sniffing)* Come on.
The camera moves to a closer view of Tom, his fists raised, then to a closer view of Monk, swinging his fists.

TOM *(Offscreen)* Time for the old one-two.
The camera is back on the two fighters, as Tom gives Monk a jab in the stomach, on his jaw. Monk falls to the floor, groaning as the film cuts quickly to Cecilia, wincing.

TOM *(Offscreen)* Up. Hope . . .
As Tom speaks, the film moves back to the altar. A sniffing, groaning Monk is pulling himself up from the floor as Tom stands nearby, looking at the offscreen Cecilia. He adjusts his helmet.

TOM *(Continuing onscreen)* . . . he's had enough.
Monk leans on a railing, feeling his nose. He sniffs, out of breath.

TOM *(Extending his hand to Monk)* Sorry, pal. Sorry about the rough stuff. You all right?

MONK *(Sighing)* Yeah.

TOM Let me give you a hand. *(Pulling Monk up)* There's a—Oh! *(Groans as the now standing Monk knees him in the crotch)* God, it's not fair! *(Groans again)*
The music stops. Monk again knees the groaning Tom, who drops to the floor in pain. Grunting, his back to the camera, Monk squats on the floor. He punches Tom in the face—again and again and again. Tom groans.

Cecilia runs onscreen, to Monk, trying to grab him, trying to stop the fight.

CECILIA Tom! *(To Monk)* What are you doing?!
Monk gets up. He grabs Cecilia and pulls her away from the groaning and sighing Tom, who is offscreen on the floor.

MONK *(Holding Cecilia's arm in an iron grip)* You're coming home with me now.

CECILIA *(Trying to pull away)* No, I'm not!

MONK *(Abruptly letting go of Cecilia's arm)* What'd you say?

CECILIA *(Gasping)* No, I'm going to stay and see that Tom's okay.

MONK *(Pointing at Cecilia)* I—

CECILIA *(Interrupting)* You're a bully, Monk.

MONK *(Pointing)* I gave you an order.

CECILIA *(Rubbing her arm)* I don't care, I'm tired of taking your orders. *(Looking at the offscreen Tom)* You could've killed him.

MONK *(Gesturing)* All right. I'm sorry. I didn't mean it. I hit hard.

CECILIA *(Overlapping, gesturing)* You can't just, you can't just go through life beating people up.

MONK *(Gesturing)* Look, I'm telling you one more time. Are you coming with me?

CECILIA *(Shaking her head)* No, I'm not.

MONK *(After a beat, gesturing)* I'm telling you one more time. You comin'?

CECILIA No!

MONK *(Grabbing Cecilia's arm)* Come on!

CECILIA *(Overlapping, pulling her arm away, and gasping)* No, I'm not!

MONK *(After a beat)* The hell with you. *(Pauses, gesturing)* I need a beer anyway. *(Turning and walking away, towards the offscreen camera)* I'll see you later.

Cecilia sighs, moving backwards as she rubs her arm, as she watches Monk depart offscreen. Tom is partially seen in the background, sprawled out on the floor. Cecilia turns around and kneels down by Tom, concerned.

CECILIA *(Worried, putting her arm around Tom)* Oh, are you okay?

TOM *(Taking off his pith helmet and sitting up)* Oh, oh, yeah. I'm fine. *(Brushing himself off)* Huh.

CECILIA *(Sitting on the floor next to Tom, looking at him)* You're not even marked. *(Gesturing)* Your, your hair is in place.

TOM *(Picking dust off his helmet)* No, no. I don't get hurt or bleed. *(Smoothing back his hair)* Hair doesn't muss. *(Chuckling)* It's one of the advantages of being imaginary. *(Laughs, putting his pith helmet back on)*

CECILIA *(Sighing)* You were very brave.

TOM *(Shrugging)* Yeah, well, I had him too, till he started fighting dirty.

The film cuts back and forth from Cecilia to Tom's face as each one speaks.

CECILIA *(Looking at the offscreen Tom)* That's why you'll never survive off the screen.

TOM *(Looking at the offscreen Cecilia)* You were pretty brave, too. You stood right up to him.

CECILIA *(Smiling, looking at the offscreen Tom)* You inspired me.

CUT TO:
EXTERIOR. CECILIA'S HOUSE—DAY

Gil stands on the weathered, gray-shingled porch. He paces, his scarf and fedora in place. He looks out over the porch; he leans near the door. He impatiently fingers the frame of the window set in the door. Nearby windows reflect the blue sky; a wooden storage bin is set on the side of the partially seen house. Upbeat music is playing; the chatter and shouts of offscreen children playing are heard in the back-

ground. Gil walks over to the steps, leaning against the porch railing, looking out offscreen.

CECILIA *(Offscreen)* Mr. Shepherd!
Gil starts, looking behind him, then he runs down the porch steps. He turns, walking out on the sidewalk, where Cecilia is walking, headed towards the house. Other gray, weathered houses line the street; a car is parked in a driveway, another on the street. The suspension bridge is seen in the distance; two women walk on the sidewalk in the background, their backs to the camera.

GIL *(Running over to Cecilia)* Oh, Cecilia, look, I gotta, I gotta speak to you.

CECILIA *(Shaking her head, gesturing)* Oh, listen, I, I-I, I've had a crazy morning. I-I'm still shaking.

GIL *(Overlapping, walking with Cecilia to the house)* I . . . look, I don't know what to do, all right? I've, I've struggled . . .

CECILIA *(Overlapping, looking for her keys)* Yeah . . .

GIL *(Walking up the porch steps with Cecilia, their backs to the camera, continuing)* . . . my whole life. And now I'm finally beginning to break through *(Gesturing)* and my whole career's going right down the drain.
The film cuts to a close-up of Cecilia's face as she opens the door behind her.

CECILIA *(Looking at the offscreen Gil)* You don't have to worry about that. You, *(Shaking her head)* you'll always be a great movie star.
The camera moves back to reveal Gil leaning against the door frame, talking to Cecilia, whose back is to the camera.

GIL *(Trying not to show his pride)* Oh, well, that's, that's very nice of you to, to, uh, say, *(Gesturing)* but technically, I'm not

really a star yet. *(Laughing)* Cecilia, don't, um, you know, I mean, I try to carry myself like one. *(Touching his lapels)* You know, I do the best I can as far as that, but "star"? *(Whistles, gesturing)* That's a big word, isn't it? *(Laughing, Cecilia joining in)* Star? *(Inhaling)* Yeah. Uh . . . *(Laughing)* no, no, no, star, no, no. *(Sighs)*
The film cuts back to Cecilia's face; she is beaming.

CECILIA Uh, and, and you're not, you're not just a, uh, a pretty face, you're also a peach of an actor.
As Cecilia talks, the film cuts to Gil, still trying to look humble, his cheeks puffed. He leans against the door, looking away for a moment, listening. Cecilia's back is to the camera.

CECILIA Really, I've seen you. I've seen you a lot. You, you've got something.

GIL *(Smiling, looking at Cecilia, then reacting, pulling his head erect)* I-is that your opinion?

CECILIA Sure, and I see, I see all the movies. You, you've got, oh . . . *(Sighing as Gil gestures to her, trying to draw her words out)* how can I describe it?
The camera is back on Cecilia's face, framed by the open door.

CECILIA You've got a magical glow.
The camera moves back to Gil, taking it all in. Cecilia's back is to the camera.

GIL *(After a beat, overwhelmed)* Oh, boy. Oh, oh. *(Laughing)* To hear that from a real person, that is just . . . *(Sighing, sitting down on the porch railing and gesturing)* It's not one of those movie colony bimbos, you know, *(Nodding his head, gesturing)* with the fancy dresses, filling you full of hot air. *(Pointing a finger up emphatically)* That's ju— *(Gesturing and patting the railing next to him, smiling)* Wo-would you get over here and sit down, please? Just for a . . . *(Sighs)*

CECILIA *(Overlapping, laughing as she closes the door and sits down next to Gil)* Oh, you know, you, you can take it from me. *(Shaking her head)* I, you're not just a flash in the pan.

GIL No, I'm— *(Gesturing, looking at Cecilia)* You know, it-it'd be very easy for me to trade on my looks. *(Snapping the fingers of both hands)* Just, like that.

CECILIA *(Overlapping, gesturing, looking at Gil)* Oh, sure.

GIL But I have some serious acting ambitions.

CECILIA *(Gesturing, loudly)* You should.

GIL I'd—

CECILIA *(Interrupting)* You should. You, I, you know, I-I think you're great in, in all the funny movies. *(Gesturing)* Now that's—

GIL *(Overlapping)* Thank you, that's . . . *(Chuckles)*

CECILIA *(Overlapping, stuttering)* Really, I was thinking you should, you should play some of the more heroic parts.

GIL I want— *(Gesturing)* I tell my agent that a hundred times!

CECILIA Yeah? Well, you know, you, t-, uh, well, *(Shaking her head, looking away for a moment, thinking)* I, you could play, you could play, like, Daniel Boone . . .

GIL *(Overlapping, nodding)* Oh.

CECILIA *(Overlapping)* . . . or someone . . . *(Looking at Gil)* Lindbergh! Oh, you . . .

GIL *(Overlapping)* Oh.

CECILIA *(Stuttering, overlapping)* . . . you'd be wonderful as Lindbergh.

GIL *(Gesturing)* My God! You are a mind reader.

CECILIA *(Looking at Gil)* We had the same thought? Really?

GIL *(Overlapping, looking at Cecilia and gesturing)* You . . . I am on the verge of signing for that part.

CECILIA *(Squealing in disbelief)* No!

GIL *(Exultantly jumping in his seat, gesturing)* I'm, I am! I can taste it. *(Closes his eyes and mouths a prayer)*

CECILIA *(Overlapping)* Really?! *(Touching her face and shaking her head)* Oh, you'll be wonderful.

GIL *(Sighing and shrugging)* Well, thank you.

CECILIA *(Gesturing)* Oh, there's something inside you that, you have that same kind of lone, heroic quality. I—

GIL *(Interrupting, gesturing)* Lone— You're exactly right. *(Pointing)* Everyone . . .

CECILIA *(Overlapping)* Yes?

GIL *(Overlapping)* . . . has been telling me not to— *(Waving his pointed finger)* You are right.

CECILIA *(Shaking her head)* Don't you listen.

GIL *(Gesturing)* Basically, I have been a loner my entire life. *(Crosses his arms over his chest)*

CECILIA Well, sure, anyone can see that.

GIL *(Nodding)* Sure.

CECILIA You know, you're deep, and probably complicated.

GIL *(Turning to Cecilia, gesturing)* Can I buy you lunch?

CECILIA Me?

GIL *(Starting to stand, his hand on Cecilia's shoulder)* Please. Can I?
They both stand up; the sound of a nearby train is heard in the background.

GIL Please. *(Gesturing)* Look, I love, I love talking to you.

CECILIA Oh, uh, I was just going to go upstairs and—

GIL *(Interrupting, gesturing as he walks down the porch stairs)* Don't, no, really, come on. I, uh, I just, I open . . .

CECILIA *(Overlapping, following him down the stairs)* Really?

GIL . . . I open myself up around you.

CECILIA *(Overlapping)* Oh . . .
They turn and walk up the sidewalk past the house. Their backs are to the camera. As they walk and talk, deep in conversation, they move farther and farther away from the offscreen camera, past the rows of houses and parked cars; a bicycle sits in front of one of the homes. Background jazz begins to play.

GIL I no— Have you ever been to Hollywood?

CECILIA Uh, *(Laughing)* come on, no, of course not.

GIL You, well, I *(Gesturing)* would love to just take you around Hollywood. I would real—

CECILIA *(Overlapping, chuckling)* Oh.

GIL *(Touching his hat, then putting his hands in his pockets)* Could I make a confession?

CECILIA Sure.

GIL Look, my real name, it's not Gil Shepherd. It's, uh, Herman Bardebedian.

CECILIA Really?

GIL I've, yeah, I've been a cab driver for . . . *(Gesturing)* oh . . . *(Pauses, pointing to Cecilia)* Boy, do you have a pretty face.

CECILIA *(Laughing)* Come on.

GIL You do!

They continue walking away from the camera, their conversation no longer heard. The music plays on for a beat and then the film cuts to:

EXTERIOR/INTERIOR. ROLLER COASTER PLATFORM—DAY.

Tom, in pith helmet and khakis, stands on the enclosed wooden starter platform of the roller coaster in the deserted amusement park. The curving tracks can be seen through the open sides of the platform. A motionless car is lined up in the foreground, on the tracks, ready to go. The jazz music continues as the curious Tom first looks at the car, then sits down in it, shaking it by holding onto the handles of the seat in front of him. He looks around for a beat, then steps out, brushing off his pants.

EMMA *(Offscreen)* Hi, big boy!

Tom turns and looks over his shoulder, and the camera moves to his point of view, to show Emma, the prostitute, standing outside the picket fence that surrounds the park. A winter-brown city park is in the background, past a curving street. Emma looks up at the offscreen Tom, stepping up to the fence and leaning over it.

EMMA *((To the offscreen Tom)* You alone?

The film cuts back to Tom, on the platform. He turns around and starts to walk towards its edge as he talks to the offscreen Emma.

TOM *(Smiling, putting his hand in his pocket)* Oh, hello. Uh, well, I'm, uh, I'm alone for now *(Leaning against the platform's off-screen railing)* but, uh, later I have an appointment, or, uh, should I say rendezvous? *(Laughs)*

The film cuts to a closer view of Emma at the picket fence. Her face is made up; she wears a red hat and holds a cigarette.

EMMA *(Chewing gum)* Good for you. *(After a beat)* Where'd you get the funny suit?

The camera is back on Tom—seen farther away, on the enclosed platform, which weaves like an open tunnel. In the foreground is seen the wooden roller coaster structure and the picket fence.

TOM *(Looking down at his safari suit, pointing at it)* What, this?

The camera now cuts back and forth between Emma, seen close up, leaning on the fence, and Tom, on the roller coaster platform.

EMMA Yeah. You coming from a costume party?

TOM *(Laughing, shaking his head and gesturing)* No, no, I'm Tom Baxter of the Chicago Baxters. *(Offscreen as the camera cuts back to the listening Emma, smoking her cigarette)* Explorer, poet, adventurer. Just back from Cairo, where I, uh, searched in vain for the legendary purple rose.

EMMA *(Nodding)* How 'bout that?

TOM *(Offscreen)* Well, uh, who are you?

EMMA *(Smiling)* My name's Emma.

TOM *(Offscreen)* Oh, that's lovely. What do you do, Emma?

EMMA I'm a working girl.

TOM *(Onscreen, the camera back on the roller coaster platform)* And what do you do, you delicate creature?

EMMA *(Laughing slightly)* Anything that'll make a buck.

TOM *(Leaning on the railing)* Well, we Baxters never really had to worry about money.

EMMA *(Looking off for a moment, taking a drag on her cigarette)* I'll bet. You want to come along with me?

TOM *(Offscreen, the camera staying on Emma briefly)* Where to, Emma?

EMMA *(Smiling)* Where I work. I think you might have a good time.

TOM *(Onscreen, gesturing)* Sounds enchanting. I'm up for new experiences.

EMMA *(Grinning, shrugging)* I may be able to help.

A ragtime piano begins to play as the film cuts to a bordello, dimly lit with a yellow cast from a background standing lamp. Four prostitutes are posed in the living room looking towards the offscreen Tom and Emma. In sheer robes and lingerie are: Martha and Laura on the sofa, one languidly sprawled, the other leaning forward, her legs crossed, a cigarette in hand; Polly, only partially seen, sitting on a chair holding a drink; and a large, stocky prostitute standing in the middle of the room, smoking a cigarette. A fifth woman, Nancy, can be seen in a background room, through a curtained doorway, doing some paperwork at a desk. A bureau stands in the background near the wall.

EMMA *(Offscreen)* Hi, girls. This is Tom.

TOM *(Offscreen)* Hi . . .
As Tom speaks the film cuts to him and Emma, looking at the offscreen prostitutes. Emma, slightly behind Tom, starts to undo her coat.

TOM *(Continuing, smiling)* . . . there, ladies. Don't you all look enticing?
The camera is back on the prostitutes. Polly is no longer sitting. She stands, looking at the offscreen Tom; she smokes a cigarette.

POLLY I know what you want. *(Laughing)* You want to be the great white hunter and you want me to be the tiger.
The camera moves back to Emma and Tom; she's shrugging out of her coat. Drapes hide a window in the background.

TOM *(Laughing, shaking his head)* Uh, I don't get it.
The film cuts to a closer view of Martha, lounging on the couch in a low-cut gown. A bowl of fruit sits on a nearby end table.

MARTHA *(Gesturing with a cigarette in hand)* You will if you can afford it.
The camera is back on Emma and Tom. The piano music continues in the background.

EMMA *(Tossing her coat aside)* I met Tom out at the amusement park. *(Starts to take off Tom's pith helmet)*

TOM *(Exclaiming, holding it down on his head)* Oh, no, that's, uh, my hat. *(Chuckles, pausing, as Emma nods back, then to the prostitutes)* Uh, yes, I was, uh, I was thinking about something.
The camera moves back to the couch; both Laura, leaning forward, cigarette in hand, and the languid Martha look offscreen at Tom. The stocky standing prostitute's hand, holding a cigarette, is seen near them.

MARTHA I can imagine.

LAURA Two of us at the same time?

Martha moves over to Laura, laughing, her hand on Laura's arm, as the film cuts back to Tom and Emma, seen this time in profile. A shelf of knickknacks hangs on the side wall.

TOM *(Gesturing)* You know, I was thinking about some very deep things. *(To Emma)* About God and his relation with Irving Sachs and R. H. Levine. And . . .

As Tom speaks, a seductively smiling Martha and Laura gently take him by the shoulders and glide him farther into the room, their backs to the camera. Polly, holding a bottle of beer, sits down, watching him, as he passes, obliviously chattering, en route to a nearby armchair. The heavy prostitute is seen in the background, walking in front of the trio, into the back room.

TOM *(Continuing)* . . . I-I-I was thinking about life in general. The, the origin of everything we see about us. The, uh, the finality of death *(Sighing)* and how almost magical it seems in the, in the real world as, uh, as opposed to the world of . . .

Laura picks up a magazine from the armchair; she pats the pillow.

LAURA *(Overlapping Tom, gesturing to the chair)* Right here.

TOM *(Continuing, oblivious, sitting down)* . . . celluloid and flickering shadows.

Laura settles down on the arm of the chair, holding the magazine to her chest. Martha crouches down on the other side, next to Tom. They all look at him as he chatters on. Nancy continues to do her paperwork in the back room; the silhouette of the heavy prostitute is indistinctly seen by the window near the piano; she turns and walks down a hallway offscreen.

POLLY *(Looking at the offscreen Emma)* Where did you find this clown? *(Chuckles)*

TOM *(Warming to his subject, looking at Laura)* For example, the miracle of birth. *(Gesturing)* Now, I suppo-, I suppose some of you lovely ladies are married.

MARTHA Not anymore. *(Laughs, as Tom turns to her)*

LAURA *(Overlapping)* No.

The women laugh. Martha moves on the floor, her head on the side of the armchair, laughing hysterically.

TOM *(Overlapping Martha, gesturing)* No? Then, the absolutely astonishing miracle of childbirth . . .

As Tom talks, as Laura's laughter is heard, the camera moves to Polly's face. She is listening intently. It then moves to Emma, her hand on the knickknack shelf. She, too, is listening intently as the camera moves back to Tom, looking up at the offscreen Laura, her arm on Tom's shoulder. Martha sits on the floor as before. Nancy is seen at the desk in the back room. The piano music continues, not missing a beat.

TOM *(Offscreen, continuing)* . . . with all its attendant feelings of humanity and pathos. *(Onscreen, to Laura)* I stand in awe of existence.

MARTHA Do you want to tie me up?

TOM *(Turning to Martha)* Tie you up?

MARTHA *(Chuckling)* Yeah.

TOM *(Laughing, looking back and forth between the offscreen Laura and Martha)* Oh, that i— She is . . . That's very funny. She's very funny. *(To Martha, gesturing)* That's a nice sense of humor.

Martha laughs.

TOM *(Laughing, to Martha)* The absurd non sequitur. What, what's your name, sweetheart?

MARTHA Martha.

TOM That's the same name as the Ambassador's wife.

MARTHA Well, why didn't you bring the Ambassador by?

TOM Well, he, he's still up on the screen. *(Gesturing)* But, d-do you share my sense of wonderment at the very fabric of being? *(Clasps his hands on his knee)*
Martha looks reflective.

TOM The smell of a rose. Real food. Sensuous music.
The film quickly cuts to Laura's face . . .

LAURA *(Nodding, looking at the now offscreen Tom)* I've got a child.

. . . as the camera moves down her arm to Tom. The base of a lamp sits behind them.

TOM *(Looking up at the now offscreen Laura)* You do?

LAURA *(Her hand kneading his shoulder)* Mmmm.

TOM *(Looking up at the offscreen Laura)* Oh, I see. You're a widow. Uh, oh, poor thing.
The film cuts to Nancy in the back room, as seen through the curtained doorway. A Tiffany lamp hangs down near her desk.

NANCY *(Turning to the group)* I got two kids and he's right about giving birth. It is a *beautiful* experience.
The film cuts to Emma, as she sits down on the sofa.

EMMA I never had a baby. I was pregnant, but I lost it.

TOM *(Offscreen)* Sorry to hear that, Emma.
Tom comes onscreen and sits down next to Emma, wrapping his arm around her shoulder, comforting her.

EMMA Mm. It always makes me cry to think about it. *(Sighs)*

TOM *(Hugging Emma)* Oh, there, there, now. You'll have another chance. Come on. *(To the others offscreen)* I'd be surprised if all you ladies weren't married soon. Especially by the way you dress. It's so seductive to a man. *(Laughs)*
Polly's silk-stockinged leg suddenly appears, seductively posed across Emma and Tom.

POLLY *(Laughing, only her leg onscreen)* Do you like these stockings, Tom?

TOM *(Looking at Polly's leg, then up at her, offscreen)* Oh, they're just divine. *(Laughing with Polly)* What kind of a club is this, anyhow?

POLLY *(Laughing, sprawling across Tom)* God, Tom, you're a scream. *(Laughs as she sits down on the sofa on the other side of Tom)*

EMMA He's terribly sweet.

Emma, Polly, and Tom laugh on the sofa. Emma and Polly, looking at Tom, are all eyes, seductive and being seduced themselves by the unwitting Tom.

MARTHA *(Offscreen)* He is. *(Onscreen as the camera moves to her face)* I wouldn't mind doin' him for nothin'.

The film cuts quickly to Laura's face, the lamp in the background.

LAURA Me neither, plus he's cute.

The air is charged. The piano music continues as the film cuts back to Tom, Emma, and Polly on the sofa.

POLLY *(Patting Tom's shoulder, looking into his eyes)* Okay, you can count me in. Come on, Tom, we're going to take you into the bedroom and give you an experience you'll never forget. *(Jumps up from the couch, offscreen, grabbing Tom's hand)*

EMMA And . . .

TOM *(Overlapping Emma)* W—

EMMA *(Overlapping, Tom and Polly, continuing)* . . . it's on the house. *(Laughs)*

TOM *(Being pulled off the sofa offscreen)* I came here for a new experience.

EMMA *(Smiling, looking up at the offscreen Tom)* Well, now you're going to get a champion roll in the hay.

The camera moves to Tom, standing next to Polly and Martha; the curtained doorway to the back room is behind them.

TOM *(To the offscreen Emma)* What? There's hay in the bedroom?

POLLY *(Laughing, patting Tom on the chest)* You ever been to a brothel before?

TOM *(Laughing with Polly)* What's a brothel?

MARTHA *(Overlapping Polly and Tom's laughter)* You must be kidding.

EMMA *(Offscreen)* A brothel, a . . . *(Onscreen as the film cuts to her, on the sofa)* bordello, a whorehouse.
The camera moves back to Tom, standing with Martha and Polly . . .

TOM *(To the offscreen Emma, shaking his head)* I'm not following. *(Chuckling)* Wha—?

. . . then back to Emma on the couch . . .

EMMA *(To the offscreen Tom)* We go to bed with you and make love, and you pay us.

. . . and then to Laura's face.

LAURA *(To the offscreen Tom)* Only because you're so sweet, we want to treat you to a party.
The film moves back to Tom, standing with Polly and Martha.

TOM *(After a beat, looking at the women, then grinning)* Really?

POLLY *(Laughing and nodding)* Uh-huh.

TOM *(After a beat)* Boy, this doesn't ring a bell with anything I know. *(Laughs as he sits down on the arm of the offscreen chair)*

NANCY *(Walking onscreen from the back room, to Tom)* Oh, come on, buddy. You know about makin' love, don'tcha?

TOM *(Earnestly)* I can't make love with you.

The film cuts back to Emma on the sofa.

EMMA Don't tell me you don't like women.

POLLY *(Sitting on the sofa next to Emma, the camera close to her face)* Or you were wounded in the war.
The women start to laugh as the film cuts back and forth between Tom, on the armrest, Nancy in the background, and Emma, on the couch, as each one speaks.

TOM *(To the offscreen Emma)* No, n-, I'm in love with someone else.

EMMA *(To the offscreen Tom)* No, we're not talking about *in* love, we're talking about *making* love.

TOM *(To the offscreen Emma)* But, I love Cecilia.

EMMA *(Offscreen)* Well, so what? *(Onscreen, to the offscreen Tom)* Marry Cecilia. This is just for fun.
The film cuts back to Tom, to a wider view of him, resting on the arm of the chair. Nancy leans against the curtained doorway; Martha stands near her. Polly is sitting forward on the sofa. Laura is partially seen on the arm of a chair near Tom. They all look at Tom as he talks. They don't move.

TOM *(To the offscreen Emma)* Oh, I couldn't do that, Emma. *(Looking at all the women)* Ladies, my, my gracious! *(Gesturing)* N-, uh, look, I, don't think I'm not appreciative of your offer. *(Laughing)* I must say the, the concept is totally new to me, but, uh, I'm just— *(Inhaling)* I'm hopelessly head over heels in love with Cecilia. She is all I want. My devotion is to her, my loyalties . . . Every breath she takes makes my heart dance.
The film cuts to Emma, on the sofa, visibly moved. The piano plays on.

EMMA *(Softly)* This guy just kills me. Are there any other guys like you out there?

CUT TO:
EXTERIOR. MUSIC STORE—DAY.

A music store's display window fills the screen. Behind the glass pane, a guitar, several harmonicas, and some records are arranged on a display table. As Cecilia's voice is heard, the film cuts farther away, to reveal Cecilia and Gil, their backs to the camera, looking into the window. Near them is the music store's entrance, with LAWSON'S *printed on a sign above the door. A bench is partially seen on the other side of the entrance. People pass by on the sidewalk as they talk; a car drives down the street.*

CECILIA *(Offscreen)* Lawson's Music Store. This *(Onscreen, her back to the camera)* s-s-s-store has been here since I was a kid.

GIL *(His back to the camera, his hands clasped behind him)* Yeah. I wish I could play an instrument. That's my other ambition in life, is to be a great classical violinist. Thousands cheering me, night after night.

CECILIA I can . . .

GIL *(Overlapping)* Mm.

CECILIA . . . play the ukulele.

GIL You can?

CECILIA Uh-huh. *(Looking at Gil)* My father taught me before he ran away.

As the stunning sounds of "I'm Alabamy Bound" are heard, the film moves inside, to a close-up of Cecilia sitting on a stool, playing the song on a ukulele. Gil crouches down next to her, singing the words. Only their torsos are seen on the screen.

GIL *(Singing, his face offscreen)* "I'm Alabamy bound. / There'll be no *(Onscreen)* heebie jeebies hanging round. / Just gave the meanest ticket-man on earth / All I'm worth / To put my

tootsies in an upper berth. / Just hear that choo-choo sound / Whoo-whoo!" *(Pulls an imaginary train whistle)*
As Gil sings, the camera moves farther and farther away, revealing the smiling couple in the store, the stool set up in the corner by a glass display case. The walls are cluttered with photographs; the cases are full of instruments. An elderly woman, the store's owner, stands behind the display case, leaning over the counter, smiling and rocking her head in time to the music. Cecilia's coat is flung over a table in the foreground; a fan sits on top of a tall cabinet behind the counter. A curtained stairway leading upstairs offscreen is seen in the background behind the store owner's head. Cecilia is beaming; she laughs as she plays.

GIL *(Continuing, singing, and gesturing)* "I know that soon *(Laughing)* we're going to cover ground. / And then I'll holler / *(Kneeling on one knee in front of Cecilia, Al Jolson–style)* 'Cause the world will know, / Here I go, / I'm Alabamy bound! / *(Exclaiming as Cecilia plays a riff, as the store owner walks offscreen)* I'm Alabamy bound! / (Pah!)"

CECILIA That was just wonderful.

GIL Oh. *(Sighs, smoothing back his hair and smiling)*

CECILIA *(Overlapping Gil)* That's wonderful.

GIL Oh, thanks.

CECILIA *(Overlapping Gil)* Oh, I was never *(Putting her hand to her mouth)* It's like a dream. *(Gesturing to the offscreen store owner as the piano notes of "I Love My Baby" are heard)* Oh, listen.
Gil turns, his arm on Cecilia's shoulder. They both quickly rise and walk over to the now onscreen store owner at the piano. A shelf of sheet music sits on the wall behind the counter. Cecilia starts to accompany the store owner on the ukulele.

GIL *(Reacting to the music, excited, snapping his fingers)* "I Love My Ba—" *(Singing, leaning over the top of the piano)* "My baby loves me. / I don't know nobody / As happy as me. / She's only twenty / And I'm twenty-one. / We never worry, / We're just havin' fun. / *(Beating time with his fingers on the piano top)* (Bum-bum-bum) / Sometimes we quarrel / *(Pointing at Cecilia)* And maybe we fight. / *(Putting his arm around Cecilia, bouncing to the music)* But then we make up / The following night. / When we're together / *(Gesturing)* We're great company. / *(Affecting a pose)* I love my baby / And my baby loves me."

The song ends with a flourish on the piano.

CECILIA *(Chuckling, reacting)* Oh!

GIL *(Overlapping, laughing)* Oh!

An offscreen telephone begins to ring. Everyone is talking at once.

CECILIA *(Overlapping Gil)* That was wonderful. Oh, you—

MUSIC STORE OWNER *(Laughing, as she stands up to answer the phone)* Telephone.

GIL *(Overlapping Cecilia)* Aw, that was, you know.

CECILIA *(Overlapping the music store owner and Gil, to Gil)* Well, oh, after the Lindbergh movie you should do . . .

MUSIC STORE OWNER *(Overlapping, walking between the couple towards the ringing phone)* The phone.

GIL *(Overlapping Cecilia, turning briefly as the owner walks between them, to the owner)* Oh.

CECILIA *(Continuing, overlapping Gil)* . . . a musical, really.

The store owner walks off in the background, hastily moving around the counter, disappearing behind the curtained stairwell to answer the phone. Gil and Cecilia continue their animated discussion; they look at each other. The camera slowly moves in closer and closer to their faces as they talk.

GIL *(Overlapping Cecilia, gesturing)* Do you think, do you think, you know, you know my, you know I did a, one bit in one once. It's uh . . .

CECILIA *(Overlapping Gil, gesturing)* Oh, yeah. . . . I know, I, I-I saw *Dancing Doughboys*, sure.

GIL *(Overlapping, laughing)* *Dancing Doughboys.*

CECILIA *(Overlapping)* Yeah!

GIL You remembered!

CECILIA Yeah, that was great. I remember you-you-you turned to Ina Beasley and you said: "I won't be going south with you this winter."

GIL *(Gesturing, moving closer to Cecilia)* That's exact— Right, right!
Cecilia laughs; she hugs the ukulele. The camera moves in closer to the couple.

GIL *(Reciting his lines from* Doughboys, *his hands on his hips, intensely)* "I won't, I won't, I won't be going south with you this winter. We have a little, uh, score to settle on the other side of the Atlantic."

CECILIA *(Reciting the heroine's lines from the movie, her eyes on Gil, her hand moving up and down the ukulele's neck)* "Does this mean I won't be seeing you ever again?"

GIL *(Reciting his lines, his eyes on Cecilia)* "Well, 'ever' is a long time."

CECILIA *(With emotion, reciting the heroine's lines)* "When you leave, don't look back."

GILL *(Laughing after a beat)* You remember that, you remember it perfectly. *(Gestures)*

CECILIA *(Overlapping Gil, her eyes not leaving his face)* Oh, sure.

GIL *(Taking Cecilia into his arms)* And then, and then I took her in my arms, and, and I kissed her, knowing it was for the last time. *(Pauses, sighing)* God, you're beautiful, Cecilia.

CECILIA *(Shaking her head, the ukulele still to her chest)* Was it fun? Kissing Ina Beasley?

GIL *(Shrugging)* Oh, it was jus—, you know, it's a movie kiss. You know, we professionals, we can put that, that stuff on just like that.

CECILIA *(Overlapping, sighing)* It looked like you loved her.

Gil gives Cecilia a lingering kiss. Romantic music begins to play.

CECILIA Mm.

GIL *(After a beat)* Oh, my goodness! *(Laughing, sighing)* Feel my heart. *(Gestures to his chest, laughing nervously)*

CECILIA *(Touching Gil's heart for a moment, then quickly drawing it away)* Uh, I, I, boy, I . . .

Gil rubs his forehead and sighs, as if overcome with emotion.

CECILIA *(Stunned, turning away from Gil)* . . . I have to, I should, I, thank you so much for the ukulele. *(Picks up her coat from the table)*

GIL Oh, w-well, don't be offended. I didn't mean to— Tch.

CECILIA *(Interrupting, putting on her coat)* Oh, no. I'm not offended. I'm just, uh, I'm confused. I . . .

Gil sighs; he helps Cecilia with her coat. He stands behind her; Cecilia's head is down. She holds the ukulele.

CECILIA I'm married. I-I-I just met a wonderful new man. He's fictional, but you can't have everything.

GIL Look, ca-can I see you later?

CECILIA *(Shaking her head)* No, no, I'm-I'm meeting Tom.
Cecilia exits offscreen. Gil takes a few steps towards her. He looks after her.

GIL *(Annoyed)* My own creation plagues me.
The music stops and the film cuts to the inside of the Jewel Theater. The movie screen is seen, over the rows of seats, which are empty. The black-and-white movie characters are seen on the screen, gathered in the penthouse living room. Larry is slouched in an armchair; Jason sits in a chair next to him. Rita is sprawled in another armchair, playing with Henry's tie. He sits on the armrest, leaning on the chair's back. He smokes a cigarette. The Countess is on the background sofa. Delilah sits at the white piano, Father Donnelly stands against the wall, Bible in hand, and the Communist sits offscreen near Rita and Henry. They all look bored, tired.

RITA Anything happening out there?

HENRY Not a thing.

LARRY Life is amazing, isn't it? One little minor character takes some action . . .

HENRY *(Interrupting)* Minor?

LARRY . . . and the whole world is turned upside down.

JASON *(Overlapping Larry)* Yeah.
The film cuts to the very last rows of the theater, in color, where the usherette sits in a seat, her head in her hand, fast asleep.

COUNTESS *(Offscreen)* What if he never comes back? We just drift until they shut the projector.
The film moves back to the movie characters. The black-and-white screen fills the frame.

HENRY *(Turning to the Countess, reacting)* Will you shut up? And stop that!

JASON *(Overlapping, gesturing to Henry)* Now calm down, calm down.

FATHER DONNELLY *(Overlapping the men)* He'll be back. I feel it.

HENRY *(Overlapping, to Jason, pointing at the Countess)* Was she always like that?

THE COMMUNIST *(Offscreen)* I don't want to sit around and wait. That's exactly what they want.

JASON Who?

THE COMMUNIST *(Jumping up onscreen from his offscreen chair)* The bosses.

OTHER MOVIE CHARACTERS *(In unison, reacting)* Ohhhh.

The characters, groaning, affect various disgusted poses. Rita picks up a nail file.

THE COMMUNIST *(Overlapping them, pacing across the room and gesturing)* Look at us!

COUNTESS *(Overlapping)* Not again.

THE COMMUNIST Sitting around, slave to some stupid scenario.

HENRY *(Overlapping, gesturing, aside to Rita)* Hey, you know, he's tedious.

THE COMMUNIST *(Emphatically pointing to a booklet he holds in his hands)* Meanwhile, the fat cats in Hollywood are getting rich on our work!

HENRY *(Overlapping, mumbling)* He's really tedious.

RITA *(Overlapping, reacting, hitting the arm of her chair)* Oh, please stop it!

THE COMMUNIST *(Overlapping Rita)* Studio heads, writers, movie stars!

RITA *(Throwing her nail file at the Communist)* Stop it!

THE COMMUNIST *(Shouting)* Uh, but we're the ones who sweat!

Rita sighs, giving up. She lays her head down on the armrest. Jason covers his head with his hand. Henry shakes his crossed leg, a cigarette and ashtray in hand.

THE COMMUNIST We're the characters on the screen, not them.

COUNTESS You're a Red!

THE COMMUNIST *(Shouting)* I say unite, brothers, unite, and take action!

DELILAH *(Overlapping)* Why don't you shut up and sit down?!

JASON *(Interrupting Delilah)* What possible action?

HENRY *(Interrupting, shouting)* Wait a minute! Wait a minute!

DELILAH *(Continuing)* You're working my last nerve!

Everyone is talking at once. Rita stretches in her chair, settling into a different position. The Communist, muttering, walks back to his offscreen seat.

HENRY *(Continuing to shout over everyone else, gesturing)* Wait a minute, wait a minute! Shut up, will you?!

DELILAH *(Overlapping Henry, continuing)* Lord, have mercy, I can't take no shit in there. Hmmp!

HENRY *(Overlapping Delilah, getting everyone's attention)* What if all this is merely a matter of semantics?

LARRY *(With annoyance)* How can it be semantics?

HENRY *(Gesturing)* Well, wait a minute. Let's, let's just readjust our definitions. Let's redefine ourselves as the real world *(Pointing towards the offscreen theater)* and them as the world of illusion and shadow. *(Gesturing)* You see, we're reality, they're a dream.

COUNTESS *(After a beat)* You better calm down. You've been up on the screen flickering too long.

CUT TO:
INTERIOR. THEATER MANAGER'S OFFICE—DAY.

The manager, sprawled out on his couch and fast asleep, fills the screen, a blanket draped over his body; his arm is flung up in sleep. The sound of a phone hanging up is heard. As the offscreen press agent and lawyer begin to talk, the camera leaves the manager, moving towards his desk—behind which the press agent sits, with Hirsch in a chair opposite him. Hirsch's girlfriend is sitting in her chair next to Hirsch; she lights a cigarette. The lawyer leans against a window, smoking a cigarette. The men are deep in discussion.

PRESS AGENT *(Offscreen)* It's confirmed.

LAWYER *(Offscreen)* It is? I was afraid this might happen.

PRESS AGENT *(Offscreen)* The Tom Baxter character tried to leave the screen in four *(Onscreen, counting off the cities in his fingers)* theaters, St. Louis, Chicago, Denver, and Detroit, *(Gesturing)* and he almost made it in Detroit.

LAWYER It looks bad.

PRESS AGENT *(Gesturing)* The movie houses in those towns are in a state of pandemonium. There's no way to keep the lid on it.

LAWYER *(Gesturing, walking over to the desk)* I see lawsuits, hundreds of lawsuits!

PRESS AGENT Oh, yeah.

HIRSCH *(Overlapping the press agent, gesturing)* We better pull the picture out of release.

PRESS AGENT What, in those towns?

HIRSCH *(Gesturing)* No, everywhere. Something's obviously gone very wrong here, and the best course of action is to shut down, take our losses, and get out of this mess before it really gets out of hand.

PRESS AGENT *(Looking around the group)* Sure, can you imagine hundreds of Tom Baxters flying around wild?

GIRLFRIEND *(To Hirsch)* Right, and *you* responsible for every one of them.

HIRSCH *(Gesturing, to his girlfriend)* Well, the best thing to do is to quit while there's only one of them out there. *(To the men)* But what do we do about him?

LAWYER *(Gesturing)* We've got to get him back in the picture. *(Stuttering, looking at the group)* Then we turn off the projector and . . . burn the prints.

PRESS AGENT *(Pointing for emphasis)* And the negative.

THEATER MANAGER *(Offscreen)* What a shame. *(Onscreen as the film cuts to him on the couch, half-asleep)* It was such a good picture.
The film leaves the sleepy manager, cutting to the amusement park, where an anxious Tom is standing near the Ferris wheel. He holds a bouquet of flowers in his hand; he looks out at the camera. Romantic music begins anew.

TOM *(Gesturing)* I missed you! You're late!
Tom walks a few steps towards the camera.

CECILIA *(Offscreen)* I'm sorry, I-I just, I . . . *(Onscreen as she rushes over to Tom)* I came as quickly as I could.

TOM *(Giving the bouquet to Cecilia)* I love you.

CECILIA *(Reacting to the bouquet)* Oh! *(Looking at Tom)* Oh, thank you.

TOM *(Overlapping, chuckling)* It's—

CECILIA *(Interrupting, gesturing)* Tom, u-uh . . . my feelings are so jumbled.

TOM Oh, I know, I know. *(Gesturing)* You're married and you're old-fashioned, and I'm a whole new idea. *(Taking Cecilia's arm)* But the truth is, you're unhappily married. And I'm gonna take you away from all this.

CECILIA *(Looking down)* Yeah, I . . . I know you love me.

TOM *(Putting his arms around Cecilia, bending down slightly, intensely)* Cecilia, I do love you. Don't you share my feelings?

CECILIA *(Looking up at Tom)* Well, I, eh . . . that-that's just it, I-I, y-you're-you're some kind of phantom.

TOM *(Sighing, taking Cecilia's hand)* Look, I'd— I don't want to talk any more about what-what's real and what's illusion. *(Gesturing)* Life's too short to spend time thinking about life. Let's just live it.

CECILIA Live it how?

TOM *(Putting his arm around Cecilia, leading her away and chuckling)* Well, we'll begin with dinner.

CECILIA *(Gesturing)* Oh, well, listen. No, we can— I-I've only got a few dollars.

TOM Well, we're not gonna use your money.

CECILIA Well, that's all we have! Unless you've done something.

TOM Well, say no more. *(Looking up at the sky)* The moon'll be full, the stars will be out, and we're going stepping.
They walk offscreen; the camera stays behind, remaining on the deserted Ferris wheel in the darkening dusk.

CECILIA *(Offscreen)* But we're broke!

TOM *(Offscreen)* Leave that to me.
The music stops as the film cuts to the back lot behind the theater, as seen through the alley. It's night; the alley is dark. A stationary train caboose sits in the background; the light in its window illuminates the back lot, as does a streetlamp in the lot. A railroad worker, carrying a lantern, walks across the lot, past the caboose. He's whistling. As soon as he's gone, Tom and Cecilia emerge from behind the caboose, Tom in the lead. He holds Cecilia's hand, pulling her into the alley. Their footsteps are the only noise. She holds her hat. He walks over to the theater's back door in the alley. He jiggles the lock. He holds the door open for Cecilia, following close behind. He shuts the door behind them; the alley is empty now. Crickets are softly heard.

After a beat, the film moves inside the theater. The black-and-white screen is seen over the rows of empty seats. The black-and-white movie characters are lounging about in the penthouse living room. Rita is sitting in a chair in the foreground; Jason sits in a chair nearby. The Countess, Larry, and Father Donnelly are on the couch. Henry, reading a paper, and the Communist stand near the wall. Delilah is still sitting at the piano. Everyone looks drained.

While the black-and-white characters move about on the screen, Tom and Cecilia, in color, emerge through the curtained side exit door. Tom gestures Cecilia forward as he walks over to the edge of the screen, in front of the rows of seats. They stand directly beneath the screen, looking up, their backs to the camera. Tom waves.

JASON *(Seeing Tom)* I-it's him! Tom! *(Stands up)* You're back! *(Seeing Tom, jumping up)*

TOM *(To the now perked-up movie characters, who are all looking out at Tom)* I want you to meet my fiancée, Cecilia.

CECILIA *(Murmuring)* Tom . . .

TOM *(To Cecilia)* This— Oh, well, you know all these people.

RITA *(Looking out from the screen)* It's not possible!

TOM Are you ki— I'm in the world of the possible!

HENRY *(Shouting, looking out at Tom)* Yeah? Well, you better get back in the story, you little weasel!
The film cuts to a closer view of Tom and Cecilia, in color, looking up at the offscreen movie characters, the rows of empty seats behind them. Cecilia stands slightly back from Tom, holding back.

TOM *(Laughing, clapping his hands)* Ah! You anticipate me!

CECILIA *(Softly)* Tom . . .

TOM *(Ignoring Cecilia's protestations, glancing back at her as he climbs up on the stage)* Follow me! *(Extends his hand to Cecilia)*

FATHER DONNELLY *(Offscreen)* Saints preserve us.

TOM *(Only his hand seen onscreen, to Cecilia)* Trust me.

LARRY *(Offscreen)* He just comes and goes like he pleases.

RITA *(Offscreen, overlapping Larry)* Not again.

Cecilia, holding her hat on with one hand, takes Tom's hand. He starts to pull her up onto the stage. As the movie characters angrily react, talking at once, the film cuts to the black-and-white screen. It fills the frame. Tom, his back to the camera, climbs up directly in front of his black-and-white colleagues, pulling Cecilia along with him. Now black-and-white, they enter the world of The Purple Rose of Cairo, *stumbling past Jason, who is at the edge of the screen, to the middle of the penthouse living room. The others are all gathered around them.*

TOM *(Running into the screen world, to Cecilia)* Come on.

CECILIA *(Gasping, looking around the penthouse living room)* Where am I?

LARRY *(Overlapping)* But she can't be in here!

TOM *(Gesturing)* Why not? Come on!

HENRY *(Overlapping Tom)* He's just dumb enough to think . . .

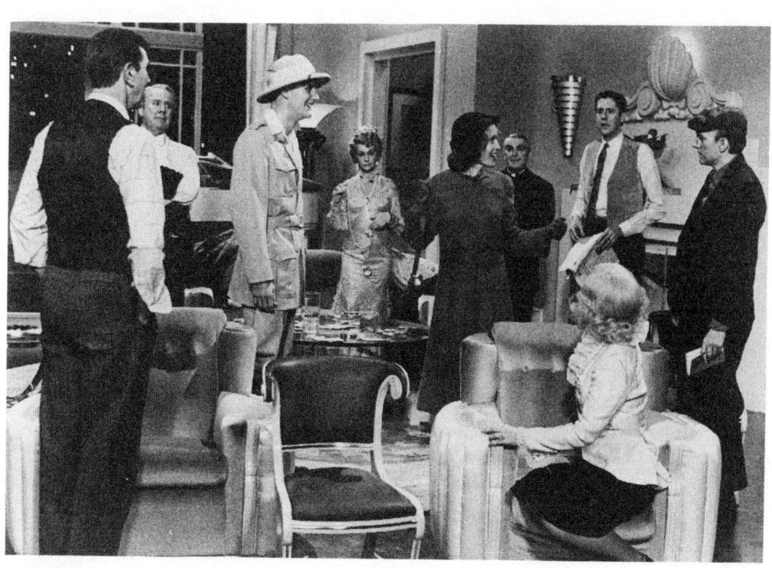

CECILIA *(Overlapping, looking around, enraptured)* I feel so light!

TOM *(Reaching over towards Cecilia, gesturing)* Cecilia, my money is good up here.

THE COMMUNIST You've got too much money.

CECILIA *(Overlapping, turning around in amazement)* Like I'm floating on air!

Everyone is talking at once now, reacting to the new situation. Cecilia can't stop looking around her; she giggles; she gasps. Rita sits in her chair, her hand to her forehead; she looks like she's about to swoon. Henry's paper dangles in his hand. Delilah gets up from the piano bench; she stands in front of the piano.

HENRY What?

LARRY *(Gesturing)* But it'll upset the balance!

HENRY It sure does.

COUNTESS *(Stubbing out a cigarette)* What's the difference? He's back, isn't he?

FATHER DONNELLY *(Tapping Henry's shoulder)* I told you he'd be back.

HENRY *(To the Father)* Oh, you didn't know that!

RITA *(Overlapping, loudly, as she stands up from her chair)* Can we get on with the plot now?

HENRY *(Gesturing)* How can we with her here?

THE COMMUNIST *(Overlapping)* Look at her. Look what he did.

RITA Oh, I—

TOM *(Interrupting, pointing emphatically)* But she's here with me, and I'll sock any man in the jaw who makes her feel unwanted!

HENRY *(Gesturing, turning from Tom)* Oh, drat!

DELILAH *(Overlapping, her hands on her hips)* Well, it's about time you got back here!

COUNTESS *(Holding up her hand)* Right! Now we finally go to the Copacabana. *(Picking up her fur wrap from the couch)* None of us have eaten in ages.

CECILIA *(Gasping)* Oh, the Copacabana!

TOM *(Overlapping)* Good, I'm bringing a guest.

JASON *(Putting his hands together, prayer-style)* Well, won't Kitty Haynes be surprised!

Big-band music begins in the background. Cecilia continues to squeal in excitement. Father Donnelly rubs his hands together in anticipation of food. Henry puts down his paper; Rita, her back to the camera, looks around at the group, her hands on her hips. Everyone is ready—for anything—as the penthouse dissolves to a close-up of a trumpet player blowing his horn at the Copacabana, in black-and-white.

The movie cuts to the Purple Rose *group clustered around Arturo, the maitre d': Rita, Jason, Larry, Henry, Tom in his pith helmet, the Countess—and the beaming Cecilia, wearing her everyday cloche hat. Arturo holds some menus.*

JASON Table for *seven*, please, Arturo.

ARTURO *(Bowing slightly)* Yes, sir. *(Pauses)* Seven?

JASON Seven.

ARTURO That's impossible. It's *always* six.

RITA *(Gesturing towards Cecilia)* We have an extra.

Cecilia turns and looks at Tom.

TOM *(Standing up on his toes to emphasize his position)* *Seven*, Arturo.

ARTURO *(Gesturing to Cecilia with disdain)* This person?
Cecilia shrugs, still smiling, and the movie cuts to Kitty Haynes, onstage at the Copacabana. She wears her sleek black dress; the big band plays behind her, the conductor in a white tux, his back to the camera, as she sings "One Day At a Time."

KITTY *(Singing)* "So let's not speak of love sublime, because time Brings on a breakup. / There'll be no tears and no emotional scenes to spoil my makeup."
Kitty looks offscreen, smiling, as the film cuts to her point of view: the Purple Rose *table, listening to her singing. Jason smiles offscreen to her, then glances around the circular table. Larry sits next to him, then Henry, and Rita; Tom and Cecilia sit with their backs to the camera; they all turn their heads to watch the offscreen Kitty. There's a railing behind their table; the Copacabana is crowded with other patrons, at other tables. Henry smokes a cigarette.*

KITTY *(Offscreen, singing)* "And when the end comes, I'll take up the slack / Until you call and say you want to come back!"

JASON *(Whispering, under the singing, to Cecilia)* Would you like some more champagne?

CECILIA *(Turning, to Jason)* Oh, thank you. *(Holding out her glass to Jason, as she whispers to Tom)* Listen . . . Tom, I don't know what they're charging you, but those champagne bottles are filled with ginger ale.

RITA *(Loudly, as Jason pours more "champagne" in Larry's glass)* That's the movies, kid!

HENRY *(To Rita)* Shh!

CECILIA *(Overlapping Henry, sipping her "champagne")* Oh, I don't care. I love every minute of it.
Tom turns and grins at her, then turns back to watch the offscreen Kitty. Cecilia watches her too, sipping her "champagne" and beaming,

as the movie cuts to a panoramic view of the singing Kitty, across the crowded nightclub, past some potted palms. The large big band plays on the stage, the conductor in front of them, as the movie cuts to a closer view of the singing Kitty, a scarf swirled in her gloved hands, as she finishes the number with a flourish. A portion of the band, with its conductor, is seen behind her.

KITTY *(Singing)* "Till then I'm waiting, domesticating, / Every Sunday, Monday, one day at a time. / Let's take it one day at a time. / Let's take it one day at a ti-i-ime!"
Cheers, applause, and scattered "bravos" are heard as the movie cuts back to the Purple Rose *table, to Cecilia, enthusiastically applauding and smiling. She glances at Tom, who is only partially seen, then back, looking out at the offscreen camera and stage. Henry and Rita are seen in the background, wildly applauding as well.*

MAN IN CROWD *(Offscreen)* Bravo!
The movie cuts back to Kitty on the stage, the band behind her. She smiles, her long dress shimmering on the floor, as she walks off, past several tables of applauding patrons, past a sweeping wall with potted palms, towards the offscreen Purple Rose *contingent—as the movie cuts to their table, to Tom, Cecilia, Jason, and Rita, seen in profile, applauding the approaching offscreen Kitty. Tom, Jason, and Cecilia stand up, still applauding, smiling. Other patrons at other tables are clapping in their seats, looking at Kitty with admiration.*

JASON *(To the approaching Kitty)* Bravo! Bravo!
Kitty walks up to Tom, Jason, and Cecilia, nodding at her appreciative audience and smiling. The club settles down; the din of continuous conversation can be heard.

KITTY *(Smiling, to Tom and Jason)* Thank you, thank you. *(After a beat, to Cecilia)* Who are you?

CECILIA *(Stammering and gesturing, clutching her pocketbook)* Oh, no, I'm, I just, I-I came with Tom. *(Looking at Kitty, shaking her head)* You sing so beautifully.

KITTY *(After a beat, staring at Cecilia, her smile frozen)* What the hell is this? *(To Tom)* We're supposed to meet and marry. *(Stops smiling)* Who's the skirt?

TOM *(Patting Cecilia's arm)* My fiancée.

KITTY What?

CECILIA *(Overlapping Kitty)* Oh, no, wait, I . . .

HENRY *(Offscreen, overlapping Cecilia)* He met her in New Jersey.

KITTY *(Looking at the offscreen Henry)* What is this?!

JASON Kitty, she's *real.*

Tom looks on, smiling, as Kitty pauses, puzzled for a moment, then reaches out and tentatively touches Cecilia's shoulder. She screams—and faints, falling down offscreen. The background patrons react; there are gasps and shouting amidst the din of excited conversation.

COUNTESS *(Offscreen)* Kitty!

JASON *(Looking around)* Quick! Pour . . . pour ginger ale on her!

HENRY *(Offscreen)* Call Father Donnelly.

The place is in an uproar. The offscreen Henry mutters indistinctly. Some of the background patrons stand up. Someone screams. Arturo comes up to the table, a worried look on his face, as Tom, muttering, pulls out some money and tosses it on the table.

ARTURO What's all the fuss about?

TOM *(Over the noise)* Uh, nothing, nothing, Arturo. *(Handing Arturo some money)* We were, we were just leaving. *(To Cecilia, taking her hand and pulling her away)* Come on. Let's go.

RITA *(Standing up, her back to the camera)* Leaving? Leaving where? *(Shaking her head)* Hey, I'm all mixed up!

Tom leads Cecilia by the hand past their table, past Rita, the Countess, Larry, and Henry, who are standing up, watching them go. He walks up the few stairs to the upper level of the club and, near the railing, surrounded by patrons and other tables, he stops and turns to the offscreen group.

TOM *(Loudly)* I'm gonna show Cecilia the town!

The movie cuts quickly to Arturo, standing by the Purple Rose *table, the band, dance floor, and surrounding tables seen behind him. Jason is partially seen, standing next to him. The buzz of the patrons creates a steady, continuous din.*

ARTURO *(Gesturing with his bill-stuffed hand)* Are we just chucking out the plot, sir?

TOM *(Offscreen)* Exactly. *(Onscreen as the camera moves back to him and Cecilia by the railing, gesturing)* It's every man for himself!

ARTURO *(Looking off, intensely, as he drops his menus)* Then I don't have to seat people anymore. *(Putting the tip money in his pocket)* I can do what it is I've always wanted to do!

JASON *(His face offscreen)* What's that?

ARTURO *(Looking at Jason for a beat, then turning around to the band)* Hit it, boys!

The band starts to play fast-tempoed swing music as Arturo tap-dances away from the Purple Rose *table, spinning his way to the dance floor in front of the band. He does a jaunty tap-dance routine to the gasps, laughter, and subsequent applause of the nightclub patrons.*

As Arturo dances on, a diamond shape appears in the center of the screen. Inside is a glittering panoramic view of Times Square. The diamond gets bigger and bigger, wiping away the Copacabana scene. Brash, high-stepping music begins to play as HARLEQUIN CLUB, *in big letters on a slant, appears on the screen, along with its logo, an outline of a martini glass. Tom and Cecilia, her hand on her hat, appear on the screen as well, superimposed on the Times Square landscape. They are both looking around and up, two awed tourists on the scene.*

The Harlequin Club sign moves offscreen, replaced by the sign for THE HOT BOX, *with its squiggly lines; it flashes off and on the right-hand corner of the screen, on a slant. As the superimposed Tom and Cecilia continue to look around them, the Times Square view starts to move, traveling up Broadway, past lit-up theaters, the Times Square tower in the distance.*

Tom and Cecilia walk offscreen as the BROADWAY DANCE PALACE *sign, with its musical notes, moves onto the center of the screen, as a waiter's white-gloved hands chilling a bottle of champagne in an ice bucket move onscreen, wiping away the Times Square view. Rising bubbles appear, superimposed on the screen, as a dancing, prismlike circle of champagne glasses fades in on the scene. The sign fades out, the champagne glasses become more noticeable, and the champagne bottle and waiter's hands dissolve to Tom and Cecilia, dancing in each other's arms; the couple is superimposed over two stationary champagne glasses, and with the dancing glasses moving in a circle, the whole screen has a kaleidoscopic effect.*

The dancing scene dissolves into the awning of a nightclub, its PURPLE GROTTO *sign emblazoned on its awning at a tilt. The camera moves down on a slant, revealing Tom and Cecilia just walking out of the club. They hail a taxi. A couple is seen walking in, the entrance bright with light. Superimposed over the scene, giving it a surreal montage effect, is a sophisticated couple dancing cheek to cheek.*

The brash, romantic music continues as a hand glides down a piano keyboard, wiping away the Purple Grotto scene as it moves down the keys. A small CLUB HARLEM *sign appears in the center of the screen, becoming larger and larger as it flashes on and off. Tom and Cecilia next appear, jitterbugging, superimposed over the hands playing the keyboard.*

The music gets a Latin beat as the striped, Eastern-style doors come into view—on a slant. Above them is a neon sign: CLUB MOROCCO. *Tom and Cecilia, their backs to the camera, appear, walking hand in hand to the doors. They, too, are seen on a slant.*

As Tom opens the doors for Cecilia, they dissolve to the inside of the club where Tom and Cecilia are doing a mean rhumba. Superimposed over their dancing forms are a pair of hands shaking two maracas. The hands dissolve to a Latin band. The sign LATIN QUARTER, *with its palm tree outlines, splashes on the screen. The couple dances on.*

The Latin beat continues as the band disappears. In its place is a tilted glass being filled with champagne. The couple fades away as rising bottles surround the glass, filling the screen. Champagne pours over the sides of the glass, and the scene dissolves to:

Cecilia and Tom riding and chatting in a taxi, as seen through its rear window, through a curtain of rising bubbles. The driver's back is seen. Tom's arm is around Cecilia; she smiles at him, nestling her head on his shoulder. He holds her tightly, the bubbles disappear, and the scene dissolves to:

The penthouse foyer, with its spiral staircase in the background. Tom and Cecilia walk onscreen, arm in arm. Piano music plays in the background.

CECILIA I had such a wonderful time.

TOM *(Laughing)* Me, too.
They walk into the living room. Through the windows, the breaking dawn can be seen.

CECILIA *(Glancing around)* Where are all the others?

TOM Oh, I don't know. *(Casually taking his arm off Cecilia, putting his hands into his pockets)* Well, probably just still dancing away.

CECILIA *(Draping her coat over her shoulder)* Oh.

TOM *(Turning to Cecilia)* Why? Does it matter? I wanted to get you alone.

CECILIA *(Shaking her head no)* It's so beautiful here. *(Looking around)* Oh! The white telephone! Oh! *(Walking over to the phone, near the windows)* I've dreamed of having a white telephone. *(Touches the phone)*

TOM *(Walking over to Cecilia, his hands clasped behind his back)* Your dreams are my dreams.

CECILIA *(Looking up at Tom, still touching the phone)* My whole life I've wondered what it would be like to be this side of the screen.

TOM *(Looking out the windows)* You see that city out there waking up?

CECILIA *(Turning to look out the windows)* Hmm?

TOM That's yours for the asking.

CECILIA *(Gasping)* My heart's beating so fast!

The music swells. Tom puts his hands on Cecilia's shoulders, turning her towards him. They kiss, lingering, the Manhattan skyline a compelling backdrop.

GIL *(Offscreen, loudly)* Cecilia!

The music stops, the mood broken. Cecilia turns and faces the camera, her hand on her hat. Tom, too, turns and faces straight ahead.

CECILIA *(Astonished)* Gil!

The film cuts to the theater, in color, with its rows of empty seats. Gil stands in the aisle, in the back, partially obscured by the glaring projectionist's light.

CECILIA *(Offscreen)* What are you doing here?

GIL *(Walking down the aisle, towards the offscreen movie screen)* Oh, I . . . I came in here to think. What are you doing here?
The film cuts back to the black-and-white screen, as seen over the rows of empty theater seats. The black-and-white Tom and Cecilia walk away from the windows, towards the center of the room.

TOM I t-, I took her on a date . . . all right? *(Gesturing)* Now can't you just leave us alone?

GIL *(Offscreen)* No, I-I can't leave her *(Onscreen, walking towards the screen, his back to the camera)* alone. I'm . . . *(Sighing)* I'm jealous.

CECILIA *(Walking closer to the edge of the screen, briefly silhouetted by the breaking dawn through the penthouse windows.)* You're jealous?

GIL Well, what do you want me to say? *(Gesturing)* I-I can't get Cecilia out of my mind. It just . . .

CECILIA *(Interrupting, walking to the screen's edge, looking out at Gil)* Gil . . . do-do you mean that?

TOM *(Walking over to the screen edge, gesturing and reacting)* Oh, for God's sake, would you go back to Hollywood? Please.

GIL *(Looking up at the screen, gesturing)* Look, I'm embarrassed to admit it, Cecilia. I . . .
The film cuts to Gil's face, looking up at the screen. As he talks, Cecilia walks over to him, her back to the camera, having stepped out of the black-and-white off-camera movie screen.

GIL *(Continuing, gesturing)* You know, you said I had a magical glow? But that . . . it's you, you're the one that has one. *(Looking at Cecilia, who is standing in front of him now)* And . . . even though we've just met, I just, I know that this is the real thing.
The film cuts to Tom, in color, facing the two offscreen. He too has stepped out of the black-and-white movie screen, which can be seen, empty of characters, behind him.

TOM You can't be in love with Cecilia. *(Walking closer to the offscreen Gil and Cecilia)* She's in love with me!
The camera is back on Gil and Cecilia, in profile . . .

GIL I'll tell you what, why don't you turn around and reenter the film?

. . . then back on Tom, the movie screen behind him.

TOM I'm never going back!
The film cuts to the black-and-white movie screen. It fills the frame. Henry and the Countess have just entered the living room. They stand at the edge of the screen, looking down at the offscreen Tom, Gil, and Cecilia.

COUNTESS I can't believe it, they're at it again.

HENRY *(Shouting)* Tom, will you get back up here?
The film moves back to the theater, in color, to Gil and Cecilia, standing next to each other, and Tom, a few steps away, his back to the camera.

GIL *(Pointing, shaking his head)* See, there you go, Tom. You're ruining everything.

TOM You are! You're the one who's ruining everything.

GIL *(Pointing to himself)* You know, if it wasn't for me, there wouldn't be any you!

TOM *(Putting his hands on his hips)* Don't be so sure! I coulda been played by Frederic March or Leslie Howard!

COUNTESS *(Offscreen)* You're wrong.
The film cuts back to Henry and the Countess, looking down at the offscreen standoff. Rita enters and stands behind them, watching the action.

COUNTESS *(Continuing, onscreen)* The part's too insignificant to attract a major star.

The film cuts back to Gil and Cecilia, standing together, and Tom in the aisle, in color.

TOM *(Turning towards the off-camera movie screen)* Insignificant! She called me a minor character . . . a minor character!

GIL *(Overlapping, looking up at the off-camera movie screen)* Like hell it is! What are you talking about?

TOM *(To the off-camera Countess, on the movie screen, pointing)* I am not a minor character!

GIL *(Overlapping, looking up towards the screen)* What do you mean, a minor character?

While Gil talks the film cuts briefly to Tom, who looks skeptical as he listens to the offscreen Gil, then back to Gil and Cecilia, seen now in close-up. Cecilia's face is in profile looking off, perhaps at the offscreen Tom; Gil faces the camera.

GIL *(Continuing, after a beat, to Cecilia as he takes her hands)* Jeez! You know, I haven't been able to think of anything since we met. I j— *(Offscreen, the camera on Tom)* I just, I have to have some time with you to-to show you what real life can be like if-if two *(Onscreen, the camera on his and Cecilia's face)* people really care for each other.

CECILIA *(Gesturing)* Oh . . . I . . . last week I was unloved. *(Turning to Gil, her back to the camera briefly)* Now . . . *two* people love me, and i-it's-it's the same two people.

COUNTESS *(Offscreen)* Go with the real guy . . .

As the Countess starts to speak, the film cuts to the black-and-white movie screen, filling the frame. The Countess and Henry stand at its edge as before, Rita behind them. They look down at the offscreen Cecilia.

COUNTESS *(Continuing, onscreen)* . . . honey. We're limited.

RITA *(Pushing Henry aside as she steps forward)* Go with Tom. He's got no flaws.

DELILAH *(Walking onscreen, joining the others at the edge)* Go with somebody, child, 'cause I's getting bored.
The film moves back to Tom, looking at the offscreen Gil . . .

TOM *(Gesturing)* She's gonna marry me. You're just, you're wasting your time.

. . . then back to Gil, Cecilia at his side. . . .

GIL *(Looking at the offscreen Tom)* Will you get back on the screen? I'm trying to tell Cecilia I'm in love with her.

. . . and then back to Tom, in close-up, looking at the offscreen Cecilia; a theater wall lamp in the background casts a golden glow.

TOM *(To the offscreen Cecilia)* I love you. I'm honest, dependable, courageous, romantic, and a great kisser.
The film cuts abruptly back to Tom, standing with Cecilia.

GIL And I'm real! *(Looks at Cecilia)*

LARRY *(Offscreen)* Let's go, Cecilia! Choose one of them so we can settle this thing.
As Larry talks to a dazed-looking Cecilia, the film cuts to the black-and-white screen, as seen over the theater seats. Cecilia, Tom, and Gil are in the aisle, their backs to the camera, looking up at the screen. Larry has joined the others at the edge of the movie screen. He, Henry, Delilah, Rita, and the Countess look down at the group in the aisle.

LARRY The most human of all attributes is your ability to choose.

COUNTESS *(Nodding, with Rita)* Mm-hmm.

HENRY *(Gesturing, looking at his fellow movie characters)* Well, wait a minute. Wait a minute. If she chooses Tom, how are we gonna end the story? We'll be stuck here forever.

TOM *(Turning in the aisle to face Cecilia, his arms outstretched)* Father Donnelly can marry us right here in the movie house.

The film cuts to Tom's point of view: Gil and Cecilia, standing farther up the aisle.

GIL *(Gesturing)* No, that won't stand up in court. The priest has to be human.
The camera is back on the black-and-white movie screen. Father Donnelly walks up to the Purple Rose *group at the edge of the screen from the offscreen background living room.*

FATHER DONNELLY The Bible never says a priest can't be on film!
The film cuts back to Tom and Cecilia; they are facing each other. Cecilia, silent for so long, finally speaks.

CECILIA *(Gesturing)* No, uh, I'm-I'm already married!

GIL *(Taking Cecilia's hands, pleading with her)* Come away with me to Hollywood!
The film cuts briefly to Tom, standing alone, his hands on his hips, staring in openmouthed disbelief as he watches Gil and Cecilia . . .

CECILIA *(Offscreen)* Just . . . like that?

GIL *(Offscreen)* Just like that.

. . . then moves back to Gil and Cecilia; he's still holding her hands, pleading. Cecilia, looking stunned, unsure, groans softly.

GIL *(Continuing, onscreen)* Oh, do something impulsive for once in your life! I mean, j-j-just throw your stuff in a valise an-and come away with me. Really, j— And don't forget that ukulele. *(Chuckles)*
The film quickly cuts to Tom, his hands still on his hips . . .

TOM *(Suspiciously, his brow furrowed)* What ukulele?

. . . then moves back to Gil, holding Cecilia's hands in his.

GIL *(Glaring at Tom, momentarily interrupted, then back to Ceci-*

lia) Look, I-I love you. I know, I know that o-only happens in movies, *(Gesturing)* but . . . *(Sighing)* I do.
A piano concerto begins to play. Cecilia looks into Gil's eyes, silent, then turns to the offscreen Tom.

CECILIA Tom?
The film cuts to Tom, his hands still on his hips—now with a confused look on his face.

RITA *(Offscreen)* Cecilia . . .
As Rita speaks, the film cuts back to the black-and-white movie screen. Henry, Rita, and the Countess are at the edge. Delilah, Father Donnelly, and Larry stand behind them. The Countess and Henry look at Rita while she talks to the offscreen Cecilia.

RITA *(Onscreen, continuing)* You're throwing away perfection!

HENRY *(Gesturing, a cigarette in his hand)* Don't tell her that! We need Tom back!

RITA *(Looking at Henry, then back at the offscreen Cecilia, with feeling)* It's so romantic!

HENRY *(With disgust, looking away)* Ohh, women!
The others on the black-and-white screen react as well, Larry with a poignant smile, the Countess with set lips; the film cuts to a hurting Tom, his hands still on his hips; he hasn't moved.

TOM *(After a beat, pausing and sighing)* Well, I'm-I'm-I'm crushed, *(Gesturing)* I'm devastated. It's . . .
Tom sighs, unable to continue. He puts his hands in his pockets. He starts to cry as the film cuts to Cecilia looking at the offscreen Tom. Gil, standing next to Cecilia, looks first at the offscreen Tom, then intently at Cecilia. He is silent.

CECILIA *(Shaking her head)* Tom, try to understand.
The film moves back to the shattered Tom, standing as before, not moving, watching the offscreen Cecilia as she talks. There are tears in his eyes.

CECILIA *(Offscreen, continuing)* You'll be fine. In your world things have a way of working out right. See, I'm a real person. No matter how . . . how tempted I am, I have to choose the real world.

As Cecilia continues to talk, the film goes back up to the black-and-white screen, where Henry, Delilah, Rita, Father Donnelly, Larry, and the Countess stand as before, at the edge of the screen. They watch the drama unfolding down on the theater floor. The Countess's head is down; Rita stares offscreen, caught up in Cecilia's words, her mouth open. They all listen; they all react.

CECILIA *(Offscreen)* I loved every minute with you.

And the film is back on Cecilia, in a close-up of her face looking at the offscreen Tom.

CECILIA *(Shaking her head, smiling)* And I'll never forget our night on the town.

The film moves back to Tom, standing as before, immobile. He stares at the offscreen Cecilia for an infinite moment. The concerto plays on.

TOM Good-bye.

He slowly turns and walks down the aisle, towards the waiting theater screen, offscreen, as the film moves back to Gil and Cecilia, looking at the offscreen Tom's retreating back. After a moment, they turn and head up the aisle. Gil puts his arm around Cecilia. The concerto plays on as they walk to the back of the theater, as they turn and walk out the exit, as the movie characters soon begin to chatter and laugh onscreen, indistinctly welcoming the returning Tom. Cecilia turns once and looks back; the bright projector light obscures their retreating figures.

HENRY *(Offscreen)* Well, you're better off with us, old sport . . . you really are.

COUNTESS *(Offscreen, overlapping)* Don't do it again.

JASON *(Offscreen)* Can we get on with *The Purple Rose of Cairo*, please?

DELILAH *(Offscreen)* If anyone wants me, I'll be in reel six.

The film moves back to the black-and-white movie screen, as seen across the empty theater. Tom stands near the edge, looking out at the offscreen Cecilia. Rita is by his side. The other characters, laughing, excited, begin to disperse, walking offscreen.

RITA *(To Tom)* Kitty's waiting for you.

DELILAH *(Beginning to walk away towards the bedroom door)* Lord have mercy!

HENRY *(Giving his arm to Rita)* Come on, Rita. *(Walks her offscreen in the direction of the foyer)*

DELILAH What a day! *(Offscreen)* What a day!

Soon the last footsteps are heard. Tom remains alone on the screen. He stands still for a brief moment, staring out at the theater. Then he, too, turns and walks offscreen. The penthouse living room is empty.

CUT TO:
EXTERIOR. CECILIA'S HOUSE—DAY.

Cecilia is running down the sidewalk towards her house, her hand holding her hat on her head. The bridge is behind her in the background; action movie music is heard. Cecilia runs past a few houses, then, reaching her own, she fumbles for her keys in her bag. She turns and walks up the steps, then opens the front door and enters. She shuts the door behind her.

The film moves inside, to Cecilia's darkened bedroom; a portion of the bedspread shows on the screen. Through the doorway, Cecilia is seen opening the front door of the apartment and shutting it behind her. She heads straight for the bedroom, towards the camera, turning on the light and dumping her pocketbook on the bed. She bends down, pulling a suitcase out from under her bed. She unstraps the suitcase and opens it, placing it on the bed. Her movements are hurried, determined. The music fades out.

MONK *(Offscreen)* So your explorer friend's *(Onscreen, walking to the bedroom doorway)* okay? I saw him walking around town with you.

CECILIA *(Offscreen, busily gathering her clothes from an offscreen closet)* Yeah, he's okay . . . no thanks to you.

MONK *(Standing in the doorway, sipping a beer and looking at the offscreen Cecilia)* I didn't mean to be so rough on him. *(Gesturing)* It's just that I get jealous when it comes to you.

Cecilia scurries back onscreen, holding two dresses. She flings one down on the bed and begins to fold the other. She doesn't look at Monk; his shadow plays on the open door in the dim light.

CECILIA *(Folding her dress)* Do you?

MONK Christ, you know I do. I know I treat you rough. It's my way. *(Fingering his beer bottle)* It doesn't mean I don't feel for you.

CECILIA *(Sighing, putting the folded dress in the suitcase, starting on the other one)* Oh.

MONK *(Sipping his beer, after a beat)* What are you doin'?

CECILIA *(Packing her dresses)* Leaving.

MONK *(Gesturing)* Here we go again. *(Sniffs, looking off for a moment)*

CECILIA *(Turning around to Monk, shouting)* You don't feel for me, Monk. All you feel is for yourself! *(Folding her dress angrily)* Your . . . your beer, your-your card games, your women!

MONK *(Putting down his now empty beer bottle)* Okay . . . I'm gonna turn over a new leaf. No, I'm not kidding, I *(Offscreen as the camera follows Cecilia to a dresser; farther in the room, the now empty closet behind her)* swear it!

CECILIA *(Overlapping Monk)* It's too late, Monk. *(Opening a drawer, taking out some underwear and socks)* It's too late, I'm going. I shoulda left a long time ago. I would've, except I was scared of being alone.

MONK *(Offscreen)* So what now? *(Onscreen as the film moves back to him in the doorway, gesturing)* You found some chump who's filling your head with big ideas!

CECILIA *(Overlapping, hurrying onscreen to the bed, her arms filled with underwear)* No, no, I got a chance to change my life. *(Packing her things, loudly)* I'm moving to Hollywood.
Cecilia turns and walks out of the room, not glancing at Monk as she walks by him, offscreen. He follows her offscreen, his shadow seen on the open door as he talks to her in the offscreen hall.

MONK All right, now listen, Cecilia, I said I was *(Offscreen, following Cecilia)* sorry about being rough with your friend, now let's shape up!

CECILIA *(Offscreen)* It's too late, Monk!

Cecilia returns to the bedroom as she talks, her arms stuffed with clothes, headed for the suitcase on the bed—until Monk, following her, enters the room, grabbing her violently by the arms.

MONK *(Shouting, shaking Cecilia)* Look, like hell it is! You . . . I said like hell it is! And don't be giving me that big-headed stuff, you hear?! Because I'm the guy that can slap you down!

CECILIA *(Overlapping, reacting and gasping as she clutches her hat)* Go ahead and hit me, Monk! *(Screaming)* Just go ahead and hit me!
Monk grunts. He lets go of Cecilia.

CECILIA *(Packing the clothes that had been in her arms)* I'm leaving anyway!

MONK *(Pointing at Cecilia, her back to him)* Yeah, well, this never woulda happened if you didn't meet that guy.

CECILIA That's probably right, and we woulda just gone on the same way till we were too old to even hope for something better. *(Shutting the suitcase)* But I did meet him! I did meet him *(Wrapping a strap around the suitcase)* and I have feelings for him! And he has for me!

MONK What about me?

CECILIA *(Panting, turning to Monk for a moment as she ties the strap)* I still care for you, Monk, if you can believe that. But sud—*(Gasps, shaking her head)* Out of the blue, for the first time in my life, somebody's in love with me! *(Looks quickly at Monk)*

MONK *(Gesturing)* No, bu-bu-but you just met each other.

CECILIA *(Panting, turning to Monk)* Love at first sight doesn't only happen just in the movies.
Cecilia pushes Monk aside and, hurrying to a shelf, pulls down the ukulele. As Monk talks, she goes back to the bed for the suitcase.

MONK *(Putting his hand up, reacting)* Hey, Cecilia, don't go. You hear me? I said don't go! Now wait a minute. I— *(Turning around as Cecilia picks up her suitcase and, ukulele in hand, walks out the bedroom door)* Don't! *(Shouting)* I said, I said don't go!

CECILIA *(Overlapping, turning slightly to Monk)* So long, Monk.
Cecilia walks to the apartment door, as seen through the doorway of the bedroom. Monk follows her, his back to the camera.

MONK *(Shouting)* You stay here, you hear?!

CECILIA *(Overlapping)* You take care of yourself.
Cecilia opens the door and leaves. Daylight pours in through the doorway.

MONK Oh, yeah. All right, well . . . *(Holding the door open, shouting down the stairs at the offscreen Cecilia)* well, go, go! See if I care. Go, see what it is out there. *(Yelling, his hand at his mouth)* It ain't the movies! It's real life! It's real life, and you'll be back! You mark my words! You'll be back!
The sound of the front door slamming closed is heard as the film cuts to the outside of the Jewel Theater, to a man, standing on a ladder, as he takes down the Purple Rose of Cairo *letters from the marquee. The camera moves away from him, past the marquee, past the sidewalk and across the street—where Cecilia is seen, making her way to the theater, her ukulele and suitcase in hand. Sweeping music is heard in the background; a car passes down the street. A car is parked near the theater.*

Cecilia crosses the street at an angle and, half-walking, half-running, moves to the front of the theater. She looks slowly around. The theater front is deserted; the ticket booth is closed. The ladder is seen in the foreground; the music plays on. Cecilia continues to look around, down the street, at the theater's glass doors. No one.

The glass doors swing open; the theater manager walks outside, carrying some marquee letters. The music stops.

CECILIA Hi, Sam.

THEATER MANAGER *(Overlapping)* Cecilia, what are you doing here?

CECILIA Meeting Gil Shepherd.

THEATER MANAGER They all gone.
The camera moves in on Cecilia's face. She looks stunned. A breeze blows in her hair.

CECILIA *(Reacting)* They . . . What do, what do you mean?
The film cuts quickly to the theater manager. . . .

THEATER MANAGER Went back to Hollywood.

. . . then back to Cecilia, staring at the offscreen theater manager. Her head doesn't move; she doesn't blink.

CECILIA Gil, too?

THEATER MANAGER *(Offscreen)* Mr. Shepherd, yeah. As soon as Tom Baxter went back up on the movie screen, he couldn't wait to get outta here. He said this was a close call for his career. I think he's gonna play Charles Lindbergh.
Romantic music begins to play. Cecilia finally looks down, in shock, as the theater manager passes her, blocking her face momentarily. She begins to cry.

THEATER MANAGER *(Offscreen)* Don't forget, Cecilia, Fred Astaire and Ginger Rogers start today.
Cecilia slowly, slowly turns around, as her face dissolves to Gil's face. He sits in a plane, by a window. He's looking out the window; he turns and looks out at the offscreen camera, which moves farther away to reveal a man fast asleep in the seat behind him. Gil looks down, his hand to his mouth. He stares off, lost in his own thoughts, alone. The music stops. Only the whir of the plane is heard. The camera stays on his face, in the quiet plane, as Fred Astaire, singing "Cheek to Cheek," is heard over the whir, and the film cuts to:

Fred Astaire dancing cheek to cheek with Ginger Rogers in the sophisticated, black-and-white Top Hat. *They are in a glamorous nightclub; other dancers glide by on the crowded dance floor.*

FRED ASTAIRE *(Singing)* "Heaven, I'm in heaven / And my heart beats so that I can hardly speak. / And I seem to find the happiness I seek . . . "
While Fred Astaire continues to sing, the film cuts to the inside of the theater, in color, near the back. Several people are seen watching the offscreen movie in their seats as the swinging doors open, and Cecilia enters, carrying her purse, her suitcase, and her ukulele. She walks near the back wall, to the aisle. Dejected, her shoulders slumped, Cecilia walks down the aisle, sitting in a seat. She looks down, her eyes sad, as the camera moves closer to her face.

FRED ASTAIRE *(Offscreen, singing)* "When we're out together dancing cheek to cheek . . ."
The film cuts back to the black-and-white screen, to Fred Astaire, leaning against a nightclub wall, singing to an enraptured, glamorous Ginger Rogers.

FRED ASTAIRE *(Singing)* "Oh I love to climb a mountain / And to reach the highest peak / But it doesn't thrill me half as much as dancing cheek to cheek."
As Fred Astaire finishes his song the film moves briefly back to Cecilia in her seat, in color. She is looking up at the offscreen movie now, her cheeks wet. She clutches the ukulele as the film goes back to Fred Astaire and Ginger Rogers on the black-and-white screen. They're swirling across a fantasylike bridge, dancing onto a huge circular dance floor, high up on a platform. Urns dot a background terrace; the "Cheek to Cheek" musical arrangement is as lavish as the glamorous Hollywood set, as lush as the dancing.

The film cuts back to Cecilia, in color, in her seat. She's engrossed in the offscreen movie now, its pull strong. Her expression is yearning, sad. She is no longer crying.The camera stays on her face, which is subtly changing. Cecilia settles down in her seat as the film moves back to the black-and-white movie screen, to a closer view of Fred Astaire and Ginger Rogers on the circular dance floor, in the midst of a spectacular, graceful duet. They dance on, the music reaching a crescendo, as Fred Astaire twirls Ginger Rogers in his arms, clasping her around the waist; she does a beautiful dip, almost to the floor, as the film moves back to Cecilia, in color, watching the offscreen movie. She is totally engrossed, totally immersed in the movie. The music plays on. Cecilia starts to smile. The film fades to black and the song ends.

As jazzy music from the movie begins to play, white credits appear on a black background, popping in and out:

Production Manager
MICHAEL PEYSER

First Assistant Director
THOMAS REILLY

Second Assistant Director
JAMES CHORY

Production Coordinator	HELEN ROBIN
Script Supervisor	KAY CHAPIN
Assistant to Mr. Allen	JANE READ MARTIN
Production Auditor	JOSEPH HARTWICK
Art Director	EDWARD PISONI
Assistant Art Director	W. STEVEN GRAHAM
Master Scenic Artist	JAMES SORICE
Chief Carpenter	RON PETAGNA
Set Decorator	CAROL JOFFE
Additional Set Decorator	JUSTIN SCOPPA
Chief Set Dresser	DAVE WEINMAN

Set Dresser	KEVIN McCARTHY
Camera Operator	DICK MINGALONE
Assistant Cameraman	DOUGLAS C. HART
Second Assistant Cameraman	BOB PAONE
Still Photographer	BRIAN HAMILL
Production Sound Mixer	JAMES SABAT
Boom Man	LOUIS SABAT
Sound Recordist	FRANK GRAZIADEI
Re-recording Mixer	RICHARD DIOR
	TRANS/AUDIO INC.
Music Coordinator	JOE MALIN
Music Recording Supervisor	WALTER LEVINSKY
Music Recording Engineer	ROY B. YOKELSON
	NATIONAL RECORDING STUDIOS, INC.
Property Master	JAMES MAZZOLA
Property Man	KENNETH VOGT
Construction Grip	JAMES GARTLAND, JR.
Standby Scenic Artist	COSMO SORICE
Gaffer	RAY QUINLAN
Best Boy	JAMES FITZPATRICK
Key Grip	BOB WARD
Grip	RONALD BURKE
Make-up Design	FERN BUCHNER
Hair Design	ROMAINE GREENE
Men's Wardrobe Supervisor	BILL CHRISTIANS
Women's Wardrobe Supervisor	PATRICIA EIBEN
Associate to Mr. Kurland	TOM McKINLEY
Costume Assistant	ISIS MUSSENDEN
Location Manager	JONATHAN FILLEY
Assistant Production Auditor	PETER LOMBARDI
D.G.A. Trainee	LIZ RYAN
Location Scouts	MARY KANE
	JOHN HEALY
	DANA ROBIN

	BARRY STRUGATZ
Casting Assistant	ELLEN LEWIS
Additional Casting	TODD MICHAEL THALER
Assistant to Mr. Wurtzel	DAN LEIGH
Art Department Coordinator	PRUDENCE FARROW
Studio Manager	STEVE ROSE
Transportation Captain	HARRY LEAVEY
Assistant Film Editor	RICHARD NORD
Sound Editor	DAN LIEBERSTEIN
Assistant Sound Editors	STUART LIEBERMAN
	MARTIN LEVENSTEIN
Apprentice Film Editor	KRIS COLE
Apprentice Sound Editor	KATHLEEN EARLE KILLEEN
Dailies Processing	DU ART FILM LABORATORIES, INC.
Opticals	R/GREENBERG ASSOCIATES
	THE OPTICAL HOUSE, N.Y.
Negative Matching	J.G. FILMS, INC.
Projectionist	CARL TURNQUEST, JR.
Process Coordinator	DON HANSARD
Process Projectionist	ANDREW HANSARD
Production Staff	TONY ADLER
	JAMES DAVIS
	JAMES GREENHUT
	AMY HERMAN
	JOSEPH PIERSON
	MICHAEL WILD

"Cheek to Cheek"	written by Irving Berlin vocal by Fred Astaire
"I Love My Baby, My Baby Loves Me"	by Bud Green & Harry Warren
"Alabamy Bound"	by Ray Henderson, B. G. DeSylva & Bud Green

The Cast

MIA FARROW	*Cecilia*
JEFF DANIELS	*Tom Baxter, Gil Shepherd*
DANNY AIELLO	*Monk*
IRVING METZMAN	*Theater Manager*
STEPHANIE FARROW	*Cecilia's Sister*
DAVID KIESERMAN	*Diner Boss*
ELAINE GROLLMAN	*Diner Patrons*
VICTORIA ZUSSIN	
MARK HAMMOND	
WADE BARNES	
JOSEPH G. GRAHAM	
DON QUIGLEY	
MAURICE BRENNER	
PAUL HERMAN	*Penny Pitchers*
RICK PETRUCELLI	
PETER CASTELLOTTI	
MILTON SEAMAN	*Ticket Buyers*
MIMI WEDDELL	
TOM DEGIDON	*Ticket Taker*
MARY HEDAHL	*Popcorn Seller*
EDWARD HERRMANN	*Henry*
JOHN WOOD	*Jason*
DEBORAH RUSH	*Rita*
VAN JOHNSON	*Larry*
ZOE CALDWELL	*The Countess*
EUGENE ANTHONY	*Arturo*
EBB MILLER	*Bandleader*
KAREN AKERS	*Kitty Haynes*
ANNIE JOE EDWARDS	*Delilah*
MILO O'SHEA	*Father Donnelly*
PETER McROBBIE	*The Communist*
CAMILLE SAVIOLA	*Olga*
JULIANA DONALD	*Usherette*

DIANNE WIEST	*Emma*
MARGARET THOMPSON	*Movie Audience*
GEORGE HAMLIN	
HELEN HANFT	
LEO POSTREL	
HELEN MILLER	
GEORGE MARTIN	
CRYSTAL FIELD	
KEN CHAPIN	*Reporters*
ROBERT TREBOR	
BENJAMIN RAYSON	*Movie Goers*
JEAN SHEVLIN	
ALBERT S. BENNETT	
MARTHA SHERRILL	
GRETCHEN MACLANE	
EDWIN BORDO	
ANDREW MURPHY	*Policeman #1*
THOMAS KUBIAK	*Policeman #2*
ALEXANDER COHEN	*Raoul Hirsh*
JOHN ROTHMAN	*Mr. Hirsch's Lawyer*
RAYMOND SERRA	*Hollywood Executive*
GEORGE J. MANOS	*Press Agent*
DAVID TICE	*Waiter*
JAMES LYNCH	*Maitre D'*
SYDNEY BLAKE	*Variety Reporter*
MICHAEL TUCKER	*Gil's Agent*
PETER VON BERG	*Drugstore Customer*
DAVID WEBER	*Photo Double*
GLENNE HEADLEY	*Hookers*
WILLIE TJAN	
LELA IVEY	
DRINDA LA LUMIA	
LORETTA TUPPER	*Music Store Owner*

The Producers Gratefully Acknowledge and
Wish To Thank the Following for Their Assistance:

The Mayor's Office of Film, Theater and Broadcasting
The New York State Office of Motion Picture
and Television Development
The Village of Piermont, New York
The New Jersey Motion Picture and Television
Commission
Conrail
Parks and Recreation Department of New York City
Lenses and Panaflex® Cameras by Panavision®

And Also Thank:
General Camera Corp.
Prints by DeLuxe®
Albert G. Ruben Insurance Co., Inc.
The R.K.O. Radio Pictures Service Mark and Logo
furnished courtesy of R.K.O. General, Inc.

Sculptures from the Encore Collection courtesy of
the Dyansen Galleries of New York City
Erte Sculpture Collection courtesy of the
Publisher Fine Art Acquisitions, Ltd.

And Also Thank:
Paintings courtesy of Kennedy Galleries, Inc.
Period Cars—Donna Motors
Mars, Inc.
Miles Laboratories, Inc.
Jack Richards—Betrand Island Park
Bob Lefcovich—Modern Telecommunications, Inc.
and
Fred Astaire

The story, all names, characters, and incidents portrayed in this production are fictitious. No identification with actual persons is intended or should be inferred.

(emblem) (I.A.T.S.E. emblem)

MOTION PICTURE ASSOCIATION OF AMERICA

Approved No. 27334

ORION PICTURES CORPORATION

ABOUT THE AUTHOR

After he was rejected from both New York University and City College, Woody Allen turned to a professional writing career, at first for television and comedians. In 1964 he decided to become a comedian himself. Woody Allen's first screenplay, written in 1964, was the enormously popular *What's New, Pussycat?* He has also written, directed, and starred in thirteen films to date: *Take the Money and Run*, *Bananas*, *Everything You Always Wanted to Know About Sex*, *Sleeper*, *Love and Death*, *Annie Hall*, *Manhattan*, *Stardust Memories*, *A Midsummer Night's Sex Comedy*, *Broadway Danny Rose*, *Zelig*, *The Purpose Rose of Cairo*, and *Hannah and Her Sisters*. Mr. Allen also wrote and directed *Interiors*. In addition, Mr. Allen has written three plays for Broadway: *Don't Drink the Water*, *Play It Again, Sam* (the latter starring himself in both the play and the subsequent film version), and *The Floating Lightbulb*.

Mr. Allen has written and appeared in his own television specials and has been a frequent contributor to *The New Yorker*, among other periodicals.